FOREST SERVICE ANIMAL TALES

More Than 200 Stories About Animals in Our National Forests

Edited by
Gilbert W. Davies and **Florice M. Frank**

HiStory ink Books
P.O. BOX 52
HAT CREEK, CA 96040

© 1998 by Gilbert W. Davies and Florice M. Frank
Front Cover by William R. Friday
Library of Congress Catalog Card Number: 98-70116
ISBN 1-887200-05-3
Printed in the United States of America

CONTENTS

INDIVIDUAL STORIES

Dogs

Felines

Range and Grazing

Reptiles (mostly snakes)

*Refer to Page xvi of the Preface

PREFACE

"All animals are equal, but some animals are more equal than others." Little did George Orwell know how famous and prophetic these words would become when he wrote them years ago. The stories (tales) in this book help to prove his insight.

There are many stories about dogs, mules, horses, bears, cattle and deer, however, the numbers are sparse when it comes to rodents, insects and reptiles (except snakes). It doesn't necessarily mean there are any fewer happenings out there from the latter group. It means that humans (animals too) have retained and observed far more incidents relating to the interaction among themselves and the larger mammals. Our lives are interwoven with these creatures, whether it has to do with domestic pets, hunting or ranching.

We accept these stories as true. The adventures and events are often humorous, sometimes serious or poignant. A few are sad or tragic and a handful are amazing or approach the unbelievable.

The stories are from all over the United States. Reference is made to 75 specific national forests. There are 216 titled stories, poems and memos from 114 contributors. The tales were edited for spelling, punctuation and capitalization. Some were abridged or edited for clarification, but not at the expense of changing the facts or language of the writer.

The contributors (many deceased) were retirees, spouses or current employees. Some of the earlier dated tales were previously printed in two Forest Service retiree newsletters: Region 5, with its FSX Retiree Club Newsletter and Region 6, with its Thirty Year Club Timberlines. We abridged and edited where necessary.

Several stories are taken from other books with permission from the authors. They are as follows, with the authors listed alphabetically by last name.

Jay H. Cravens: Two stories are from his book *A Well Worn Path*, published by University Editions, 1994.

Bob Gray: Five stories are from his *Forests, Fires, and Wild Things*.

Les Joslin: "Ninemile Remount Depot" is adapted from his book *Uncle Sam's Cabins* published by Wilderness Associates, 1995. "No Buckaroo" is from his book *Toiyabe Patrol* published by Wilderness Associates, 1993.

James R. Pratley: Three stories are from his book *Shorty*.

Stan Tixier: One poem is from his book *A Good Lookin' Horse: Cowboy Poetry and Other Verse*.

The two poems by A. R. Iven and James H. Sizer came from a 1919 book titled *The Forest Ranger and Other Verse* collected and edited by John D. Guthrie and published by The Gorham Press.

Finally, we decided to include some of the animal stories from two earlier books published by HiStory ink Books titled *Forest Service Humor* and *Forest Service Memories*. These are identified by an asterisk (*) in the contents listing. There are U.S. Forest Service photographs in the center of the book. They were all taken between 1910 and 1950.

Animals have always played an important and necessary role in the Forest Service and in the lives of field people from the start. Wildlife management in the area of habitat and range management relating to cattle, sheep, horses and even goats are major responsibilities. In the past it would be normal to have several dogs or cats around the ranger stations, guard stations or work centers of the Service. We believe that one way to preserve the rich history of the Forest Service is to issue books such as this, the seventh in a series about the Agency and its people.

GWD & FMF

Dedicated to:

All things bright and beautiful,
　　All creatures great and small,
All things wise and wonderful,
　　The Lord God made them all.

Cecil Frances Alexander
(1848)

QUOTATIONS

The old hound wags his shaggy tail,
  And I know what he would say:
It's over the hills we'll bound, old hound,
  Over the hills, and away.

> From *Over the Hills*
> By George Meredith

Let dogs delight to bark and bite,
  For God hath made them so;
Let bears and lions growl and fight,
  For 'tis their nature too.

> From *Divine Songs*
> By Isaac Watts

I heard a bird at break of day
  Sing from the autumn trees
A song so mystical and calm,
  So full of certainties.

> From *Overtones*
> By William Alexander Percy

The night comes down, the lights burn blue;
And at my door the Pale Horse stands,
To bear me forth to unknown lands.

> From *The Stirrup Cup*
> By John Hay

A wise old owl sat on an oak,
The more he saw the less he spoke;
The less he spoke the more the heard;
Why aren't we like that wise old bird?

> From *A Wise Old Owl*
> By Edward Hersey Richards

You have to believe in happiness.
Or happiness never comes.....
Ah, that's the reason a bird can sing
On his darkest day he believes in Spring.

> From *You Have to Believe*
> By Douglas Mallock

BEARS

BEARLY ENOUGH TO EAT

Jack Spencer

Kathump! Kathump! Kathump! Dimly I became aware of a nagging sound as I struggled out of the depths of a deep sleep around midnight in my sleeping bag. It should have been quiet except for night sounds. We were camped on the shore of Mahlberg Lake deep in the Boundary Waters Canoe Area Wilderness in the Superior National Forest in northern Minnesota.

Befogged, I reached for a flashlight and unzipped the tent flap to look outside. The cone of light revealed a hungry, mature, athletic brown bear as the source of the sound. He stood beneath our canvas Duluth packs containing all our food for the next several days, which were hanging just out of his reach by a rope looped over a large red pine limb. Amid a cloud of dust, he performed a vigorous version of the standing high jump as he leaped on his hind legs while vainly reaching for the packs with his front legs. Undeterred by the light shining in his eyes, the bear continued his noisy quest for the source of the tantalizing smells emanating from the packs.

I yelled to Burt Essex, my tent mate and we threw on our boots and emerged from the tent in as hostile a manner as possible, considering we were clad only in our boxer shorts, to protect our food from this unwanted visitor. A voracious cloud of mosquitoes descended on our bare bodies just then causing us to reflect for a moment that it might have been wiser to have taken the time to put on our pants first. But this was a time for action, not thought! We began yelling insults, waving our arms and hurling rocks at the unresponsive beast, who regarded with amusement the two figures in front of him making such a fuss in their underwear. The noise awakened the rest of our fishing party, Bob Wray and Bob Merz, who sprang into action from their tent nearby. The sight of four unclothed, irrationally acting campers was enough to dimly penetrate the hunger-driven mind of the bear with the message that he was unwelcome. As he reluctantly shambled away up one of the many trails leading through the brush around camp, we were free to scratch our mosquito bites and to consider what to do next.

We were all foresters working at the North Central Forest Experiment Station in St. Paul, and had some idea of the persistence of bears once they have stumbled across food. The summer had been exceptionally dry, making natural food scarce for them. Our bear was simply trying to get a decent meal—our meal. As we plotted our strategy in the darkness, we occasionally pointed our lights in the direction of the trails. Soon, we spotted the shining eyes of our nemesis who had returned and was ready to resume his food plundering. Another fusillade of rocks sent him running back up the trail but we knew that he would keep this up all night. We decided that two of us would stand guard for a two-hour shift, then the other crew would relieve them, to be repeated until daylight. For the rest of the night the bear returned at an almost predictable interval of every 20 to 30 minutes, moving silently over the bone-dry litter on the ground, to be repulsed by the watchful sentries and their pile of rocks.

After breakfast the next morning we thought about moving camp to an island but decided against it since the bear hadn't been able to reach our food earlier. We even hauled the pack a little higher off the ground. Satisfied that we had outsmarted the bear, we turned our attention to the reason we were there— catching fish.

But first, Burt had to use the outdoor, wooden privy some 50 yards away, up one of the trails leading from camp. As the three of us waited for him to return, our nocturnal adversary brazenly walked into camp and tried to steal away with a nearby, small, foodless pack in his mouth. (Clearly, he was not a selective shopper.) A furious volley of stones convinced him to drop the pack and sprint up the same trail that Burt had taken. With bated breath we heard the privy cover slam in the distance, signaling Burt's completion of his task, and a few seconds later a bloodcurdling cry pierced the air. Moments later when Burt strolled a bit too nonchalantly into camp, we asked him what all the yelling was about. He explained unconvincingly to the skeptics in front of him that he had confronted the galloping hairy beast on the trail and had merely tried to frighten it further away from camp.

Certain that the bear could not reach our food packs without a stepladder, we pushed our two canoes onto the mirror like surface of the take and concentrated on catching walleyed pike. After several hours of trolling with nightcrawlers and leeches, surrounded by pristine stands of northern white cedar, quaking aspen, balsam fir, white birch and red pine, our route took Burt and me past the campsite once again. Our alarm grew as we got closer to shore—our Duluth packs were nowhere to be seen! With sinking hearts we paddled at flank speed to shore and jumped from the canoe to investigate closer.

A dangling rope was all that remained of our hope for a balanced diet—the packs were gone. Sadly we had to admit that we had been outmaneuvered. Apparently, the wily bear had rejected his earlier tactic and had simply climbed up the tree and out on the limb, then reached down to slash with his paw until our packs fell to the ground. He must have dined on the tastiest foods first (summer sausage was high on his list, cheese was low, as evidenced by the tooth marks left in the uneaten block), then dragged the rest into the brush to consume later when his appetite returned. Already feeling hunger pangs as we contemplated the possibility of our next few meals being composed of roots and berries sautéed with nightcrawlers and leeches, lightly seasoned with pine pitch and garnished with duckweed, Burt and I fanned out in the brush on the off-chance that we might find the food cache. There was little hope of success given the size of the area to search but by dumb luck we stumbled across the now shredded packs and what was left of the contents partially buried under leaves and branches about 100 yards from camp.

The bear had left enough food for a couple of meals of assorted, uncomplimentary edibles (heavy to pancake mix and cheese), so obviously we would have to leave for home earlier than we had planned. But how were we going to cross all the portages between the lakes that lay ahead of us without our Duluth packs to carry our loose gear? Cleverly, Burt thought that we might be able to jury-rig them by sewing up the tattered canvas with monofilament fishing line. When the two Bobs returned to camp later, Burt was sitting bent over one of the packs punching holes through canvas with his pocket knife and suturing fragments together like an emergency room surgeon.

On the trip home the next day we gingerly hoisted the patched packs on our backs, hoping they would hold together long enough for us to traverse the many portage trails between us and the car. They performed beautifully. The bear may have proven himself more shrewd than we were, he may have purloined our food and caused us to abbreviate our fishing trip and we may have been hungry and beaten, but we left with our dignity intact—what was left of it.

THE BEARS AMONG US

Gerry Ingco

It was early in the summer of 1956, my second field season with the Forest Service on the Sequoia National Forest. The previous year I worked as a junior forester cruising timber in very steep, rugged front country, the headwaters of South Fork of the Tule River. We worked out of pack in spike camps from where we fought and cursed for every chain of survey line gained.

The job was interesting, though, because the tract of timber we were working contained many isolated groves of Sequoia that few people had ever seen. The Sequoia groves were on lands of the Mt. Whitney Lumber Company. The purpose of the cruise was for a future land exchange whereby the Sequoias would eventually be included into the national forest.

We cruised every mature Sequoia over the entire tract. All other trees were sample cruised. When cruising Sequoias we employed different techniques than used for any other commercial forest tree, making extremely precise measurements. In spite of the adversity of the job, the work was a great learning experience.

I was prepared to spend the next field season cruising, but I got an offer I couldn't refuse. I was asked to make a survey of the range allotments on the Kern Plateau. At that time the Kern Plateau was completely roadless except for the one trail head at the end of Nine Mile Canyon which connected to highway 395 on the east side of the plateau.

Most exciting about the new job was that, for the most part, I would do all my traveling to and from the work sites on horseback. A lot of the work would be in "east-side" open pine and sage interspersed with rich green meadows. The country is scenic and perfect for traveling on horseback.

With my new boss, the venerable and colorful old time range officer, Cooper Smith, we set out from the trail head in Kennedy Meadows for Jackass Meadows. Jackass Meadows would be a base camp from where I'd work the northern portion of the Kern Plateau. The Kern Plateau was bordered on the north by an even larger expanse of wilderness on the Inyo National Forest and Kings Canyon National Park. The survey area was bordered on the west by the steep, rugged main fork of the Kern River, and on the east and south by the precipitous South Fork of the Kern River.

We were off on the trail, leaving the Kennedy Meadows Guard Station right after breakfast. Cooper was on his handsome Arabian stallion, and I was on Doc, my new chestnut gilding quarter horse. In tow, I had my gentle gray pack mule, Peanuts.

Jackass Meadows is about nine miles northwest of Kennedy Meadows and was the location of a tourist pasture. Tourist pastures were scattered throughout the back country about an easy day's ride apart. These pastures were fenced and contained several acres, more or less, of quality forage.

A fenced pasture was a great convenience. Lacking a fenced enclosure, it would be necessary to hobble the livestock every night to allow them the ability to find forage and water on their own. In spite of being hobbled stock can, and often do, travel a long way during the night; and be difficult to locate in the morning. For me, if I didn't have the benefit of a fenced pasture, I'd have to take Peanuts with me every day, making for an awkward work situation

Like many mountain meadows, Jackass Meadows was encircled by a dense, tangled stand of lodgepole pine. There was a clear, cold spring on the east edge of the meadow. Opposite the spring on the west side was a small grove of mature Jeffrey pine. The whole setting was a very nice location for a base camp. We were planning to occupy the Jeffery pine grove which would receive the early morning sun and be shady during the heat of the day.

By early afternoon our train entered the band of dense lodgepole pine which surrounded Jackass Meadows. In the trees the trail narrowed so that Peanut's pack barely cleared the tree trunks on either side. Overhead the tree canopy closed and shut out most of the sunlight. I was riding Doc, Peanuts was behind me; pulling up the rear was Cooper. As I was about to break out of the semidarkness and enter the meadow, there was a loud sound of breaking branches to my left. Instantly, fifty feet ahead on the trail, two large bears crashed through the wall of trees, bounded across the trail and forced their way into the wall of trees on the right. The bears were out of sight in an instant but could be heard punching through the strip of timber toward the meadow.

When Doc saw the bears he reared slightly, then settled into a head tossing, quick stepping, little dance and I set about trying to calm him down. Peanuts kicked the air with his hind legs and tried to execute an about-face. While I was trying to reorganize my charges, Cooper rode up, chuckling and amused at the event We opened the gate and entered the meadow heading along the western edge toward the Jeffrey pine grove.

6

As we neared the pine grove we reined in quickly to observe something very unusual in the deep shade under the trees. What we saw appeared as a dense, dark, combined mass of mingling life forms, moving but not going anywhere. Something very strange indeed.

From our vantage point we began accessing the nature of the strange scene before us. Darn! We were looking at a number of bears feeding on the carcasses of about a half dozen cows lying together in a tight group. Also, we saw green foliage on branches scattered about on the meadow around the pine grove. Associated with the debris on the ground, we saw a telltale sign on one of the trees; a narrow gouge torn through the tree's bark and extending along the length of one side of the trunk.

It was immediately obvious that the unfortunate cows sought shelter from a thunderstorm and were killed by the lightning bolt which struck the newly scarred trunk. It was likewise obvious that bears from some distance around Jackass Meadows became informed of the awaiting banquet. The bears we encountered on the trail were late comers. We also wondered if other bears may, at this instant, also be in transit. Would every bear on the Kern Plateau eventually come here?

It was now obvious that this spot in the meadow was not, after all, the best place for a campsite—at least not during an electrical storm. Those tall Jeffrey pine trees stood as natural lightning rods head and shoulders over all the other shorter lodgepoles in the neighborhood.

It was painfully clear to me that if I were to camp at this location, I would to have share the site with those bears. They would be there continuously, participating in a feeding frenzy until the last bone was stripped. I'd not only have to see the event in the daylight; throughout the darkness of future nights I'd have to listen to the tearing of flesh and the sounds of scuffling among the bears.

Prior to being employed by the Forest Service I had other jobs working in the woods. I had a few encounters with bears. I never considered them to be a serious threat. These were black bears which are ordinarily reclusive and not supposed to be aggressive toward humans. It appeared, though, that these animals in this situation, might not fit the usual behavioral pattern. We felt they might be extremely aggressive if they felt their food supply might be threatened. We witnessed frequent arguments of a very physical nature, and there was a general feeling of extreme tension there in the pine grove.

Also I wondered about the safety of my animals. The meadow was not large, shaped like a thin rectangle, and my animals were always less than a few hundred feet from the pine grove which was halfway along the border on one long side of the meadow. I would be on hand during the night in the event of trouble, but I was worried for Peanuts, alone in the pasture with the bears while I was away working.

We decided there was no other convenient campsite. The next location with similar amenities would entail much additional travel time to most of my work sites. The only alternative was to share the meadow with the rowdy visitors in the grove, and hope for the best. My camp would be at the spring across the narrow part of the meadow from where the bears were partying.

I took some comfort in the fact that, in a worst case scenario, I had a rifle which might be of some help. I brought my Remington Rolling Block carbine, a turn of the century single shot made for the 7mm Spanish Mauser cartridge. In those days, people working alone with livestock often chose to carry, a firearm. In an emergency, a gun could be useful in sending a signal of distress. In the back country, only fire guards carried radios. They were heavy, bulky, and not too reliable anyway. Also, because we had to travel in difficult terrain, serious accidents with livestock were not uncommon. A firearm could be used effectively to humanely terminate the lingering suffering of horse or mule resulting from a mishap.

Coincidentally, for me, there was an equally good reason to pack a rifle. I would still be working after deer season had started and the country was prime habitat for mule deer.

The first night, as expected, I didn't get much sleep. Because of the normal quietness of the forest at night, sounds coming from across the meadow were much amplified and impossible to ignore. There were a variety of rather unpleasant sounds associated with the feeding habits of large carnivorous mammals. To the accompaniment of the sounds of the bears feeding there were growls, snarls, blaring roars, and related sounds of physical altercations as the diners vied for the choice morsels. Through the night I also listened apprehensively for indications that our livestock might be in jeopardy, or that the bears would be paying us a visit.

Dawn finally arrived and the night, surprisingly, proved uneventful. The bears kept to themselves, contented where they were. Our animals were calm and collected. They seemed to have handled the situation better than me. Cooper looked like he got a normal night's sleep. Nothing could ever phase that man.

The presence of the bears entailed a lot of extra precautionary work each day before leaving camp. I had a ten day's food supply which had to be secured while I was away from camp. The goods needing protection were put in the center of my ground cloth. I gathered the supplies into a bundle and tied it off the corners of the ground cloth with a lead rope. I'd toss the loose end of the rope over a sturdy tree branch at a point far out from the trunk, and away from other branches that might support a bear. The bundle of food had to be lifted above the reach of a bear standing on the ground, and still dangle out of reach from above. Considering the combination of necessary requisites for a qualifying tree branch, it is usually hard to find such a branch at any potential campsite. The tree selected was nearby, but outside the campsite.

The food bag was very heavy. Since I had no block and tackle, I had to pull it up using horsepower with the rope attached to the pommel. Repeated twice a day, this necessary precaution was quite an inconvenience.

The afternoon of the second work day Cooper took off for Kennedy Meadows from where he would be leaving for the supervisor's office. I would be alone camping at Jackass Meadows until I finished surveying the area to be worked from Jackass Meadow. I estimated I'd work there about twenty-four days. I hoped the bears would consume their supply of beef as soon as possible.

The days actually went by uneventfully as far as camp life was concerned. After one week the bears were still present at the continuing banquet. The bears had enough to occupy themselves and ignored the other occupants of the meadow. I actually got used to all the noisy goings on across the way. I slept each night away, accepting the sounds of tearing flesh, crunching of bones, and the grunting and growling as normal sounds of the night.

After another three or four days the cows were almost reduced to a heap of bare bones. Over that amount of time the bears began leaving and were finally replaced by a few buzzards picking over the leftovers. These birds would scatter and disappear when I entered camp. I figured I had weathered the crisis. I could now enjoy this perfect natural setting for relaxation after a hard day at work. I still remained diligent in my precautions to protect my livestock and supplies.

My campsite was very simple but quite adequate. I slept in the open in a comfortable cowboy's bedroll. A bedroll consisted of several interfolded woolen blankets which were arranged to reduce creeping up at the foot or coming apart at the edges. I could sleep under, or over, more than one layer of blankets depending whether I chose to use the blankets for warmth or as a mattress. The blankets were contained inside a very large piece of very heavy canvas, folded so there were a minimum of two layers of canvas over the blankets. Strips of cloth were sewn at locations so the loose edges could be tied in place. At the upper edge there was an extension of canvas serving as a flap which could serve as a head shelter or canopy. The flap had sewn in pockets to store personal effects. This bedroll was the forerunner of the sleeping bag of today but it was much more comfortable and almost totally weatherproof. Its drawback was its weight, probably thirty pounds, but that didn't matter, pack mules could carry two hundred pounds of gear and supplies.

I had one item of camp furniture. A rustic table made by former campers. The table had poles for legs and a top consisting of a single slab of wood. The table top was hand split to shape and the finished product was not very flat. The outside edges of the plank were higher than the center. Also the table was slightly lower at one end due to uneven legs.

During the night I tried to provide some measure of protection to whatever supplies I thought would be tempting to a bear. I did not want to go through the laborious routine I used to secure the camp during the day. My food was folded in the ground cloth placed nearby, but at a tactfully selected distance from where I would be sleeping. For obvious reasons, I didn't want to sleep right next to that stuff. To provide some means of alarm, I tied several empty cans to the bundle so I would hear an intruder's first attempt to steal my provisions.

After dinner and washing dishes, I would stack utensils, cookware, condiments and miscellaneous items on the table. At the end of the table, I kept a bucket-sized aluminum pot filled with cold water to keep a head of cabbage fresh.

When the after dinner chores were completed, I would use the remaining light of day to work up my survey data and work with aerial photos. After darkness had set in I would read for pleasure, lying in my bedroll by the light of my gasoline lantern. The lantern stood in a cleared spot on one end of the table. I would sleep at the end of the table with my head directly under the lantern. My rifle was placed conveniently at my side with the barrel resting on my saddle bags.

I kept the rifle unloaded because when there was a cartridge in the chamber, the firing pin (which was attached to an exposed hammer) rested directly on the cartridge's primer—a hazardous situation that invited accidental discharge. I kept a few loose cartridges handy in one of the pockets in the bedroll's top flap.

One night while sleeping soundly, I was instantly startled by a loud sounding metallic clattering. Then immediately something very heavy and hard fell on my head so hard that I saw stars that were definitely not part of the night's sky. Next in rapid succession, came down a cascade of very cold water onto my head and into the bedroll's opening. All the while the clattering sounds continued nearby.

The instant the disturbance started I knew a bear was into the things I had on the table. Those clanging sounds were my pots and pans being scattered around. Each succeeding disturbance, however, prevented me from reacting more rapidly. But when I regained my composure, which may only have been a few seconds, I reached for my rifle with one hand and groped for the cartridges with my other hand. After seemingly an endless time, I succeeded in placing a cartridge into the rifle's chamber. I closed the breach block and pulled the hammer back with my thumb. Continuing my progression of reactions, I started to rapidly squeeze the trigger while elevating the rifle's muzzle skyward (I wasn't about to shoot directly at something I couldn't define in the darkness).

As I applied pressure on the trigger of the rifle I simultaneously made an attempt to bring fourth a cry as menacing and threatening as possible. The yell came first, instantly followed by the ear splitting rifle's report. An orange flame with a spewing of sparks issued forth from the muzzle of the carbine's short barrel. In an instant darkness returned but the rifle's report continued to echo repeatedly in the distance.

As soon as I was aware of the return of silence to the night, the stillness was again broken by the sound of rapidly pounding footsteps. I didn't know whether this animal was running toward me or away from me—hoping it was the latter. I was thankful to hear the cracking sound of breaking branches as the bear hit the tangled wall of dense lodgepoles. The crashing sound continued until the bear finally forced his way into the adjacent open forest surrounding our meadow.

It was all over now. I surveyed the effect of the commotion with the aid of my flashlight. Nothing was damaged, just things rearranged in an extremely untidy manner. The thing that hit me on my head was the base of my lantern which was laying on the ground with the glass shattered. I had a big bump on my head, but it was a good thing I wasn't cut by the glass. When the big pot was tipped over, the table's depressed center conveyed all the water in a single stream and the torrent of water was directed right at me. My head was directly below the low end of the table.

I set to work to dry my bedding and picked up most of the clutter left by the incident. I then tried to get some rest during what remained of the night.

For the remainder of my stay in that camp, there would be no more encounters with bears.

Over a period of thirty-five years of working in the outdoors, and additional years in the forest for recreational purposes, I have had a fair number of interesting experiences with bears. Once I even had to have a pesky critter relocated from our own backyard. I've experienced other intrusions into back country campsites, some with serious and costly damage to supplies and property. The encounter at Jackass Meadows, for me though, was most curious.

I remember this old Gypsy proverb: "Sometimes you *get* the bear, but sometimes he *gets* you."

BEARS AT THE ANIMAL FAIR

Abe G. Turley

During 1934, I was a member of a blister rust crew, pulling ribes in the white pine stands of the Little North Fork of the Coeur d'Alene River in the Coeur d'Alene National Forest. We worked the country in strips, one chain wide, six men to a crew. The worked area was marked by ordinary string as we moved. Strips usually started and ended at a clearly defined point; a ridge, road, river or creek. In our case, our strips started at a road and ended at a creek.

For lunch, the cooks set out the makings and we made our own sandwiches. Dessert was an eight ounce can of fruit. Lunch was carried in a cloth sack which we tied to the back of our suspenders.

With experience, we found we could estimate pretty accurately where we would be by lunch time. We also found the constant swinging and banging of the lunch bag soon formed it into the shape of a cantaloupe. So, we would tie our lunch in a tree by the creek and when we worked our way back down, had a little picnic. It worked very well for a few days. Apparently, Bear had been watching us and had pulled all the lunches from the tree and torn each one open. He ignored the sandwiches, preferring the dessert. Each can had been neatly punctured in several places and the heavy syrup sucked from each one.

We tried leaving our lunches in a tree one more time, but it was clear that Bear would have his way. We learned something from this experience, though. Bear can read labels.

———————•◦•———————

Next spring, 1935, I started working on the Wallace District. The first job was presuppression work; road, trail and telephone maintenance. On this particular day, I was patrolling a trail alone, checking signs and section line markers, when I became aware I was being followed. When I reached a spot where I could view a good stretch of trail behind me, I stopped. Sure enough, about 300 yards behind me in the trail, was ol' Bear, still coming. I was getting nervous, when he stopped about 100 yards away, stood up, moving his radar from side to side, then zeroed in on me. I was the first to move. I turned and headed up the trail, somewhat faster this time, hoping Bear would change his mind. After half a mile, though, he was still behind me. We both stopped and he gave me the old once-over with his radar. This time I went straight up the mountainside, maybe 100 yards, and sat down to see what Bear would do. He dropped to all fours and ambled up to where I had left the trail, stopped, stood up and illuminated me again. He knew exactly where I was, but dropped back on all fours and disappeared up the trail.

I sat there for half an hour, then decided to give the rest of the afternoon to Bear and headed down the trail for home.

———————•◦•———————

Later, I was assigned to King's Pass Lookout as lookout fireman. King's Pass Lookout was sited at the end of a spur of the Bitterroot Range. It started at Granite Peak and dog-legged its way about 20 miles west into the Coeur d'Alene National Forest. At King's Pass Lookout, it dropped steeply away to finally dissolve in the mingled waters of Beaver Creek, Prichard Creek and the North Fork of the Coeur d'Alene River.

The spur was breached at King's Pass. Originally a wagon road, it provided a shortcut from Beaver Creek to Murray for wagons and stage coaches and eventually for cars and trucks. To facilitate construction of the lookout, a road was bulldozed from the pass along the spur to the lookout site, about three miles.

Because of the poor "water chance" at the lookout, it was deemed advisable for the lookout to water up at a spring on the outskirts of Murray. It was a good flow and someone had laid an iron pipe to bring the water to the edge of the road, a great place to fill up. Of course, this meant the lookout had to have a car, which I had. And that's how I became the lookout at King's Pass lookout for two seasons.

I had a 1930 Ford Model A Cabriolet. It had all the appearance of a convertible, rag top and all, but it didn't convert. The windshield opened and the rear flap could be opened, providing a form of flow through system of air conditioning, complete with grasshoppers and other forms of hurtling insects. Access to the rumble seat was provided by a step plate atop each rear fender. Watching young ladies climb into it was always a heartwarming sight.

The lookout was built in 1934, for occupancy in 1935. When I arrived to open the place, everything to get it running was stacked at the bottom of the stairs; folding canvas cot, three blankets, new captain's chair, gas lantern, utensils, china, silverware, rations and the niftiest little cast-iron stove I had ever seen. With stovepipe. And, a shiny, new Osborne firefinder. It took me two hours to get it all upstairs and set up.

I was resting in my new captain's chair when it occurred to me that something was missing; water. I was instantly thirsty. "Water me now," came to mind. So, I collected the water hauling gear and drove the six miles to the spring where I took on water and started back.

It was a pleasant, warm afternoon, so I rolled down the windows, opened the windshield and enjoyed the trip as I ground my way up the hill to the pass. I shifted into first as I turned onto the lookout road, which was rough and narrow. I had driven out of the timber and around a sharp bend when suddenly, about twenty feet away, in the center of the road, I saw Big Mama Bear with two cubs.

We saw each other at the same time. I stopped and Big Mama took off up the hill followed by one cub. Number two cub took off, too, in the opposite direction. I sat there. I remembered hearing that the most dangerous place in the world to be was between Big Mama and her cub. That was exactly where I was. I rolled up the windows. I had also heard that Bear regarded rag tops as easy pickings. I closed the windshield.

About that time, number two cub, discovering he was alone and receiving some signal from Big Mama inaudible to human ears, came tearing through the brush to the road, running so hard his back feet were passing his front feet with each step, bawling, "Maa! Maa! Maa!" as he scrambled up the bank and out of sight.

That was the last time I saw Big Mama and her cubs. In fact, it was the last time I saw anything with four feet and fur during the time I was at King's Pass Lookout. No chipmunks, no squirrels, no rabbits, not even a mouse. I did see about 60 jillion yellow jackets that summer, though.

I often wandered if maybe Big Mama ever had me on her radar while I was batting yellow jackets.

———— · · · ————

Before ending this saga of Bear, I have two more encounters to relate. These took place sometime after I had left the Forest Service.

My family and I were camped in a single unit Forest Service campsite near the upper end of Priest Lake in the Kaniksu National Forest in the Idaho panhandle. Our daughter, age fourteen and her friend, Connie, decided to sleep under a large, spreading pine at the edge of the beach, a short distance from our tent. Sometime early in the morning I was awakened by sounds of something messing around the table. I grabbed a flashlight, poked my head through the tent flap and lit up a small black bear. He took off at once and scampered by me, right toward the tree and the girls. I ran as fast as I could in bare feet. The girls were sitting bolt upright, wide-eyed and scared. "What was that?" they yelled in unison. What could I say? I said that it was a bear. Connie said, "It ran right between us. I think it stepped on my pillow." Well, Connie had spread a clean, white hand towel over her pillow. When I lit it up, we could see the dirty, black, unmistakably plantigrade print of a bear's paw. There was a shocked silence. Then, Connie said, as she carefully folded the evidence, "I will never, NEVER wash this towel!"

Same lake, different location, different time. A bear had gotten into a neighboring camper's camp and mangled a metal barbecue, definitely making his presence known. The following evening we had a fire on the beach, about 50 yards from our camp. We had, or thought we had, stored our food in the car. Returning later to the campsite, I led the way with the flashlight. I swept it with the light and there, standing beside a tree, leaning against it with one front paw, was a small brown bear. He wasted no time getting out of there. When we checked out the site, we found we had overlooked a small, plastic, insulated zipper bag. Bear had cleaned it out; a brick of cheese, six eggs and a jar of sweet pickles, which had a screw top lid. There were teeth marks an the lid and at first I thought Bear may have pried it off, like a bottle cap. But no. Close examination showed that the lid had not been bent and the threads were not distorted. Bear had dug a small hole in the sand, put the jar in the hole, tamped it firmly with sand and managed to get the lid off. By unscrewing it! The jar was still in the hole, clean as a whistle.

Now, I'm the guy who scoffed at park rangers' stories about the bear that opened car trunks by bounding on the lid until they sprung open. And the one about the bear that entered a ranger station by opening a double hung window, then left by the same window, closing it behind him. And the one about the rangers who were concerned about the number of bear/hiker encounters, so issued a bulletin suggesting that hikers wear something noisy like bells, thus warning Bear that something was coming. The suggestion was quietly rescinded when some little harness bells were found in some bear feces.

I laughed at these stories as palpable nonsense concocted for the entertainment of gullible tourists, yet here I was, with a story every bit as incredible, a story I could not repeat. Ridicule is something I would have trouble bearing, until now! I have reached an age where such things don't bother me. Especially when I know my story is true.

THE BLACK BEARS OF THE SHASTA

Don Blackburn

I was suppose to be checking behind the contractor crews in the Shasta National Forest. That summer, 1956, the Forest Service employed me as one of a number of college students working on the gooseberry (ribes) eradication project in the sugar pine country of the Shasta. We were living in a rustic camp at the Bartle Guard Station, east of McCloud, California. Quartered in army squad tents framed in wood and with wood floors, we began each working day by being dropped on lengthy survey lines paralleling each other a mile apart. We would count and measure the inches of live ribes plants missed by the contract crews to see if contract standards were met.

The project supervisor told us that the area contained a good population of black bears, very curious by nature, having a keen sense of smell but poor eyesight. He issued each of us a whistle. If you get treed he said, just blow your whistle until someone on an adjoining survey line comes to your rescue. Armed with this assuring information and our trusty whistle, we went to work each morning confidant of our safety among the friendly Shasta bears.

He forgot to warn us about lunches left in pickup trucks with open windows. I learned that lesson quickly. It was a long time between breakfast and supper. Ambling along my survey line on another day, I climbed onto the slippery limbs of a manzanita bush at the edge of a small rocky bluff, took my handy compass hanging from a string around my neck and began looking for a reference point to continue forward on my survey line. Suddenly my foot slipped and I dropped a few feet onto the rump of a very startled yearling black bear. Neither of us stood our ground. So much for a black bear's keen sense of smell.

A couple of weeks later, waltzing along my survey line through a mature sugar pine forest, I suddenly encountered a mama bear with two large cubs. She made one menacing growl and I made one flying leap into the safety of a nearby fir sapling. This particular sapling was maybe 12 to 14 inches diameter and 30 to 40 feet high. From my perch half way up this tree, I withdrew my trusty whistle and begin blowing on it. This seemed to have a different effect on the mama bear and on her cubs. It seemed to irritate mama while enticing the cubs. The cubs started up the tree, I climbed higher, mama bear went berserk on the ground. I blew my whistle while climbing as high as this sapling would support me. When the lead cub reached my perch, I popped its nose with the toe of my boot. It squealed and retreated a few feet, mama bear vented her feelings with some awfully profane bear talk. The cubs got her message and withdrew to the ground. Some 30 minutes after I quit blowing my trusty whistle, mama and her cubs finally declared a truce and withdrew. Not wanting to spend the night in a fur sapling, I descended from my perch, returned to by survey line and completed another uneventful day in the Shasta. My partners, working lines a mile on either side of me, told me they never heard my whistle. They also said that had they heard, they would have had more sense than to approach a nut in a tree, serenading a mad adult bear, using a loud and irritating whistle.

Remember our sleeping tent at camp? Well, you see, just a few yards beyond the tent was our camp trash dump. Most nights, we could hear the bears rummaging for a midnight snack, rattling tin cans, woofing and bear talking to each other about how poor scavenging in a Forest Service dump could be. Four of us slept in each tent, one in each corner. You could roll up the canvas sides during the hot weekend days when we were in camp but we kept the canvas sides rolled down at night for some protection from the night air, which was cold enough in July to freeze the water in our canteens, which made mighty good drinking along our survey line the following day. One of those nights I dreamed that a nice warm breeze had wafted into my tent. I could feet it blowing across my face. A sudden racket beside me and I awoke to find another yearling bear in my face. While exploring the wonders of this human habitat, he must have gotten tangled between the canvas side and the ropes used to secure the tent. He reacted as any normal, intelligent bear teenager would. And I reacted as any normal student, awakened from a pleasant dream with a bear in my face, would react. I succeeded in tearing the zipper out of a sleeping bag, collapsing one end of an army squad tent, scaring the daylights out of three tent mates and ruining one young bear's nighttime exploring. On the following weekend, we relocated our trash dump, and covered up the old one.

My other compelling encounter with a black bear that summer occurred on a Saturday night. Returning to camp after an exciting evening in McCloud, Weed, and Mt. Shasta, we were cruising along the black asphalt road to camp, on a moonless night. Suddenly a dark form arose on the road in front of us. I stood on the brakes, but still managed to bump the dark form before coming to a stop. Have you ever heard a black bear running through the forest on a dark night, after he has been rudely bumped by a Plymouth while he was enjoying his road kill? We examined the bumper on my car, no damage, but did note an odorous wet accumulation on the road, steam arising, visible evidence of one bear's version of "guess who's coming to dinner."

I will always remember the beautiful Shasta National Forest of northern California, and its curious denizens who kept us (close) company in the summer of 1956.

THE BLUE NOSED BEAR

John H. Ayers

This story started when I became the district ranger of the Winthrop Ranger District, on the Okanogan National Forest in the spring of 1952. Ranger Putt Darling had been transferred to the Union Greek District on the Rogue River National Forest in Oregon.

As soon as weather permitted I made my first trip into the primitive area as it was then called. A cabin had been built in the Spanish Camp area two and one half miles south of the Canadian border, for administrative use. This was surely a very necessary cabin because it could snow there any month of the year and often did.

There is nothing like being pelted with several inches of wet snow in July or August. Not only does everyone get cold and wet but all your gear gets soaked as well. I have dried out in the Spanish Camp cabin on numerous occasions.

I am not sure but I think the first district ranger was Frank Burg and he built the cabin. He lived to be 103 years old. Certainly this must say something good about the values of being a district ranger.

Well best get to the story. I took my horse and pack string and the district packer, Mr. Lewis Cornwell, and headed into the back country, eventually arriving at the Spanish Camp cabin. The door was open and a bear had torn off its hinges. The inside was in a terrible mess.

This was not vandalism, as we have found it today, but the results of a hungry bear, probably just out of hibernation. We made a practice of leaving food in the cabin just in case someone were to get caught and have to lay out a winter storm. The bear knocked down the stove, the shelves and bit into every one of the canned goods, Following him came the porcupines and packrats. What a mess. It took us most of a day to get the place cleaned up.

Right then I decided that I'd put an end to this so on the next trip I took extra boards, nails, strapping etc., and built a stronger door. When we left in the fall, I felt sure this would not happen again.

By now I'll bet you have guessed it did happen again next spring. This time, however, the bear pushed out a window, there were two of them, and he went in through one of the windows. I didn't think he would do this as he had left paw prints on the windows before but didn't attempt to break the glass. I told Mr. Howard Weller, Logging Superintendent for the Wagner Lumber Company, about my problem and he offered to give me two of the old heavy radiator screens off D-8 tractors.

This seemed like a good idea so I made arrangements with Mr. Francis Lufkin of the North Cascade Smokejumper Project, to have them dropped in at the cabin on my next trip to Spanish Camp. I picked them up at the camp and using lag screws secured them to each window, People visiting the area probably thought that we were trying to protect something valuable in the cabin, however, there was very little of value in the cabin. Now I was sure that I had a secure bear proof cabin.

You guessed it, there was still another way for a bear to gain entrance. However, this time when leaving in the fall, I left several pressurized blue paint cans laying about the cabin. I thought if he comes back again I'll know him from the other bears by his blue nose.

To make this long story short, when we went back the next spring the bear had climbed onto the roof and torn off the shakes and went in again.

This time, at last, we had a way of marking the bear. At least this was different. We had paint cans with teeth holes and blue paint all over on the ceiling rafters and on the walls and floor.

Surely now we would learn which bear was the culprit. However, no blue nosed bear was ever located. Maybe the bear left the area having had enough of the paint. He never showed up at the cabin again.

This about ends the story, except that summer I had Mr. Lufkin drop several sheet of corrugated iron roofing at Spanish Camp which we secured to the roof and that did end the bears fun of destroying the inside of the Spanish Camp cabin every spring.

THE BEAR

Philip Lee

The Targhee National Forest in northeastern Idaho borders both the Grand Teton and Yellowstone National Parks. As a result, grizzly bears occasionally wander onto the forest seeking food or just a place to hang out for awhile. Sheep herders freely admitted shooting grizzly bears during the years before they were listed as a threatened species. They also guardedly spoke of shooting a few after they were listed. This story took place while I was range and wildlife staff on the forest.

The rancher called me at home late one evening complaining about a grizzly bear harassing his sheep on Two Top Mountain. His herder had seen fresh tracks and the sheep were highly disturbed the night before. I thanked him for calling me and giving us a chance to manage the situation to prevent either the loss of the bear or the loss of his sheep.

The sheep were grazing under Forest Service permit in an area that had recently been designated as important grizzly bear habitat. Most of the eastern portion of the forest had been so designated in an attempt to provide protection for the bear and to avoid having the area listed as critical habitat by the fish and wildlife service. Such a listing would automatically have resulted in the area being closed to livestock use. We were hopeful that we could continue to graze sheep and cattle in the area while protecting the bear.

The next morning I called the biologist doing research on grizzly bears in Yellowstone Park to find out if he knew of any bears in that general area. He checked his sighting list and found that a radio collared female grizzly was last recorded just west of West Yellowstone. We borrowed a radio receiver from the local Idaho Fish and Game officer and set it for the frequency of the bear's radio so we could track her.

The forest biologist and I spent the next two days trying to locate the bear. In the meantime the rancher had set up a propane cannon by his sheep bed grounds. The cannon, plus shots from the sheep herders pistol, had kept the bear out of the sheep for two nights but the bear was becoming bolder. We finally located the bear during daylight hours and with an airplane were able to see that the bear had two cubs with her. She would bed down each day a couple of miles up the mountain from the sheep.

The biologist and I decided to spend the next few nights with the sheep in their bed grounds and assist the permittee and herder in keeping the bear from killing any sheep. Hopefully she would move back into the park in a few days. We would use the radio to follow the movements of the bear each evening as she started for the band of sheep. Up to this time she had been feeding on ants and berries. We also discovered that she was eating sheep droppings.

We would park our pickup near the sheep and shine our headlights and spotlights into the timber when we could determine the presence of the bear near the sheep. We would also drive around the area hoping the activity of humans would scare the bears away and they would leave the forest and go back into the park.

As I approached the bed grounds late one night I found the biologist parked in his pickup along a creek. I could see the receiver antenna sticking out of the pickup window. I stopped my pickup behind him and walked around to his window. I asked him if he had the bear located. He said he did. I asked him where she was and he pointed into some willows about twenty feet away. Needless to say I was back into my pickup in about two jumps.

After a few more nights it was obvious the bear was not going to leave the sheep alone and was becoming more aggressive. We convinced the fish and game officer to help us trap the bear and move her back into the park. That next day we got two culvert traps and set them up near the sheep. During this time the sheep had been moved every day and were in the vicinity of the rancher's home.

We baited the traps with bread, fish from a hatchery and other food items to attract the bear. She did not come near the traps the next night. The following day the rancher provided us with a dead sheep. We cut her open and dragged her carcass around the area behind our pickup hoping the bear would pick up the scent in her wanderings. We then put parts of her into the two traps.

That night about midnight we located the bear with our receiver and she was working toward the traps. The fish and game biologist and I were sitting in his pickup about two hundred feet from the traps. A while later we heard one of the traps slam shut. About an hour later we heard the other trap slam shut. I jumped out of the pickup to run and see if we had caught the bears. The fish and game biologist warned me not to go near in the dark. He said the two cubs could each have gone into a trap and the sow could be staying nearby. We could no longer pickup the radio signal so we did not know where she was.

When daylight came we could see that both traps had been sprung and no bears were in sight. We cautiously approached the traps. Much to our joy the two cubs were in one trap and the sow was in the other one. Apparently the cubs had been less cautious and had entered the first trap together. After not being able to get them out the sow herself had entered the other trap. We could not believe our luck.

We tranquilized the bears and put collars on the cubs. We took the old radio off the sow and placed a new one on her. We weighed them, put tatoos on the cubs and put them back into the traps before they revived. They were then hauled back into Yellowstone Park over one hundred miles away.

I had been involved in trapping and snaring other grizzly bears but this was the most exciting episode for me. Unfortunately the bears were back the next year. The sow had to be killed because she would not stay within designated habitat. Later both cubs were also killed. The sheep were removed from the range on Two Top Mountain and relocated outside grizzly bear habitat.

BOB'S BEAR RESCUE

Chuck Smay

My first job was on the Hume Lake Ranger District on the Sequoia National Forest. During the time I worked there from 1955 to 1959, I learned many things about the Forest Service. Some of them served as lessons on what not to do in a given situation. One of my supervisors was Assistant Ranger Bob Werner. As a new forest worker I was impressed with the energy that Bob put into his job, He seemed to always do everything "full speed ahead." I spent several days with him marking timber. His lunch eating habits were an example of his fast approach to everything. Every day he had the same thing for lunch. It consisted of a can of sardines and a banana. At lunch break, he would reach in the back pocket of its cruiser vest and pull out the can of sardines. Still standing up he would use the can key to roll back the top of the can. From his vest pocket he took out a small plastic fork and proceeded to eat the contents of the can without stopping. Next he would pull out the banana, peal it and eat it in about four bites. He would then neatly fold up the banana peel, place it into the empty sardine can, roll the top shut and place the empty container back in his cruiser vest. Lunch was over! By now I usually had sat down and perhaps eaten most of my sandwich, usually faster than I wanted to since I knew after the first couple of days working with Bob that this was not to be a leisurely picnic. Bob would pace around giving me a few more minutes to bolt down the remainder of my lunch. Lunch was usually 15 to 20 minutes long due to my inability or unwillingness to chew any faster. Lunch over, off we would go to mark some more trees. I learned a lot from Bob, including how to eat faster!

Fortunately, I was not with Bob the day he decided to implement one of his wildlife management strategies. I can only imagine what actions he might have expected me to take in this situation. It seems that Bob was driving down the road from highway 180 to the Pinehurst Ranger Station when he was presented with an opportunity that seemed too good to pass up. He came around a corner and spotted a bear cub in the top of a small cedar tree. Bob quickly (how else) stopped the Jeep, opened the back compartment, grabbed an ax and chopped down the tree. The bear cub, not having much experience with foresters, just watched until the tree toppled and landed in the middle of the road. Bob, apparently not having much experience with bear cubs, grabbed the bear by the back of the neck and rump to place him into the Jeep. About then the bear's fear instincts "kicked in" and it started scratching, biting, and according to Bob's account, generally expressing its unhappiness. Bob's leather work gloves were no match for the teeth and claws of a very scared bear. Being a man of action, Bob quickly (how else) managed to throw the bear cub into the open back door of the 1/4 ton Jeep and slammed the door closed. Visualize the picture for a minute. We have a full cab Jeep in which there is no separation between the front driver's seat and the remainder of the enclosed cab. Into this limited space we have placed a very frightened and possibly very angry bear cub that has a strong physical desire to be back in the wild. We have the rescuer of the bear, standing outside of the vehicle. He is a bit reluctant to enter the vehicle and proceed to the ranger station with his passenger. We have the mother of the bear, who fortunately for the driver of the vehicle, did not make an appearance during this rescue process. During this time of indecision, the bear cub proceeded to autograph the inside of the vehicle with tooth, claw, and some other deposits. Until the day the district traded the Jeep, it had very evident claw marks all over the inside of the cab. Not every ranger can train a bear to mark its territory in this manner.

While Bob was deciding on his next bold move, the local school bus came upon the scene. Fortunately, the driver was on the return run and had time to stop to lend assistance. Somehow, the two of them subdued the bear cub. The school bus driver took charge of the bear and took it to a local business. The bear was on display for a few days before it was released.

You can imagine how much fun Bob's co-workers had in teasing him about this wildlife adventure and just what his overall plan was in the first place. I don't recall that he ever revealed his master plan in this bit of wildlife management.

BEAR MY SOUL

Susan Menanno

Pizza before leaving home is always a delight. With leftovers I knew I would have some for the trail the next day. I was heading in for my usual four day tour. It was time to walk up the Butte Fork Trail and enjoy the diversity from canyon to lake to ridge.

Usually my week begins by talking with my supervisor about my planned travel plan and projects I plan to work on while in the wilderness. With that done, I arranged to be dropped off Friday morning and picked up Monday afternoon. This is always great because I can cover more of the wilderness and not have to rewalk any trails.

Must have been the pizza (pesto and artichoke) that attracted the wildlife to me this day. The canyon trail is eight miles long where I began my journey at Shoofly Trailhead. Having passed the "Guardian" trees, two sugar pine in which the trail walks through; both are so big that six people joining hands can encircle these elders, always greet me. A mid-sized bear ran across my path only ten feet in front of me. WOW!

such a gift. A mile later, another bear crossed my path. I must have bear medicine with me this day. Such a delight, for in this part of California, bear pursuit season is still legal and the bears are more elusive each year. To see two within three miles of the trailhead is a gift for this ranger!

I can smell that foil wrapped pizza and it must be time to have a slice. But my body stops. It's that wonderful sensation when the body/mind are working in partnership with one another. Usually the mind interfers with the wisdom of the body and clouds the reaction time. Ah, when that dimension is reversed or shall I say, when the true essence of body wisdom comes forth and the body reacts, it is a sensation like childbirth. The body simply begins to do its thing. I stop. Look up .... there's a black bear with a white "V" across its chest looking at me very intently. This is bear sighting number three. "Hello," I say as she looks at me and neither of us move. Again, with pursuit season these bears are usually on the run, but she and I have contact and wonder which one of us is going to move first. Lucky for me she slowly walks deeper into the canyon. I am glad she's not running, for it is much too hot for that. WOW! The ole adrenaline .... can I have my pizza now? Well, maybe I will just get a little farther up canyon before I do that.

But two more bears crossed my path before I have any pizza. What a day! Five bears. It's nearly 2 p.m. and its been several hours since breakfast. I want pizza! Finally, a big incense cedar and I take my pack off. I hear a cracking of brush behind me as I yell, "Okay, I know you're there, but I am going to have my pizza now!"

Finally, with belly full I begin to head on up canyon again. Moving a little slower now, day getting hotter, pack feeling heavier, I round a bend in the river and the eastern piece of Cedar Basin. I love these magnificent giants! Looking at the trail, the sensation happens again! What is that? It's so small that my body stops and my mind reels to catch up. It's the smallest bear cub I have ever seen. Look at those pointy little ears! And there's mom... and she's the biggest bear I have seen back here in some time. Guess I will just stand here and she holds my gaze and my heart beats harder. Suddenly baby moves, and mama still holds my gaze and I see baby now looking at me with renewed interest. My heart pounds louder, as mama stands over her new cub and I say, "I will be moving through now." Finally braking the concentrated gaze of mama, I move quickly and wonder if indeed I did just see seven bears within the past eight miles. And will I see another to make it eight bears, one for each mile. But who am I to tempt fate. How lucky am I to see even seven bears. Any one of them could have had my pizza or me for their lunch. But each shared my gaze and my path as I shared their home.

That was three years ago. This year I have not seen a bear in Red Buttes. Plenty of signs, but no sighting. I realize today just how lucky I was to share a moment in time with seven bears.

BOAT TRANSPORTATION AND GAME

M. L. Merritt

Local travel in southeastern Alaska in 1921 was by gas powered boats. There were no roads, except near settlements and few trails, so the Forest Service maintained a fleet of eight or nine boats (from 35 to 60 feet long). These were comfortable and seaworthy and provided living quarters in the field. During my time, one boat (The Ranger III) was wrecked on a reef southwest of Admiralty Island. Two others were sunk and raised but generally boat travel was pleasant and relaxing. In the fall, when it was necessary to tie up or anchor during bad weather, opportunity was afforded for duck and goose shooting. This hunting was excellent and everyone had all the birds they could use. Deer hunting was also good in season.

Bears were numerous, particularly black bears, though very shy. I remember some tremendous bear tracks in the Martin River flats north of Katella. The individual footprints seemed nearly as wide as my foot was long but I suppose memory of size is unreliable. Anyway, the bears were huge by any standards. On Afognac Island were extensive grasslands. The brown bears there would beat down trails through the dense grass as they went up and downhill. These trails were double ones, with a separate path for the feet on either side of the body. One of our young foresters, Jack Thayer, was killed while cruising on Admiralty Island. He had shot at and wounded a large brownie that had reared up in his path. It immediately rushed him and cuffed, scratched and bit him to death. The bear escaped. After that, all of our men carried rifles while in bear country and usually did not travel alone.

ONE TOUGH TMA

Phil Kromer

It was dark when I arrived at the Lumberyard Ranger Station on the Amador District, Eldorado National Forest. I was there for a weekend of deer hunting with my friend Dave Jones in that fall in the early 1960s. I had replaced Dave as TMA on the Georgetown District when he moved to Amador and we made good hunting partners.

There was a light on in the office so I stopped there first to see if it was Dave working late. TMA Bill Cotter looked up from his desk when I walked in. As we exchanged greetings I could tell Bill was really excited about something.

"You'll never guess what I did today!" he exclaimed.

"No, what did you do today?" I asked.

"I killed a bear with a shovel!" he fairly shouted.

It seems that he had an appointment earlier in the day with a salvage logger to go out and mark some bug trees for a small sale. They left in the logger's old Dodge Power Wagon which was driven by the logger's helper. When they spotted a patch of bug trees above the road they parked the truck and Bill and the logger started up the hill while the helper slid down behind the wheel to catch a few winks.

Up in the woods they heard some strange noises. On investigating, they found a bear which had been shot some days before. It was badly injured and would stagger along for a few feet then fall down.

"Do you have a gun in the truck?" Bill asked.

"No, I sure don't," the logger answered.

They found that, by throwing rocks and sticks at the bear, they could pretty well steer it in a particular direction.

"Tell you what," Bill said. "You go back to the truck. I'll steer him down to the road and when he gets there, you run over him with the truck."

Being an excitable little fellow, the logger tore off down the mountain. He ran up to the truck, yanked open the driver's door and hollered, "Move over! Move Over!"

As he slid across the seat the startled driver asked, "What'sa matter?"

"Cotter's running a bear down the hill and when it hits the road we're going to run over it with the truck!" the logger explained.

Not knowing that the bear could hardly walk, the helper scrambled all the way across the cab and right on out the passenger door. "You're crazy as hell! Cotter might be bad but he ain't that bad. I don't know what's going on, but I don't want any part of it."

The logger fired up the Power Wagon and waited. In a few minutes Bill and the bear approached the road. The bear was even weaker than when they had first found it. Bill trotted over to the truck.

"That poor fellow's about had it. You got any tools?" he asked.

The logger motioned toward the back, "Yeah, there's some back there."

Bill picked out a shovel and returned to where the bear had fallen on the road. With a few well placed whacks behind the neck, he put the bear out of its misery.

And that's how it came to be that Bill Cotter killed a bear with a shovel.

BEARS IN THE CLEARWATER
NATIONAL FOREST

R. W. Smith

In the summer of 1953, I worked as a surveying aid on the Canyon Ranger District. The Canyon Ranger Station at that time was at the dead end of a low standard road, about two hours drive from Pierce, Idaho.

On a sunny Saturday morning I decided to go for a hike up the trail that followed the North Fork of the Clearwater River. I had been walking about an hour and a half when the trail passed through an open area with a lot of huckleberry bushes. The bushes were loaded with berries and on seeing them I said, "Ah ha!" I immediately heard a loud crashing noise and saw a medium sized black bear take off running in the opposite direction. I don't know whether the bear was as scared as I but we both ran in different directions.

After walking back toward the ranger station for about five minutes, I suddenly thought, "Why head back, the bear ran away from me, when he heard my voice." I turned around and continued on up the trail.

In the summer of 1959, I was designing bridges for the Oregon Highway Department. My new wife and I took a vacation on the Clearwater National Forest where I had worked six summers before. We camped at a Forest Service campground where Beaver Creek enters the North Fork of the Clearwater River. The campground was rather primitive. There were several three inch diameter western red cedars and some western white pine trees along with 20 foot high alders. The two outhouses were the old fashioned two holers with no pains taken to ventilate the odors.

We spread out our sleeping bags that night on a level patch of ground about 75 feet southeast of one of the outhouses. I woke up about an hour or two before sunup. Looking to the northwest, I saw the dark silhouette of what appeared to be a bear standing on his hind legs. I woke up my wife and we made a mad dash for the car. Two or three hours later I woke up and saw by daylight that what had appeared to be a bear was one of the outhouses in the campground.

BEARS AND THE ANGELES NATIONAL FOREST

David M. Waite

Generally, one would not associate wild bears with a national forest located within a day's drive of a metropolitan area teeming with over eight million people. However, the Angeles National Forest is unique in many ways and supports a respectable population of bears.

Historically, this area was home to the California grizzly bear but they were exterminated early in the twentieth century. Sometime in the 1920s, a group of wildlife enthusiasts persuaded the California Fish and Game authorities to introduce some black bears into the Angeles National Forest. About the same time, the Yosemite National Park was having an abundance of bears in the Merced River drainage and the Angeles NF, along with other Southern California forests, were the recipients of several pairs of bears. Over the years, this population took root and survived the usual fire, flood, draught and the famine which followed the three natural disasters.

By the late sixties and early seventies, a combination of factors resulted in larger than normal bear population and they became somewhat of a problem to the rangers. During the late fifties and early sixties there were several major wildfires that burned over large areas of the Angeles NF. The chaparral regrowth produced an abundance of wildlife food and cover. Deer and small game thrived. Manzanita, scrub oak and other shrubs and trees produced good crops of mast. End result was a noticeable increase in bear sightings and encounters, more complaints of break-ins by cabin owners, and bear damage to apiaries by beekeepers. Campgrounds and picnic areas were becoming prime targets as the bears found easy pickings in the garbage cans and pits.

The California Fish and Game officials worked closely with Forest Service wildlife biologists to solve the problems without killing the offending bears. In the years before the use of tranquilizing dart guns, they devised large traps made out of a section of culvert pipe, four feet in diameter, mounted on wheels. It worked like a box trap and when the bear was inside they hauled the trapped bear to a new location where it was released. This was quite successful in most cases, however, there was one young male bear that was a frequent visitor at the Charlton Picnic Area on the former Arroyo Seco Ranger District that was caught and moved more than forty air miles away. He was back at Charlton three days later. He was so used to being near humans that he was easy prey for a lucky hunter. The Charlton bears were quite a nuisance to the district recreation officer as they were the cause of rapid turnover in maintenance personnel. One occurrence vividly illustrates the problem. The Monday morning cleanup crew had collected a pickup truck load of full garbage cans and backed up to the collection bin to empty the cans. As they got out of the truck, the lid on the bin suddenly flew open and a good sized bear stood up and jumped out. The garbage haulers dived back into the truck and sped away, spilling garbage and trash in their wake. The bear took off into the brush and did not come back for several days. It was too much for the newly employed clean up people. They had been recruited from the Los Angeles Inner City State Employment Office and the bugs and snakes were enough to endure, but the bears were just too much. They resigned on the spot and vowed never again to set foot outside of civilization.

Another incident was more serious and shows that bears, even young yearling cubs, can be dangerous. A small group of teenage boys were spending a weekend in a trail camp on the West Fork of the San Gabriel River, just below Cogswell Dam. Early in the morning of the second day the group was suddenly awakened by the frantic screams of one of the boys. In the dim light they could see a bear dashing out of the camp, and scrambled out of their sleeping bags to check on their wounded friend. The boy's head had scrapes and bruises that needed medical attention but he had suffered no life threatening injuries. Mt. Baldy District Ranger, Anselmo Lewis, investigated the incident and his report indicated that the campers may have attracted the bear by not keeping their site clean and tidy. He reported finding discarded foods, including ham or bacon grease, partly eaten sandwiches and chicken bones scattered near the sleeping bags. There was also offal left where they had cleaned some trout nearby along the edge of the creek. Ranger Lewis concluded his report by stating, "The bear probably thought he was biting into a large chunk of ham or bacon which was actually the boy's head protruding from the sleeping bag."

There were, and continue to be, incidents where the uneducated forest users provoke wild animals into situations where the human can be severely injured. This situation often occurs where bears are seen along forest area roads or highways. Many times people will stop and get out of their vehicles to get photographs. In one case a mother had her two small children pose beside a small bear cub. She did not associate the cub with an adult mother bear being in the nearby brush. Fortunately in this case a ranger came along just in time to get the children and mother safely back in their car before the mother bear made an attack. In other cases, people leave pet food and small pets outside exposed to foraging bears, coyotes, mountain lions and other wild animals looking for an easy meal.

Bears continue to conflict with humans as more and more people move into their domain. Wildlife confrontations are just part of the problems urban foresters must solve in many parts of the country in the twenty-first century. The Angeles National Forest officers have had these problems for many years and will continue to face these problems into the next millennium.

EARLY LOOKOUT EXPERIENCE

Carl Albrecht

The most exciting events I experienced were on the lookout. The first year was 1930. A packer packed me into Beaver Butte on the Mt. Hood National Forest.

There was a cougar that would follow me when I went after water. The trail being dusty where the cattle walked, I would see the cougar's tracks in my track when I came from the spring. I tried all summer to see him. I would hide in the brush or I would wait on a high point overlooking the trail but never got to see him.

Bears would visit the spring also. I would get to see them once in awhile. I had a camera that year and tried to get a picture of them but could never get close enough. One day, when going after water I saw what I thought was a big black cow coming through the pole patch. I kept going and looked up. It was not a cow but a huge bear! It did not see me or hear me and we met on the trail. I hollered at him and he gave a big woof and took off down through the trees on a dead run then turned around and came back to the trail, reared up on his hind feet and came toward me. I let him get within about 15 feet from me and I figured I must do something so I fired my 22 over the top of his head. He let out a woof and took off down through the pole patch but turned around and came back again three more times. Each time I would fire over his head. The last time he followed alongside about 30 feet away, frothing at the mouth and snapping his teeth. He followed until I came out in the opening at the lookout, then sat there swinging his head back and forth. A few days later an Indian rider came by and I told him about the bear. He said, "Oh, you seen that old grizzly!" It scared me then but I never saw him again.

The tracks of his front feet were as large as a dinner plate and the toes of his hind foot tracks were longer than my shoe tracks and I wear a size 12 shoe! When he reared up on his hind feet it looked like I could lay my two hands spread out between his ears.

About two weeks later an Indian was fishing in one of the lakes not too far from there and he said he saw a huge bear that came after him. He had a raft on the lake and he jumped on it and shoved it out on the lake. He emptied his .32 caliber revolver into him and only got a grunt each time he fired. The bear waded out in the lake to where he had to swim, then turned back and disappeared. The Indian paddled to the other side of the lake where his horse was and hightailed for camp. I believe this is one of the last grizzlies ever seen in Oregon.

THE CASE OF THE BRASSY BEAR

Emil Sabol

In 1964, when I was district ranger at Union Creek on the Rogue River National Forest, the station compound was being visited nocturnally by a hungry black bear. He rummaged through the residential garbage cans and left a mess, as you can imagine. This happened on several nights. It appeared that the problem was not going to be resolved without some sort of action by the residents.

Thinking that it was an errant bruin from the garbage dumps at Crater Lake National Park, we decided to seek the aid of our park service friends. Buck Evans, who was then chief ranger, agreed to lend us their trailer mounted live trap. This consisted of a section of a six-foot culvert mounted on wheels, with a trap door spring loaded to a bait can which hung at the rear of the culvert. The culvert was closed on that end. We loaded the bait can with bacon chunks and drippings and other goodies which were considered sumptuous bear fare.

We parked that rig in various locations on the station for several nights but the bear wouldn't bite. Meanwhile, he continued to sample the garbage cans of the station personnel. We despaired of ever catching that guy alive and were considering turning loose some of the mighty hunters among the station's work force.

Well, this bear solved the problem for us in the wee hours of the next day. He decided to do a little marauding around the cabins behind Beckie's Cafe, a special use which was situated (and still is) adjacent to Union Creek Ranger Station. It so happened that Mrs. Gene Arias, the wife of our blister rust control foreman, worked part time at Beckie's and was staying in one of the cabins along with another waitress. The bear strolled across the porch of the cabin and began to sniff and snort near the door. It was about 3 a.m.

What the bear didn't know was that Mrs. Arias was an accomplished hunter and kept a .300 Savage handy in the cabin. Her girlfriend had a .32 Winchester and together they dispatched the bear right there on the cabin porch. In the morning when I came to Beckie's Cafe for coffee, the ladies showed me their trophy which had already been "skun out" and dressed.

While we were a little embarrassed by our failure with the trap, we were pleased that the problem had been solved by one of our own. I don't remember that anyone had written an environmental analysis for the project.

B-B-B-BEARS

Chuck Hill

Back in 1945, we four R5, Shasta National Forest, McCloud District trail crewmen were bedded down and asleep in Rinkel's Cabin on the McCloud River, five miles below Hearst Ranch. My cot was beside and below a four foot square window.

We were awakened sometime in the middle of the night by a terrible racket. Someone said in a shakey voice, "What's that?"

I finally gutted up, turned over and saw a bear's silhouette spread-eagled all over the window above me. "It's a b-b-b-bear," I said.

All four of us quieted down. In a little bit the uproar stopped and the silhouette disappeared.

Next morning we went out to see what the bear had been up to. No damage was apparent. Tracks in the dust didn't add up to a bear covering a four foot window three feet off the ground.

Then Bert Norris, our WWI vet crew boss chuckled. "'Twas only a yearlin' cub," he said. It stood on that upside-down wash tub on that bench below the window.

In 1943 or 1944 at McCloud District's Bartle Guard Station, Jay Free the cook, heard someone messing around in the kitchen of the mess hall in the middle of the night. Jay was bunking in another room of the building. He thought, "Those kids are raidin' the icebox again. I'm gonna scare 'em."

He grabbed his flashlight and .22 pistol and snuck through the dining room to the kitchen with the flashlight turned off and the pistol poked out in front of him. The pistol came up against a body and Jay turned on the flashlight to see a hairy bear belly at the pistol's muzzle. Without thinking he pumped the pistol dry. Killed that sucker right there in the kitchen.

Needless to say, there were no more midnight raids of the Bartle kitchen by the fire crew.

THE BREAK-IN AT BOWERY FLAT

Chuck Smay

In the late 1960s, the Stonyford District on the Mendocino National Forest established several temporary field stations to provide extra fire protection in areas that had been recently logged. Funds were collected from timber sales to pay for the added fire protection. Bowery Flat was selected as a site where a fire prevention technician (FPT) would be stationed to patrol the area. Everyone knew this was going to be a temporary station so in the legendary fashion of the Forest Service an outstanding collection of used materials was assembled to create the Bowery Flat Station. The keystone of the station was a small trailer for a living quarters. I intentionally avoided using the term travel trailer, since to the modern mind this might imply the unit was self-contained. It definitely was not a self-contained unit. Basic shelter might more adequately describe the trailer. The main redeeming feature of the Bowery Flat Station was the setting at a small seasonal meadow surrounded by a mixed stand of ponderosa pine and Douglas fir.

One year the station was opened in mid-May and the seasonal FPT, who's name I cannot recall and his faithful dog, went about his duties checking the logging activities, issuing campfire permits, replacing directional signs, talking with visitors and responding to an occasional smoke report. Given the remote setting and the low number of visitors in the area, the FPT's dog provided much needed companionship, It is generally more acceptable for humans to talk to their dog than to be caught talking to the squirrels after a few months of duty at an isolated station! The social life at Bowery Flat was a bit limited for the average 18-25 year old summer FPT. On their days off they generally left the area for the excitement of the city.

Upon returning to Bowery Flat late one evening after being gone on his days off, the FPT was surprised to find the trailer door standing wide open. Vandalism was generally not a problem then so he was surprised to find that the general respect for property had been violated. It was evident the intruder had tried to open several windows on the trailer before finally deciding to break open the door. The door lock was not just broken but literally ripped out of the light aluminum frame on the trailer door Once inside, the intruder ransacked the place! The FPT's evaluation of the situation soon revealed that hunger was the motive for the break-in as the cupboards and refrigerator seemed to be the main target. Some of the food had been eaten on the spot and it appeared that other items had been carried off. While there were no witnesses to the break in, the evidence left no doubt about the identity of the responsible party. Hidden in the genetic make-up of the mind of a bear is the answer to why it chose to create a new door in the location of a window! Based on the size of the newly created opening it seems the bear thought an opening at least twice the size of the original door better suited his needs. In any event the thin interior plywood and exterior aluminum skin of an old trailer was no match for a determined bear.

As part of the post-break in analysis, the FPT was advised he could file a claim for the food he lost as a result of the bears raid on his home. His claim included his food and the dog food for his faithful patrol companion. The value of the dog food was greater than the food for the patrolman. Several months later the official action came back approving the claim for the FPT's food but denying the claim for the dog food. There was an unofficial note attached to the claim by the reviewer to the supervisor of the FPT indicating, "We noticed with concern that the dog seems to be eating better than the employee!"

BEAR REMOVAL

C. Rod Bacon

Outside the cookshack at Roundtop Work Center on the St. Joe National Forest, there are two trees about five feet apart. In 1968, Vern Richardson had a black lab that scared a young black bear up one of those trees. The commotion brought the camp inhabitants. It was hopeful that by holding back the dog, the bear would come down. This having failed, a fireman by the nickname of "Cap" got a canvas canteen cover, filled it with rocks and climbed the second tree. When Cap got above the bear, he began throwing rocks down, starting the bear's descent, followed by Cap. When the bear was about four feet from the ground, the dog broke lose from its hold. The bear leapt into Cap's tree where they had a race to the top. At about the twenty-foot level, the bear decided it didn't want to tangle with Cap's flailing feet. The bear went airborne and hit the ground running.

It was an effective method of bear removal, as he never returned. However, Cap never used that method again.

KODIAK BEAR

W. G. Weigle

One day Ranger McDonald of Cordova took his boat, "The Restless," to go out to Hinchinbrook Island to scale some timber. He anchored his boat and walked a mile to the timber and just as he reached the timber he ran into a big Kodiak bear. His monthly report card read, "I went to Hinchinbrook Island to scale some timber. I was fully a mile from the boat and met a big Kodiak bear at 12:01. Reached the boat at 12:02."

THE RANGER'S CASE AGAINST "SMOKEY"

Fritz Moisio

There was this mangy bear who entered Desolation Lookout by breaking through the roof. He left the place a shambles. Shortly afterward, a big black bear that claimed the territory around Ruby Creek, busted into Ruby Guard Station. He broke the cook stove and thoroughly ransacked the station.

It didn't take long for a red bear that roamed the upper Thunder Creek area to get wind of John Dayo's trap line cache in Meadow Cabin. This bear did away with John's food supply and his medical kit containing a quart of high proof Canadian rum.

One evening on our way to seek a better trail route in the area of the Skagit Queen Mine, Slim Welch and I stopped at Middle Cabin shelter. We had supper with the trail crew. The cook served meat loaf which may have been bear meat, but was too well disguised with onion and garlic to tell. Since the crew occupied the shelter, Slim and I unrolled our sleeping bags in a small opening away from the trail and shelter. During the night I was awakened by Slim's yell. Being zipped in a mummy bag with arms pinned inside, I arose to a sitting position directly from the hips. Slim's flash beam showed this big lop-eared bear between us—it was eyeball to eyeball with us. Without use of arms or legs, I thought I was a goner. About then the bear said "WOOF" and his halitosis almost got us. All we could do was to "woof" back and to our surprise the bear turned tail and lumbered off. Thanks to the gourmet trail crew cook, we had acquired a powerful lifesaving "WOOF."

On the Okanogan Forest a bear broke into the Forest Service cabin at Spanish Camp. Before leaving he bit into a pressurized can of blue paint and strip painted the interior. This bear made the March 1961 issue of *National Geographic* where on page 354, Avon Denham comments: "Probably the only blue-nosed bear in the Cascades," and, "I bet he turned himself inside out getting out of there."

Finally, the most dastardly of all dastardly bears, was the one that set a forest fire. This happened when Walt Elsbury and I were holding down the ranger station—the other guys were on annual leave. They had taken off for the early fall season high country deer hunt. We were working on a timber sales plan when Gabe Turner, a prospector returning from his claim, reported sighting smoke which appeared to be drifting down the North Fork of the Cascade River. Walt and I took off in a pickup. From the end of the Cascade River road we hiked to Mineral Park. Commencing at Mineral Park shelter we noted bear tracks along the trail. The signs indicated a bear was dragging something. At various points along the trail we picked up a knife, fork, spoon and a crushed milk can with teeth punctures. Upon reaching the fire all evidence fell into place. The bear had taken a fisherman's pack from the shelter and dragged it a mile up the trail. At this point he broke the pack frame, tore and buffed the packsack until all contents were spilled, including a large box of matches. This violent action caused the matches to ignite and set fire to forest fuels on the uphill side of the trail. With routine effort we controlled and mopped the fire.

On our return to the station, we discussed the trespass and the evidence we had against "Smokey." We concluded "Smokey Bear" had evaded the Civil Service System—that he was occupying his position by political appointment, and that our objective should be to get this impostor canned. In submitting the fire report 929, we prepared a strong case against "Smokey." We were unsuccessful; "Smokey's" political status and his stacked up propaganda prevailed. We had to "cease and desist."

A BARE BEAR TREE

R. S. Shelley

A long time ago, when the Roman Nose Lookout was being built, I left the head of Smith River soon after daylight. The boys said, "Take a gun—a lot of bear are in that berry patch five miles up." "No gun," I said, "I'll tree him and you bring the gun with the pack train."

When I reached the berry patch, I suddenly stopped moving. Here came a big, black bear crossing the road about 50 feet ahead of me, eating berries as he went. As he disappeared into the brush, I started barking like a dog and ran after him. In a hundred yards I had him treed and kept him treed for a long half-hour. Bears, as you know, come down backwards. As he saw he had been hoaxed he started backing down and I grabbed a long fir limb, which had blown off in the wind, and slid the sharp point up the tree. Down came the bear—up went the limb—down came the limb and down came the bear. Then, up went the limb again and up, up went the bear. Finally, I left him to the boys. I'm the last one left of that gang, but for those who doubt my story, the marks are still on the tree.

FIRE AND WILDLIFE

Dick Worthington

Around Labor Day of 1955, northern California and southern Oregon experienced a series of the most severe lightning storms ever recorded in that area. Many major fires were started, including the Haystack Fire on the Oak Knoll Ranger District of the Klamath National Forest which was eventually to exceed 150,000 acres. With the normal air flow in the area, the Rogue River Valley quickly filled with smoke. Not only were the airports closed, most of the state and Forest Service lookouts could not see.

On the Rogue River National Forest we had a lot of fires but because of the smoke no one really knew how many, how big or where they all were. All of us were pretty busy for more than a week on a minimum sleep and maximum effort basis. I remember getting home for the first time in a week after it all started. It was for the first full night's sleep I had for the period, only to be rousted out about 4 a.m. to take a logging crew into Crater Lake Park to take over one of their fires.

The fire, about a mile from the highway, was smoldering in very heavy duff. No water was anywhere near, so it was a dry mopup show, just the kind of operation a logging crew absolutely hates! I remember about 10 or 10:30 a.m., as we were eating lunch, a yearling bear showed up. We threw him some sandwiches and he thought we were great. Then we noticed that his paws were burnt and he was obviously in pain because he'd lick them frequently.

One of the crew hiked out to their crew wagon and picked up an old end hook rope. Then, much to my consternation, they lassoed the bear and tied him between a couple of small hemlocks. After using all the burn ointment in our first aid kits, the next problem was to let him loose. Well, we got the rope off of him, but I'm quite sure the bear had fewer cuts, scratches and bruises than most of us. The last we saw of him he was just getting into high gear. His hind legs were reaching up about his ears and his front paws were just visible under his rump.

I was always real partial to young bears after that, for this one kept a logging crew working on a fire they didn't like by providing an hour or so diversion.

THE BOGARD SKUNK MONSTER

Bruce Barron

The old Forest Service Ranger Station at Bogard (on the Lassen National Forest) was nestled in the evening shadows from those rugged peaks of the Caribou Wilderness Area. Huge Eagle Lake trout migrated up meandering Pine Creek to spawn in the deep vernal pools east of the station. Herds of antelope cavorted in the lush meadows, while trophy sized mule deer came down from nearby hillsides to water and forage along the creek bed.

The area was so copious with wildlife, it is no wonder rumors began to spread about a huge striped skunk that had been sighted by local woodsmen. It was often seen out in the meadows shuffling along the streambed. It was of monstrous size. There was conjecture that it was some kind of mutation, and since skunks were known to be carriers of rabies, people talked of forming a posse to hunt it down. There were also suggestions that "maybe it should be captured and sent to a university for scientific study."

Finally, a contingent of concerned woodsmen descended on the U.S. Forest Service Ranger Station at Bogard to confer with Ranger P.D. (Pete) Hook as to what action should be taken.

It was then that Ranger Hook got a sheepish look on his face and confessed that just as spring was beginning to break, he had been cruising a stand of timber in the nearby area. He chanced upon a bear still in the torpor of hibernation sprawled under the protection of a large pile of downed logs. Ranger Hook admitted that he had succumbed to a whim and had used his tree marking spray gun to paint the white stripes down the back of the hibernating bear.

It was midsummer before the hapless bear completely shed his winter coat with the white stripes and rumors of the giant skunk finally faded into the obscurity of time.

SMOKEY BEAR IS SAVED

Jay H. Cravens

In 1950 I was dispatched to a large forest fire on the Lincoln National Forest in New Mexico along with Harlow Yaeger and four other Coconino crew bosses. Harlow supervised project crews on the Elden District and had visited us at the Elden Guard Station. While he never talked about it, Harlow had been a prisoner of war when he was captured by the Japanese in the Philippines during World War II. He was an excellent person to work with and get to know. He taught me a great deal. En route to New Mexico we saw a series of large fires burning on the Sitgreaves and Apache National Forests. Our fire on the Lincoln National Forest was known as the Capitan Gap Fire. A very experienced forest officer by the name of Dean Earl was fire boss. Harlow and I were assigned separate sectors that burned hot all night and crowned and ran during the day. The temperature was very high; it was extremely dry and windy. The fire camp and our food was constantly buffeted by gale force winds. Wind blown debris and sand were in everything we ate. It was a very dangerous fire.

Harlow was in charge of a group of soldiers from Ft. Bliss and was assigned to the southwest sector running up on to Capitan Mountain. His company of soldiers were endangered by a crown fire and almost trapped before Harlow led them to safety on a rock slide. When the fire had passed around them, one of the soldiers heard mournful crying and whimpering sounds. He found a tiny black bear cub clinging to the trunk of a burned tree. The cub's paws were badly burned and one of the soldiers carried him back to the fire camp. I was there when they arrived and the bear was handed to me. It was crying, whimpering and licking its burned paws. I recall it crying as it chewed my leather gloves. I did not know at the time this 10 inch ball of black fur I held in my hands was to become the original Smokey Bear. For years afterwards, my daughters Melissa and Cindy asked me to tell them the true story of Smokey the Bear. Many people think that I found him. I did not find him, but I held the little creature for a short time before he was taken away to become that famous symbol for fire prevention.

BIRDS

THE STORY OF NIGEL

Kelly Andersson

We had a pygmy owl with us for awhile one summer. We were driving back down the old logging road up above McIntyre Creek on the Wallowa-Whitman; a car had evidently dusted the little owl, and he lay there mid-road, ruffled and confused. We picked him up and took him home and named him Nigel. (Everyone knows how owls are supposed to be wise. I had a philosophy professor once whose name was John Hofer. He wrote under the pseudonym of Nigel Fischbein, so I thought Nigel would be a good name, and no one argued me out of it.)

It took us awhile to figure out that he was a pygmy owl. While Nigel rested on a deer antler on a shelf behind and above the wood stove, we paged through the Field Guide to North American Birds. Reading of a "sparrow-sized" owl with "two white-edged black spots resembling eyes" at the back of the neck, we knew we had a pygmy. He really did look like he had eyes in the back of his head, as if the surrealistic pale-yellow orbs in front weren't intimidating enough.

Nigel began his recovery. He seemed depressed at first, and I was afraid every morning that he wouldn't be with us anymore. But I'd find him somewhere, usually on the upstairs railing or in the loft, often perched on one of the large house plants there.

"How is Nigel this morning?" I'd ask. He'd reply that he was hungry, which in owl language sounds like a loud click, like the obnoxious snap teenage girls make with their gum. I'd click back, and then set Nigel on my arm, just near the crook of my elbow, and carry him to the kitchen. Opening the refrigerator door, I'd say, "What'll it be today, Nigel? We have chicken, pork, or fresh venison steak." He always said he wanted venison steak. Steve at that time was cutting up deer for the freezer, and Nigel preferred his rare—as in not cooked—so he was a lucky boy.

Pygmy owls are only about seven inches tall when they are grown up, and Nigel was just a squirt; he didn't appear to have been long out of the nest. He was the most enchanting creature I had ever encountered. I had never been around a wild animal that LIKED to be touched and talked to.

I've rescued a bird or two—a grosbeak kamikazed into my studio window the year before, and lay disheveled on the grass, wondering, I'm sure, what on earth (or in the sky) had got him. I also am one of the few people who have held a hummingbird in their hands: a tiny calliope hummingbird flew through an open door into the living room some years ago. It couldn't find its way back out, because it got up above the door near the transom window. Steve climbed up there, wrapped the tiny creature in a shirt, and handed the package down to me. I took it outside and unfolded it, and in a blur of color it streaked away. I considered it an omen.

Nigel, however, was more like an adopted child. He would sit on my arm, waiting to be fed, and stretch his beak WIDE, eyes squinted shut. I would stuff him with the tiny pieces of venison till I was sure he would burst. I'd stroke his miniature head and trace the feather pattern on his back and smooth the feathers under his chin and down his tiny owl breast. I said hoot to him, like I imagined his mom had, and though he never said hoot back, Nigel looked as though he were hypnotized. It was hard to imagine this toy-sized bantam attacking anything, but his references in the field guide say that pygmy owls attack birds larger than themselves.

I had been a little worried about Nigel's diet, not having previously been too familiar with owls. I made inquiries of a friendly local wildlife biologist, and discovered that Nigel needed more than just venison on his menu. Owls require bone and fiber and feather for the manufacture of pellets. They swallow their prey whole, and then cough up pellets, and if they can't do this I suppose their little systems shut down. So I kept a sharp eye on the barn cats and, sure enough, caught one with a pocket gopher. I negotiated it from her on Nigel's behalf. A pocket gopher is bigger than a pygmy owl and this one was inert so I wasn't sure that Nigel would find it interesting, especially since meals had been thus far forthcoming with no effort on his part.

I set it near his favorite rubber plant in the loft, an offering from his human. He ignored it for a time, but I had cut off his venison rations and hunger soon won out. Nigel spent two days eating up that gopher and began producing pellets like a pro.

Nigel was an ace pilot and could fly from my elbow launch site across the open beam living room to a landing spot thirty feet distant. Often he made for the antler behind the wood stove. He looked quite natural there, naturally stuffed that is, a tribute to a skilled taxidermist. Sometimes, though, he'd sit on the fig tree by the window and gaze outside. That began to bother me.

One morning I walked past Nigel (who was sitting on the railing) on my way into the bedroom. I'd been thinking about why I was feeling guilty about keeping Nigel, and began to examine my motives. I realized that the reason I didn't want to let him go was that I wanted to keep him for myself because I enjoyed him so. I realized that that was selfish, that I was being small. I knew there was no way to justify the thing, but it didn't make it any easier. I began to cry, wanting him to stay, wishing he wanted to. And as if I had called for him, he sailed into the room and landed on the window sill. He looked out at the yard and the forest beyond and then at me. I couldn't meet his tiny predator gaze; I felt wicked and mean-spirited.

Tears streaming down my cheeks, I plucked Nigel from the window. I set him on my arm and ran my finger over his head and down his soft and mottled back. I said hoot to him, opened the window and held my arm outside.

PHEASANTS

Joe Church

In September 1958, I was detailed to Fort Jones as acting district ranger, temporarily replacing Lou Hahn, the sitting ranger, who had been detailed to the Klamath Forest Supervisor's Office to head up the Klamath portion of the nationwide outdoor recreation resource review (ORRR). Lou and his family continued to live on the station, so Ginny and I, with family, rented the Fred Williams' farmhouse in Hungry Hollow Valley, a couple of miles south of Fort Jones. We lived there until the following May when we moved to Orleans on the Six Rivers National Forest.

The farmhouse was located about a quarter mile east of the Eastside Road, had a wood plank fence around the front yard and several shade trees to shield the front and west sides of the house. A pretty nice place and we enjoyed it even though it was a cold place in the winter because it was mostly brick. However, before winter came, there was autumn and with autumn, in particular October, came the pheasants. The big barn up the driveway toward town housed a family of barn owls who would give us the eye as we walked by, but basically, as owls do, kept to themselves. The pheasants were more social, however, and they would often come up to the house and parade on the front yard fence. It was pretty common to see six or eight birds on the fence in the morning, including a couple of beautiful cocks. Autumn also was hunting season and two friends, Bob Sharf and Bob Devlin, new foresters on the Klamath, were looking for a sure place to hunt. I described the situation at our house. Immediately interested, they arranged to come to the farm the following Saturday.

The day dawned clear and cold. We got up early to get ready for the visit and noted the pheasant parade was in full swing. Birds galore. Bob and Bob got there early and, after come coffee and chatter, went out to hunt. They went here, they went there and they went everywhere, but didn't see bird one. By the time they gave up, clouds had rolled in, the wind had picked up and it was cold. They came in to thaw out, have some more coffee and complain loudly about being led to believe there were pheasants actually there. Ginny and I both insisted that there were birds, but they weren't buying any of it. So, off they went, muttering and grumbling about phantom birds. They were gone about fifteen minutes when we looked out into the front yard where there was a line of beautiful pheasants parading along the top slat of the fence. Sharf and Devlin never believed that one either.

AN INHOSPITABLE CAVE

Howard W. Burnett

When you work in the woods, you expect to get good and wet sometimes, but it is always a good policy to find a place to get out of the storm for awhile, just to see if it is a shower that might blow over, or if you are going to have to just take another soaking. (This policy usually only results in delaying the inevitable dousing.) Clouds started to blow in one day when I was checking a logging road on the head of Hightower Creek, high on the south face of the Blue Ridge in the Chattahoochee NF, in Georgia. As the sky darkened, I started to look around for a place where I might stay dry for awhile.

The logging road had a head high bank on the left side, and above that I could see two huge boulders that appeared to have a sort of a cave beneath them. Perhaps I could squeeze in there for a bit. I put my hands on the top of the bank, and tried to raise up enough to see if there truly was a sheltered spot there, when I was rudely greeted by a severe hissing. Thoughts of "rattlesnake," "bobcat" and "bear" passed through my mind in mid-air, as I jumped back away from the bank. It was a jump to be proud of, a classic jump of maybe 12 or 15 feet, as only the adrenaline rush of a nasty surprise can generate!

After circling the area, I could see who was occupying the cave. It was a family of two buzzard chicks, almost fully grown, but still covered with snow white down. That was enough for me—they could have the shelter and I would (and did) get wet! Buzzard nests are nasty, at best, what with leftovers from the good dead things brought to the chicks, plus the youngsters droppings. In addition, a cornered buzzard's inherent defense mechanism is to regurgitate the contents of its stomach at you. Which these chicks did. Can there be any place more gross than a buzzard's nest? I'll take the rain!

I suppose not many people get to see a buzzard's nest, and my education was furthered by my visit that day. But I sure paid for that education with a good wetting!

THE CHICKEN MOVE

Gail C. Baker

It happened when we were being transferred from John Day to the Gasquet Ranger District in 1939. Gasquet District was still part of the Siskiyou National Forest in R6 at that time. It has since been transferred to the Six Rivers National Forest in R5.

In those days, most transfers of personnel were made in the spring before fire season. The Forest Service did the moving by using one of the big red fire trucks that was used in the summer to move regional fire cache equipment to fires throughout the region. The regional fire cache was then on Yeon Street in Portland and Roy Walker was in charge of the caches. When my move came up Roy brought over one of the big red fire trucks to move us from John Day to Gasquet.

We were living in a small rental house on the outskirts of John Day. There was an old barn on the place and the owner who lived there before us had chickens. When they moved they left one old hen on the place. Soon she wanted to set so we sent to Montgomery Ward and got a dozen day old Rhode Island chicks and gave them to her.

At that time we had only a handful of belongings and, wanting to make a somewhat decent load for Roy and the big red truck, I crated the dozen chickens and added them to the load. Even that did not make much of a load. So we arranged, through Ranger Mike Palmer, who knew the Langs who owned the Rose City Upholstery on Sandy Boulevard in Portland, to pick up a sofa and matching chair on our way through. We also arranged to pick up a set of springs and mattress and other things a short distance from the Rose City establishment on Sandy Boulevard.

I had Roy drive the truck via Portland and stop first at the Rose City Upholstery where I would meet him and help load the living room set. Everything worked out fine but, since it was only a short distance from the Rose City Upholstery to the next stop, we did not bother to tie the load on securely. As Roy drove the truck down Sandy, the chicken crate fell off and broke wide open. The dozen chickens were loose in the middle of busy Sandy Boulevard. I honked the horn and got Roy's attention. He and I caught every one of those chickens without losing a one! That was in 1939. What do you think would happen if you tried to do that today?

The chickens and the rest of our things arrived safely at Gasquet and we served fresh eggs and fried chicken to dignitaries from the regional office and to the Forest Supervisor Ed Cliff on their inspection trips to the district. Probably helped me get a "satisfactory rating."

ENCOUNTER WITH AN OWL

Bob Gray

I'm not really sure what kind it was, except that it was big and mean. Anyway, here's the story:

Robert Pratt, a co-worker with me on the old Sacramento (Mt. Shasta) Ranger District and I were looking for a late night lightning fire near the Military Pass Road. While driving slowly up the dusty, sandy road this owl flew ahead in the glow of our headlights and landed in the middle of the road about sixty feet or so ahead of us. We stopped and looked at him for awhile and then drove on ahead causing him to fly on up the road a hundred yards or so before alighting again in the middle of the road where he sat and glared at our headlights. He did this several time until I finally said to Robert, "Let's see if we can catch him." Robert stammered a little and said, "You catch him, I'll drive." So, with the plan in mind to get out of the pickup and creep around through the scattered brush and juniper, I'd get beyond him and sneak up to his blind side and grab him from behind. All was going well as I crawled up behind him on hands and knees, while he continued to stare into the headlights. I think the motor noise kept him from hearing me. Well, I got within reaching distance before I realized how big the prey was. I made my lunge and grabbed a leg and foot. The struggle didn't last long. His free foot had great talons and his strong wings nearly beat me to death before I managed to release him. Fortunately, only my ego was bruised and battered from the incident, but believe me, "an owl ain't something to be messed with."

About that fire; we never found it as it probably burned itself out in the sparse vegetation.

A DUCK DAY'S WORK

Harvey Mack

It never entered my head that one could have more than their fill of ducks and geese. When we moved to the Modoc in 1954, we soon learned that we were in a waterfowl paradise and that the hunters on the staff were more than willing to share. We soon found out that it was the hunt, not the waterfowl, that was important to them. Bob Cron was the most generous of the bunch. He made regular hunting trips to Tule Lake and always came home with a lot of birds. Since he was not too excited about cleaning and eating all of his birds, he regularly would drop them off on our front porch where I would find them when I came home from the office. I had made the mistake of telling him that we enjoyed ducks and geese, but not as a steady diet. We finally got to the point where even our cat no longer was excited about duck meat so we had to politely discourage his leaving many more and, if I recall correctly, the last bunch included a woodpecker. To this day, I never have gotten back a taste for ducks or geese, even for special holidays.

In 1955, I had another very unusual duck experience. Three members of the RO staff from San Francisco had come to the Modoc to make a limited GI inspection, mostly in the nature of field trips. They seemed to have a special interest in waterfowl, lakes, recreation, etc., near Tule Lake. One evening they returned to Alturas with their vehicle loaded with dead ducks and the problem began. What do you do with three or more limits of ducks during the hot summer and they were going to the Klamath the next day.

The hotel owner was a good friend of the forest so we turned to him for help. He managed to find several cardboard boxes and some dry ice so we were able to pack the birds away for the night. The next morning Supervisor Rahm broke the news to me that I was to take his sedan, load it with the ducks, and deliver them to Yreka with the hopes that I could find some way to have them frozen. Now remember, I was not a hunter, I did not have a hunting license and I had three or more limits in boxes in a Forest Service sedan. Neal cautioned me not to get involved in any way with a game warden!

I made it without incident to Yreka and promptly called upon the supervisor for assistance. I explained the situation and he was somewhat trapped as they were now spending time on the Klamath Forest. He called around and finally found a friend, the manager of the local grocery market, who agreed to store the boxes of ducks in his freezer until arrangements could be made to get them to San Francisco. Now relieved of my cargo, I returned to Alturas and reported that my "other duties as assigned" responsibility had been met without even a sign of a bad odor from any of the ducks.

QUAIL, OATS, AND COMMUNITY RECOGNITION

Bob Spivey

I grew up on the Hume Lake District of the Sequoia NF where my father Paul Spivey was a technician. We lived on the Pinehurst Ranger Station during the school year, and dad would move up to the Hume Lake Guard Station as soon as the snow was off the roads in the spring. My mother Dorothy and sister Kathie and I would follow as soon as school was out. In the fall the process was reversed.

The CCC era ranger station at Pinehurst had the usual collection of buildings, including residences, office, garages, warehouses and cookhouse. A rather large area had been fenced in to contain the Forest Service stock. As a young boy, the ranger station and environs offered lots of interesting people, activities and places to explore.

Occasionally, after a storm had left a foot or two of snow, I would go down to where the oats were stored and put a couple handfuls in my coat pocket and wander down into the pasture to find the animals and offer them a little snack.

On one of these excursions I came upon a bunch of quail trying to scratch down through the snow to get to the soil and find something to eat. I sprinkled out some oats under a big manzanita bush and noted that the quail relished this source of food.

At the time I was in the eighth grade at the Miramonte School, there were two others students along with me in that grade. I mentioned to them my experience, and that information got to the teacher of the four upper grades, my teacher. She thought this was a good example of a young man helping the wild creatures, so she told the local game warden. He spread the word around the mountain area served by the small Miramonte School and I received recognition for my care of the quail.

My family was proud of me of course. And at the same time my dad made sure that I understood a couple of important lessons. First was that doing good for natural resources would always bring a positive reaction. He suggested maybe I would want to make a career of that. And second, I should never give away what wasn't mine to give.

RED-TAILED FRICASSEE

Bruce Barron

During World War II the Forest Service was in desperate need for bodies to fill seasonal fire control positions. Remote locations on the Goosenest District of the old Shasta Forest were especially hard to fill.

One summer we hired a young boy fresh out of New York City to man the Ball Mountain Lookout Station west of Mt. Hebron. He had read stories about Daniel Boone and other frontiersmen, so he came equipped with a .22 rifle and lots of ammunition. His intent was to supplement his larder with wild game and "live off the fat of the land!"

He would frequently call on the telephone and describe a Stellar jay, woodpecker, red-shafted flicker, or some other hapless bird that he had unceremoniously tossed into the stew pot. (He was definitely not a candidate for an honorary membership in the Audubon Society or Sierra Club.) One day he called with a note of desperation in his voice. He had killed a big bird a couple of days before and complained of the tough, sinewy meat. He described a red-tailed hawk that had evidently been riding the thermals around Ball Mountain for several years. He also complained of a swollen tongue, stomach ache, flatulence and chronic constipation.

He was advised to look into his first aid kit for a small round box filled with little pink pills labeled cascara, and to take two of these pills with a large glass of water per instructions of the label.

All was quiet for an hour or two; then we got another call. This time he complained of severe stomach cramps, gut-rumblings, loose bowels and a myriad of other gastrointestinal malfunctions. After we asked if he had taken a couple of the cascara pills, his response was that he had taken the whole box full of two or three dozen pills. He said, "The pills were so small that he didn't think that just two pills would do the job."

Fearing that he may have coincidentally suffered an attack of appendicitis, we rushed him to a local clinic, where the doctor "pumped out his stomach" and purged the superfluity of pills and stringy hawk meat. After he rested his badly abused intestinal tract for a day or two (and laundered his messy underwear), he returned to the lookout and thankfully put the offending rifle in storage for the rest of the season.

CATTLE AND SHEEP

THE WHITE-FACE STEER

Harold E. Smith

In 1911, I was the newly appointed ranger assigned to the newly created Pine Mountain District of the Deschutes National Forest. The district comprised all of Newberry Crater, the west slope of the Paulinas down to the Deschutes River, the north and east slope of the Paulinas to the high desert and south to the Lake County line.

Fish life was nonexistent in both Paulina and East Lakes in 1911. Stocking of the two lakes took place in 1913.

With the opening of the field season in 1912, the district boundaries were changed. Newberry Crater was added to the LaPine District in charge of Ranger John Curl. My headquarters were moved eastward to Antelope Springs.

During Ranger Curl's reign over the Newberry area, the hot springs at the southeast corner of East Lake was discovered. A lease for the site was taken out by one Fred Shintaffer and a start was made toward setting up a lodge. Financially speaking, Shintaffer was operating on a shoestring. Because of limited finances, progress was slow. Lodgepole pine was abundant in the area and Shintaffer was allowed almost unrestricted free use of the logs for building purposes. Thus, within a short period of time, the lodge began to take shape in a series of log cabins.

Late in the fall of 1916, my official duties took me into East Lake. I drove the Model T Ford to the end of one of the pole roads on the north slope of the Paulinas, parked the car and drained the radiator to prevent freezing. From there I hoofed it over the rim and around the lake to the Shintaffer Lodge. As I proceeded toward the divide I met numerous small bands of Millican cattle heading for the lower country. It was snowing heavily. By the time I reached the crater rim, I was kicking my way through 18 inches of the fluffy snow. Two hundred yards or so above the lake shore I came upon a freshly broken trail. A casual examination revealed that it was a man's track and that the traveler had made at least one round trip, up and back. I followed the trail around the lake to where it ended at the Shintaffer cabins. When asked about the trail, Fred said he had been over there attending a bear trap. Knowing that he had trapped bear in the area, I accepted the story as truth. I should have known better, however, for it was not likely that a bear would be out that late in the season.

Next spring, with the snow partially gone from the Paulinas, I made a trip into East Lake to put the telephone line in order. Again I stayed all night at the Shintaffer camp. While there, I noticed some scavenger birds busy with something down along the lake shore. I inquired about the reason for the concentration of birds and was told that they were eating some corned beef that had spoiled during the winter and had been dumped. Asked where the beef came from, Fred said he had bought it at LaPine the previous fall.

Leaving the lake the next morning, I took a shortcut over the north rim. Near the summit, in a thicket of dwarfed lodgepole, I came into a blazed trail. Not blazed in the usual way that larger trees are blazed, though. This was merely brush hacking, lopping off small branches along the way. My first thought was that I had stumbled on a trappers' trail, yet I knew of no trapper having been in there. The trail was leading in my general direction, so I followed it. On top of the ridge, where the trail ended, I found the remains of a white-face steer. Pieces of hide, lower leg bones and skull were in evidence. Instead of being severed at the joints, the leg bones and neck had been chopped off with an axe, indicating a hurried and sloppy job of butchering. Feeling the hide from the forehead, I found a bullet hole. Probing

63

into the neck joint I found a 30-30 bullet which I carefully preserved.

Shintaffer, as we all knew, was short of cash and probably short of supplies. He could have killed a beef any time prior to the November snow but the weather would have been unfavorable. He waited for the freeze-up. When the snow came, the cattle started to move. This was the last chance of the season and conditions were right. Shintaffer, with his 30-30 Marlin, overtook the cattle on the divide, butchered the steer and carried the meat into camp, thereby leaving his tracks in the snow. Only by the mere timing of a few minutes did I miss running into him with his load of meat. Had this happened the story might have been a different ending. He might have shot me in order to conceal his lesser crime.

At my first opportunity, I reported to George Millican. I gave him only the bare facts without revealing my suspicions. The old man told me there was a standing offer, by the Oregon Cattlemen's Association, of $500 for information leading to conviction for crimes of this kind. At that time, $500 looked like big money, especially since my salary, $91.66 per month, was barely enough to sustain my family at a substandard level. Momentarily, I was seized with the ambition of bringing Shintaffer to the bar of justice. First, I would have to take a packhorse to the scene of the butchering and bring out the leg bones and whatever other evidence was available. Second, go to LaPine and check with the merchants to see if Shintaffer had bought any beef there the previous fall. Third, swear out a warrant for the suspect's arrest and seize his rifle for comparison with the bullet I had removed from the steer's head. Fourth, search the Shintaffer premises for bones to match those recovered earlier. I had no doubt that I could gather enough evidence for a conviction. On the other hand, what could I gain? Whether conviction or acquittal, I would lose the friendship and cooperation of Fred, both valuable assets to one in my position. I was reasonably sure that my employment with the government would bar me from accepting the reward.

Finally, I would be spending a lot of time and some money, delving into a case where I could lose much and gain nothing.

The verdict which I imposed on myself was, "Forget the white-face steer and tend to your own business."

THE CARING CATTLEMAN

Robert W. Cermak

We were on the Black Hills Forest for most of 1968 and part of 1969. I was deputy supervisor which meant that mine was the complaint department. Dave Wright was the Nemo District Ranger and reminded me that he had worked for me on a slash crew at Tonasket on the Okanogan (R-6) during the summer of 1953. He also shamefacedly admitted that he was the dumbass crewman who had cut his foot resulting in a lost time accident for Ranger Everett Lynch and a thorough chewing out for TMA Bert Wells and for me. Every district has its characters and the Nemo District, headquarters Deadwood, was no exception. Lawrence F. Heath lived in the Nemo Valley and ran cattle on a nearby allotment. Dave had had trouble with Lawrence for three years running because he left stock on the range for weeks after the end of the season. Finally, in exasperation he recommended the supervisor send Heath a letter stating that he was in trespass and that his allotment numbers would be cut 10% for repeated violations. The response from Heath was a four page handwritten letter detailing his problems with trees from "the forest reserve" falling and knocking down his fences, with his bouts with the "flu" which kept him from removing said trees, with his travails in pursuing his livestock, with his troubles with doctors in Rapid and with assorted other complaints. His letter quoted rangers long since passed to their reward to the effect that he had never committed an offense.

I wrote back to Lawrence suggesting that he come see me and make his case in person. Bad mistake! A few days later our resource clerk came to the door and said that Lawrence Heath was there to see me. As she turned to leave she pinched her nose and said "Phew! " Deputy was an important job as anyone could tell by my "office. " It was a one time closet that was just big enough for a desk and a chair opposite with a window that refused to open. Into this cubicle shuffled Lawrence Heath. He wore gray chambray trousers and shirt and a gray fedora. His face was gray as were his hand. I thought that maybe he had a skin condition. Then he removed his hat disclosing a pasty white forehead that contrasted with the rest of his body. I blinked and realized that this guy was so dirty that all of him was gray, so dirty that his stench filled the little room and made me choke. I shook his gray hand and then sat back as far away from him as I could get, not very far. He began his tale of woe as I tried to breathe through my mouth. He talked and talked. I listened and nodded and listened and nodded, sucking the rancid air in through my mouth and hoping that it wouldn't shrivel my lungs. Finally, after nearly an hour, he ran down and I was able to politely usher him past the resource clerk who grimaced in sympathy and out the door. Later I wondered if he had deliberately not washed for six months in preparation for the interview. Nope!

I called Dave and charged him with sending the walking effluvia to me just because I was the deputy. "Oh no," claimed Dave, "He's always like that." Then he went on to prove his case. He had visited Lawrence one winter to give him pluperfect hell for leaving his cows on the range to starve. When he entered the house he was assaulted with a smell something like a cross between a slaughterhouse and an ill kept barn. He chastised Lawrence, who protested that he was misunderstood. As proof he pointed to a young calf laying behind the stove. He was keeping the calf warm and out of the frigid South Dakota winter. Dave had to leave before he lost consciousness but returned the following spring to get Lawrence's signature on his grazing permit. Lawrence invited him in while he found his specs and laboriously signed the form. Meanwhile, Dave held his breath. He happened to glance casually toward the stove. There was something behind it. He looked more carefully and realized in shock that it was the mummified remains of the calf that Lawrence had "saved" the winter before, still lying behind the stove.

SHEEP

Rudo L. Fromme

It was in the spring of 1912, as I remember, that I reached the Mule Creek Hotel late one evening from a walking inspection down the Rogue River Trail. Here I learned that a band of 200 sheep were being unloaded from the railroad at Westfork for driving via Ninemile and Marial to this point and on down river for experimental summer grazing along the coast near Gold Beach.

The Mule Creek Hotel, by the way, deserves a brief description as to its facilities around 1910 and '12. It was a very plain pole and shake building of two stories. The lower floor accommodated a small store and dining arrangements, while the upper floor served as sleeping quarters for the family and guests. There were no partitions, rooms being blocked off with old sheets or other such material spread between roof supporting posts. Candle and lantern light often furnished early to bed folks some weird and occasionally exciting silhouettes of the bedtime preparations of later arrivers.

The hotel was a nightly playground for fleas. The only peaceful night I ever had there in that respect was when I bunked with the then supervisor McDaniels some years later in connection with a short inspection assignment. There was some enticing allure about his body that caused these little bed companions to flock to him and leave me alone. Bedbugs didn't appear to be so ambitious here. The Galice Hotel was their favorite rendezvous and they did their tribe real justice.

In the morning, I started on foot toward Westfork to head off those rumored sheep or to try to find out "how come," without a crossing permit. For a light pocket lunch, I purchased a small paper sack of bulk raisins. Around midmorning, I started shooting them into my hungry mouth while hiking along. "Ah, sweet elixir of life," thought I, as I stepped gaily along, eyes front, and with increasing deliveries by ever larger handfuls. But not for long. "Am I getting fed up already?" I wondered. Then suspicion began to take the place of pleasure so I stopped and stared into the sack. Could I believe my eyes? Well, you can guess. The residue was on the go, for sure, each little white worm trying to get on top to contribute to my sustenance. I threw the almost finished sack as far as I could and cursed those dirty Mule Creek savages.

Sure enough, here came a flock of sheep heading right toward me. The leaders stopped, then deflected, and their followers scattered in all directions with several dogs yipping at their tails to try to get them in line again. The next instant, I was looking into the barrel of a rifle or shotgun held at the shoulder of the meanest looking man on horseback I ever hope to see. The reins were over the saddle horn and he was ready for action.

Fortunately, he didn't hold the bead on me for long. He had to speak, or rather yell, "What's the big idea? Scatterin' them sheep all over hell! I thought when the dogs started yapping they had met up with a wild cat'r somepin. You're damn lucky you came around that bush when you did. Just look at them sheep now. Couldn't you have given 'em a little room to get by?" All of this, or something like it, seemed to came out in one long breath.

Then I told him who I was and my reason for coming to see him. He didn't appear to know that he was expected to have a permit "just to drive a couple hundred sheep over a damn rocky trail down Rogue River," where he was having to tote feed on packhorses behind him to keep them from starving to death on the way. As his helpers and packhorses arrived, he was persuaded to return to Westfork so we could contact Portland to have him put up $100 (I believe) for probably trail repairs below Mule Creek. In fact, he got a horse from one of his men for me to ride so we could hurry the job as much as possible. Told the men to round up the flock and bed down right there till he got back in the morning. A three-way telephone conversation did the trick, as he had business connections in Portland. After an "all's forgiven" toddy, I caught the evening train back to Grants Pass.

CITY BOY COUNTS CATTLE

Denny Bungarz

In the late 1950s, I was stationed on the Trinity National Forest at the Minersville Guard Station as a seasonal fire foreman. Early one spring morning, Jim McKnight, District FCO called and told me that the Wilsons of Lewiston were driving their cattle onto the forest and they would be coming by our station sometime that day and I was to count the cattle as they were driven by. And by the way, I was to count the cows, cows with calves, cows with calves over six months old, cows with calves under six months old, the steers and the bulls! Now keep in mind that I was about 20 years old and was born and raised in Oakland, California. About the only thing I knew about cattle was that they were responsible for the milk I found in the cartons in the grocery store or the hamburgers I enjoyed.

The first mistake I made was to park our "fire engine" (not anything like the FS has today) on the road in a narrow place. My thought was to have the cattle go by one at a time so I could count them as I had been directed. Well, the cattle had other ideas. They did not like the sight of a green power wagon parked in the road. Needless to say, a complete stopping of the cattle drive, one of Harold Wilson's cowboys rode up on his horse and suggested that I move the vehicle. He was not as nice as that but this is a family book. After moving the vehicle and getting the drive back on track I attempted to count the cattle as I had been directed as they went by. First one or two at a time and then eight or ten and then many more rushing to get by that vehicle in the road. Needless to say I had no clue as to the number of cattle that went by that day. But a very nice Harold Wilson rode up at the end of the drive and asked if I had the count. He could see that I was a bit confused so he pulled out a notebook from his shirt pocket and said "Young fella, this is the count I have, is it the same as yours ?" Naturally my count and his came out exactly the same !

IMPOUND THEM!

Mark Petty

While I was on the Klamath National Forest in northern California, a new rancher near Hilt next to the Oregon border decided that the way to utilize the brushy front country was to get Mexican cattle. So he bought several car loads and dumped them on the district's scattered lands a little west of Hornbrook. These were as wild, long-legged, long-horned, skinny a cattle as you had ever seen. We wrote him several letters and met with him, telling him to get his cattle off the district. He said that he was sorry but he could not catch them. So Al Crebbin, Range and Wildlife Staff Officer, said, "Impound them!" They were running in eight foot brush. We hired six of the best cowboys we could find, complete with several horses each and their brush dogs. We built a corral and had at it. We got most of them and hauled them to the stockyard where they were fed the best feed. We told the rancher that he could have them back as soon as he paid all the costs. He did and we never had any more problems. It seems that this was the first large cattle impoundment in the region for 20 years, and this was in 1959.

COUNTING SHEEP

Bob Gray

Not all sheep counting is done while trying to go to sleep. The national forests of the West are often summer range for both cattle and sheep which spend their winters in the lowlands of the great valleys or hanging in the slaughter houses. Mountain meadows are lush with nourishing grasses and browse which are highly prized by stockmen and ranchers.

Sheep have all but disappeared on the Shasta-Trinity, but in the 40s, sheep still browsed through the McCloud flats with a dust haze continually hovering over them as they moved in large herds.

District Ranger Dutch Sullaway sent me to Bartle one spring day to count sheep as they were unloaded from the McCloud train. I stood at the bottom of the unloading chute as they were coming out of the rail cars, counting as they crowded by. A tally whacker is a counting device held in your hand with a push button to record each animal, and the total shows on the dial. After tallying several car loads, I checked the dial. I had tallied about twice as many as the sheep allotment allowed. This shook me up and I told the owner he had far too many sheep for the allotment. "No, in fact I'm a few shy," he said, then a puzzled look came on his face. "Did you count the lambs, too?" Well, no one had told me to only count the ewes, so I had counted everything. Anyway the lambs were as big as the ewes, because the ewes had been shorn and the lambs were still "wooly." Dutch laughed at our mistake and we accepted the rancher's figures. There was no fee for the lambs, so they were not to be counted. Now I know how to count sheep.

PAINTING THE CAR GREEN

Robert W. Cermak

It was the spring of 1956, and we were on our way south from the Tonasket District of the Okanogan to the Quincy District of the Plumas. Ethel and I were in high spirits driving in our little '49 Ford Tudor with our three boys, aged 3, 2 and 1, and the smallest sized U-Haul trailer loaded with all of our possessions. Away from the cold winters (no snickers please!) and back to California where we both had been raised. I had planned the trip to cross over the giant Grand Coulee Dam. As we approached the north end we saw a shiny new Cadillac in front of us and in front of the Cadillac a small herd of cattle being choused across the big dam by a couple of cowboys. We arrived behind the Cadillac driven by a very impatient middle-aged woman. She was tapping her fingers on the steering wheel and creeping closer and closer to the back of the herd which moved at its own slow and erratic pace. Finally, she could take no more and began blaring the horn. This disturbed the cattle something fierce and the cowboys almost as fiercely. One of them rode back to ask her politely to stop honking the horn. They would get the cattle out of the way as fast as possible. She slumped back into her seat fuming at the delay which probably would cost her ten minutes extra on her trip. We watched in amusement as she edged her car ever closer to the lagging cows. We were almost across the dam when she came too close to a huge old cow six or seven years old. Suddenly the cow lifted her tail and spewed a load of green all over the front of that shiny new Cadillac. Then we were really amused. Even the cowboys grinned.

SHEEP ON THE ANGELES

Jack Horton

In 1964, the Saugus District of the Angeles National Forest experienced a serious brush fire which burned entirely through the district from south to north. The burned area included Drinkwater Flat. This vicinity included a valley of perhaps two and one half or three miles long, oriented in a north-south direction. The ridges on either side of the valley were not nearly as steep as topography typical of the Angeles Forest. Vegetation was primarily chamise, a brush species common in Southern California. This species sprouts prolifically following a fire.

Following the fire a suggestion was made to graze sheep on the burned area to retard regrowth of chamise. This suggestion was studied and it was decided to give the proposal a try. We hoped to establish a fuelbreak to aid in the control of future fires as well as to create a more attractive and open area.

The burned area was sprayed with 2-4D (at a time "herbicide" was not generally considered to be a bad word). This treatment greatly suppressed regrowth in the months following the fire. The following year a permit was issued to a local rancher to run sheep on the area, about 3,000 animals I believe. The experiment was still in progress when I transferred from the district in 1969. Without retreatment with chemicals or prescribed burning, chamise will come back eventually but grazing will delay the process. The project convinced me that grazing could be a useful tool in the management of vegetation in Southern California under some circumstances.

The project offered some interesting and sometimes amusing (and revolting) experiences. The rancher hired Basque sheepherders. None spoke English. I used to stop at one herder's trailer and have lunch with him. He was a big guy—maybe 250 pounds and good natured. The menu was usually the same; lamb stew, cheese, sheepherder bread and red wine. Since we could not speak each other's language, there wasn't much conversation. We sat there and grinned at one another, occasionally attempting some sign language, like pass the stew. The food was always good.

Each year we counted the sheep when they were turned onto the allotment. I took the district clerk along on one of these occasions. She stood next to the chute as the sheep were unloaded and tried to pet sheep as they came off the trucks. She wound up with sheep stuff splattered all down her front. A bad clothes day for her, no doubt.

Male lambs were castrated before being turned onto the range. Basque herders harvest the "oysters" with their teeth, a method Americans don't have the stomach for. The sack is slit with a knife, the herder takes the "oysters" in his teeth, extracts them and drops them into a bucket. Since several other herders bring him the lambs, one herder can harvest an impressive number of "oysters" in a day. These so-called "mountain oysters" were later cooked and eaten at a lamb barbecue. They were yummy.

DEER, ELK AND ANTELOPE

WINTER GAME COUNTING

Corwin E. "Slim" Hein

Ranger Henry Tonseth and I made several winter deer counts in the mid-thirties along the desert edge of the Fort Rock District near Cabin Lake Ranger Station. It was fun and fairly easy going on webs and skis as the terrain was quite level. The timber to the west and north had been in the Paulina Game Refuge since 1924, and the deer population was at a high level. Herds of 50 to 150 were common. Following one rather strenuous day we went northeast from Cabin Lake and after about 10 miles decided we had enough and dropped in at the old Harrison Ranch where Reub Long and two other bachelors were wintering. Reub insisted that we stay overnight and, as it was snowing, we accepted and bedded down in the tackroom with horse blankets for cover.

The next morning it was still snowing as we kegged up until noon. I went out to see what the dogs were barking about and saw Jack Parker, a local trapper, approaching with a backpack and a rather suspicious "limb" sticking out the top. Jack and his partner were wintering at the Foster Well trapping coyotes and bobcats in the Devils Garden. Jack announced that they were out of spuds and coffee. Reub threw Jack's pack on the grain bags on the porch and had Jack partake of some lunch. When Jack was ready to leave, the spuds and coffee were in his pack and the "limb" was not.

74

What was it that Jack had brought in his pack? Well, when one is the guest of a neighbor it is not proper protocol to snoop in other guests' baggage.

Soon after Jack left, Henry and I headed for the Derrick Ranch via Foster Well and stopped at the trapper cabin for a drink of water. Near the cabin was a mound of coyote and bobcat carcasses bigger than their woodpile. We 'lowed that Jack and his partner's trapping had saved the lives of far more deer than we suspected they had harvested for table fare. Let sleeping dogs lie!

THE STARVING ELK PROBLEM

Rudo L. Fromme

On my first trip (1913) down the Hoh River in the North Fork Soleduck, Ranger Chris Morgenroth pointed out to me the closely cropped condition of certain small, leafy bushes and the succulent twig ends of vine maple. He explained that elk were doing this while seeking shelter from winter storms higher up. In his opinion, this was becoming serious for the maintenance of the elk herds in this particular valley, especially the rearing of new ones. Some weaker mothers and young ones, not able to nibble high enough, were already starving to death.

This, of course, was more serious during winters of heavy snows, when the winter range confined them more closely to the valley floor.

Chris and I began nosing around about the desirability, if not necessity, for some form of limited hunting of elk in certain westside valleys, particularly the Hoh. Mr. E. B. Webster, editor and publisher of the *Fort Angeles News*, promptly took exception, and ran an editorial or two denouncing this suggestion, and implying that the ranger and I were stretching the actual facts; that what we had seen was the natural old age deaths or killings by cougar or accident.

This called for a show-me trip. I think it was in the early spring of 1921-'22 that the ranger, Mr. Webster, the Oregon State game warden and I floundered our way over the snow filled upper Soleduck Trail and down into the Hoh River bottom lands. We found plenty of evidence, not only of overfeeding on brush, green moss and small tree branches, but we came across several dead elk, the condition of which indicated that they had died from starvation. Webster, an ardent nature lover, sat down on a fallen tree and practically wept. He had just recently published a book entitled, *The King of the Olympics*, referring to the elk. It also contains descriptions and many interesting accounts from local trappers and nature lovers of 28 other Peninsula animals, as I count them in my complimentary copy.

One paragraph in this book is headed, "The Oddest Sight Supervisor R. L. Fromme Ever Saw in Mountains." It is in his chapter entitled, "The True Mountaineer, the Whistling Marmot." After relating that Ranger Chris Morgenroth and I had hiked up onto the Soleduck Divide in May, 1918, and were climbing a snow slope, we "suddenly heard a shrill whistle from one side of the park, and after a moment or two, a big whistler came into view. He whistled again, when another whistle or an echo responded from below. In a moment, there was no doubt about the answer, for another marmot came out from behind some brush, still further down. Instantly, they started running toward each other, and when about ten feet apart, each reared up on his hind legs and covered the rest of the distance upright, waving their front feet in the air. They were not far away and were very plainly outlined against the snow and clearly seen to be cuffing or slapping each other's faces as they came together." "Fighting?" I asked Mr. Fromme. "Not at all. Doubtless either or both of them had that very morning tunneled out through the snow and were so glad to see each other they just didn't know what to do."

Mr. Webster quoted me correctly except that we actually saw the second marmot burst frantically up through the snow from his long winter's sleep, look around dazed for awhile in the brightness of the midmorning sun (probably the first warm day of the spring) and then answer the first one's shrill call for renewed companionship.

Through the offices of the Oregon State game warden and the House Committee on game matters, I was invited to present a lantern slide talk to a joint session of the legislature. This, an evening meeting, was well ballyhooed in advance, so that the hall and galleries were well packed. I used mostly my own Kodak efforts except for the animal views. All the slides had been hand painted in the Asahel Curtis studio in Seattle. Naturally, I took advantage of this opulent opportunity for pushing the multiple use principle of forest management and the wilderness treatment of much of the high country, but also spent some time on the elk problem and the idea of limited hunting to save the herds in certain westside valleys instead of resorting to the expense and undesirable results of artificial feeding.

BUCK FROM ABOVE

Ralph G. Johnston

Nappy Martin, a CCC foreman on the Angeles National Forest in the late 1930s, was driving his Model A roadster on which he had just had a new white canvas top installed. As he was driving through a cut bank on a single track mountain truck trail, a buck deer fell from the top of the cut and dropped feet first through the top of his new car. It not only ruined his new top but also his planned date with his girlfriend he was on the way to pick up.

TO CATCH AN ELK

Philip Lee

The helicopter circled 50 feet above the snow covered ground just north of where we lay hidden behind sagebrush plants. There were 10 of us lying there waiting for the helicopter to start moving in our direction. Below the helicopter, but out of our view was a herd of about 50 Rocky Mountain elk. The pilot was trying to herd the elk toward us and the eight foot tall nylon net we had strung some 400 feet among the sagebrush and bitterbrush plants.

Suddenly the helicopter straighten and started our way. "Get ready !"Tracy yelled. "Here they come." A minute later the herd broke over the hill and headed for the net. About 50 yards from the net they spotted it and started to turn. We had been positioned in two lines and we had the elk between us as we all jumped to our feet, waving our arms and yelling at the top of our voices. Most of the elk ignored us and broke away, free of the net. A half dozen reacted with fear and ran headlong into the net.

The Forest Service, Bureau of Land Management and the Idaho Department of Fish and Game were cooperating on a study to determine the home range of the elk that wintered near the sand dunes west of St. Anthony, Idaho. We knew they moved onto the Targhee Forest in the spring and guessed some of them might summer in Yellowstone National Park. We needed to know for sure so we could manage their numbers to avoid habitat damage to their winter range.

I had invited some friends from St. Anthony to help with the capture. Jim was particularly excited about the prospects of catching elk. He hunted them every year and when I explained the process, was even more eager. Jim had been a high school football and baseball star in California. He was ready to put a tackle on an elk.

The idea was for two or three guys to grab an elk that was tangled in the net. They were to throw them to the ground and hold them while the state biologists put radio collars on them.

The radios would last two or three years and the elk could be tracked throughout their range. When the first group of elk hit the net there were so many that some of us were on our own in bringing them down and holding them. A full grown bull elk weighs between 700 and 1,000 pounds. I doubt that any of us could have tackled one and put it down. Fortunately there were no bulls in this bunch. Cow elk are smaller and weigh about 500 pounds. A frightened cow elk is a formidable opponent

As the elk hit the fence they usually get their front feet tangled and fall down. If we were quick enough and could get to the elk before they got back up it was a simple matter for two people to hold one down. So many elk had hit the net this time that it had collapsed. Some of the elk had fallen, others had remained on their feet.

I watched as Jim raced toward a cow with her front feet tangled in the net. The net was on the ground but the elk was not. Jim hit her high and hard just in front of her shoulders. A better tackle I could not visualize. Down went the elk with Jim right on top of her. All along the net elk were being pulled down or held down where they had fallen. We were all fresh and were able to hold the elk. To keep them quiet we put our jackets over their heads so they could not see us. The collaring on this first group went pretty well. Jim got up smiling brushing the snow off. We managed to get the net back in place before the pilot had located another bunch of elk. Again we were fortunate not to get any bulls. I asked Tracy about this and he explained that the pilot was picking small groups without bulls on purpose. We couldn't handle a bull in this net and he might hurt one of us or himself and probably tear the net to pieces.

By the third elk I could see Jim was less enthusiastic. He was beginning to limp and he said his shoulder hurt. I had been lucky. The elk near me were always thrown down and I just had to get to them before they got up. It was still a job holding the big ones by myself and by late afternoon I was exhausted. The last elk to go down near me was a big one. I got to her and covered her head. I yelled at Jim to come help me as soon as he could. Everybody was busy with their own problems. My cow struggled and would not hold still. She finally worked herself over onto her back with me on top. I had my arms wrapped around her hind legs and was just laying on her hoping my weight would hold her down. She suddenly gave a hard kick with both feet. I landed 10 feet away in a sagebrush. The elk got up, shook my coat off her head and raced away. I heard a chorus of howls and laughter from the rest of the crew. I laughed too for a few seconds before I realized how fortunate I was. If I hadn't been holding the elk's feet very close to my body she probably would have broken several fibs or cut me up pretty badly.

We collared enough elk that day to complete the study. Over the next two years we knew a lot about those elk and where they spent their time. One cow had gone back to Yellowstone Park the next summer and joined with some elk from Jackson Hole, Wyoming. She spent that winter in Jackson Hole and returned to Yellowstone the following summer. The second winter she returned to the sand dunes. She had averaged 200 miles of wandering a year. It wouldn't be easy preparing a plan to manage a herd if they all did that. Fortunately she was the exception. But still, statistically that meant a portion of the herd probably went with her.

I had trapped mule deer in northern California, bighorn sheep in Oregon, small mammals in Colorado and grizzly bears in Idaho. Years later I would catch spotted owls as they came to take mice from me. That day tackling elk is one of the days that still gives me the best memories.

ED & A BUCK

Bob Gray

Ed was a fire prevention technician at Fall River in northern California when I went there. Now Ed was famous for telling tall tales but after working with him for a couple of years, I decided he was just one of those lucky people who always had interesting things happening to them.

The flats around Burney and Four Corners are a winter deer range because the snow never gets too deep and goes off early in the spring. Ed and I were marking some dead and dying pines in the area for a salvage timber sale near Four Corners. We were working strips about 50 yards apart and keeping track of each other by sight or calling back and forth. Ed called, "Hey Bob, come here, I need some help." I thought maybe he couldn't decide on whether to mark some trees or not as I walked toward him. When I got there, he was peering around a tree at something. The something was a huge buck with blue antlers. I stopped and watched as the buck followed Ed around trees and thickets while he squirted blue paint at him. That buck was definitely trying to pick a fight and Ed was equally determined to keep away from him. The whole front end of the deer was dripping blue paint and he continued to follow Ed until he saw me when he decided he couldn't cope with two humans at once. I don't know yet why the buck acted that way and only one other time have I seen a buck show hostility to people and he was obviously sick and foaming at the mouth. Nothing at all appeared to be wrong with Ed's buck.

THE ELK BUGLE

Ken Weissenborn

The Santa Fe National Forest in northern New Mexico is home to many big game animals. Among these are wapiti, or elk. The Forest Service is responsible for the management of habitat, while the New Mexico Game and Fish Department is responsible for management of the animals themselves.

These two activities are interdependent. The two agencies work in close and generally harmonious partnership. At times, the assistance of volunteers helps in the management effort.

One of the largest elk herds in New Mexico lives in the Pecos Wilderness area. This is back country—roadless, accessible by hiking or riding. Motorized access is prohibited by law.

Thousands of hikers and horsebackers visit the area every year. One of their great thrills is sighting elk in the wild. A controlled number of hunters are permitted, under close supervision by the game department.

A reasonably accurate estimate of herd numbers and composition is needed to set management goals. Various methods are used—aerial surveys, track counts and others. The most accurate (and, incidentally, the most fun) is the fall bugling survey.

In the high country, rutting season usually occurs in the latter part of September and the first few weeks of October. Usually cautious bull elk become aggressive in seeking out their harems. They make their presence known by "bugling," a shrill, high-pitched call that can be heard for long distances in the silence of the forest. This call somewhat resembles the call of a loon. Once heard, it is long remembered. It has a twofold purpose—to attract females, and to alert other males of their presence. Challenging males, also in search of a harem, respond vigorously. The end result is often a battle for supremacy—with the winner adding to his group of females and the loser going off to start anew. Hunters take advantage by replicating the bugle to attract bull elk to their site.

Bugling surveys are conducted by Forest Service and game department personnel, with help from organized sportsmen's groups from the area. Volunteers compete for the few positions available, particularly if they have been lucky enough to draw a hunt permit.

Personnel involved in the survey gather at a central point—in the case of the Pecos survey the headquarters is Beatty's cabin. This particular survey started on Thursday afternoon. A group of 25 or so people (including 10 - 12 volunteers from one of the sportsmen's clubs in Los Alamos) assembled in the early afternoon. A brief introduction of participants was followed by an orientation.

Survey parties of six people each were formed. These groups would work as a unit for each of the five days of the survey. Each group was assigned a leader, local people from the game department or Forest Service. The leaders were responsible for assignment of survey stations, for packing bedrolls for each person, for leading groups to assigned stations each afternoon and picking up men and gear for return to camp each morning. Survey crew members were to spend the night at their assigned stations. Each man was to keep his mount with him. He would spend the night sleeping out on the ground. His survey duties included recording all wildlife he had seen, and noting all elk bugles he had heard. No one was to use elk bugles while on the survey. We did not want confrontations between man and elk.

The group leader's job was to pack the parties out to their assigned station and unload their bedrolls and lunches. Each man was to be on station an hour or so before dusk. The leader manned the station furthest from camp, and spent the night in the field in the same way as his crew members. In the morning he would saddle up and lead the pack animals back over the previous afternoon's route. He would bring the group back into Beatty's cabin for a late breakfast, a chance to rest or swap stories and become organized for that afternoon. A hearty dinner was served before going back on station for the evening watch.

A few of the volunteers were ill-equipped for spending nights out under the stars, but few complained. I wound up with a good group of surveyors, with one exception. I had spent many days working from horseback in this country, and knew full well that the weather could change in a short time. I was well equipped—I carried a full-length oilskin saddle slicker and a Navy flight jacket. I always wore chaps, a sombrero, spurs and had covers (tapaderos) on my stirrups. This gear protected from brush, thorns, rain and snow.

One of the Los Alamos volunteers got on my case about being "the rough, tough cowboy" dude. By the end of day two, I had enough. The next afternoon my group was assigned to the most distant survey route. I led them off cross country— through spruce and fir trees and across tangles of fallen timber. It was a long, hard trip. My smart alec volunteer was literally in shreds when we arrived at his stand. The next morning I took pity on the group. I didn't think it was fair the good guys should suffer any more because of one man. I took them back to the cabin via a wide, smooth, easy to travel trail. When we got back to Beatty's, my "friend" dismounted, walked over to me, grinned, and said, "We could have used that trail on our way in last night!" My reply—"You got it!!" After that, we got along well.

We did have one violation of the no elk bugle order. The District Forest Ranger, A. J. Garner, had carried his bugle with him, and used it to entice a bull elk into view. This episode was the basis for the following poem:

There are strange things done 'neath the wilderness sun
    By those rangers, fearless and bold,
And their terrible tales of the forest trails
    Will turn you all shaky and old.

The high mountain lights have seen many odd sights
    But the oddest they ever did see
Was that terrible day a bull elk put AJ
    Right up a big old spruce tree.

Now the night, it was long and that bull elk was strong
    And there's an unbreakable natural rule—
Sleeping is tough, and you can't get enough—
    'Cause a spruce tree gets ungodly cool.

Well, he prayed and he prayed, but that big elk, he stayed—
    That sucker, he just hung around.
So he told the good Lord he would sure keep his word
    If he got safely back on the ground.

Soon the sun in the east slowly warmed up the beast
    The elk thought "I'd better get gone."
While the man in the tree said "At last I am free."
    And he slowly and stiffly climbed down.

If you doubt what I say, check it out with AJ.
    This caution is certainly true!
Be careful! Be frugal! Never blow your elk bugle
    If that bull elk is bigger than you!

EPILOGUE

This poem was written several years ago, while riding the Cumbres-Toltec Narrow Gauge Railroad from Antonito, Colorado to Chama, New Mexico. It was a beautiful fall day, and the sight of a bunch of elk grazing in a meadow reminded me of the incident in the Pecos.

I presented the poem at a campfire gathering of retired folks the following spring. I admitted to the group that I had not followed my own advice—I had never checked it out with A. J. Since he was present, I asked him if the story were true. His reply: "Absolutely not! That elk did not run me up a tree! I got up there of my own free will and accord!"

COUNTING ANTELOPE

A. G. Brennels

We had a project that we did by plane on the Lassen National Forest that was, what I believe to be, the first winter aerial count of antelope conducted in the State of California. This came about because many ranchers were beginning to complain about the large number of antelope that were in the area. Antelope were going into their haystacks and were really raising Cain with the range. Ranchers wanted something done. California State Fish and Game people had provided a man to make a study of the antelope herd and he really didn't do a very good job. He indicated that the herd was growing by leaps and bounds. It just didn't make sense to me. Some of my staff people and I had been spending some time in winter following antelope herds and we thought otherwise.

The region approved an aerial survey of the range and a fellow by the name of Bill Randall of Klamath Falls got the bid to do the flying. We met him in Reno in February, 1939. We found him a little apprehensive because it just happened we were having a bit of wind and on the way down from Klamath Falls he'd ripped some fabric off the wings of his biplane. However, we flew into Susanville and Bill patched them up with tape. He was still uncertain but not knowing anything about airplanes, I assured him that everything was going to be lovely. Ed Huestis, who was forest C&M foreman, would fly with us and be our photographer. We flew for two days. I began to learn what antelope were like. I said, "Now Bill, when you go down toward a band, don't get too low at first; they'll all be strung out because they're afraid of the motor noise. When I say, 'get around them Shep,' turn the lead antelope to make the band circle and bunch up and we'll get some pictures. When I say, 'lay off,' they'll string out again and then Ed can get some photos when that happens. After we get back we can kind of break the herd up into tens and we can count them." Well, Bill really got into the swing on this and he was just like an old sheep dog. I didn't think I would ever get him out of there. It's the only time in my life when I thought I was going to get air sick because of his tight turns around the head of those antelope. When we got back we had the photos developed, put our feet up on the radiator and counted the antelope one by one. We came within 300 head of what we had estimated over previous counts. And, I knew we had missed some because there was one band that I could not find for the life of me. Anyhow, this really gave some credence to the fact that you can use an aircraft in Forest Service work for something other than putting out forest fires or finding trespassers.

VALIDATING DEER

Don Bauer

Editor's Note: On September 14, 1983, former district ranger and San Bernardino NF Supervisor, Don Bauer, talked to District Ranger Danny Britt and PIO Elliott L. Graham about the Vista Grande Station on the San Jacinto Ranger District.

As we walk around here I notice just to the east of the gas house an iron pipe that a tree has about engulfed. We used to follow the practice, which I thought was a very good one, of involving the fire people. There was no functionalism on a ranger district, you couldn't afford that luxury. The ranger was responsible for everything and everybody with him were multiple use people. They were fire and campground maintenance people, surveyors, wildlife people, and one of the programs we were in was to learn more about deer management. With California Fish and Game it was our practice that people had to validate their deer tags when they got a buck. Forest officers were authorized to validate tags. As part of that program we would take measurements on each deer, his condition, weight, antler class and other material that would be useful to biologists. This meant weighing. So that iron pipe was one of those that would be hung in a tree and balancing scales would be hung on that and you'd wrestle the deer up there, hang it and weigh it and report the weight. I found it worked very good because each member of the district organization wanted to be a member of the team whether they were fire people or ran tractors. They were real interested in what makes deer grow and what the factors were. It put them in a position where they could speak with some knowledge to the hunter and the public they were dealing with. Also, it built rapport, a mutuality of interest between game managers and game wardens with the fish and game and Forest Service, which I felt was very important because all these people worked for the same taxpayers. I thought it was a loss when we didn't validate deer tags anymore. It also gave me wonderful information as ranger. I would keep a little half-inch map for the San Jacinto District which was real handy. You could carry it under your arm to go to meetings. As each deer was validated, we would put a pin on the map at the location where it was taken. We used a color system like red for forked horns, blue for three points or something like that, so you could tell at a glance where the deer were being harvested and what their antler size class was, and when you were faced with the problem of the hunter who said, "Well, where can I get a buck?" You told him he could take his chances but show him where most of the people were. You could see the patterns. There was a good pattern here in this area on Black Mountain. This was pretty tight closure on the west. Santa Rosa was always a good area. As I recall, we'd harvest between 100-150 bucks a year on this district.

DOGS

THE PINK LABRADOR

Andy Stevenson

During the early 1960s, while serving as fire prevention technician on the Beckwourth District, Plumas National Forest, I like many other employees, had a pet in the form of man's best friend. Mine was a black Labrador named Duke. We got him in the fall of 1962. He was a noble beast and a true companion. He was well known by Forest Service personnel throughout the district.

During this period of time, the Forest Service allowed an employee to take his dog to work with him and to take him into the field. Duke's letter of approval had been signed by Ranger Ed Angwin and Forest Supervisor Bill Peterson. He was a dog in good standing. As long as our work was done and the dog was no problem, then it was okay. The district ranger's dog was Lady, the ADR was Clint Tripp and his dog was Junior. Bill Sims had Chief, Frank Johnson had Jake, Martin Warne had Cleo, Dennis Graves had Rusty, Curtis Marshall had Buckley and Huston Hanson had Smokey. The dogs seemed to get along okay. I remember one time, however, when the dogs were all together in the compound at the Mohawk Ranger Station. We were loading tools and gearing up to head out to different work sites. The eight dogs were making tight circles around each other with a couple of heads over the other dogs' shoulders. All had the hair up on their backs and stepping like they were walking on eggs. Jim Seley and Rene Cavaille both said, "There's going to be a dog fight." All dog owners were there and did their best to mediate the situation. Before this could come about, someone accidentally backed up and stepped on a dog foot. The dog let out a yelp and the fight was on. It went from one end of the compound to the other. It moved from the fire warehouse over to the wash rack and up and around the gas pump. It didn't last too long and then everyone got their dogs and loaded up in the trucks and headed out to the field. It must have cleared the air because it never happened again.

Duke went along with me everywhere I went except flying, off forest training or fire assignments. When I had office work to do, he was always laying out by the Forest Service truck I drove. He was ready and loved to go. He expected to go and was really bummed out when he didn't get to. He went along when there was tree planting, thinning, soil erosion work, campground maintenance, fire prevention and suppression, site prep or slash burning. He always stayed home when I took snow surveys. He didn't handle the deep snow very well. He seemed to understand when I was gone on off forest fire assignments. He stayed home with my wife and three children. Over the years, Duke had been on hundreds of wildland fires. Many times he returned more pink and red than black. This was from the retardant. He was on so many fires, one fireman said that he should have been red carded.

One September in the late 1960s, during deer season, I rolled to a fire at the north end of the C Road and north side of highway 70, approximately five miles east of the Mohawk Ranger Station. The fire danger was extreme. The fire was located on a south slope in second growth reproduction, creating a bad situation. One thing in our favor was that there wasn't a breath of wind. We were able to get a lot of manpower and equipment to the fire early. I was the second person to arrive after Al Watson. I grabbed a shovel and canteen and left Duke inside my truck because of the fire conditions. Within minutes we had about 18 people and an engine and crew on the fire and began to make headway. One B-17 air tanker from Chester arrived overhead. The air tanker dropped one-half of its load on the head of the fire. With the hose lays along both flanks and the people with hand tools, we were able to hook the fire. It was still active several yards inside the line. The air tanker was directed to drop its remaining retardant on the inside near the top of the fire. The pilot carried the load a second too long before he dropped. Most of the load went down over the fire, hitting the vehicles that were parked on the east side of the fire. Three pickups were hit pretty hard with the retardant. My pickup was one of the three. Duke was sitting on the front seat and I had left the driver's window down when I left him there. The pickup was hit broadside with a low drop. Many gallons of goop hit the truck and a lot went through the driver's door window. The force knocked Duke off the seat and onto the floor board on the passenger side. We got the fire knocked down and in good shape before I dropped down to the road to check on Duke. He was still on the floor board and I yelled at him, "Duke, are you okay?" He was plastered with retardant. The only way he could have been wetter was if he were bigger, and he looked like something from outer space. I let him out of the truck and he could hardly walk. The retardant was setting up like plaster of Paris. The pickup wasn't much better as the retardant that went inside got all over everything. It was on the dash board, windows, seats, paperwork, steering wheel, floor boards, head liner, the Forest Service radio and everything else in its path. It took almost an hour to clean the windows inside and out so I could move the truck back to the Mohawk Ranger Station. Then it took another hour and a half at the wash rack to really get it cleaned. That evening I took Duke down to the Feather River just under the Mohawk Bridge. After an hour of retrieving pine cones, Duke was black again instead of pink.

Two months later, Vern Hunt called me from the forest auto shop in Quincy. He said, "As the shop foreman, I would like to know what in the hell you did to all the wiring up under the dash board of the Forest Service vehicle No. 2627?" He said the dried retardant was caked up under the dashboard. If there was once a color code for wiring, there wasn't now because the wires were all pink.

Duke died in September, 1974. We had him 12 years. He was always there and almost everything he did was comical. If you happen to be an owner and lover of a dog, you will know what I mean.

WILD DOGS

Brian Ballou

Three lightning fires down the ridge had been fought for the past week by an assortment of district people—timber beasts, silviculturists, wildlife specialists—and a handful of firefighters pulled in from other districts. The fires deepest in the canyon, down where there were no roads, had been fought by smokejumpers.

All the other firefighters were gone now. The fires had all been declared contained, then controlled. It was up to me to inspect them, grind out any last smokes and call them out.

My engine had a crew of three that day—the Holy Rollers. One of them, Casey, was practicing to become a preacher. I'd known him for several years—several wild years. He'd been a cusser, a drinker and a snoose chewing sourpuss. He was a fair fireman, but a whiner; then a bleeding ulcer changed more than his attitude. When he returned for his summer job on the engine crew, he brought with him a better haircut, an improved complexion and a sunny attitude.

Alas, he remained but a fair fireman.

His sweetie, Maureen, was also on the crew. She was a dark-eyed, dark-haired beauty of some Slavic descent with big black eyebrows, teeth as white as sea foam and a smile for everyone. She, too, was often found with her nose buried in The Book. As for her firefighting skills, they were steady.

The third member of the team, Otto, was religiously inclined as well, though perhaps not as clearly. Nothing, it seemed was clear to Otto. He was the youngest of my crew, as well as the youngest of three strongheaded fire fighting brothers. Along with their father, the brothers had haunted the upper reaches of the Rogue River National Forest for nearly a decade. They were all fine and knowledgeable firemen, if a bit overzealous. Otto had somehow been clipped by the furor of his elders, and was seeking solace elsewhere—precisely where or why, he didn't know.

As a fireman, he had the skill, but not the desire.

I parked the engine in the shade of some madrone, as it was midday and quite hot. I told the crew to stay put while I walked down the hill to check the fires They looked surprised but pleased. They snuggled in, cracked their Bibles and commenced grilling each other on verse and its deeper meanings.

For reasons unclear to me even now, I elected to leave behind both a shovel and a radio as I headed down the mountain to check on the fires. I guess neither seemed necessary. People who had worked on the fires had told me they were dead out and I had no reason to believe otherwise. All I expected was to take a pleasant hike through the woods, perform the professional exercise of seeing the fires with my own eyes before declaring them out and give myself a break from the Bible thumpers.

It was hot and still. My boots crackled through the stiff, dry chaff of the dried madrone leaves littering the ground on the ridgetop. Sound carried easily and other than that made by my footfalls, there wasn't a noise to be heard.

The first fire was barely a stone's throw from the engine. It was also the biggest of the three. I walked all around it, then crisscrossed it twice from different angles. There was no smoke visible and I couldn't smell anything smoldering. It was out and I noted it as such on a fire report card that I pulled from my pocket. The second fire was perhaps four hundred yards downhill from the first. A well-marked flag line led me straight to it and had it not been for the flags I might have walked right past it. The fire was no more than twenty feet wide, just a splash of black ground that could've passed for a tree's shadow. I trooped around it and scrutinized the ground for any sign of smoke. Finding none, I marked it as "out" as well.

The third fire was way down the ridge from the other two. Its flag line took off from the second fire and petered out after about an eighth of a mile—when the flag line maker discovered he was running out of flagging. He had continued to hang flags but they were far apart. The rule of thumb in making flag lines is to post flags within eyesight of each other and the alternate theory is to post flags that can be seen from the highest point between two flags. This high point could be a stump, a downed log, a boulder or any readily climbable tree. Naturally, this can make following a flag line something of an adventure.

This flag line followed the steepest drop off the ridge, going straight down into the hole. I followed the sparsely scattered flags for another full eighth of a mile before I began wondering if I was following the correct flag line; it is possible to get off track when an old flag line intersects another flag line and the flag line follower inadvertently starts following the wrong flag line. The farther I got down the hill, the more I wondered whether this situation had occurred; my verbal instructions were that the third fire was about a quarter mile down the canyon, and I'd already walked at least that far.

It was about that time, when I was standing in the crotch of an old madrone trying to see the next flag, when I heard the dogs.

Down the hill from me, perhaps a hundred yards, I could hear them growling and baying at something I couldn't see. I couldn't see the dogs, either. My first thought was that these were bear dogs, and that they were out ahead of a hunter, had found a bear and treed it, and were holding the bear in the tree until the hunter caught up with them.

But the more I listened, the more I doubted that analysis. The dogs sounded agitated—more agitated than bear dogs keeping a bear in a tree. Dogs after a bear tend to bark and yip a lot. They're excited and they raise a ruckus and they pretty much stay put around the tree until the hunter catches up to them.

These dogs, though, sounded angry. Their growling and snarling sounds moved around. As I listened, it dawned on me that they were coming up the hill toward me, one on each side of the tree I stood in.

They were flanking me.

It was at that moment I first regretted not having brought either a shovel or a radio. Though I didn't have any real reason for fearing the dogs—yet—I was decidedly uncomfortable with my undefended position.

The first thing I did was step down from the tree and find me a big, stout limb to use as a club. Then I climbed back into the madrone. I waited, and listened. One of the dogs had moved up above me. His growling was fierce—a deep throated, rattling warning. The second dog remained somewhere off to my left. As he got closer, he began barking savagely.

Maybe they didn't know I was a man, I thought. Or maybe they were after something else. Or maybe not. Maybe someone was with them. Maybe he'd call them off if he knew I was here. So I called out to the dogs.

"GET OUTTA HERE!" I yelled, sounding as big and mean as I could, hoping the dogs would realize their mistake and troop off to other business. My bigger hope was that the hunter—if there was a hunter with them—would hear me and call them off.

The silence that followed my challenge to the dogs didn't give me any hope that the latter was true. Within a couple minutes both dogs resumed their low growling and snarling, making me believe they knew what they were tracking, it was me, and I wasn't going to talk them out of it.

The dog above me circled back to my right. The one on my left hadn't moved.

As far as I could tell, I had two options. One was to stay put until someone came to rescue me. The other was to try to escape. The first option was probably the safer but it had ramifications that could be professionally embarrassing. I'd come down the hill without a radio or a shovel and this was not just contrary to policy, it was just plain stupid. And whoever came downhill to rescue me would run the risk of being attacked or shredded by the dogs. If someone did get hurt, then the repercussions would circle back to me—and deservedly so, since I'd failed to follow basic procedure.

For these reasons, the second option became the clearer of the two—though it was less appealing. It meant I had to get from high point to high point all the way up the hill, until either I reached the truck or the dogs gave up. At this point, neither seemed a safe bet.

The other possibility was growing larger in my mind as the barking and snarling and growling continued. They could also catch me out in the open, between defensible points, on my way up and they could tear me to ribbons.

I tried hard to convince myself that this would not happen. The dogs probably wouldn't attack if I didn't give them an easy opportunity. If I didn't display fear, then they probably wouldn't risk attacking me. I concentrated on not smelling like fear, and I told myself that I would not—could not—run. And I told myself I had to keep talking to them. I had to sound authoritative, in control, and unafraid. I had to get up and keep up the ruse of being the aggressor until I either bluffed them away or got to the truck.

I looked uphill at the route I had come down, and selected the next spot I could get to that would keep me high enough above the ground to avoid snapping jaws and ripping teeth. There were plenty of trees around to climb but I was one of the world's worst tree climbers. Many of the trees were madrones, like the one I was standing in; even for bad climbers, madrones are easy to climb.

I hopped down from the tree, froze and listened, then trooped deliberately and purposefully to my next high point. All the way there I told the snarling dogs how I would tear them limb from limb if they came within reach. Talking tough made me mad. Truth was, I had plenty to be mad about—the dogs had kept me from finding and checking the last fire, which could prove an embarrassment if the fire wasn't really out. It also angered me that I was being threatened by anything at all. I wasn't generally a combative sort, but I didn't like to be challenged or threatened and by now I was mad.

"Tear you limb from limb," I said. "Kick your aimless asses. Pound your heads and tear you limb from limb." I tried to sound authoritative. Firm. Not challenging, just authoritative.

I climbed steadily from the first madrone refuge to the next good one. Then to a boulder, where I made another stand. Then to a big root wad. Then to another madrone. The dogs kept pace with me, still growling and slinking and snarling, as I advanced up the hill. They stayed out of sight, but kept within what I figured was striking range.

I kept going up the hill and at about the ninth or tenth resting point, I realized the dogs were no longer following me. This made me wonder whether the dogs really did have something treed down there, and had been just warning me off. But I didn't stop to ponder the deeper reasoning of wild dogs very long. I kept going from high point to high point for another three hundred yards, then began a brisk, beeline walk toward the truck, hoping I hadn't been flummoxed by clever dogs into dropping my guard long enough for them to get me.

When I arrived at the engine, the Bible studiers were dozing. Otto woke up when I opened the driver's door. I climbed in. "Thought you'd gotten lost," he said, yawning. The others came awake at the sound of his voice.

"Find the fires?" Casey asked, not really caring.

"Yup," I lied. Well, a third of it was a lie.

"They out?"

I nodded, firing up the engine.

"That one that was way down there, did you have any trouble finding it?" Maureen asked.

I shook my head. I was sweating hard and I hoped she would think my uncommunicative behavior was due to my being out of breath. Truth was, I was doing all I could to keep from shaking. As I drove, my buttocks quivered and my knees tingled.

At home that night, I sat out on the back porch and scratched my black Labrador's ears until he was in a trance. I drank a fair number of beers and watched night close over the forest. The creek water tinkled and gurgled. A few robins got in their last licks. Some ways off, a cow mooed.

As we headed inside to go to bed, a pack of coyotes started yipping. They weren't far off, probably halfway up the ridge behind the house. Their cries carried in the summer stillness like wild spirits, looking for someone or something to instill with thoughts of fear and wonder. I lay in my bed for a long time without sleeping, communicating with the spirits of coyotes, Labradors, and wild dogs.

JUNIOR AND THE
BEARSKIN MEADOW CREW

Chuck Smay

He had more experience than any of the other crew members but he was OK with even the newest member calling him "Junior." He had several years experience in the ways of the Forest Service by the time I started my first year. Pick an area and he had been there and done that, yet he treated everyone with equal respect and everyone liked to be around him and wanted to be his friend. Junior was a natural leader who had the ability and desire to do about anything to be a part of the group. He didn't mind being the one to break the path through deep snow on a winter project or break trail through thick brush on a project fire. He would work any shift, sometimes two if that was necessary. If the rest of us were dog tired from a long shift or too much social activity, Junior would always be the first one up the next morning to make sure we made it to the cook shack for breakfast. He never let us down. Despite his hard working serious side he liked to have fun like the rest of us 18-20 year old summer employees. He could set a pace that none of us could match for long and he always got to the top of the hill or back to the truck before we did. He would just stand there and grin at us and shake his head as we would catch up. Naturally, he was fully rested by the time we got there and ready to go again. Out on the job he loved to slip up behind you and scare the daylights out of you by making some racket so you thought you were about to be devoured by a bear or some other creature of the forest. I learned his skills in this area on several night fire assignments. About the third day of boring night shift mopup work, Junior would liven things up with one of his sneak attacks designed to produce sudden fear! It is actually amazing how fast one could move, even when you thought you were tired, when properly motivated by surprise and a healthy mixture of fear for good measure.

Just like the rest of the crew, Junior liked it when we got called to a fire. It provided a great break from the routine project work and usually got us all into some country we did not normally get to see. Another great benefit was the chance to see friends from other stations and ranger districts that were also sent to the fire. I think everyone on the forest knew Junior! If there was a new employee, or someone from another agency Junior usually made the first move to get acquainted. It is humbling to be around this kind of natural talent. Our crew had the reputation of being a good hard working crew and so we usually got some challenging assignments on the fires. When we finally got to camp it was a welcome sight and we were certainly ready for something other than C-rations or stale sandwiches. Wow, could he eat. I was amazed at the food he could put away when we were on a fire assignment. After a long shift he could easily go through the chow line two or three times before he was full. He must have been the chow hound the Forest Service had in mind when they set the calorie standards for firefighter's meals.

I saw Junior show any kind of fear only once. I was a bit surprised at this reaction to our helicopter flight from the Hume Lake area into the back country for what turned out to be a weekend assignment on a lightning fire. It was one of those early rickety old helicopters, and I had flown only a couple of times by then myself. It frightened me a bit that he was so nervous. I kept thinking, what does Junior know or see about this that I am not aware of? At last the pilot and I, of all people, convinced him that everything was OK and the flight should not be any problem for the three of us to go in. I never told anyone on the crew about this incident. It seemed to me at the time to be one of those things that friends do not share with others. It turned out that the most dangerous thing that happened was our need to survive the entire weekend on only canned Dinty Moore Stew!

After a couple of summers many of the crew members went to other summer jobs on the district. I was assigned as an inspector on blister rust control contracts. This usually involved working by yourself and consisted of following a predetermined search pattern over large areas of the forest where the contractor had worked to remove undesirable plants that were the source of the disease. I was delighted to learn that Bill Prinz,

Junior's boss had designed the project so the two of us could work together. It was a great summer! We were together out in the field virtually every day and working in some beautiful country. There were just enough yellow jacket, snake and porcupine encounters to keep you alert, so that Junior did not need to pull any special surprises. We got our assigned summer's work done and had fun doing it. While I had greatly improved my woods skills, I still could not keep up with Junior. He could still walk circles around me but true to his nature he did not make a big deal about it.

I moved on to other jobs and so did Junior. We would see each other once in awhile and it was always a great time together. I regret that I lost track of him over the years. I am sure he has retired by now, and has a great many friends like me that remember him. I know that Junior was the neatest Labrador retriever that I ever worked with. A loyal and true friend and a great companion on any field assignment. Thank you Bill Prinz for having Junior on the crew and for letting me work with him in the field one summer while you were office bound!

SHORTY AND THE RATTLESNAKE

James R. Pratley

Shorty, a beautiful toy shepherd puppy, came to live with us early in 1945 when I was commuting to Oak Grove Park during my initial assignment with the Forest Service.

On her first day at Oak Grove Park she was introduced to all but the very highest brass. I was not about to risk her rejection before her feminine wiles could work their charm. She was an immediate sensation with the crew, so much so that it was a fight to see who would get to carry her to and from the job site as she was much too young to manage by herself. Not only did she have to be carried but she had to be safeguarded against all the perils of the forest; the eagles, hawks, fox, coyote, badger and, of course, the ever present rattlesnakes. This task fell to young Bill who equated the responsibility with pay raise. By the time the brass discovered that we had an unpaid member on the crew, Shorty was fully entrenched in the hearts of all who knew her.

Her first difficult experience came on a reconnaissance project in Big Tujunga Canyon between the Tujunga Tunnel and the Colby Ranch, an area infested with rattlesnakes. Being unable to walk through the brush, as tall as a house in some places, we had a choice of crawling over the top, which was very slow going, or crawling under the brush on our hands, knees and bellies. We did not relish this last approach for obvious reasons. What, however, were we going to do with Shorty? There was only one solution. She would be carried in our one knapsack along with tools, our lunch boxes and two canteens of water. The day was very hot and she began to resist this honor before we could even get her in the sack. But once in she had no way to get out. Even though she stood on her hind legs, she could barely peek out between the top of the bag and the buckled down cover. Worse yet, the canteens and the lunch boxes pinched her toes and banged against her legs as she and the bag were literally dragged through the under portions of the brush.

Before long we reached a section where the brush was just too close to the ground to allow us to crawl. Bill, along with Shorty, then began to climb on top of the rickety brush, no easy task, and to work his way to our next ground position. All of a sudden Bill disappeared from view and I heard him cry out, "I fell through and am hung up by the knapsack. I can't get out. Give me a hand." I could also hear Shorty whining and complaining as she too was unable to help herself and was trapped in that damn bag.

Between Bill's call for help and Shorty's pleas to be released from her confinement, I had every reason to hurry to the rescue. Reaching Bill was no real problem but cutting him loose was another matter. So, before trying to free Bill, I took Shorty out of the bag, put her in my shirt and was about to cut the straps when we heard the one ominous sound that changed our plan, the unmistakable sound of a rattlesnake. After careful investigation, we discovered that the snake was directly under

Bill, making his entrapment a very fortuitous happening. Had he fallen through we would have had a serious situation on our hands, a long way from medical attention and no way to summon help short of several hours away.

The only way to release Bill safely, was to move him vertically, bag and all, with nothing available but brute strength on my part. Bill was helpless and only able to extend his arms for me to grasp. But pulling him up was no solution. No matter how I might brace myself in the unstable brush, the more that I pulled, the deeper I descended. Obviously, another plan had to be devised, one where I could brace myself as best I could and he would then crawl his way up my arms and body to safety. First, I had to cut away the offending bag and drop it to the ground where it could be retrieved later. Now it was up to Bill to climb my frame despite the sweat that had come from the heat of the day but was also generated by his close call. But, being young and vigorous, and with his only safe escape over my body, he was up to the task.

Shorty, however, was still taking her lumps as Bill, in his zeal to escape, was not too careful as to what he grabbed in his hand over hand upward climb. We more than heard from our little friend, who could in no way appreciate the situation. Finally, with one last effort, Bill managed to drape himself across the brush and heave a big sigh of relief.

After a few moments of rest and reflection, we then had to retrieve the knapsack and its contents, constantly aware of our adversary and any other possible relative or friend that he, or she, might be consorting with. Fortunately, the snake that had caused the problem had moved on to a safer location so that we could pick up where we had left off. But, as you can imagine, the rest of that day was one of hair trigger responses to anything that sounded like a rattlesnake.

When the day was completed, we performed our daily ritual of inspecting each other, including Shorty, for wood ticks; had a cooling drink from Big Tujunga Creek and hiked back to the tunnel where we had left the pickup.

102

ED

Joe Church

Toward the end of our tour at Orleans on the Six Rivers National Forest, we acquired a dog who, when standing on his back legs, would have given Bigfoot a run for its money in size. His name was Mr. Ed, named after the horse in the popular TV show of that time. He was a big, long-haired German shepherd. He was gentle and friendly, especially with kids which was good since the station was loaded with kids and, come to think of it, he more likely acquired us, rather than the other way around.

In the turmoil of the December, 1964 storm and flood, one of the district families, Gin and Al Earhard, lost just about everything they owned when the Klamath swept their trailer, car and worldly goods off the bench they occupied near Ullathorne Creek. A new house was available on the station, one of several built during the 1962-64, PWA program, so the Earharts moved into it until they could get a replacement trailer for the lost one. They did get the new trailer the following spring. Meanwhile, when they did move to the station they brought Mr. Ed, or Ed for short. We had lost our dog, Lassie, an Australian shepherd, to salmon fever shortly after the flood, so Ed was a welcome visitor. The kids, especially ours, took to him as he did to them. It was a sad day for all when the Earharts moved into their new trailer and took Ed with them. The next day, though, there was Ed at our door wagging his tail furiously. Al took him home. Next day, Ed was back. Al took him home again and tied him up for two or three days, then let him go. Next day, there was Ed at our door wagging his tail furiously. Gin and Al thought it over for a day or so, for they really liked Ed. They then told us that apparently Ed would rather be on the station with us and the kids and that if we wanted him we could have him. That's how we acquired Mr. Ed. Or, did Mr. Ed acquire us?

Ed went with us to Twain Harte and the Mi-Wok District of the Stanislaus when I was transferred there in January, 1966.

Ed was a moose, but a gentle moose. When I went in the field he went too, as often as I could take him. I went through a lot of adventures with Ed, but one generally stands out more than others.

The Stanislaus Forest Transportation Plan called for the construction of a main east-west road between the town of Tuolumne and Cherry Creek Reservoir on the Groveland District. A goodly chunk of this road was already in place but did need improvement. The section crossing the Clavey River had been the only one staked. The district ranger should have some idea of what was going on on his district, I thought, so one day I drove to the west end of the staked line and hiked down it to the Clavey. Ed went with me. A tough hike—rocky, steep and brushy. Not only that, it was midsummer and hot. We did get to the river, finally, and that water was inviting. I took off my boots and socks and soaked my feet in that cool, clear water. Ed, wearing his heavy coat, probably worse off than me, stepped into the water, drank his fill for the time being, then sat down on the river bottom. There he was shoulder deep in Clavey River water, sitting down and slowly wagging his tail underwater. He was a contented moose. While there, I took sometime to explore the canyon and found, to my astonishment, some potholes six or eight feet deep with smooth vertical sides, ground out in the granite bedrock. There was no water in them, so it occurred to me that they could be deathtraps for any animals, including humans, which fell into them. None that I saw, however, contained any such remains. Nonetheless, they were scary. Later after Ed and I both resoaked ourselves in the river, we began our trek out, arriving much relieved at the pickup an hour or so later. But, my real picture of that hike is that of Ed, sitting shoulder deep in Clavey River water, contentedly wagging his tail.

As a postscript, one autumn night a couple of years later, Ed was struck and killed by a pickup in Twain Harte when he was out running with Sam. We buried him that night in the backyard of the house we were renting, with hope he is resting there yet.

RANGER STATION DOGS

Wendall L. Jones

Each ranger station always seemed to have a goodly supply of dogs. Perhaps only slightly fewer than children. We didn't have leash laws but if a dog was behaving badly, it usually mysteriously or purposely disappeared. A dog that bit kids was not long from doggie heaven (or hell). Dogs were often the underlying factor in a ranger station dispute. Some guys liked to take their dog with them to work. Then there were complaints about the doggy aroma in the truck.

HOW TO MANAGE A MENACING DOG

Rudo L. Fromme

This was demonstrated to me while en route one night in 1911 in a four-horse drawn wagon stage from Roseburg to Fort Orford via Myrtle Point in Oregon. This was the most expeditious means for reaching Ranger W. B. Millbury's MacGribble Station from Grants Pass. As we stopped to change horses around midnight, my one traveling companion, a fairly young man whom I had not known before, remarked, "Let's get out and stretch our legs and wet our guzzles with a little water." Overhearing this remark, one of the stable men promptly "threw cold water" on the water thirsty victims by saying, "There's no water here at the stable except what the horses are drinking. We have to carry it from yon house across the road. But I wouldn't advise you to try to get it there—not this time o'night, anywise, 'cause there's a watch dog sleeps by the pump that 'ud just as soon take a chunk out of you as not—perhaps liefer." "Hell! theta ain't no dog'll stop me if I can just find a couple o' stout sticks," responded my friend in a contemptuous tone. The stable hand pointed to some spare axe and shovel handles standing in a corner of the barn. "Just the thing," said the dog tamer, as he grabbed a shovel handle in the left hand and an axe handle in the right. "Come on, pal, follow me, but stay back aways, case I don't belt him right the first swing."

As we gingerly approached the front yard gate, sure enough, there was a low, menacing growl from the front porch near the pump. It was a partly moonlit night, so I could see the big fellow get up and come sneaking toward the opening gate with his neck hair "all abristle." "Nice doggy," said the thirsty one, as he approached gingerly, shovel handle to the front like an old-time Gladiator's parrying lance. But the "nice doggy" came with a rush, grabbed the interfering lance between his snarling teeth, then "whang" came the axe handle down on the doggy's head. Also, up went a front window and away to the friendly stable flew one Fromme and erstwhile dog tamer, both however, minus the cool drink of water. The fresh team of horses was raring to go, also the fresh driver, so we settled back with our dry, swollen tongues and hoped for better luck at the next stage station.

DOG DISHES

Ed A. Grosch

It was the second winter that I spent in the Covelo-Round Valley area of Mendocino County. As a seasonal lookout fireman for the Forest Service, you had to hunt up another job when laid off at the end of fire season. There was no unemployment insurance in those days.

One year, I landed a job doing "barn-dogging"—feeding horses, milking cows, and cleaning stables—for a large ranch company in the south end of the valley. The ranch foreman told me to take my horse and a couple of gentle milk cows over to a "poison oak ranch" on the Poonkinny Road. A poison oak ranch was what we called the poor soil homesteads that squatted amongst the large ranches. While there, I was supposed to pick up a couple of cows that had strayed to this place. I was not a cowboy, but the foreman said the other rancher would help me get these other cows started for home. These stray cows were a little brushy, wild and not easily herded, so I took one of the good herding McNab dogs with me. By the time I got to this other ranch, I was almost to Dos Rios and it was very late in the afternoon.

This rancher, knowing I would not be able to return to the headquarters until after midnight, invited me to spend the night at his place. I thought it would be all right, so I used the old wall phone and called the foreman, and he agreed. We proceeded to do the chores and put the various animals up for the night.

This rancher was known for being a very good "hound man," and he had about ten of them staked in his yard. On entering the house there were three more hounds lounging by the kitchen stove. This man was a bachelor and the house was more like a two room cabin. The only inside plumbing was a single water faucet over a small sink. He built up the fire and started making supper. The coffee pot was already on, so it only needed to be heated. The main meal was to be deer stew and dough-gods (biscuits) with the reboiled coffee. His small table was all ready with three settings of enamelware plates, cups and utensils. As soon as the dough-gods were out of the oven, we sat down to eat

After the usual cigarette and coffee to settle our supper, I offered to wash the dishes. As I stood up to prepare for this chore, he reached over, grabbed the plates—utensils and all— and set them on the floor. Immediately the inside hounds were there to lick them off. When they were done, he picked up the plates and turned them bottom up on the table with the silverware next to each plate. I was dumbfounded and speechless. He simply remarked that dog tongues and saliva are very good sterilizers and there was no need to wash the dishes.

I slept very fitfully on an old iron cot, wondering how many fleas I would become host to. The next morning, I was too scared of getting sick to bring myself to eat any breakfast but I did drink a little coffee to fortify me for the long ride home.

A RESCUE OPERATION

R. Kenneth Smith

I was assistant ranger on the Sonora District of the Stanislaus under Ranger Bill Spargo in 1936-37. These were depression years. Individuals and partners were trying to grub out a living by panning gold or making split products such as shakes, posts and ties. Also, there were the first faint stirrings of winter sports activities on the forest. In fact, there was a rope tow near Long Barn and some genuine imported Scandinavian ski instructors. "How do you turn on those things?" "Vel, yoose turn, that's all." Also based at Long Barn was an Alaskan dog team driver with sled and dogs. He was trying to make it by taking people an sled rides, the ride being over snow plowed highway or other plowed road.

There were some Finnish tie makers working six or eight miles out in the woods from Long Barn. They sent a messenger out to the telephone relating that one of their party was very sick. Would it be possible to have him brought out to the hospital? As fate would have it, here was a driver and dog team right at Long Barn. The dog man was eager to demonstrate his team but needed a partner. Would I like to go? Would I! We rendezvoused at Long Barn. It was beginning to get dark. Long Barn Resort gave us a nice dinner. The lady owner clucked over us, prepared roast beef sandwiches for the trip and we started.

The first half mile was on cleared, icy road. We rode the sled and just sailed along. The dogs were eager. We came to the end of the plowed road and into, not onto, a couple of feet of snow. The team pulled and the dogs broke through to their bellies. The sled was a big, heavy steel runnered one for Arctic conditions. We sort of looked at each other but there wasn't much choice but to have at it. The driver and I took turns walking ahead on our snowshoes to somewhat pack the road to the tie maker camp. The dogs pulled, stopped, panted and pulled some more until we got to the cabin. The Finns were all up. It was after midnight and everyone was talking except the sick man, the driver, me and the dogs. We decided to rest a couple of hours and with all of that hospitality I drank a big cup of black coffee. You haven't tasted strong coffee until you have had a cup of Finnish tie maker coffee. I lay down on a bunk but dozing was out of the question. I just lay there and shook.

It came time to start back. The dog man didn't feel good so asked me to feed the dogs. He had brought a sack of meat and told me to give a big chunk to each dog. He said, "Feed the leader first or they will fight over the food." I ventured out into the night with the food sack. The dogs had curled up in their traces but when they saw me every one immediately sat up. They knew what was coming and I could see that they were very intent. I will never forget all those yellow unblinking eyes fixed on me.

I tried to get the first to the leader but in an instant that pack turned into one big ball of snarling, fighting dogs, each with another dog in his teeth. The driver burst out of the cabin with a broom and flailed about until a sort of growling order had been restored.

The sick man was by now well wrapped up like a mummy, except for his nose. His partners bade him goodby; he was well padded and tied down, and we took off. In places the snow was now crusted and that helped, but usually it was just plow along. The driver went ahead to pack. I had to stay right at the sled because it would not track when we crossed the small drainages. There were culverts in the road so the roadway was there, but as the team went around a curve, the loaded sled would be pulled off the road and over the bank. I had to flop around on snowshoes and pull the sled sideways enough to stay in the track.

The dogs were magnificent. They pulled until absolutely spent, then stopped and panted. When the driver gave the signal to go again every dog was up and pulling.

We got back to Long Barn well after daylight. An ambulance was there and our adventure was over. Sadly, the man died of pneumonia the next day. The tie makers got the news and all walked out a few days later for his funeral and burial at Sonora. The team owner and his dogs drifted back to Alaska to a home and environment fitting for such a team.

BREAKING THE TENSION

R. H. "Dick" Tubman

I spent four seasons with Fred or his right hand "Aimee" McPherson. Each has a special recollection. We 12 students were camped on the Deschutes as the District Six east-side timber survey party. An OSC forester, Bill Manlove was Fred's assistant and Bill had a small mongrel dog with him in camp. It was friendly, innocent and answered natures call according to its sniff. Our days were long or reasonable according to where we went and how near the days work completed that part of the cruise assignment. The hands of the clock didn't bother us except that we were well on our way by 8 a.m.

In the evenings when all of us were in and "Old Tripp" had fed the last party stragglers, sometimes 8 p.m. and later, we gathered in the "bull tent," a big wall tent. We sat around on camp gear boxes, or blocks of wood or what have you. This particular night at dinner we had a special guest, the "DIGNITARY" of the Deschutes. He was dressed to kill, his pressed chokebores and jodphur boots all shining and aglow—all he needed was the quirt to be a full-fledged "foxhunter."

After a few pleasant remarks at the table, into the bull tent we went, but the "air" of the two key principals changed after some disagreement and we began to recognize that the big "DIGNITARY" might be picking on our boss. So we quieted down with a little apprehension. Suddenly the two principals went outside to settle their dispute and we overheard some strong statements. We kept quiet. The argument seemed to be settled and the two principals came back into the tent and we boys sat down. Not much was said.

Bill's mongrel just then wandered into the gathering, looked around, went to Bill, sniffed his boots, passed on to the next in line, sniffed, on to the next around the tent walls sniffing, came to the "DIGNITARY" jodphurs, sniffed, hesitated, went to the next boots, then suddenly he found it. He turned, walked to the jodphurs, cocked his hind leg and "let go." The beads of piddle sparkled. We became tense, the "DIGNITARY" never moved a muscle, "took it in stride," suddenly got up and walked out followed by Fred. Several words passed, a vehicle started, we held our apprehension and in walked Fred. We said "Bill's little dog didn't like our "DIGNITARY," did he?" The group roared and the tension broke.

BEAR DOG

Grover C. Blake

One summer I had a guard who brought with him to the mountains an Airedale dog named Lucky. Lucky's purpose was to frighten away bear and other troublesome animals. He was especially good at finding bacon in a pack at night when all was quiet. He just loved bacon.

His first encounter with a wild animal was with a porcupine where he came out second best. He did not hurt the porcupine at all but his owner worked overtime separating Lucky from numerous quills.

Later on, when making a field trip, I took the guard along. Lucky came also. Far out in the wilderness area we heard a very peculiar screech coming from a distance ahead. We glimpsed through the trees and over the tops of huckleberry brush and saw some rapidly moving objects. Almost instantly, around a turn in the trail, came Lucky at a speed never matched by any Airedale before or since as far as we know. About ten feet behind Lucky was a brown bear coming toward us at a speed fully equal to that of Lucky. That dog was really bringing us a bear. The bear turned from the trail and into the brush almost at my horse's head. Lucky happened to think of something he had forgotten and hurried home after it.

We soon found where the race probably started. A cub was having trouble going up the smooth side of a Western larch tree and was telling the world how unhappy he was. He kept on scrambling and crying in the bear language until he reached a limb. He then clammed up.

CANINE INTELLIGENCE

James R. Pratley

Shorty, my constant companion in the woods for twelve years, learned early on not only to obey instantly but that I would return to wherever I left the pickup at the end of the day, which in this case saved her life.

George Knowles and I, along with Shorty, were looking for the southwest corner of section 10 near the junction of Indian Creek and the South Fork of Indian Creek, north of Happy Camp on the Klamath National Forest, in order to obtain the necessary rights of way for the improvement of the Indian Creek Road for logging purposes.

Parking the pickup next to the creek, we began a traverse of the mountain slope which was a jumble of downed snags and heavy brush. After about one hour we realized that Shorty was no longer with us. Calling and whistling as we moved further away from the truck, we figured that she would soon join us as she had done on so many previous occasions. But, after about an hour of a most difficult traverse, there was still no sips of Shorty. By lunch time we both really began to worry as the area was used by the locals for bear trapping. There were coyotes, badgers and rattlesnakes, any of which could have made short work of a 24 pound, very friendly dog. Though we searched the area diligently for the section corner, it became obvious to us that it had never been established during the land surveys in the mid 1880s, typical of so many surveys of that era when the land values were considered to be very marginal.

Giving up the search for the corner in midafternoon, we began our traverse back to the truck, still without any evidence of Shorty, though we followed the same route we had used that morning. Getting close to the place where we first began to miss her presence, we began to notice traces of what appeared to be blood on the fallen snags and knew without a doubt that Shorty had either been taken by perhaps a coyote or had been hurt in some fashion. But, where was she? Neither of us had any clue.

Arriving back at the truck, we decided to cool off in the creek and have a drink of water before undertaking a thorough search in the immediate area for any possible clues as to where Shorty might be. It was then that I heard a faint and pleading whine coming from the creek. There she was, her hips buried in the sand at the edge of the water, in full view of the pickup, if we had looked. We both knew that something had happened to her that morning and that she had returned to the vicinity of the truck to await our inevitable return.

Scooping away the sand and gravel from her rear legs, we discovered that she had apparently misjudged a jump across a fallen log, and in coming down, had ripped her anus on a sharp, jagged limb. Not only was the wound painful but she must have known that she could not get our attention, could not keep up with us and that she had to return to the creek to stem the loss of blood from a very serious injury. So, she used her training and her woods sense to return to the creek and the pickup as her only salvation knowing that we would eventually return. How she managed to dig herself into the sandy beach, we can only surmise. And, luck was obviously with her all the way as she eluded any possible predators. Had they discovered her at any time during the day, she would have perished on the spot.

Cleaning Shorty off as gently as we could in the cooling water, we then raced to the ranger station, applied first aid and then began the long trip to Yreka for surgical repair at the vet's. Once again she survived to return to work after a two week leave of absence, somewhat moth-eaten as the vet had to shave off most of her backside after already undergoing a complete body clip for the hot summer weather.

CURLY REDWOOD

Gary Munsey

Curly Redwood was the district ranger's dog on the Redwood Ranger District in the 1960s. Curly was a golden retriever, at least that is what we were led to believe. Truth be known, Curly was not playing with a full deck. In fact, he was about three bricks shy of a full load—you know, the porch light was on but no one was home. The stories about Curly are legion. I will try and recall a few of the more memorable ones.

Curly liked to ride on top of the ranger's pickup. The ranger's nickname was "High-Beam Hatzi" because he drove with his headlights on and subscribed to the theory that no harm could befall you if your lights were on, but that's another book. Curly would start out in the back of the truck, work his way up to the top of the cab of the truck and subsequently a nose would appear at the top of the windshield as the dog decided to look through the windshield. This was distracting, especially if you were traveling at 60 miles per hour.

During slash burning, Curly had a disquieting habit of retrieving "grenades" that had been thrown to ignite the slash. These grenades had a 20 second fuse. Curly could usually locate and fetch the grenade in about ten seconds and with a five second run back to the person that threw it, that left five seconds before it exploded. Needless to say we would all try to either get the sputtering grenade away from Curly or try to outrun the dog in search of cover.

His retrieving was not limited to grenades. While duck hunting at the mouth of the Klamath River, Curly decided to try and catch a diving coot. The coot would dive and then Curly would dive, the coot would surface and then Curly would surface and so on. We finally had to drag the nearly drowned retriever into the boat. He had a habit of falling asleep in the blind during hunting trips so that if you shot a bird, you had to kick Curly to wake him up and get him going.

One of Curly's more bothersome habits was that of trying to occupy the same space as me on a log that I was standing on, often ten feet or more above the "jungle" floor. Being "cold nosed" from the rear by a leaping golden retriever was often enough to launch me into space.

The one incident that stands out above all the others is the time that Curly mysteriously passed out in the district office. The ranger's attempts to revive him were unsuccessful, so he picked up Curly, ran down the stairs, threw the dog in his truck and took off for the veterinarian in Crescent City. On arrival in Crescent City, Curly suddenly woke up, shook and wagged and trotted off, after apparently a nice hour's nap.

I don't miss the fog and I don't miss the rain. I don't miss the floods and I don't miss the pain. I don't miss the redwoods and I don't miss the "jungle," but I do miss many of the people I worked with on the Redwood and Gasquet districts. (I know it doesn't rhyme, but what do you expect, poetry?)

FELINES

JOE AND THE HAWK AND
SAM THE HUNTING CAT

Nancy R. Hood

One day at Dry Lake Lookout I heard an odd noise. I looked up and out the window. I saw my black cat Joe all puffed up and stalking around what looked like a pile of chicken feathers. His eyes were huge as he glared up into the air. I looked up also and saw a hawk, possibly a red-tailed doing his best to fly away.

The hawk looked like he had gone through a picking machine. He had one or two feathers left in his tail and his wings were very tattered. He was about 20 feet above the ground and was really struggling to glide away through some trees. I never saw him again so I don't know if he survived while his feathers were growing back.

Joe was unhurt. Apparently the hawk dove at him and Joe heard him. He must have flipped over and met the hawk claws to talons. His copper, penny colored eyes were really big. Later on, after we were lookouts at Collins Baldy, he would react to the buzzards the same way as they soared by. He growled loudly as if daring them to come try something!

My black cat Sam was Joe's brother from the next year's litter. The mother of both was a cross-eyed Siamese. All one-half Siamese act like dogs and follow a person around.

Joe and Sissy, his litter sister, Sam and Hercules, Sam's gray litter brother and I would go walking after hours. I would be walking along around bushes looking for obsidian pieces. Joe, Sissy and Hercules would stay fairly close. Sam was always lagging, smelling to check out all the clumps of grass and holes in the ground.

One time I had gone around a bush with Joe, Sissy and Herky close by. We were out of Sam's sight. He meowed. I said, "Over here Sam," thinking he would trot around the bush. Instead he came through the bush meowing loudly.

The bush was about eight feet by eight feet. I was almost trampled by seven deer which exploded out of it as Sam came through. He was a 15 to 18 pound black object barreling through their hiding place. I didn't know they were there. All of us had a good scare.

So, I always said that Sam would be good to take hunting as he could surely flush out game!

CAT TALES

Bob Gray

During and after thunderstorms, lookouts quite often see smoke from fires that later go out from heavy rain or lack of fuel. These smokes may puff up intermittently or show for a few minutes and disappear or show up for several hours before disappearing for good. Occasionally, one of these smokes will dissipate only to show up days or even weeks later with disastrous results. For this reason, it is important to thoroughly search out by aerial recon or even on foot these possible "sleeper" or "holdover" fires.

Verna, on Slate Mountain reported a smoke near her lookout one day thusly, "It came up just over the brow of the hill from me and a distinct column showed for several minutes before it disappeared."

Since all the other fires from this storm had been found and taken care of I decided to take Bob F. to Slate Mountain and see if we could find the fire. My plan was to walk out to Budweiser Gap, about a mile and a quarter away, get on the back azimuth reading from Slate Mountain which was visible from Budweiser

Gap, and walk straight to the lookout on the designated bearing. This way I was bound to come to the burned area or even the still smoldering fire, though the base of the smoke was hidden from the lookout by the brow of the hill.

We had one problem which I'd failed to see and that was Slate Mt. had no Shasta net radio and I had no Trinity net radio so the only solution for communications was for Bob to stay in my pickup at the foot of the 30 foot tower to talk to me and holler up to Verna to keep me on the proper azimuth as I used a signal mirror to show her my location. With this plan, I left the lookout on foot, with a shovel and portable radio to search for the fire by myself. About 10 minutes and a quarter of a mile later, as I was struggling through a dense brush patch, a mountain lion sprang from the brush less than five feet from my side. Being startled was putting it mildly, as the lion bounded away from me and when she stopped about 50 feet away and stood facing me, it was a real surprise. I really wasn't afraid, but found it quite interesting to be looking at a wild mountain lion.

We watched each other for several moments, it seemed, and soon I playfully called, "Kitty, Kitty," to which the feline creature took a couple of steps toward me.

Since I wasn't really trying to entice her any closer, I then took a couple of steps toward it. It backed off a few feet, but still didn't leave. By then, I decided I'd better get on with my business, so I detoured around the animal, and was much surprised to see it following me at about 30 or 50 feet distance. Still I wasn't unduly alarmed, as there was no sign of hostility; just curiosity on the cats part, though my own curiosity had long gone.

For about a couple of hundred yards that tawny creature followed me, with me continually looking over my shoulder. Just keeping track, you know. Suddenly, about 20 feet in front of me there was that cat again. No, because a quick glance behind assured me I was still being followed. There was a second and much larger lion just ahead of me, and it looked far less friendly than the first one. Maybe my imagination was working, but this new critter looked twice as big and definitely had a scowl on his face, though he showed no real signs of hostility.

By this time, I figured this nonsense had to stop. I raised my shovel like a rifle and went "BANG, BANG!" They didn't budge, except that the second one circled behind me to where the first one was. At least I can see them both at once, I was thinking. They continued to follow, sometimes within 20 feet, stopping when I stopped and walking when I walked. I sweated, fretted and prayed a little before deciding to call Bob on the radio to tell him a couple of mountain lions were on my tail, and that I was going to keep walking to the Budweiser Gap clearing. Well, when you talk on the Forest Service radio, everyone hears you, especially when you don't want them to. In seconds everyone was aware of my plight and the dispatchers were ready to send a copter for me. Lenore, on Sims, reminded me that once I had told her, "Don't worry, Lenore, he's as afraid of you as you are of him," when she encountered a mountain lion while on an evening walk,

I declined the copter and continued to the Gap about a half mile away. My friends stayed with me all the way, but at some greater distances. As I reached the opening in Budweiser Gap, I was startled to see a man enter the clearing from the Incline Trail. It was Mr. Mardahl, a timber cruiser for International Paper. "Man, I'm glad to see you—What do you see behind me?" "My gosh, a mountain lion," he answered, then he saw the second one as I asked him to look again. While we talked, the lions melted into the brush but I was sure thankful to have a reliable witness to this unlikely tale.

I never did look for the fire anymore and Mr. Mardahl decided he'd seen enough timber for the day, so we walked down to the road to his car and to where Bob picked me up. Yes, we looked over our shoulders occasionally on the way down the trail.

Back at the office there was a neatly wrapped and ribboned box of catnip on my desk. From my friend Bob M. and the gang.

CAT MAN ON THE KLAMATH

Chuck Burk

During the great depression of the 1930s, a number of men took up mining claims along the Klamath River and its tributaries in northern California. They weren't looking for a pot of gold at the end of a rainbow. Their hope was simply to keep body and soul together until the economy improved and then they were long gone. A few, however, stayed on, doing their thing in such a low key way that they seemed to be a part of the landscape. Charlie Everill was one of these. I became acquainted with him while serving as the D.R. on the Seiad Valley District of the Klamath National Forest in the late 1950s.

There was nothing all that unusual about Charlie. Shaving, bathing, changing clothes and laundering were not his strong points. But he did love cats and there were cats everywhere on his mining claim. He didn't take care of them in the usual sense. They had to rustle most of their grub. But, the door of his one room cabin was always left ajar and they used it as headquarters, especially when the weather was bad.

Long before the term "endangered species" was invented, Charlie became aware of the dearth of birds in his neighborhood and surmised that, somehow, his cats might be implicated. Guilt driven, he constructed a dozen bird houses, attached them to skinny, ten foot poles and planted them in his asparagus patch on a flat between the road and the Klamath River. They looked oddly like giant sunflowers on spindly stems swaying in the slightest breeze. Most importantly, they contributed greatly to Charlie's karma.

Just how many cats there were on Charlie Everill's creek claim was a matter of conjecture. He never made a "head count" as a rancher would with his cattle. Still, he had a gut feeling for quantity and, sometimes, after eyeballing the meowing mess he would opine, "I think somebody has been dumping cats here."

I don't know where Charlie was when he died but presume it happened while on a rare trip to Yreka. The district attorney called with the news and asked if I would bring in Charlie's personal effects.

I invited Bill Strait, the game warden, to visit the cabin with me. On our arrival the door was ajar as usual. Since it was my party, I knocked and walked in first, then charged out gagging and wheezing. Bill questioned my rapid exit but I couldn't talk. He then strode in and seconds later was outside hacking along with me. The cabin had a dirt floor and was one humongous kitty litter box with an aroma approaching the point of detonation. In order to accommodate the D.A.'s request, we had to hyperventilate outside, dash in and grab what we could, then get out. We filled a medium sized cardboard box with worn out clothing and paraphernalia. Charlie traveled light in this world.

With no known relatives, Charlie was buried alongside indigents and paupers who chanced to die in Siskiyou County.

Sometime later, while hiking across his claim, I discovered a cemetery on a slope above his cabin. There were several rows of rough rock headstones with less than the usual spacing and each bore a laboriously chiseled name. There was Myrna Loy, Jean Harlow, Greta Garbo, Claudette Colbert, Janette Gaynor and many more. It was a poignant tribute to Charlie's feline friends.

My only regret was that Charlie's remains were in a potter's field instead of here with his cats. Snuggled in between Greta Garbo and Janette Gaynor there should have been another rough stone chiseled "CHARLIE EVERILL, R.I.P."

MELBA GOLF LYNX

Rudo L. Fromme

Melba Golf Lynx is what I named her the first night of captivity. She was a wild baby lynx or bobcat and she seemed to have a high soprano voice. I also wondered if I would need a golf club to handle her. Roger Chris Morgonroth was with me and we were in a twin bed cabin at Singer's Resort on Lake Crescent. The cat was in a small slab top wooden box at my bedside and kept waking me up with a cry of "Eee, Eee, Eee's" every time I failed to dangle a finger through the slats for her to suck on.

We had been at Huelslock's Ranch on the Hoh the night before. In the morning their dogs treed a wild cat which was dropped with a well aimed rifle shot. Hearing the above mentioned curious cry, I pulled the baby cat out from under a fallen tree. There appeared to be no other kittens present. She was probably only a few days old, as there seemed to be a scum over her eyes. On the spur of the moment, I put her in the back pocket of my Filson shirt—no packsack this trip—which was to check on blowdown fire protective measures after several years' experience, probably the early spring of 1923 or '24. Got the small box at Forks, following our 20 plus miles walk, but took the kitten out for air quite frequently en route. We caught a lucky ride to Singers in the rather late evening. The cat was quieted down in the morning with a raw egg. Didn't seem to care much for cow's milk.

Fill her full of raw eggs and she would sleep peacefully most of the time, waking up full of coy playfulness. Took her home to Olympia via usual public means of travel and kept her until the July or August Sportsmen's Show in Seattle, at which time she was around five months of age. A piece of cow's liver would imbue her with so much eager frenzy that one dare not get his fingers too close to her. With a box of sawdust or woods duff in the basement and the door slightly ajar, she was more easily and trustingly housebroken than the usual domestic cat.

As to playfulness, her main idea of enjoyment was to slip along by the wall when she heard anyone approaching the doorway and then spring on the person as he or she entered. If the person was a stranger to her, she would drop at once and run to hide, but with me, she would hang onto my pants leg and pretend to be chewing me up. I soon taught her to jump onto me in the open from a table top. Also, to play "dead cat," in which I held her two front paws between the fingers of my right hand, soothed her eyes shut with my left hand until she dropped her head to one side in a relaxed position. Then, I would swing her in extended arm loops perpendicularly two or three rounds and up into the air. She would scream with seeming ecstasy while in the air, then come down with all claws bare to land on my stooped back or shoulders.

She refused to be cuddled or carried in one's arms unless too sleepy to resist, but she enjoyed riding on my shoulder in the house or yard. She enjoyed climbing our small cedar tree in the evening's recreation and sometimes wouldn't come down until baited with a raw egg and presented with my bent back to spring on from one of the lower limbs.

Sidewalk strolls with Melba in those days of loose dogs were always exciting. I didn't try this very often and not without a collar and short leash on her. She wouldn't follow very well but would run at my side or ahead in fair shape. As a dog approached, she seemed to watch out of the corner of one eye, allowing him to get close enough for her to reverse in a flash and send him yapping away with a scratched nose. When people approached, she would leap onto me and climb for a shoulder. You can imagine that my coat and trousers soon looked like the Wizard of Oz. My lower arms and hands were also well decorated, but the scratches never seemed to become poisonous. She refused to play when I tried wearing gloves, just got over into a corner and sulked.

Perhaps it was because I had permitted her to claw me up in play that she became more and more a one-man cat. My wife, Ruby, was not particularly infatuated, or in tune, with the moodier moods as she grew older—I mean the cat. Sometimes we put on real fights—I'm still referring to Melba—in which she screamed, clawed and bit, but I would cuff her with the flat of my hand against the side of her nose until she ran to her sulking corner. After some moments of apparent repentance and listening to my quieter voice of shaming her and offering renewed friendship, she would slowly approach my extended hand, rub the back of her neck against it, then lick a finger gently and wag her stub of a tail. In this action, she was far more like a dog than a domestic cat. However, I could not be home every evening and hold my job, so I grabbed at the invitation to display the wildcat at the Sportsmen's Show in Seattle on the opening Sunday incidental to a forest trip.

I carried Melba to Seattle in a slat top box as when bringing her home in the first place. It naturally had to be somewhat larger so I used an old fashioned shawl strap to carry it by. They were prepared for me with a 10 by 12 foot enclosure bounded by chicken wire about four feet high. Within this was a wire cage affair open at the bottom, probably a yard square and three feet high with narrow shelves three feet up. Entrance for the cat was by tipping it back so she could either walk on the grass or sleep on a shelf. Orders had been placed with the camp kitchen to supply her with two or three raw eggs per day and some variation of liver or sardines.

After a short survey of her quarters, she wanted out to play so it wasn't long till I had the fenced enclosure surrounded four or five feet deep with kids and olders watching the cat leaping from the top of her cage to my beckoning shoulder six to eight feet away. When I increased the distance too far for the shoulder, she would land on my leg somewhere and, with a seemingly savage but playful growl, pretend to tear me apart. I had to bend my shoulder toward the cage and move it up and down to coax her to jump back to the cage top.

I also put Melba through the dead cat stunt and she screamed so thrillingly when thrown in the air that the management coaxed me to put her through this act several times during the day to ballyhoo crowds to certain neglected exhibits. Of course, we couldn't pull this stunt too often. She had her moods and I didn't wish to have a fight on my hands,—or my arms, or face. She had a way of letting me know and it was usually by that stub tail of hers or the mean look in her eyes. Then I would get her onto one shoulder in a hurry and zip her back to her pen for a snooze on a shelf.

When carrying her about on the crowded grounds with no collar or leash, I was always having to push women's hands away. They would say, "Oh, look at the tiger kitty—nice kitty." Several were rewarded with scratched fingers because I couldn't dodge them all.

It was not an auction sale. A good looking 18 or 20 year old girl in our first audience asked me if I would sell the cat, to which I responded, "Yes, my home location is too confining and I'm not there steady enough to keep her under control. Have you a suitable place? And, do you think you could handle her?" She lived in the country, so she said; also, that she had taken care of several wild pets at times, including a coyote. She felt sure that after she started feeding Melba she could make friends with her. "Well," I said, "I suppose I ought to get ten or fifteen bunks for her." "I'll give you fifteen," came her prompt response. "Just wait till I find my dad for the money. But I had to tell her that this was on condition that the cat was still alive and healthy by next Sunday, as I had promised the management to leave her here in care of a city zoo attendant for the entire eight days of the program. I would give her written promise to that effect, if she would be sure to meet me here next Sunday. "Good," she said, "I'll get you the fifteen now to seal the bargain and then you can refund it if the cat fails to survive the show." Pop came through and I took the dough.

As I was giving the zoo attendant feeding instructions, I demonstrated how he might give the cat a bit of jumping exercise now and then. I held her front paws, so he would stroke the top of her head very gingerly. She growled quite menacingly far down inside which caused him to remark, "Well, I may try it once. A middle age onlooker asked if I would sell the cat. He wanted it to train his cougar hunting hounds. I told him that I doubted whether Melba would run from his hounds, as she seemed to have lots of confidence in her ability to fight back. Besides, I had already sold the cat for fifteen bucks. "Oh," he exclaimed, "I'd a given you twenty-five." "Well," I said, "You can probably buy her off her new owner within a week or so, as I have grave doubts that she's going to like her deal." I gave him her name and address.

The attendant was laying for me near the entrance gate. He said, "Look at my arms. I was a fool to be wearing a short sleeve shirt as you do. But I was a bigger fool for ever letting the damn cat out. When I tried to pet her she bit my finger and when I tried to put her back in her cage, all hell broke loose. I have to use a hooked cane to pull out her food dish and to push in the food. She tries to claw me through the chicken wire. I now wait until she's asleep. She's sure a one-man cat and you needn't worry about her health."

She was half asleep on a shelf as I entered the enclosure and some kid was trying to arouse her by poking her with a long, dry tree branch. She was growling inside but not offering to move. I stopped the kid in a hurry and she perked right up at my voice. However, she blinked her eyes and seemed unsure, until I started my soothing tone for coaxing her to play. Up she got, stretched to the limit and started wagging her stub tail to get out. After that, this Sunday was much like the last one, except that she was even less tolerant than before of would-be petters.

The new purchaser departed with the cat in the slat top box, confident that she would soon have her sitting on her lap in blissful contentment. She sent me a snap shot in a couple of weeks showing just that, but the cat looked quite sleepy. In another letter about two months later, she wrote that a man dropped by and offered to buy Melba. He wanted to use her to train his hounds. She let her go because her mean moods were becoming more frequent, if not continuous. She enclosed the man's name and address.

It was not until early spring that I got out to the new address to see if the cat was still around. I recognized the new owner from his interest at the Sportsmen's Show. He promptly stated that the cat was too civilized and mean for his purpose. He'd tried her out only once with the dogs. She ran all right, but when the dogs caught up with her she turned and clawed the hell out of them. He was now afraid that they'd never be any good for his purpose again.

She stayed away a couple of days then but came back for more civilized food. She keeps wanting to get out of her pen but won't stay gone. Gets a chicken or two and then comes back for her eggs and liver. He'd been phoning the city zoo for a couple of months to come and get her. Now they're promising to be here tomorrow. All she does anyway is to keep pacing back and forth growling at the whole world unless she's sleepin'. Come into the backyard if you want to see her.

As we approached the chicken wire pen with shed roof, Melba was pacing and growling. I went up close and started, "W'y Melba, don't you recognize your old playmate?" She stopped both growling and pacing at once and looked straight at me. The owner backed away, saying "Boy! I never saw her do that for anyone. Go closer, and talk some more." He didn't need to say that as I was already doing that very thing. After listening and looking me over a little further, the cat came up to the wire fence and rubbed the back of her neck against it for me to reach through and stroke her. "I'll bet you could go right inside that pen and really pet her," suggested the man. "I'll bet you're not going to see me try it," said I. She was just about a year old at that time, probably twice as heavy and much more menacing looking.

I had planned to try to look her up at the Seattle Zoo later, but I never got around to it. Anyway, it had been an interesting experiment and experience.

THE BOUNTY

Phil Weinzinger

On the Salmon River District of the Klamath National Forest, I took the mail down to the post office in the evening. Coming home one evening in February, 1941, I spotted a mountain lion in the car lights. All I had was a .22 pistol in the seat alongside me in a new Plymouth coupe of my own. I had just made a holster for the gun. I finally got the .22 pistol out and the lion jumped up on a bank. I leaned out of the car and went like that—bango. I didn't think I got it. I ran up with the flashlight, making a lot of noise to scare it up a tree. It damn near bit me. It was down. I'd hit it in the shoulder. Two more shots.

The next day an Indian boy walked by and said, "Hey, Weinzinger, did you get some meat last night?" He was hoping for a hind quarter. They thought I'd killed a deer. I told him I'd killed a lion but he didn't believe me. I sent the hide off to San

Francisco and got a $55 bounty on a female. The next year they stopped all bounties.

TRAVELING CATS

Nancy R. Hood

I went to Collins Baldy Lookout on the Klamath National Forest in 1970 after Dry Lake Lookout was closed. My cats did not like it as well as Dry Lake was rocky and lower elevation, steeper and hotter.

There were only two roads up to Collins Baldy in 1970, McKinney Creek, which was 35 miles from home and Columbia Mine Road off Mill Creek which was 11 miles. Not knowing if I could use the short route, I took all three cats up by way of McKinney Creek.

Joe, who was eight years old, always rode in the back window or on the top of the front seat looking out. Sometime in June, Joe decided to go home. It took him 19 days! He must have gone the 35 mile route. My friend, who lived with me at Scott Bar, called to let me know he was there.

I went down to get him the next evening and brought him back up Mill Creek and the Columbia Mine Road on which I had moved rocks so I could use it with my 1953 Buick as well as my 1951 Jeep. The next time it took him three days.

Then, his brother Sam who was seven years old, tried it and took one day to make it. They never went together but for the next three summers they would go home at least three times a summer. Sam apparently told Joe to just go down the ridge to Scott Bar three miles, wait for darkness at the Quartz Hill Mine, then dash across the bridge, through Scott Bar and one mile home up Scott River Road. If they left before midnight they were home in the morning, or if too late they had to hold up at the mine during the day and be home shortly after dark.

All my cats were used to just me and were terrified of people and dogs. They would hide every time someone came to visit.

THE COUGAR—MYTH OF THE FOREST

Norman F. Mathews

Legends, myths, truths and half-truths combined have made the cougar or mountain lion one of the most interesting, mysterious and fascinating mammals of the Western World.

Many are the tales of children being carried off into the unknown by the wilderness demon. Of adults being shadowed along a lonely trail, or the screams heard during the night, not unlike a woman's cry in mortal fear.

Blood-thirsty man-killer? Maybe on rare occasions, but far less than the accounts credited to this shy, quiet, furtive animal. The questions are endless and intriguing, but the answers are few and largely inconclusive.

No mammal in North America has been labeled with as many common names as the cougar. In the Eastern United States, panther was, and still may be, the most common name used to describe the cougar. Jaguar, tiger, often spelled tigre, were terms often used. Calamount, "cat of the mountain," was also applied, along with gastos montes to the Spanish speaking people. Even today, it is difficult to convince many people that a mountain lion, cougar, panther, puma are one and the same animal.

Puma was long favored by many wildlife specialist as the most desirable common name. But in recent years, the names mountain lion and cougar are the most frequently used, with cougar growing in popularity.

The origin of the name cougar is not known, but may have been coined by early French explorers when first setting foot in the New World.

The cougar belongs to the order CARNIVORA (meat eating), and to the cat family FELIDAE. Large males may attain a length of eight feet—nose to end of tail—with weights of 150 to 180 pounds. Females are generally somewhat smaller in stature. Both size and weight can vary greatly in both sexes depending on environmental and genetic factors.

At one time, this great cat had a geographical range extending from coast to coast in the Western Hemisphere. Today, the east-west range is a narrow corridor that follows mountain ranges though Canada, Western United States, Mexico and into South America.

During the early pioneer days, predatory animals were a major drawback to the establishment of the livestock industry and a serious competition with early settlers for venison and other wild game. To assist in the control of the large number of such animals, most territorial governments established a bounty fee to be paid for each predator taken. This bounty system was to continue in most of the western states well into the 1960s.

Along about that time, some states began to realize that the cougar deserved to occupy a niche in the total environmental scheme. The idea was supported by many sportsmen groups, and eventually by the Federal land managing agencies. The cougar was given big game status protection, and most important of all, research was initiated to learn more about the numbers, habits, and distribution of this animal.

Since that time, studies have shown that the cougar seems to be holding his own in the rough mountainous regions of the West and Southwest, and many biologists believe that they are now increasing in numbers. This trend will probably continue as long as mankind spares these sanctuaries from encroachment and development.

Over the years, studies have been made of the food habits of the cougar with deer being high on the list of preferables. When the deer population decreases substantially in any given area, the big cats will either move to another region or select other available prey. Quite often this can be domestic livestock, both sheep and cattle, and occasionally a young horse. He is also not adverse to taking smaller prey such as ground squirrel and porcupines.

The cougar is seldom a scavenger, preferring to make its own kill. The exception to this may be a young or starving animal. Seldom will the cougar eat tainted or spoiled meat, and almost always covers the kill with leaves, twigs and other debris to hide the remains from other animals. As long as the kill remains fresh, the cougar may consume the entire carcass, especially if accompanied by young.

I well remember the first live cougars that I encountered in the wild. At the time, I was working as a summer employee for the U.S. Forest Service, and was returning to my duty station after attending to a small lightning fire. Rounding a bend in the road, I encountered a large female accompanied by a pair of half-grown kittens. At a very short distance we eyed each other for several seconds, before the female turned and quickly bounded into the forest. The kittens watched their mother disappear, but made no effort to follow.

In a few moments they were back to scampering about and seemed not a bit concerned about my presence. Rarely will the cougar attempt to defend her young from man, to the extent that the female bear will.

Contrary to popular belief, the cougar seeks its prey through silent stalking on the ground. Long, patient hours may be required before the cat is close enough to spring upon its prey. If the cougar fails in its initial attempt, its inadequate lung capacity does not permit a long chase.

The big question of course, is the cougar directly selective in predation? I personally do not believe so. The animal is an opportunist, knows its own limitations, and will usually take the easiest prey available. Sometimes this will be no more than a ground squirrel or a porcupine. The cougar is quite adept at turning a porcupine on its back to expose the soft underbelly, thus avoiding the dangerous quills.

Over the past forty years, I have had the opportunity to examine many cougar kills. Most of the large kills have been deer, with an occasional one being domestic livestock. In the deer category, the majority were does, fawns or young bucks. Yet on several instances, there have been large, mature bucks preyed upon. Whether these big bucks were previously injured, I could not determine, but almost all appeared to have put up a terrific struggle against the cougar.

One cold January day in 1959, I came upon just such an encounter, while working as a ranger on the Gila National

Forest in Southwestern New Mexico. Myself and two companions were on our way to a timber harvesting area early in the morning. About six inches of new snow had fallen during the night, and the landscape was truly a winter wonderland.

The road that we were traveling followed along the bottom of a large, timbered canyon; along which flowed a small stream, now mostly frozen over. Some few minutes before our arrival, a large four-point buck (western count) had descended the canyon side and crossed the stream. Possibly he had stopped to drink at an unfrozen spot. The cougar, a fine large male, had been making his way along the edge of the roadway, when he detected the presence of the buck. Crouching, he remained motionless, and waited for the buck to come within striking distance.

One running jump put the lion square on the buck's back, and the battle was on. The fight had been a terrific one as evidenced by the amount of debris thrown about, and the hair and blood upon the new snow. But the cougar was the eventual winner, although suffering some lost hide and bruises in the encounter.

When we drove upon the scene, the cougar had dragged the buck upon the roadbed and was attempting to carry its prey up a steep embankment. Seeing the vehicle approach, the lion crouched by the kill, reluctant to leave his hard earned prize. But as we came closer, he soon lost his nerve and bounded away. Later examination showed that the cougar returned to feed on the buck after we had departed from the area. This proved to be the lion's undoing, as my companions were able to track him up and thus obtained a prime cougar trophy.

As far as the sportsman is concerned, cougar hunting is in a class by itself. Being a nocturnal animal, the cougar prowls about during the night, and then finds a secluded spot to lay up during the daylight hours. Thus the casual hunter rarely sees a cougar, unless the animal is accidentally flushed from its resting place.

The majority of the lions that I have seen in my lifetime were no more than fleeting glimpses as the animal bounded across in the glare of my vehicle headlights.

Most successful cougar hunting is done with the use of hounds and horses, at least in my area of the country. In any region where dogs can travel swiftly and which is damp enough to hold the scent, the hound has an excellent chance to tree or corner the quarry. But in most of the high, rugged mountain country of the Western United States, the lion can often escape pursuit by taking to country so rough that no man or dog can follow. Often the air is dry and the ground so dusty that scent will last for only a short period of time. Then the chase is likely to fizzle out on some hot, dry, wind-swept ridge.

For the hunter, who by one means or another, is successful in the taking of a cougar, there is no finer big game trophy. Although I have hunted the animal on many occasions, the failures have far outnumbered the successes. Yet, I never tire of the chase and have great admiration for this mystic beast. May the cougar forever travel the wilderness path and provide a unique challenge to the dedicated sportsman.

A STAND BY ME STORY

Bob Ziegler

Two forest officers on the Prescott National Forest in Region 3 were gathering information on mining claims when they came across an abandoned shack, the door standing ajar. Hoyt slipped inside with Wayne following close behind. Once inside, they discovered a bobcat had taken up residence. The cat growled and started to stalk menacingly toward them. Quick thinking Wayne hastily backed out the open door and slammed it shut—on Hoyt and the bobcat.

A COUGAR AT LAIRDS VALLEY

Tom Harris

In early June 1931, we packed into our first camp at Lairds Valley, about 23 miles by trail west of Orleans in the Bluff Creek basin. Lairds Valley at that time was a beautiful little meadow on a shelf not far from the western ridge. It offered few amenities. Several of the boys took advantage of a small shake cabin at the edge of the timber and moved into it. An 8 x 10 tent served as cook shack. Supplies did not reach us by pack train often enough to satisfy the prodigious appetites of the crew. At one point we were forced to supplement our food supply with a little local fresh meat. To keep it cool at night we hung a haunch from the cook tent ridge pole that extended out from the front of the tent. Directly in front, Jimmy Sowder and I had our bedrolls on the ground under the stars.

The first night after obtaining the meat, Jimmy and I had crawled into our sleeping bags just as it was getting dark. After some few minutes, I happened to glance out and there, not eight feet way, was a large dark form with a long tail swishing slowly from side to side, sniffing the air expectantly—it could be only one thing—a cougar! The alarm was given. The boys spilled out of the cabin and we all watched the cougar in the gathering dark amble across the meadow and slowly disappear into the timber. It was in no hurry. After it vanished, we took stock of ourselves.

At the alarm, no one had stopped to put on clothes. Standing in a little group peering after the cougar, we must have presented a weird sight. Bob Mansfield, stark naked but for a pair of sox and gripping a .38 revolver in one hand, was shaking like a leaf with excitement. And the rest of us were in various stages of undress and suppressed emotion. Not a shot was fired; our cougar's visit was short but safe

The episode furnished talk at campfires for the rest of the season.

EARLY DAYS

Fred Wehmeyer

The early days were a historical period in forestry development. Those who took an active part can well remember the early pioneering—the seemingly endless lodgepole thickets; the bottomless swamps of the river and creek bottoms; the miles of debris left through snow slides; the yellow jackets; the devil clubs; the Swede killers; the month-long pack horse trips with the many privations, miseries and frustrations. After being almost sucked dry of blood by clouds of mosquitoes, no-see-ums, gnats, deer flies and horse flies all day and night, grown men have been seen to set down and bawl, then grit their teeth, get up and resume whatever they were doing with added vigor. Members of the Service seemed to have a fierce determination of accomplishment, and Uncle Jimmy Wilson's instruction "to carry on, keeping in mind the greatest good to the greatest number in the long run" took its place in the scheme of things as the Eleventh Commandment.

Life also had its lighter moments. To those looking for a bit of humor, there was always sufficient time for an occasional chuckle. One of the early guards woke up and thought he heard some kind of machinery running. He had been clearing trail on the head of Ransay Creek on the Upper Methow. Worn out from a heavy day, he lay there and listened and conjectured on what he heard. Then he got a whiff of an odor that was especially fetid and opened his eyes to see a large puma standing straddle his body with its head a matter of inches from his own. The animal, evidently pleased to have found company, was purring but had evidently failed to use a mouth wash for its breath was even beyond the halitosis stage. Archie, for that was the guard's name, reached up under his pillow and grabbed his revolver and in his excitement pulled the trigger, blowing most all the feathers out of his pillow. The puma threw large quantities of pine needles, cones and twigs over the bed as it left the area in a series of great leaps.

HORSES, MULES AND DONKEYS

THE GRANDEST MIXUP OF ALL

Charlie Shaw
(edited by Les Joslin)

The late Charlie Shaw of the Flathead National Forest, who was district ranger at Spotted Bear Ranger Station from 1945 to 1958, left vivid impressions of life there in *The Flathead Story* published by that national forest. Some of these stories, of course, involved animals.

Spotted Bear Ranger Station was a center of Flathead National Forest horse and mule packing before roads began to replace mountain trails. Packing wasn't always smooth going, and once in the late 1920s—when Ranger Shaw was Spotted Bear fire dispatcher—produced what he called "the grandest mixup of all." As he wrote it:

"Eleven full strings (10 head each) were packing out of there for the Spotted Bear, Black Bear, and Big Prairie districts. One morning, nine of these strings were going to leave the station for various destinations. The strings were packed and ready to leave at about the same time. Packstrings were tied up all over the place when Jack Langtree, the station cook, asked the packers to come in for a cup of coffee before they pulled out.

"While they were in the kitchen tent drinking their coffee, something spooked one string. They broke loose and started bucking, bawling, and running through the other eight strings. This caused every string to break apart and stampede. There were mules and horses bucking and running all over Spotted Bear Ranger Station. Ninety head of horses and mules were involved in this mixup. Some of them became tangled up. Some were down. But most of them stampeded into the woods, trailing packs and equipment as they ran.

"This happened about 9 a.m. But nobody got his outfit together that day. Mules and packs were found the next day as far away as Harrison Creek, eight miles south of the station. Some were found on Horse Ridge and in Twin Flats in the other direction. They next day, some were found still carrying their packs. Others lost their packs, saddles, and halters."

The packers had a big job putting that mixup right, but "the mess was eventually straightened out, and the packers were on their way. The packers, in a class by themselves, accepted the mishap as part of the work of moving Forest Service supplies over mountain trails."

NINEMILE REMOUNT DEPOT

Les Joslin

For almost a quarter century, from 1930 to 1953, Ninemile Remount Depot—set up about five years before Ninemile Ranger Station was built at the same Lolo National Forest site about 25 miles west of Missoula, Montana—provided packers and pack stock for fire control and project work throughout the roadless reaches of the northern Rockies. Even today, at historic Ninemile Remount Depot and Ranger Station, the tradition of Forest Service packing lives on.

"When Congress set aside forest reserves in 1891," as the 1991 Forest Service publication *Miles By Mule*—quoted throughout—tells it so well, "people took horses and mules for granted much the way we take automobiles for granted today. The first forest rangers packed all of their belongings onto a horse or mule and saddled up to travel to their assignments. They gave little thought about the impossibility of managing the land without their animal partners."

But, while rangers and fire crews in the rugged and roadless national forests of the West depended almost entirely on pack strings of horses and mules, times were changing elsewhere. "Trucks and tractors started to replace pack and draft animals on farms. And as automobiles and good roads increased, many people sold their saddle horses in favor of more modern transportation. Local supplies of pack and saddle stock started to disappear.

"Then in 1929, during an unusually bad fire season, the Forest Service awakened to a new challenge. With the mechanization of rural America, there were no longer enough pack horses and mules available for hire to supply fire crews fighting forest fires in remote areas.

"Driven by the need to supply their own demand, the Forest Service established Ninemile Remount Depot to raise and train quality pack and saddle stock." From 1930 to 1953, a once run-down ranch on Ninemile Creek within the Lolo National Forest evolved into a unique Forest Service "ranch." Modeled after U.S. Army cavalry remount depots that supplied horses for troopers, this facility bred saddle horses for forest rangers and "maintained 20 pack trains of nine mules each, experienced packers and transportation, ready to mobilize in minutes for firefighting" and to support back country work projects. "When not fighting fire, the mules packed supplies to trail crews and freighted construction materials to remote mountain tops to build fire lookouts. The depot's pack trains packed just about everything imaginable that is essential for managing a national forest.

"Professional packers at the remount depot developed packing equipment and perfected the art of packing to its highest level. They standardized methods and equipment so that any trained packer could pack all of the tools and supplies needed for a twenty-five person crew with just nine mules. Their methods were the most humane for keeping pack animals healthy."

In the early 1940s, when aerial firefighting was pioneered at Camp Menard, an early smokejumper base about a mile north of the remount depot, the mules got into the act. Smokejumpers trained at Ninemile's so-called airport pasture. Often, droning Ford Trimotor airplanes had to buzz the field to clear it of grazing mules before the jumpers could hit the silk. And there was another tie-in. About one mule per smokejumper was needed to pack out the jumpers' gear, stashed along mountain trails after fires for pickup. Smokejumpers based at the aerial fire depot in Missoula continue to practice at the airport pasture, where the Ninemile Ranger District that now operates the historic remount depot still grazes livestock and cuts hay.

In 1953, the regional forester decided to close Ninemile Remount Depot because of the increasing effectiveness of aerial firefighting—smokejumpers and helicopters—and improved road access. Remount depot facilities were incorporated into the Ninemile Ranger District operation the next year.

"Then in 1964, just as it started to look as though pack mules might become obsolete, Congress passed the Wilderness Act. This law directs the Forest Service to manage some special areas to preserve their wild character; no roads, no mechanized equipment are appropriate in wilderness." In these areas, horses and pack mules continue to play their historic roles.

Today, the Ninemile Remount Depot, a Ninemile Ranger District unit, is home to the Northern Region Pack Train of nine pack mules and two expert Forest Service packers. In addition to providing packing services on national forests throughout the region, the pack train is used to help educate Forest Service personnel and the public on low-impact livestock use in wilderness and to represent the Forest Service at parades, fairs, rodeos, and other special events. At the Ninemile Remount Depot Visitor Center, which opened in 1989, visitors see how America's biggest pack station operated in the 1930s and 1940s.

The Ninemile Remount Depot

The Ninemile Remount was, at one time, the center for U.S. Forest Service packing activities in the Northern Rockies. Completed by the Civilian Conservation Corps (CCC) in 1935, the Remount was the home roost for more than 1500 Rocky Mountain Canaries (also known as mules), as well as prime breeding stock for the Forest Service. Firefighting, trail and fire lookout building, and many other kinds of backcountry work was done with Ninemile packstock wearing US brands on their hips and diamond hitches cinching down their cargo. The pack strings were spurred on by packers who had reputations for never sparing the adjectives when the going got tough.

The Remount's upper hayfield was used to train smokejumpers in the early years of the famous firefighting crews. More often than not,
dressing Ford Tri-Motor airplanes had to buzz the field to clear it of grazing livestock before the jumpers could hit the silk.

In 1980, Ninemile was listed on the National Register of Historic Places for its traditional architecture and its role in Forest Service, Civilian Conservation Corps and local history. Ninemile is still a working ranger station and pack depot, the home for a number of USFS activities, combining history and practicality. Mules and horses are still run through the chutes and corrals on their way to perform important work in the backcountry. And if you listen very carefully, you can still hear the canaries sing!

Ninemile Ranger District
Lolo National Forest

A 1955 ENVIRONMENTAL PROBLEM

George W. Kansky

There are a number of ways one can dispose of a dead horse in a remote public area. Bury it, let the coyotes eat it or maybe just walk away in revulsion and helplessness. This story is about an effective way to do it.

It happened in the Rogue River in southern Oregon at a place called Natural Bridge within the Rogue River National Forest. The place is an interesting geologic attraction; a place where the whole volume of the upper Rogue River swirls in a powerful vortex and drops down underground instantly as into a funnel and disappears. One can walk across to the other side, dry shod. Several hundred feet downstream it spews out of its cave an outraged, angry torrent, confined in a vertical lava rock gorge. Visitors on the rim look down in amazement.

On a Sunday afternoon, two Rogue River Valley boys, each riding a horse, attempted to cross the river above Natural Bridge. It was a mistake. The river is deceptively deep and powerful. The horses lost footing on the slippery lava and floundered frantically. One boy got his horse out. The other drifting rapidly, slipped off and made it to shore but his young mare was swept into the whirlpool and was sucked under.

The boys reported the accident at the Union Creek Ranger Station to the district fire control assistant (DA) on duty. That evening he and the district ranger went down to look into the gorge.

Unbelievable as it may seem, that drowned mare had been disgorged from the underground maelstrom and had lodged across a ten foot boulder. She was balanced there in the middle of the river with roaring, foaming rapids on both sides and at least 50 feet below the rim of the gorge. It was a sorry sight and, for the moment, left the two foresters sorely perplexed. This was no place for a casual let "nature take its course" dismissal.

Princes and kings had fished this river. People drank the water. Water pollution was unthinkable. The two went home to wait for daylight.

Meanwhile, the event got down valley, probably faster than any modern e-mail could move it, and fell on the ears of one of the Rogue River Forest's friendly "key people," a well-known man who was listed in forest plans, may be on the forest supervisor's advisory board, and was taken on show-me trips. This key person was a kindly businessman who often talked with rangers and there were good vibes. It was a little difficult to talk with him since he was nearly stone deaf. Next morning, early, he came storming into the ranger station saying that he had seen the horse and was outraged at the threat to downriver values and the Forest Service must, at once, do everything in its power to "—get that carcass out of the river—" and he would tell the county sheriff to enforce this on the Forest Service! The ranger spoke of the great difficulty it presented but the key person was adamant and so we assured him that it would be taken care of. Within an hour the sheriff phoned to say, "Let me know when you have removed the horse."

Right away the ranger and assistant went back to the gorge to sit on a rock for awhile looking at the options. It was inconceivable to lower anyone in a sling, rope him over that torrent or throw a lasso so far. Almost wistfully, the ranger said, "If we could just nudge her loose from the rock with a little dynamite." The assistant picked that up immediately saying, "I know just the guy who can do it." But WHOA now! On cooler reflection, how sensible is this? Then and there, they completed an environmental assessment for the whole 90 miles of the Rogue River Valley in about ten minutes and decided to go for it.

The assistant quickly contacted the forest road foreman who was a certified blaster and who really knew his stuff. He was delighted at the challenge and came up at once, fully equipped. It wasn't even noon. Together they lofted a tag line across the gorge to draw a one quarter inch rope across. In the middle of the rope they had moulded a soft plastic explosive about two inches thick and four feet long. This was the old WWII Army surplus C-3 demolition plastic. It could be shaped into any form.

It was plentiful then and devastatingly powerful stuff. No one present knew how much to use but they used a calculated wad. An electric cap was inserted and wired to the rope. Then the whole harness was carefully lowered from the sides of the river to drape the charge evenly over the horse. It took a lot of wire to get far out of the way.

The ranger had a crew moving about to clear the river and area of any people for a half mile around. Finally, all was set. With a last "FIRE IN THE HOLE" called in warning, the road foreman cranked the detonator. The initial effect was a deep down-in-the-earth BOOM and a seismic thump that shook the rock under the men. Then came a thunderous explosion that sent water and debris towering, followed by reverberations and aftershocks for seemingly miles around. An atomic bomb no less! The district assistant thought, good Lord, what have I done? What if it shook something down or changed the river or damned it? Oh no!—there's a diversion dam and a flume into a power plant ten miles downstream!

People looked at each other. Things settled down. They tentatively approached the rim and looked over. The gorge appeared unchanged, intact. The river ran white and pure— merciful GOD! The horse had disappeared—just gone. The rock under her was gone. The rapids ran evenly there. So where were the pieces? None appeared plastered to the walls or rocks. She just vanished. Subsequent search of the river and banks downstream revealed no legs or bones, no guts, no ears— nothing. Vaporized? Fish food maybe. The awed and astounded crew quietly rolled up the equipment and dispersed. No one cheered. Their feelings were short of outright jubilation, although for his part, the road foreman was certainly proud. Like a job successfully done with a leftover nagging concern about where that horse might show up again.

Well, she never did. A week went by with little comment. Then on Sunday, who should appear but their Mr. Key person, striding up the lane to the district ranger's house. After greetings, he sidled up comfortably close. He said he had seen to his unbounded pleasure that the horse had been removed. Pleased at this, the ranger said that it had been dangerous, but successful. There would be no problem. He then scrambled for some way to change the subject, offering, "Have you tried fishing the good pool at Farewell Bend?" But Mr. Key person had heard part of the story and pondered for a long minute. Then, in a rush of curiosity, he asked, "Well say, just how in hell *did* you get rid of it?" Whereupon the ranger, in a rush of self-defense, muttered things like the horse was gone, the threat removed, he wouldn't report on it anymore and it would be prudent to close the subject. If you talked sort of fast downwind from Mr. Key person, he would miss a lot of it. After a sociable visit, Mr. Key person left in good spirits but seemed vaguely dissatisfied.

There was no follow-up and no media interest. The boys who lost the horse were too embarrassed to be inquisitive, and there was no evidence. As you might expect, Forest Supervisor Jack heard the story at staff coffee breaks or somewhere. Next tine he came to Union Creek, he mentioned it kind of offhand and the district ranger couldn't do much better than to just look sheepish. But Jack didn't say a single unhappy word. Good ol' Jack!

YOU HAD BETTER CHECK THE HORSES

Dwain Nebeker

The trail crew foreman did the cooking. It was my job to take care of the horses. As he prepared the evening meal, the foreman suggested that I might check on the horses. I didn't think it was necessary as I thought I could hear the "bell mare." I would do it after supper.

The Boise National Forest had an agreement with the forestry school at Logan, Utah to provide summer employment for interested forestry students. A few of us reported for work at the Boise National Forest headquarters. We were asked if anyone was familiar with working with horses. I was raised on a farm where real horse power was still used so I volunteered to go to the Bear Valley District to work on a trail crew. At that time (early 1950s) the district personnel consisted of the district ranger, assistant ranger, trail crew fireman and trail crew. I was the crew and we would work trails 10 days at a time. We had two riding horses and two pack animals.

We had camped in a large meadow the day before where forage and mosquitoes were plentiful. Now we were camped in a timbered area where there wasn't much for the horses to eat. Our food supply, except for some moldy bread was gone. During the day we had come on some "fool" hens in some low bushes. After some rock throwing we were able to get enough hens to eat. The smell of something good cooking was enough to keep me near the campfire until after supper. Now it was time to check on the horses.

The horses were long gone. There was still enough light so that I was able to check their tracks which were headed back down the trail. I thought I might be able to catch up with them by maintaining a slow run. In the process I almost ran over a bear. He got off the trail just in time. He ran one way, I ran the other. After awhile I had to slow to a walk. It was now dark and I realized that I would have to pace myself and just keep going.

I finally came on the meadow where we had been the night before. The three horses and one mule had found what they wanted—something to eat. Unfortunately for them, I had to interrupt their meal. I caught one horse to ride and then spent a good part of the night trying to drive the others back to camp. The mule would keep trying to go back to the meadow. The light from the moon would sometimes make it difficult to tell which way the trail went. At 3:30 in the morning we finally arrived back in camp. The foreman allowed me to sleep a few extra hours the next morning before we again continued our work. The horses didn't get away from me again. I will always remember the long night on the trail spent chasing horses.

BEATING A DEAD HORSE

Robert W. Cermak

In the early 1960s, when I was district ranger at Challenge District on the Plumas, we were expected to winter forest horses. Forest Supervisor Bill Peterson had his own mount that he rode the range along with permittees, and the eastside rangers from the Milford, Beckwourth and Greenville districts also had horses. A few of the folks on the eastside, like Chet Cannon, were cowboys. I think the rest just chased the romantic image of the old ranger on horseback. At any rate, the eastside districts had the fun of riding horseback in the summer. The two westside districts had no horses and as junior ranger I had the chore of caring for them in the milder winter on the westside.

We found good pasture at the Beever Ranch several miles west of the ranger station and then hoped that the horses would stay inside the fences and not pester us all winter. That was not to be. Every week or so the phone would ring and district clerk, Maxine Arrendale, would come to my office and report, "The horses are out." I always tried to send an assistant, or almost anybody but me to round up the horses and fix the fence. The trouble was that as soon as Maxine heard the news everybody disappeared. It was magic. How did they know? I began to hate those horses. Poor beasts, it wasn't their fault that their landlord was afraid of big animals like elephants, walruses and horses and hated fixing barbed wire in the pouring rain.

One night I was awakened out of a sound sleep by the telephone ringing. I looked at the clock, 1 a. m., and mentally prepared myself for another house fire. But it was Pike County Peak Lookout telling me in her lilting tones that one of our horses had got out and been hit by a car. The California Highway Patrol was on the scene and wanted the ranger. I got up, dressed in my uniform and grumbled at my wife something about "those damn horses." It was raining as I drove my Chevy pickup to the scene and stopped behind the CHP cruiser. The officer and the driver who had hit the horse were standing by its head. The horse was Coalie, a big, black gelding.

I introduced myself to the officer and the driver and saw that Coalie had a broken front leg. All of my irritation at the horses vanished when I saw that poor old horse, his head hanging low. I knew what had to be done. The CHP officer unholstered his .357 Magnum and handed it to me. "He'll have to be destroyed," he said. I said, "I know." I looked at Coalie, looked at the heavy pistol and then looked at the officer. I had probably said, "I wish those damn horses were dead," a dozen times in the previous few years. The CHP officer saw that I could not shoot Coalie. He said kindly, "Do you want me to do it?" Wordless, I handed the pistol back to him. He pointed the barrel at the center of Coalie's head and pulled the trigger. Coalie collapsed in a heap just like one of those buildings taken down with explosives that you see on TV.

The driver's car was not damaged. He gave me his address and phone number and left. The CHP officer took some notes and also left. I stood there in the rain looking at the poor old dead horse. I now had found out that there was something worse than a horse outside a fence. It was a dead horse. I found the spot in the fence where Coalie had escaped, made a temporary fix and was pretty well soaked when I finished. I didn't sleep much the rest of the night.

The next morning I realized that I had two choices, bury the dead horse with a hired dozer if I could get permission from the owner of the Beever Ranch, or see if a rendering outfit would come after him. As luck would have it, there was a rendering company in Marysville. I called and spoke to the manager who told me that he would be glad to pick up the dead horse, but he couldn't pay me anything because it was 40 miles from town. "Come and get him," I said. It was bad enough to tell the SO that one of the horses was dead because Bill Pete had a soft spot for each one of them. But if I had to hire a dozer to bury him I was going to catch hell for sure. Now I had a way out at no cost. I congratulated myself for getting out of a potentially bad smelling situation.

I decided to call Administrative Officer Ernie Smith and ask him to tell the boss. If you knew Ernie, you knew that he was a stickler for following the rules. I wasn't worried, I had this situation covered. Ernie came on the phone and I explained that the horse had been hit by a car and had to be destroyed. I explained how I had solved the problem by calling the rendering company.

"You can't do that," Ernie said in a peremptory tone of voice.

"What? I can't do what?" I asked, shocked that my brilliant solution was rejected.

"You can't give that horse to the rendering company."

"I already have."

"Call them and tell them that you made a mistake"

"Why? Why can't I give away a dead horse? It's dead, for crying out loud."

"Because it's property. It's on the property record and a form has to be completed and approved in this office before you can dispose of any property."

I nearly jumped through the phone. "Before that's done he'll be all swelled up, he'll stink like $700, and we'll have to bury him. It will cost a mint! Where do I get the money?"

This went on for some minutes. Finally, we compromised. I was to fill out a Form AD-112 Report of Lost, Stolen or Destroyed Property and send it with someone to Quincy where he would approve it on the assumption that the renderer would arrive afterwards. Old Coalie, even in death proved that he could give the ranger fits. I'm sure now that Ernie also enjoyed giving the ranger fits, not to mention a lesson in following the rules. I'll bet he was grinning during the entire conversation.

MOUNT BARNEY

Victor H. Flach

During my early days of service I became acquainted with Lage Wernstedt and had the privilege of working with him in succeeding years. Lage, pronounced "Loggy," was not only a pioneer forester, having graduated from Yale in 1905, but he also became a pioneer in photogrammetry and developed new trends in the use of photography for mapping.

In 1917, using panoramic terrestrial photographs, taken from mountain tops on the Columbia (now Gifford Pinchot) National Forest, he mapped, almost single handed, an area of about 700 square miles, and this work was accepted by the U.S. Geological Survey.

Lage did a lot of drainage mapping in the early 1920s, notably on the Willamette, Umpqua, Mt. Baker and Chelan forests. He took terrestrial panoramic photographs from appropriate mountain points, which were supplemented by transit triangulation to orient the pictures for subsequent office mapping operations. There were few high mountain roads in those days, and a typical party consisted of three men mounted with six pack horses.

Roland C. (Bud) Burgess and I accompanied Wernstedt in the summer of 1923 to the Willamette (old Santiam and Cascade) and Umpqua forests. It was a highlight in my career and I'm sure Bud found it so, too.

Lage depended almost entirely on natural grazing for the horses. That summer we occupied about 38 mountain peaks and lookouts. All day we would ride and ride, Lage saying nothing until late afternoon when he would spot, simultaneously, our next point of occupation and a nearby pasture site. Even in unfamiliar country he could keep this double purpose in mind. As a result, we almost always got located in country suitable to the uses of both men and horses.

Lage had one quirk however—he didn't believe in hobbling his horses. That meant our horses would sometimes stray away in search of better forage. This meant Bud and I had to chase through the hills in pursuit of them. Sometimes this would use up a full day or more.

Near Oakridge one day Lage startled me by saying, "Vic, I need another horse, here's fifty dollars to buy one." Why me? Bud was the horse expert. Sure, I could ride and even learned to throw a diamond hitch but other than that, I was a city boy.

Lage insisted, however, and told me to go up the road toward Lowell and talk to the farmers about a horse. He added, "Be sure you get one that's gentle and is both a good saddle and pack horse."

That turned out to be a difficult assignment. There were horses for sale, all right, but at prices of $85 and $100 with nothing said about their abilities as saddle or pack horses. About noon, having walked eight or nine miles, I came across a man plowing his field with a heavy maned, swaybacked horse weighing perhaps 1,200 pounds. We struck up a conversation. The horse was gentle enough but had never been ridden with a saddle, only bareback around the place by the farmer's children. And, he had never been used for packing. Even worse, the farmer felt he couldn't part with him for less than $75.

I was about to give up when I was invited in for lunch. Maybe it was the mellowing effect of the food. Or, being an amateur magician, it was the magic tricks I showed to his children. But after lunch, the farmer said he'd sell me "Old Barney" for the fifty.

I'd never ridden bareback and Barney proved too much for me. He was so swaybacked and so wide in the back that my legs straddled him at about a 100 degree angle. I couldn't take it so I got off and led him back to the ranger station.

Lage was standing on the porch. It was late evening. For a few seconds he said nothing, just looked at the swaybacked plow horse. Then he exploded, "What in the hell you got there?"

"Lage, you gave me fifty bucks to get a real gentle horse, one that could be saddled or packed and this is the best I could do. I'll guarantee he's gentle or I never could have gotten back. And, with a high enough saddle, he ought to ride all right at the speed we'll be going."

Old Barney turned out to be one of Lage's best all-around horses, one of the few he held over to the next season. The following year, working on the Okanogan (Chelan) Forest, Barney got tangled up in some fallen telephone lines and fell over a cliff. In his memory, Lage named that point, "Mount Barney."

MULES AND HORSES ON
THE KLAMATH FOREST

Bob Buttery

I transferred to the Klamath from research in 1960 and worked out of the supervisor's office as range conservationist. Charlie Yates was forest supervisor and my boss was Al Crebbin, the range and wildlife staff officer. The majority of my work was range analysis of grazing allotments in the Marble Mountain Wilderness, so, although I had a pickup and horse trailer, most of my travel was by horseback, led by my pack mule, Judy. In retrospect, it seems as though my two and one-half years on the Klamath consisted of one long pack trip with short breaks for winter, fires, returning to town for supplies and to reintroduce myself to my family. I was gone so much that whenever a phone call came for me at home while I was gone, my wife would tell the caller that I was out in the bushes with Judy.

Packing on the Klamath was, and may still be, a little different than other forests. The pack saddle we used was a regular sawbuck, but was different in that it was fitted with an aparejo, which is a solid, A-shaped device which keeps the alforjases and pack boxes from rubbing the mule. This arrangement seemed to be peculiar to the Klamath because I have packed all up and down the Rockies and Sierra Nevadas and have never seen it used elsewhere. Even the diamond hitch was different on the Klamath and was called the Salmon River diamond. Al showed me how to pack the Klamath way, then turned me loose and left me alone after he was satisfied that I knew what I was doing. As I remember, this occurred on our second pack trip when he saddled up one morning and rode away alone, after telling me to break camp, pack the mules and meet him in the evening at a place I had never been, about 15 trail miles away. This I did and the packing instructions ended.

I must have ridden a thousand miles with Al and was always amazed at his toughness and knowledge of wilderness camping and travel. He rode a big sorrel, proud-cut gelding named Red

Rocks, who was always number one in the pecking order of any string of saddle horses and pack mules (both Forest Service and permittee animals). He was high-spirited and always kept Al busy. Late one June evening in 1960, while returning to Marble Valley from Big Elk Lake, we rode down a very steep slope to go around a big red fir which had fallen across the trail. As the horses struggled back up to the trail, Red Rocks lunged and fell. Al kicked loose but hung up on a fishing rod tied behind the saddle. He hit the ground hard and rolled down the slope under my horse and started her bucking. I stayed aboard but Al's fall cost him a cracked rib. All we could do for him back in camp was to give him aspirin. He rode in rough country for two more days without complaint before we got back to town and saw a doctor.

For a big timber northern California forest, the Klamath had a lot of horses and mules, and there were bound to be accidents. In July, 1960, as we were leaving Carter Meadows on a pack trip, we heard on the radio that Charlie Davis got bucked off at Shackleford corral and broke his leg. Later on that summer, Paul Leimbach lost part of a finger while tying up a horse in a trailer at the Callahan Ranger Station. Paul was a tough kid and they had to make him take the rest of the day off after he got back from the doctor. I benefited from his accident, in that it caused me to design a safe manger knot, for which I got two $25 awards when it was adopted for Forest Service-wide use. Still later, Ernie White broke a hip up in the Marble Mountains when his horse went over backwards with him. He was flown out by helicopter.

A forest GFI was held in October. Al Crebbin, Charlie Yates, Lou Haan and I took Ev Doman and Bill Dasmann of the RO on a pack trip into the Marble Mountains in order to inspect some of our grazing allotment management and my analysis work. The day we left on the trip was one of those days you would rather forget, but never do. I was up at 5 a.m., and off to Fort Jones where Lou and I loaded our horses and mules and drove to the Kelsey Creek Guard Station. The rest of the party got up much later and drove up to Lovers Camp, while we brought the horses (Sundown and Tobe) and four mules (Maude, Jake, Hope and Judy) up the Canyon Creek Trail. Maude got away and I had to chase her clear back to the Kelsey Creek Guard Station. When I caught up with the string again, Tobe got away, and I had to chase him back to Pratt's Pack Station. While I was gone, Hope hid out in the brush and we rode away without her. When we discovered that she was missing, I rode back and found her but had to chase her all the way back to the Kelsey Creek Guard Station as well. While fording the Scott River, she balked and jerked the lead rope out of my hand and in the process jerked my cantina off the saddle horn. Unfortunately, the cantina contained my camera, binoculars, dark glasses, compass, maps and allotment records. In addition, the water was eighteen inches deep and I was wearing fourteen inch boots. To top things off, my horse decided to stand on the cantina which pretty well wrecked everything that the water did not. The rest of the inspection party was fresh and ready to go when we got to Lovers Camp. I do not think El Doman was too impressed with the soggy map that I handed to him or the allotment records, which were all stuck together.

In those days, Forest Service people were still allowed to carry a rifle during deer season and take advantage of opportunities to get their winter meat. Charlie Yates was carrying a .30-.30 in his saddle boot and telling us how good the deer liver was going to taste for supper. In the pass between Little Elk Creek and Deep Lake, he took three shots from his horse at a deer. None of the horses were too happy about the shooting, especially Charlie's. Charlie missed with all three shots. As we rode away, Al said that hereafter, the pass would be known as "No Liver Pass."

JUMPING CACTUS

Duane G. Breon

In 1958, I was the assistant ranger on the Mesa District of the Tonto National Forest in Arizona. One of my major jobs was surface rights determination. A new federal law prohibited the patenting of mining claims through mining of common varieties of minerals. This included sand, gravel, rock, etc. Our job was to locate mining claims, determine ownership and location then contact the miner and let the person know they could no longer gain title of their claims by mining common variety minerals.

On Monday mornings, Bill Stewart, the general district assistant, would pull the Jeep drawn horse trailer as far into the Four Peak country as we could go. We would then unload the horse and my gear, set up the pup tent and have a cup of campfire coffee. Bill would then take off down the mountain with Jeep and trailer. He would be back to pick me up Friday afternoon. Ranger Randolph R. Riley (nicknamed "Railroad Riley") expected me to spend at least 40 hours a week in the field.

No other human being would be seen all week. I would see an occasional prospector's smoldering fire but no prospector. They would stay in hiding partly because they were usually recluses and partly because they thought I might be a claim jumper.

I would grid the country on horseback, locate the four corner monuments of rock and search for the claim notice, usually in a Prince Albert tobacco can in one of the corners. The miner's name and address would be copied from the claim notice and the claim monument location would be pinpricked on an aerial photo. Later, the court records would be checked to see if the prospector had filed his claim. If he had, a letter would be sent him or her, notifying them the mine could not be patented with common varieties of minerals.

One night I was asleep in the pup tent and I heard a heck of a commotion. My first thought was a bear or mountain lion was attacking my horse. I grabbed my revolver and flashlight and, in shorts, headed into the dark to save my horse. He had been tied to a paloverde tree about twenty yards from the tent.

The horse, still tied, was laying on his back and threshing in a cholla cactus patch. Cholla cactus are called jumping cactus because cowboys swear the cactus balls will jump at you in passing. The truth is, you have to rub up against a cholla and the balls will come loose and stick to your clothes or the horse.

I untied the horse and got him standing up. I led him to an open area and proceeded to remove the cactus balls from his back and sides. A stick with two nails sticking out the end in a "V" was the homemade tool. The nails would be worked under the balls and then they would be flipped off. Some thorns remained in his hide. No saddle blanket or saddle on him for a few days.

After working the rest of the night to remove the cactus balls I started walking down the mountain leading the horse. A line cabin and corral was only five miles away. It was Thursday so I only had to wait one day to have my horse, gear and me picked up.

It took approximately ten days for the remaining cactus thorns to work out of the horse's hide. An exciting experience for both of us.

LOST IN A BLIZZARD

Grover C. Blake

On the afternoon of April 19, 1928, I was near Cloverland on the Umatilla Forest in eastern Washington, and had just purchased a new saddle horse. I started to go through the mountains to Iron Springs Ranger Station, riding the newly purchased horse and leading my other saddle animal. Before reaching the edge of the timber on the Iron Springs side I found myself in a blinding snowstorm and darkness was coming on. Soon the snowstorm, darkness and the high wind, which had sprung up, created conditions like a Colorado blizzard. I was soon hopelessly lost. After a time I knew I was in the settlements but could see nothing and could find no shelter. I passed by Iron Springs Ranger Station gate without knowing it and kept going. After awhile I realized that I was becoming exhausted and that the horses were tiring. I was soaking wet and badly chilled. I felt that I should keep moving to keep up circulation. The snowdrifts were quite deep by this time and it was quite a struggle for the horses at times to get through them. Just as I concluded that neither the horses nor I could keep going until daylight and I would have to figure out some solution quickly, I discovered we (the horses and I) were within a few feet of a building. It was painted red. If it had been white I could not have seen it. I found a door and entered a large barn with stock inside and plenty of hay. Oh, how pleasant was the feeling to be inside out of that wind and blinding snow. I had some dry matches and got the horses located and fed. It was near midnight. I went outside to look for a house but, in the storm, I had no luck. I returned to the barn and found some empty grain sacks and wrapped them around me and my wet clothing and eventually became warm. When daylight came, the wind had ceased and I soon got myself oriented. I then made my way to Iron Springs to warmth, food and dry clothing.

It eventually occurred to me how stupid I had been. If I had changed mounts after the storm struck, the other horse would have taken me directly to Iron Springs Ranger Station. She had been owned by the forest ranger who preceded me on the district and had long known Iron Springs as home. I was once saved in a Colorado blizzard by a horse which took me to camp in the face of a blinding blizzard such as once were so deadly to travelers on the plains and I knew how dependable a horse could be in such a situation. I had "goofed" again and paid dearly for not using my head.

A TALE OF A HORSE'S TAIL!

Bruce Barron

Immediately after I entered the Forest Service in the early 1940s, the Shasta Forest personnel were gathering for their annual fire suppression training school at Camp Leaf (an abandoned CCC Camp south of Mt. Hebron on the Goosenest District). The training session had just gotten underway when a "preseason" fire broke out on the William Randolph Hearst estate at Wyntoon on the McCloud River. Because of the prestige of the Hearst family and its powerful newspaper enterprise, it was deemed prudent to hit this fire hard and fast and the entire Camp Leaf forces converged on Wyntoon.

The fire was on top of a ridge with access over a steep talus slope of fragmented shale. I was packing a cumbersome shovel and for every three steps forward, I would slide back two on this slick frangible terrain. I was becoming weary of the ordeal when I was forced to step aside to allow three mounted horsemen to pass by. Having four legs gave the horses an advantage and as a stout pinto pony started to pass, I grabbed its tail and let him tow me on up to the top of the ridge. It was an added struggle for the pony and the rider often looked back at me with quizzical and somewhat disdainful look on his face.

As we gathered around to discuss fire suppression strategy, I became extremely apprehensive when introduced to the man on the pinto pony. He was our fire boss, Shasta Forest Supervisor Norman Farrell. I knew things were going to be okay when Norm said "we've met" and gave a big grin and conciliatory chuckle during our introduction.

A SHAKY MULE

Lee Morford

In 1928, the day before Thanksgiving, the carpenter foreman on the McCloud District of the Shasta National Forest told me there was no more work for the winter months. I spent that time until about February trying to find a carpenter's job any place in the State of California. I could not find a job, so I went back to McCloud to the ranger station and asked District Ranger Dutch Sullaway if he had a job for me and he said that he did. I was to be headquarter's fireman.

On April 1, I went to work for Dutch. That day he took me down to the Hearst Ranch and introduced me to three mules and a horse and said there was five tons of hay that he wanted me to pack down to Rinkle's river cabin which was five miles down the river. I was making two trips a day with the mules, carrying two bales of hay on each mule. One day, I either had an extra heavy bale or I did not get it high enough. It was pretty low and there was a bad place in the trail which was about six feet above the river. Straight down from the trail into the river was a deep hole. This mule had been going back and forth and I had not had any trouble with him but there was a jagged rock sticking out. He hit the rock with a bale of hay that was too low and fell over the side into the river. I thought that was the end of my career in the Forest Service. The mule got up and was struggling around. The water was about three feet deep where he was. I jumped into the river, grabbed the rope and led him to a place where he could get out. He was standing there with his legs spread. He was shaking and could barely stand. I thought he was scared but then realized those bales had soaked up another three hundred pounds of water. I jerked the hitches loose and let the bales of hay fall off. The mule was unhurt.

THE LOPSIDED MULE

Joe Ely

William "Andy" Anderson was ranger on one of the nastiest districts in the nation in terms of incendiarism and lots of real big fires. I was forest fire control officer and we worked harmoniously on the fire problem for a number of years. But we could not agree on how to pack a mule.

Neither of us had ever learned to throw a diamond. We both used a squaw hitch but we both did it differently. When we shared a pack mule to carry our camp and shared the job of packing the mule, the result was a lopsided mule.

To tie a squaw hitch, you first throw the cinch and lash rope across the packs and the mule. Then you reach under and catch the little cinch hook with a twist in the lash rope and pull it up right. Then you bring the rope up across the middle outside of both packs and the mule and go around the other side. Then you throw a loop between the pack and the mule with the remaining rope coming out behind the lower side of the loop at the bottom of the pack. Then you lift the pack with the lash rope, secure it temporarily and go back to the first side and repeat. If you have a partner, you each do one side. Then you don't have to go back and forth.

The problem was that Andy would always do his side the other way around. He would bring the rope out behind the top of the pack and then pull the pack down. Try as I might to explain the virtues of the two level packs riding high and neat on the mule, he would persist in doing it his way and I, mine. The result was that we had that mule all day with one pack high and the other pack low; a lopsided mule.

FRED GROOM BECOMES A FOREST RANGER

Jack Groom

Fred Groom was a self-educated man having attended school near Ukiah, Oregon, only until the age of 12. At that time it was necessary for him to drop out of school to help make a life for himself and his mother following the death of his father. However, during the remainder of his formative years he read everything he could get his hands on, including many of the classics. And so it was, at the age of 28, he heard that there were some openings with the Forest Service for a job as forest ranger. He studied hard to master the subjects he would have to know in order to pass the ranger's examination. In 1911, along with about fifteen others, he took the test at the Forest Service headquarters in Sumpter, Oregon. All who took the examination were local men like himself except for two forestry graduates from an Eastern school.

Besides the technical examination, part of the test had to do with the requirement that each one demonstrate his ability to saddle and pack two horses as if he were going on a trip into the back country. All the materials including blankets, tarps, ropes, eggs, canned goods and other provisions were stacked alongside the saddles and packbags. Two fairly gentle horses were provided. This, of course, was "old hat" for local boys. Fred was the first to volunteer. He quickly completed the loading, got on the horse and galloped down to the end of the lane and back. The two Eastern boys waited until the last, carefully observing each of the others. Finally, one of them took his turn. By that time old Nell, the pack horse, had become considerably disenchanted with the whole setup. She had been forced to gallop down this same lane and back over a dozen times and couldn't really see that she was getting anywhere. So when she started out with this young man's pack, the cinches not being in their usual place and the pack not feeling too solid, she must have decided that this was her opportunity to unload. She started bucking and the pack came apart, throwing cans and everything else in the load out into the brush alongside the road. Old-timers reported years later finding unopened cans at a considerable distance from the old road and wondering how in the world they ever got there.

THE MULE WHO WOULD BE FIRST

Jack Spencer

Paul Meischke rode a saddle horse up the Kelsey Creek Trail, followed by two pack mules. I brought up the rear on another saddle horse. Paul was the range conservationist on the Klamath National Forest in northern California in the late 1950s, and I was a young forester not long out of the Army. We were heading in to the Marble Mountain Wilderness Area for ten days to establish permanent range transects in some of the many high country grassy meadows there. I knew little about range management, being a timber beast and Paul was to help me learn some of the fundamentals.

The purpose of our work (some would call it a vacation) was to help track the long-term health of the meadows, and to figure the level of cattle grazing they could support. To do this, we stretched a 100 foot metal tape between two angle irons driven into the ground at places representing average conditions in the meadow, and recorded the species of vegetation or lack of vegetation inside a small metal ring we placed at one foot intervals along it. Later, when the results from each of these transects and other temporary plots scattered over the meadow were analyzed, Paul could estimate the number of cows and their calves that could graze in the meadow during a summer season without over using the grass. The locations of these transects were pinpricked on aerial photos so others could return from year to year to remeasure them to see if things had changed for the better or worse.

Our two government mules performed like loyal public servants, except for a short lapse the first night when they felt a great longing to return to their home corral and headed down the trail on their own to find it. We had put hobbles on their front legs and turned them loose in a 20 acre meadow of green grass before we went to sleep, thinking they would consider themselves to be in mule heaven. The next morning only the two horses remained—the mules were AWOL! Paul thought he knew where the independent minded animals had gone and, saddling a horse, he took off at a gallop back down the trail after them. A few hours later he returned to camp leading the unrepentant deserters. He had found them several miles down the trail, still in their hobbles, taking short little hops with their front feet as they moved patiently and determinedly toward their goal.

It was important to the mules to establish dominance by being the first one in line behind the lead horse, when all four animals were strung out on the trail. Each tried to out race the other to claim the prized position initially, and once there, had to protect his place by fending off the other mule who tried to push and shove his way ahead of him. The competition reached its peak when we finished our stay and started toward home. There was much jockeying among pack animals as the lead changed hands many times while the topography was gentle enough to permit the second animal to run up alongside the first one and make his bid to muscle into the choice spot. But when the trail steepened, the second mule had to wait for one of the few wide places in the trail before he could attempt his assault once again. At these times the first mule would push his nose as close to the lead horse's tail as the horse would permit, then furiously stand his ground. In this way he successfully maintained his post all the way down to the Kelsey Creek Guard Station, much to the frustration and growing anger of the second mule.

Paul and I unsaddled the animals and brushed them down before releasing them in the corral. Both mules headed straight for a dust hole and wallowed in it on their backs, then stand up and shake themselves. The humiliated and unforgiving second mule then walked slowly up to his partner, turned quickly and kicked the mule who was first squarely in the ribs with his hind legs, clearly making a statement about his feelings on mule dominance.

HORSES AND MULES AT THE ANIMAL FAIR

Abe G. Turley

In 1938, I was assigned to Wallace Ranger Station as headquarter's guard. Got a raise this time to $140 per month. Again, payday was once a month. The ranger station was located second floor rear of the new post office building. The office was upstairs, over the garage-warehouse. Rolling stock consisted of a Chevrolet pickup, a Ford pickup, a Chevrolet station wagon and a GMC one and one half ton stake body. Sleeping quarters were in a rented house across the alley. The pack string was quartered at Montgomery Gulch Guard Station, about 12 miles west. I reported to Henry Kottkey (Hank, to his friends), the alternate ranger, and a man for whom I developed the greatest respect.

Among other things, the stake body provided transport for the pack string. Hauling the string was a learning experience that required an extremely soft touch on the wheel, the brakes and the shift. The animals were loaded laterally, heads alternating left and right. They were individually lashed in place to provide support during forward movement. Our string was limited to four animals because that was all we could carry in the truck. The trail heads were equipped with dirt ramps that we could back up to for loading and unloading. In spite of efforts to stabilize the load, it was still pretty fluid. I can still remember the sound of four shod animals struggling to maintain footing on the bare deck of the truck, no matter how careful the driver was. I felt sorry for them.

The headquarter's guard was expected to be a jack-of-all-trades; carpenter, blacksmith, mechanic, driver, painter, maintenance man and, of course, smokechaser. But, I was nonplussed when I learned I was to take the pack string into Kellogg Peak to open the lookout for the season. The regular packer, Bobby Connors, had been disabled when a mule rolled over him while he was attempting to disentangle it from some telephone wire. He was on the mend but in no shape to load up or mount a horse. The plan was that we would load the stake body with the lookout gear (this was a first year opening so there was extra gear), drop me off at Montgomery, where Bobby would help us prepare the pack string. Hank and Bobby would drive to the trail head while I trailed the string by another route. This was a first for me, but Bobby assured me there would be no problem. The horse knew the way.

I didn't say so, but I was privately dubious, even worried about the whole thing. I had never been around horses, didn't understand them, didn't even like them very much. And, I had heard some wild stories about mules; they were cunning, they were stubborn, they always knew what you were thinking, things like that, but I was committed. Maybe condemned would be a better word.

I got into the saddle with no slip-ups and from there I just let the horse lead the way, as Bobby said it would. The route took us down the gulch to the highway, then down the shoulder about a mile, then across the South Fork on a rickety bridge. I was feeling pretty good by then. People were waving at me as they passed, and I straightened a bit in the saddle, and wished I had borrowed Bobby's hat. We approached the big flume and the only place we could get under it. The horse stopped, I dismounted, the horse led the string through and I remounted. So simple. I may as well have caught up on some sleep.

We arrived at the trail head in good tine. Hank had unloaded the gear and Bobby had overseen the makeup of the loads. This was a three mule string and, because there was extra gear the horse was packed too. George Howard, an old-timer who fought fire during the great fire of 1910 (he told me he had little time for fighting fire, he was too busy running) was to be the lookout. So, between all of us, we had everything ready to Bobby's satisfaction. I led off, taking it slow, per instructions, and George brought up the rear, keeping an eye on the packs. It was a long climb, uphill all the way but we made it without a single mishap. I helped George get his stuff into the lookout, which was in a short tower. Then there was naught to do but get in the saddle and let ol' Dobbin take us home. We met the truck at the trail head, hauled the string back to Montgomery and headed home. I got a pat on the back from Hank who sensed how worried I had been about the whole thing.

———◆———

Now I am an old man. I have brown spots and I can't hold my water as well as a once could. I snarl at the neighbor's pets when they use my yard. I snarl at my neighbor. I curse the raccoon that fouls my patio. I have mental bouts with the mole that inhabits my parking strip. I never win because it is smarter than I am. I admire the bald eagles that occasionally perch in the big deodar cedar at the end of the street. I chuckle at the news stories about the wolves in Yellowstone, the cougars in the city parks, the moose in the streets of Spokane, the grizzlies in the high country and the Canada honkers that hiss at joggers on the jogging paths. I make friends with the strange dogs I meet on my morning walk and, in winter, I feed the birds. And, I'm happy because I know

The Animal Fair is doing fine.

DIRTYFACE

Philip Lee

The following account is about my first job with the Forest Service and a horse named Dirtyface.

Twenty miles at a lope on a fat, bowlegged horse had peeled the skin off the insides of my thighs. Blood was drying and my jeans were sticking to my legs. It was mid-morning and I had been in the saddle since daylight. The cowboys riding with me had gathered a hundred head of cows and calves from the high Oregon desert east of Lakeview. I hadn't had a drink since breakfast at four that morning and the steak and eggs had long been converted to energy and expended. While these cowboys never carried food or water when they rode, at least they rode young strong horses even if they did buck every chance they got. My horse had resisted the ride from the start and by mid-morning was doing his best to get me off his back. He was probably hurting as much as I was. How had I gotten myself into this situation? It was simple, I was eager to learn about managing cattle on the forest, eager to ride and ignorant of the shortcomings of my horse. His name was Dirtyface but I called him everything else but during that ride.

My first full time job with the U.S. Forest Service had started a few days earlier. I was working as a range conservationist and was responsible for administering the permits of a dozen ranchers. The ranchers I was riding with that day were gathering cattle from their spring range on the Bureau of Land Management. This range covered thousands of acres in the high desert. We would ride 40 miles that day before we finished and there would be two more days just like this one. We had 500 head of cattle to roundup and move to the forest.

The week before my boss, Ranger Clyde, had taken me out to the horse barn and shown me the tack and the horse trailer and told me how to find my horse. Ranger Clyde was a good boss. He told me what I had to do and where to find the equipment I needed. When he asked me if I could ride a horse I nodded yes. I was on my own. My first job was to ride the north end of the district and check that all the fences had been maintained before the cattle were turned onto the range. My horse was in a pasture at Willow Creek where we had a guard station. There was one man living there and he was a fire guard for the south part of the district.

When I arrived at Willow Creek I was really excited. The cabin was made of logs and was as picturesque as a postcard. I could see my horse standing in the pasture, belly high in grass, behind the cabin.

It had been several years since I had ridden a horse but I had learned the basics from high school and college friends who had horses. I sure couldn't call myself an experienced horseman. Even 25 years later and thousands of miles of riding and packing, I did not consider myself an expert. I had spent too many years with real cowhands and packers to fool myself that way.

The fire guard came out to greet me as I drove up to the cabin. "Hi!, I'm Bill. Looks like you are planning on a ride today." I introduced myself and explained where I was going to ride. "I was just leaving on my patrol and don't have time to help you with the horse." he said. "You might have a little trouble with him. He hasn't been ridden this year. I think he is a little hard to catch." With that he jumped into his pumper truck and drove off. I didn't notice him stop behind some trees at the far end of the pasture.

I knew enough about horses to bring a bucket of oats along. Few horses can resist a snack on rolled oats. I got my halter and the bucket and climbed the fence into the pasture. I was happy and excited. My own horse to ride and care for. Thousands of acres to ride him in and the whole summer ahead of me. As I got close to the horse I could see why they had named him "Dirtyface." It wasn't a very becoming name, but it fit. His face was blazed but the blaze looked like someone had rubbed dirt into it. He was not a tall horse, but he certainly was wide. It was obvious he had not had much riding lately. The other district rangers all had horses of their own and seldom borrowed another ranger's horse. I would soon find out why no one borrowed Dirtyface.

166

By the time I got near the horse I was soaked past the knees. The grass was deep and still wet from morning dew. The pasture had water standing three inches deep in places. It was a lush wet meadow. Along the south end of the pasture there were lodgepole pine trees. Along the west edge there was a large clump of willows. The entire pasture of about three acres was enclosed with a buck and pole fence. There was no corral.

Dirtyface kept on eating grass as I approached. He barely looked up. This should be easy, I thought. When I got within ten feet of him he raised his head, looked at me as if to say hello and goodbye, and trotted toward the other end of the pasture. When he felt a safe distance he began to feed again. I rattled the oats in the bucket and he looked up. "Now I'll get you," I said.

An hour later the dew was off the grass. Sweat was on my forehead and running down my back. I was no closer to catching Dirtyface than when I started. About that time I noticed the pumper truck pull out onto the road. I guess Bill had enough laughs for one day. "Go ahead and laugh, Bill. We will be gone when you come back for lunch," I muttered to myself. I was not to be beaten by that horse. I went to the truck and got a 50 foot rope. That got Dirtyface excited and he began to run. I chased him around the pasture a couple of times trying to lasso him until he tired of that game. However, he had a new game to play. He hid behind the willows along the west fence. As I approached him he would just sidestep around the willows away from me. By then I knew it would take some fancy work to fool that horse.

I went into the lodgepole stand and found a couple of downed trees about four inches in diameter and 20 feet long. I carried them to the willow patch and laid them on the ground between the fence and the willows. They were just long enough to reach into the willows. I tied the rope onto the fence about 20 feet from the poles and laid it on the ground. Dirtyface was out feeding again. I grabbed my halter and ran toward him. Just as I expected, he raced to the willows where he stood and watched me. I chased him around the willows about three times. On the third time around I stopped and put the two poles across the rails in the fence and stuck the other ends into the willows. I ran around the willows again and Dirtyface ran around them also.

He came to the poles and realized he had been tricked. He spun around and headed back toward me, but by then I had the end of the rope and I pulled it chest high. I finally had my horse.

I learned a few lessons that day. Always take rubber boots when catching a horse in a wet meadow. Never leave Dirtyface in the pasture without hobbles, and always give yourself an extra hour to catch a horse, even if he is hobbled. I also learned a few lessons on that first ride in the desert. The first—never ride a fat, bowlegged horse when riding with the cowboys, and the second just as important—never depend on someone else for food or water when in the saddle.

But here I was, out on the desert in the hot sun, no food (except for two tootsie rolls), no water and no shade. I'd give anything to be wading knee deep in the horse pasture now. Worse of all I was riding Dirtyface, a bowlegged horse who stumbled often. I was sorry I had ever caught him that first time. Should have just let him retire in peace at Willow Creek, I thought.

By late afternoon we had moved the cows to a good holding area where they could water, feed and mother-up their calves. I rode on into camp, too tired to eat, and collapsed onto my bedroll. I was determined to have a different horse the next time I made that ride. That's another story.

WIND POWER BY MAUDE

Ed A. Grosch

About Labor Day 1951, I was returning to the Indian Dick Guard Station (Covelo Ranger District, Mendocino National Forest) after almost a week on some small lightning fires near Washington Rock and Four Corners Rock. I was riding Goldie with my mules Red and Covelo carrying my few tools and my bed. The trail off Little Butte led down through Henthorne Lake

(Richard Wilson's Ranch) to the Middle Fork of the Eel River at Hoxie Crossing.

Nobody was staying at the lodge that summer. The gates were thrown open so visiting cattle would not get caught behind any fences. The orchard was thriving for some reason and there were lots of red apples and some figs. The deer and other varmints were apparently already enjoying themselves, although the bears seemed not to have found the fruit yet.

I knew the trail crew and other visitors were probably waiting at the guard station for a resupply coming in by pack train from the Eel River Ranger Station. Because of this, I stopped in the orchard and off-loaded my equipment and other possessions from Covelo. Then I filled each kayak (pannier) with these beautiful red apples. I must have had close to 100 pounds, all told. After arriving at Indian Dick, I put the apples in a box in the meat safe and later the trail crew and I fixed enough apples to make baked apples for dessert that evening.

The next day we sharpened saws, axes, McLeods and repaired any broken handles, etc. We worked hard as we were in anticipation of the pack train that afternoon. Two forest visitors came by right after lunch. On seeing all those apples, the lady guest suggested she would help us to make some applesauce. After we finished our chores, we all pitched in to core and quarter the fruit. As the first kettle began to boil, we realized that we were going to have many gallons of sauce, so I grabbed the big old washtub off the shed wall and cleaned it with bleach and soap.

By the time I'd finished this, the packer arrived and we helped him with unloading and caring for his nine mules. That done, the others returned to the applesauce business while I did the honors of preparing supper. When I had dinner ready, the wash tub was about half full of applesauce. Since it was very hot, we set the tub on a bench near the rail yard fence to cool.

The horses and mules were in the surrounding pasture and we were chowing down on our summer steelhead and fresh veggies. Over our coffee and baked apples, we head a funny slurping noise coming from the area near the tub of applesauce. I rushed out the door of the house to see a mare mule named

Maude with her head through the fence rails and her nose in the tub. I yelled and her ears came forward and she slowly withdrew her head through the rails. As I ran to the tub and looked in, I realized there was not even a pint of applesauce left! Maude stuck her nose in the air, gave a snort/whistle and trotted off.

The next day the packer tied her to the rear of his line of mules. I knew that Maude would provide the necessary "jet propulsion" for his trip to Hammerhorn Lookout.

THE WILLAMETTE MULE DRIVE

Al Kreger

In the mid 1950s, the Willamette National Forest was using about 60 head of pack mules and saddle horses. Each ranger district used one or more pack strings (a saddle horse and five or six mules) to supply the many fire lookouts and move and supply trail maintenance crew, forest inventory crew and survey crew camps. The old Cascadia Ranger District, now the Sweet Home Ranger District, was using ten lookouts at that time. There was a road to only one, Sand Mountain. The rest were pack trips. It kept two pack strings busy all summer, supplying these lookouts and all the crews that were camped out in the roadless back country.

All these pack animals were wintered (fed and cared for) by a cattle ranch somewhere in central Oregon. This location would change, depending on which ranch was the successful bidder. Usually, the location was somewhere in the vicinity of Powell Buttes or Prineville, Oregon. Each spring, the pack stock would be trucked into the Fish Lake Remount Station, as it was known then. Each animal was fitted (shod) with a new set of shoes. This shoeing was done by Bob Gage, who was the forest lead packer and Tex White, who was the other Cascadia District packer. They were usually helped by one or two packers from other districts.

After all the animals were shod, each string was trucked to the other ranger districts with the exception of the McKenzie Ranger District. Their packer would "trail" the string down the old Belnap Road, now highway 126, to the McKenzie Bridge Ranger Station.

In the fall, the process would be reversed. All the pack stock would be returned to Fish Lake, the shoes would be pulled and the animals trucked back to winter pasture. The hauling would be contracted by a freight company using two large truck and trailer rigs. I helped load one September morning when we loaded out 57 head.

In the spring of 1960, Warren Pressinten, the forest fire staff who was also responsible for all pack stock, was reviewing the cost of hauling these animals. The cost was over $700 each spring and fall. A lot of money in a 1960 budget.

Pressinten, "Press" as we called him, asked three ranch raised employees, Rex Resler, Bob Mealey and me, if we would be interested in donating our three day Memorial Day and Labor Day weekends to drive the mules from winter pasture to Fish Lake and back again in the fall. The forest agreed to buy the groceries for the three day trip. (We had to buy our own whiskey.)

We rode our own horses. Resler usually rode a Tennessee walker, Mealey rode a brown and white paint named Bingo and I rode a black and white paint called Tony. We would trailer our horses to Fish Lake on Friday night. Early Saturday morning we would load our horses, all the camp gear and groceries in a Forest Service stock truck, ride into Sisters, Oregon, eat breakfast at a restaurant, on to the ranch and the mule drive would begin.

We designated Press the trail boss and Press also was the chief cook. He and Resler usually rode the lead and kept the mules as bunched up as possible. Mealey and I would bring up the rear. My job was keeping strays from going into some ranch gate or an alfalfa field and flagging vehicle traffic if we were on a busy road or highway. Bob Gage drove the stock truck (we called it the "chuck wagon"). He would block traffic, where necessary, and haul the camp gear on to the next camp. The entire trip covered about 75 miles over a period of three days and involved two campouts, one near Rumalo, Oregon, and the other at the Cattlemen's Corral on the old Santiam Wagon Road, seven miles west of Sisters, Oregon.

The first day we would follow back country roads where we could. Sometimes, we were on highway 126. We would cross highway 97 just south of Redmond, Oregon, and camp at a ranch a few miles west of the highway.

The second day we followed country roads, crossed a lot of open range land, and on to highway 20, east of Sisters. We skirted the south side of the town of Sisters, but had to come back to highway 20 near the Sisters Ranger Station, then follow the Old Santiam Wagon Road seven miles to Graham Corral.

The third day we followed the Old Santiam Wagon Road from Graham Corral to Big Lake and the Old Santiam airstrip, crossed the northern side of Sand Mountain and down to Fish Lake and home.

After the first trip, other forest employees got the idea that they would like to make the trip, usually two or three each trip. Press called these guys, "chee-chock-oos." He said it was an Indian name for a tenderfoot in the Alaska gold fields. We would pick out the most gentle horses in the herd for these fellows, help them saddle up and we would begin the trip. Some were pretty good riders and some were not. Very few made it past the first or second day and then they were willing to finish the trip riding with Bob Gage in the stock truck.

I remember one fellow who I think had never been on a horse in his life. He showed up in his Forest Service uniform, flat shoes and of all things, his hard hat. (The rest of us wore the garb we had grownup with, boots, Levis and Stetsons.) We put this fellow on the most gentle horse and helped him mount up. He grasped the saddle horn and we started down the road. He made no attempt to guide the horse, so the horse decided he wanted to stay in the center of the herd and that's where they stayed, hard hat and all.

In 1965 or '66, I decided to take my oldest son Dick along for the ride. He was in seventh grade. We mounted him on a gentle old horse we called, "Annie Mare."

172

As I mentioned earlier, our second day's ride took us through some open range land. There were usually cattle and calves grazing in this area. It should be mentioned here that some mules have a mean habit of attacking any small animal, a dog, a calf or even a colt. My job, as we traveled through this area, was to ride ahead and drive any cattle away from the road and out of sight of the mules. On this day, however, I missed a saddle mare with a very small colt.

Before we knew what was happening, a half dozen mules broke from the herd and attacked this small colt, viciously kicking and biting this helpless little critter. As Rex Resler and I tried to separate the colt from the mules, I saw Bob Gage leave the stock truck, mount up on Annie Mare and leave Dick standing by an old corral. We tried to get the colt and its mother to this corral and separate them from the mules. As we approached the corral, I saw my seventh grade son pick up a pine limb and start swinging it at the mules and trying to protect the colt. I dismounted, and as Rex kept the mules back, Dick and I managed to get the colt inside the corral.

As we rejoined the mule drive, Bob Gage returned to his truck and located the mare and colt's owner. They hauled the colt to the nearest veterinary but to no avail. The poor, little fellow died of internal injuries.

On one trip, as we passed the Sisters Ranger Station on highway 20, some of the mules smelled those nice, green lawns and decided to have a bite of fresh grass. Wendall Jones, a well known Region 6 employee, was stationed at the Sisters Ranger Station at that time. As I gathered the mules, I had to drive them between some of the dwellings and across the lawns. And, there was Wendall's wife, Jesse, shaking her fist and yelling at me to get those mules out of her flower beds.

On another trip, as we traveled the highway just east of Sisters, I was bringing up the rear and flagging traffic. As I stopped, there was a pickup occupied by a couple of ranch hands. One leaned out the window and yelled, "Where did you get that big spotted horse?" I replied, "I bought him from Little Joe Cartwright." Little Joe rode a horse on the well known TV show,

Bonanza, that was a dead ringer for my horse, Tony. I'll bet that fellow still believes that he saw Little Joe's horse.

As mentioned before, we followed the Old Santiam Wagon Road from Graham Corral over the Cascade summit just south of Hoodoo Ski area and on to Fish Lake. This 25 mile part of the trip could be a joy ride or a hard day's work, depending on the winter's snow pack. One year we started to encounter snow soon after we left Graham Corral. A few more miles and we were getting into snow drifts so deep that the mules refused to break their own trail. Bob Mealey, who was riding the lead with Press, started breaking trail with his trusty horse Bingo. After several miles, Bingo began to wear down. When we reached a spot of bare ground at Santiam airstrip, Bob asked me if I would break trail with Tony. Tony was a big, strong horse that stood 16 hands high and weighed 1,500 pounds. I would think nothing about riding him 25 to 30 miles a day on other trail rides. The farther we went, the worse it got until we were breaking through snow drifts five and six feet deep. Some places my horse had to step across large blown down logs buried beneath the snow. My worse fear was that Tony would rupture his belly on a broken limb protruding upward from these fallen logs as he crawled across them, but he never faltered. After four or five miles of tough going, we started to go downhill and began to see more and more bare ground. Some of the mules ran past me and headed for the corrals at Fish Lake. They knew that Bob Gage would be there with the gates open and feed racks full of hay. After a 75 mile trip, they were heading home.

I continued to make the mule drive trip both ways from 1960 to 1968. I missed the Memorial Day trip in 1969 because of illness and by Labor Day I had transferred to another forest.

I don't know how long the mule drive continued. Rex Resler did a tour of duty in Washington, DC. Mealey was transferred to the Siuslaw National Forest and I was on the Umatilla National Forest. More and more fire lookouts were abandoned and trail maintenance and other campout work was contracted. The only saddle horse and pack mules that are still around are used to pack garbage out of the wilderness areas and for Forest Service dignitaries to ride on wilderness trips. Then, many of these animals are contracted.

The helicopter has replaced the trusty mule but the helicopter will never replace the memories of those trail rides. As I rode side by side with Rex Resler one day, he took a deep breath and explained, "Nothing smells better than a mixture of the smell of horse sweat, sage brush and horse ____."

I continued to use ol' Tony on hunting trips on the Umatilla and Malheur forests until he succumbed of old age in 1976.

Modern machinery has replaced the horses and mules of yesteryear but they will never replace their memories.

A STICKY SITUATION

Ed Masonheimer

This story took place on the Hot Springs Ranger District, Sequoia National Forest, during the 1963 season. Location was the trail between Frog Meadow Guard Station and Baker Point Lookout.

Part of my duties required me to take supplies to the district lookouts within my patrol unit, which included using stock. Baker Point Lookout was at the end of a very steep and treacherous trail that overlooked a lot of the upper Kern River area above Kernville.

I should explain that there was a road (of sorts) that you could truck the stock to within about a mile of the lookout. However, considerable time could be saved by using the trail from the station (Frog Meadow) to the lookout.

I had made several trips using this trail and was familiar with most of the hazards along the way and negotiated them without incident. However, this particular time I was packing a couple of propane bottles along with other badly needed supplies.

We had gone about one half mile from Frog Station and were lined out fairly well when entering a steep section of the trail going downhill. As a lot of you know, on steep sections of trails, holes develop from stock stepping in and over rocks and roots, etc. We were just entering one of these areas when I felt a tug on my lead rope. Turning to see what the problem was I noticed my lead mule's front feet weren't touching the ground. Needless to say, I about panicked as she was stuck between two trees. Thank God, she stood there without making a fuss, as I'm not sure I would have gotten her out without major help.

I tied my horse and the other mule out of the way and tried to calmly assess the situation. "*GULP!*" Can you imagine calling the boss on the radio and telling him that you have a mule hopelessly stuck between two trees and need help.

Because of the way she had settled between the two trees I couldn't get to the cinch and couldn't loosen the lash rope, but could get it untied. Being wedged the way she was, rocking the pack was out of the question. However, I was able to move the front of one of the propane bottles a little by lifting up, then going around behind the tree and moving the rear of the bottle up a little at the same time, being very careful not to get kicked. After what seemed like an hour (probably only 10 or 15 minutes) of nerve-racking work, I got her feet on the ground and, with a little wiggling, she was able to get free of the trees.

Other than my wife, I'm not sure I told anyone of this situation for sometime. Besides, how do you tell your boss something like that?

ALMOST THE END OF AN ERA

Gordon Jesse Walker

Big Red, a government mule, was born in 1949. No one seems to know exactly where but it could have been in Missoula, Montana.

There used to be a remount station there where they broke mules to pack and then sold them to various agencies.

Big Red came to me in the late 1960s. We traveled hundreds of miles together clear up to the fall of 1981 when he made his last trip packing a cast iron stove on his back. Big Red and I put on several shows at the Union Creek Campground amphitheater over the years and we enjoyed every one of them. He liked having his picture taken best of all because he'd pose just like a professional.

Big Red showed signs of ailing about the first of March after wintering quite well. He was taken to Crater Animal Clinic for treatment. The vets floated his teeth and he was dewormed. I gave him some liquid vitamins mixed with oats. His appetite picked up but he still didn't gain any weight.

On March 31, he started to slow down on eating. By Friday, April 2, he wouldn't touch a thing. On April 3, I took him back to the clinic. When he climbed into the trailer he fell, never to stand again. At the clinic two doctors worked on him and tried to save his life. He couldn't get up and it was quite evident that he was suffering a lot of pain. The doctors agreed he would never stand again and there was only one choice and that was to put Big Red to sleep. It was I who had to say "go ahead." I would take care of his remains myself. I was by him when he died.

He was put to sleep in the big six horse 5th wheel trailer he dearly loved. He was 33 years old and probably worked for the Forest Service longer than any Rogue River mule, though I don't know for sure.

I picked a site for his grave about one half mile northwest of the Prospect Ranger Station and he was buried there on Monday, April 5, 1982.

Sarah mule from Butte Falls preceded Big Red in death. Stella mule at the Prospect Ranger Station is the sole survivor and the last of the Rogue River National Forest mules. When she dies it will mark the end of an era, never to be revived.

The good old days of the colorful, rough and tumble life of a packer has almost come to an end. I should know because I'm the last of the old Rogue River Packers.

LIFE WITH CHOPPO, MY FIRST AND ONLY HORSE

Harvey Mack

WWII had just begun and in the spring of 1942, there was considerable fear of Japanese attacks that could result in forest fires along the Southern California coast. Jack Smith and I were selected to maintain a horse patrol from the San Juan Guard Station on the Ortega Highway north of San Juan Capistrano east to highway 395. Much of this area was just north of the Camp Pendleton Marine Base. Ranger Albright required each of us to purchase a horse, saddle, etc., to be used on the patrol with the Forest Service furnishing hay, oats, shoes, etc. I knew absolutely nothing about horses so I bought a three year old gelding, Choppo, from Arlee Leck, a local rancher for $125, a lot of money then for a forest guard. Choppo was a small horse, only 14 hands high and had been raised somewhat as a family pet. I rode him once around the ranch and found him to be very spirited and responsive but once we left his happy home at the ranch, he became an entirely different horse.

First, he immediately figured out how to unlatch the corral gate and headed back to the ranch where he was raised. After several such escapes we finally made it complicated enough that he could not open it. Next, he had to be shod and really put up a fight. We had to drop him on his side and tie his feet but he finally relaxed and let us proceed.

He did seem to take a liking to my wife as she would feed him little tidbits, scratch his nose and make him feel more like he was at home on the ranch. We lived in a cabin in the middle of a summer home special use track and our plumbing was an outhouse on the other side of the road from the cabin. Every time she came out to make the crossing, Choppo would go into a loud series of whinnies with accompanying stomping which very often proved embarrassing to her when cabin owners were in the area as he announced what was going on.

One evening I had the horse at the guard station and my wife decided she wanted to try riding him. She petted and talked to him and we all decided he was in a good mood and agreed to let her ride around the station. She got mounted and Choppo turned his head and looked at her and decided to give her a good ride. He took off down the Ortega Highway with us running after her and trying to catch up. One of the crew took off after her in the tanker and when he passed her, we feared for the worst. Suddenly Choppo stopped, turned around and very slowly walked back to the station as if he had given her a real treat.

Now getting down to the patrol business, the only reason I had the horse. He was very docile while being saddled but as soon as I would get into the saddle, he would go into violent "crow topping" with an appropriate release of gasses and then break into a wild run down the road for about a half mile through the special use area. People would wait to see me and the horse. He then would have it out of his system and became manageable for the rest of the day. However, when it was time to go back up the canyon to the cabin, he would refuse to go with me on his back but when I would get off and start walking, he would put his head over my shoulder and walk back with me with a certain look that let everyone know who really was the boss.

The patrol was a different matter that he seemed to like. He was a strong horse and we would cover the 20 miles each way with enthusiasm. However, all that I carried was a shovel, single bit hand axe, a canteen and a lunch. There were no telephone lines or radio so there was no way to communicate with anyone all day. I often wondered what I would have done if I had come onto a fire or person that should not be there. At least I knew that Choppo probably could have outrun almost anything. One day when returning I got a late start from Tenaja and it got dark while we still were a couple of miles from home. Choppo slowed and gently laid down with me still on his back. No amount of prodding, kicking, shoving or swearing did any good— he was done for the day. When he finally stood up, I hobbled him, took off the saddle and used the blanket for the night. Come daylight, be was raring to go as he had not had hay or oats and was glad to be on his way back.

After about two months of the patrol, it was decided that they were of little value and we were ordered to sell the horses as the Forest Service would no longer pay for the maintenance. I sold Choppo to a couple of fellows that were very impressed with his willingness to run and they raced him at local fairs and other events where he did pretty good but died of a heart attack during a race.

NO BUCKAROO

Les Joslin

Back in the early 1960s, when I was fire prevention guard on the Bridgeport Ranger District of the Toiyabe National Forest, I spent a few days each summer in the Hoover Wilderness where increasing visitation was compounding the risk of wildfire. The job of wilderness ranger was yet to be created and wilderness patrol and public contact were otherwise left to the district's three-man trail crew.

Most of my wilderness patrols were on foot, but on rare occasions I rode a horse.

I never claimed to be a cowboy. My only previous experience with horses had been gained during summer visits to an uncle's farm and most of what I knew about them had been learned from books and movies. But I knew enough to get by and, in spite of my shortcomings as a bunkaroo, most of those horseback patrols went well.

I say "most of those horseback patrols went well" because I darn near wound up finishing one of them—the only one that didn't go well—on foot.

That was the time Marion Hysell, the district's fire control officer and my boss and I rode in to a little unnamed lake above Barney Lake and below Hunewill Peak to rebuild rock fire rings and erect a sign. I hoped to show Marion, a Wyoming cowboy, that I'd learned a thing or two about horses.

After finishing the work and lunch we began the return trip on the two big black horses hired from the Mono Village pack station. About half way down to the junction with the Barney

Lake Trail, Marion and I met a group of hikers. They were bound for the little lake we'd just left and we dismounted to talk with them. About what, I can't remember. What I can remember is that my mount suddenly decided to quit the country. He reared, yanked the loosely held reins from my hand and bolted down the trail toward the pack station about five miles away.

"Now you're a hiker, too!" one of the hikers observed with what seemed thinly veiled satisfaction.

Instead of explaining my preference for shank's mare, I excused myself with something like, "Darned if I'll walk back to Mono Village!" and lit out after the horse.

"He'll never catch it," another of the hikers predicted.

But there was a chance. I recalled the series of switchbacks in the trail up this steep slope and hoped they'd work in my favor. I plunged off the trail and down slope over boulders and through thickets to head off the fugitive mount.

The first time I tumbled back onto the trail I was just too late. Down the trail to my right, the horse was hightailing it into the next switchback. Back into the woods I plunged, again careening downhill as aspen branches slapped my face and mountain mahogany slowed my progress.

Within moments I was back on the trail and this time ahead of the game. Off to my right, the horse was just turning out of the switchback and thundering toward me, eyes wild and ears back in what looked a lot like determination. I was determined too, and as the big black tried to evade me, I grabbed its reins just below the bit, yanked down hard and wrestled it to a kicking, snorting, dusty stop.

Reins tight in my grasp, I led the horse back up the trail. Would catching this runaway redeem me in Marion's eyes? In the eyes of the hikers?

By the time I had led the recaptured mount up the trail to where Marion and the hikers were waiting to see if I would walk or ride home, I had managed to brush off dust and leaves and tuck in my shirt. I had also reviewed and rejected every alibi east of the Sierra. The truth of what had happened was plain to see. Marion grinned his good natured grin. He seemed satisfied at the fact I'd caught the horse. The hikers seemed impressed by the same fact.

We mounted up to resume the ride to the pack station. I told myself I was finished with horses.

But it was one of those days and those horses hadn't finished with us. Almost back to the pack station, we met a woman and two little girls sitting on boulders beside the trail and stopped to speak with them. Marion was soon engaged in polite conversation with the woman while the little girls admired our mounts.

"I like horsies," the younger girl beamed at me.

Woosh! Her fond words were drowned as Marion's big black, standing spraddle legged directly in front of her, proceeded to relieve himself.

This didn't do much for the conversation and horses just don't move on while responding to nature's call. So there we were, all trying our darndest not to appear to notice the steady stream splashing and steaming in the trail dust not six feet from the woman and the little girls. Except of course, the little girls whose eyes widened at the spectacle.

I had to bite my tongue to keep from laughing as I watched Marion, close to laughter himself and the woman affect an immediate interest in virtually every aspect of our surroundings—Ah! The glories of nature!—save the cascade that held the little girls in awe. Finally, after what seemed eons, the downpour abated. And the big black snorted satisfaction.

"Well, we better be gettin' on down the trail," Marion rather disingeniously excused us and on we rode. Once around the bend and out of sight and—I'm sure—earshot, we doubled over in our saddles with laughter.

MEMORIES OF HORSES AND MULES

Bob Spivey

From the summer following graduation from high school, until I graduated from Humboldt State University and got my first permanent professional position as a forester at Orleans on the Six Rivers National Forest, I had summer jobs. Fire crewman, fire guard, timber inventory crewman, slash patrolman, timber inventory crew foreman, a wonderful set of experiences. (Throughout this piece I'm using the terms in use at the times these events took place.)

Starting with those summer jobs and flowing through my career, there are many memories of the use of Forest Service and rented stock to complete work projects. Moving men and equipment in to remote areas for fire fighting, planting fingerling fish in high mountain lakes, assessing resource conditions, supplying lookouts, doing various types of inventories, achieving work projects such as trail construction including bridges, handling all the work related to the range and the range permittees; these are examples of the types of work that I remember getting done with the help of these tremendous partners.

Sometimes I was by myself with a single animal, other times there were hundreds of animals moving tons of tools and food into very remote large fire camps, and every kind of situation in between.

I felt then, and I feel now, a tremendous appreciation for the capability of horses, mules, and even some burros, to accomplish sometimes very difficult tasks. The skill of the Forest Service packer was a major part of the equation, and I remember so many wonderful packers. Their knowledge and skill at packing these animals to achieve major work while showing great care for the animals always impressed me.

During my career time the situation of course changed dramatically. Additional roads greatly increased the ability of recreationists and others to access the forest along with facilitating the administrative needs of the agency And the use of helicopters to move men and equipment into remote locations became commonplace.

But I'll always remember the tremendous work achieved when livestock were integral partners in Forest Service work accomplishments.

HORSE LOGGING WITH SOME EXCITEMENT!

Ralph A. "Sparky" Reeves

There was the time in 1937, when we were stationed at Big Camas Ranger Station in charge of a 50 man CCC side camp out of Diamond Lake on the Umpqua National Forest.

Margaret and I lived in a tent house one quarter mile from the ranger station along with our new son, Rich. The ranger was Harold Bowerman, with assistant Kelly Churchill and office helper, Winnie Churchill. The 50 man crew and one powder foreman, Van Cleveland, in charge of stump blasting, were building road from Big Camas Ranger Station toward the Steamboat Ranger Station on the Umpqua River.

The brushing crews had cut out the brush on the right-of-way, the fallers cut the trees and the buckers cut the logs to length so that they could be logged by a Forest Service team of matched black horses driven by teamster Guy Fender.

One day after the CCC crew had finished their day and returned to camp, Guy had a few more logs to move so that the dozer could push out some stumps so that another section of truck trail or pioneer road could be built.

While pulling a log, one horse slipped and fell onto a one inch stob that one of the brush cutters had cut off at about six inches above the ground at an angle of about 60 degrees. The stob punctured the horse's stomach, and when the horse regained its feet, about 18 inches of intestine was protruding from the wound.

Guy ripped off his undershirt, wet it from a canteen hanging on the mane of one horse, removed a line from the harness, pushed the intestine back in, wrapped the line around the horse and pad—truss fashion—and radioed the ranger station from the stock truck.

The phone lines were abuzz with the news, and the supervisor's office in Roseburg, with Vern Harpham, Forest Supervisor, was advised by a local vet to destroy the horse. The doctor at the CCC camp at Diamond Lake got word of the situation and said, "Let me try!" The Doc received permission from the supervisor's office. J. R. Montgomery drove him from Diamond Lake to Big Camas where he picked up water, ropes, about ten CCC boys and myself and drove the two miles out to the job.

The doctor brought along a bottle of tranquilizers from the camp infirmary and asked Guy if he could get a handful into the horse's mouth, which he did. In about five minutes we pushed the horse over into a bed of fir boughs, wound side up, removed the undershirt that was used for the pad, removed the lines and Doc cut away the hair as best he could.

After tying the horse's rear feet to a stump, and with the CCC boys holding the horse's head and front feet, the doctor washed the wound and stitched it up. We made a girdle of canvas and copper blasting wire. We got the horse up and into the stock truck and to the ranger station just as dark set in.

Prognosis: No feed for 12 hours; if after that the horse got around for two days, he would be OK.

The horse and his mate were subsequently transferred to the Tiller Ranger Station for the winter. I lost track of the team there, also Guy Fender who knew the proper first aid for his charge. Yes, we did horse log in the Forest Service in those days back in '37 and '38, and it was sometimes exciting!

MULE STORIES

Bob Gray

Granite Peak was a long days trip from Weaverville on the Trinity National Forest. Loading the stock about daylight, driving for two hours in the stock truck to the trail head, unloading the truck and saddling and packing the broncs usually lasted until 10 a.m. It was a steep four mile climb and in the springtime much of the trail was covered with hard packed snow, which necessitated digging tracks for the mules to walk in across the steep barren snow covered slopes.

On one occasion, before learning the need to dig steps, one of my two mules slipped on the rock hard snow and slid about 100 feet down the hill. Sheer luck resulted in him sliding into a soft brush patch rather than into one of the huge granite boulders. Except for a few hairs rubbed off and the load being scattered, Doc was all right. Dexter, from the top of the snowback, looked in contempt at the mule who lost his footing and patiently waited the hour it took Doc and me to recoup and regroup.

I later found out that another mule had been killed a few years earlier at this same location under the same snow conditions.

I seldom went anywhere with the packstring without some misadventure. The most memorable one was my own fault for not using the best judgment.

It was late summer, the trail crew had finished its work in the Stuart's Fork drainage, and I took my horse King, with seven mules to Morris Meadow to pick up camp and haul out garbage.

The day was beautiful, the mules were at their best possessing most of the virtues of the Boy Scout law excepting "thrifty" and "reverent." Ten out of twelve ain't bad in anybody's book.

We got to the meadow in mid-afternoon, with lots of daylight left. The trail crew had already left and I'd planned to camp overnight, leaving in the early morning. Well, I got to thinking,

I'm not tired, the mules are already saddled and with a little luck I can make it back to the Trinity Alps Resort shortly after dark.

The mules' dispositions started to change as I loaded them and even King looked at me in a strange way. No doubt they had anticipated a good roll in the meadow and an evening of feeding themselves on the tall grasses which they could eat without stretching their necks. With about two hours of daylight left, we headed down the trail. In my hurrying, I didn't balance the packs as well as I should have and within a mile I was already adjusting, balancing and retying my self-designed diamond hitches. With darkness gaining on us, we settled into a slow trot with packs bouncing and lead ropes straining between the animals.

My lack of wisdom in trying to do two days work in one was rapidly becoming more apparent to me as we rounded a bend, coming face to face with a bear. I reined up and the mules piled up behind me on the narrow trail. The lead mule was probably the only one to see the bear but that was enough. He whirled around, pulling the lead rope from my hand and crashed into the mule behind him. Like falling dominoes, the reaction took place. Each mule whirled into the next one and in seconds lead ropes were broken, packs were flying, saddles hanging under bellies and mules scattering into the trees and up the trail. Fortunately, it took more than a bear to get King upset so I dismounted and tied him to a tree as the bear disappeared up the hill.

When I walked back up the trail to survey the damage I was appalled to find packs, saddles and broken harness scattered for a quarter of a mile up the trail and some of the mules disappeared into the woods.

Darkness was rapidly approaching and I couldn't find a flashlight, so I had better take care of the animals first and worry about the gear later, I thought. Catching the mules wasn't too difficult and as I caught then, I removed what was left of their saddles and tied them to the nearest tree. By the time the first four were taken care of, it was dark and all I could see were dark shadows as I approached the others. Never being sure which end of the creature I was approaching, I talked gently and soothingly to them so that if it was the kicking end maybe they'd kick gently and soothingly.

Finally, I had found and tied up six of the seven but could not find the seventh. "He'll just have to wait until daylight," I said to myself, hoping that he was not tangled up in the brush somewhere.

Finding a sleeping bag and something to eat was not too difficult as I remembered where they were laying along the trail before darkness came. A cold can of beans and some crackers sufficed before crawling into the sleeping bag for the night but I didn't sleep too well wondering where the seventh mule was.

Daylight came and I shivered as I came out of the warm bag. "Gotta find that mule," I muttered to no one in particular. "One,–two, wonder which is missing, –three, four, –five, –six, seven!" They were all there. Somehow I'd forgotten to count the first one I tied up after the bear. "Darn, I sure could have slept better if I'd known all were accounted for."

A half sack of grain was distributed to the eight animals, and they "ate like horses," if I may make a joke. The grain didn't fill their empty stomachs but helped until I could get the saddles patched up and loaded, which took about four hours.

I was tired and the animals hungry and the packs pretty scraggly looking when we arrived at Trinity Alps about two hours later. A couple of bales of hay and a late breakfast furnished by the resort restored the mules, the horse and my spirits.

When I arrived at the barn at Weaverville, Joe and Bernie were there to help me unload, bless their souls. "How did it go?" they asked. "You made good time," not yet knowing what I'd been through. "Had a good trip," I lied. "Oh yeah, then what the hell happened to this pack gear?" asked Joe, who was going to have a few days' repair job ahead of him. Then I told them the story. "It couldn't have happened to a nicer guy," they agreed. A couple of sadists, I thought, as they obviously enjoyed the story of my trauma of the past 24 hours.

THE LAST OF OLD ROOSTER

George W. Morey

I well remember one trip with Hugh White in 1943. It was late in November and we were moving the pack stock to winter pasture at the Al Powers Ranch on the Fort Orford District in Oregon. Our starting place was the Redwood Ranger Station. There were 60 pack animals besides our five saddle horses. Our route was down the Illinois River to Agness. The first day was without incident and we camped at Briggs Creek. During the night a southwester swept in from the coast with gale force winds and much rain. We only made 11 miles that day. We spent the night at Bald Mountain, trying to sleep in the old "prune dryer type" lookout building. We were glad to be on our way at the streak of day in that driving wind and rain.

By the time we arrived at Silver Creek all of the small streams, as well as the Illinois River were at flood stage. The water was about three feet over the Silver Creek low water bridge. All of the mules followed the leader across but when an old pack horse named Rooster got about halfway over, he made a ninety degree turn and stepped out into that raging current. In about two minutes he was out in the middle of the Illinois River and going full speed ahead. We got to see him once more about one half mile down stream but by then he was going end over end. It turned out to be the last we ever saw of Rooster.

FADED HOOFPRINTS IN
THE SANDS OF TIME

Bruce Barron

When I joined the Forest Service in the early 1940s, the Forest Service was still using horses and mules for riding and packing into the "back country." On many of the ranger districts, horse trailers and stock trucks were scarce, so horses were often lead to the job site trotting behind the pickup tethered by a long halter rope. One absentminded "cowboy" started leading a horse out of the fenced in ranger headquarters at Mt. Hebron. All of a sudden he felt a tug on the rope. Like Pegasus, the horse made a giant leap and landed out in front of. his vehicle. It was then that the "cowboy" realized he had driven across the steel rails of the cattle guard, and the horse had been smart and agile enough to vault over the guard rails to avoid the possibility of breaking his legs!

Mules are often referred to as being stupid, however, there were a pair of mules on the Shasta Forest that were exceptionally well trained. The Black Butte Lookout north of Mt. Shasta city was accessible by a narrow serpentine trail that spiraled its way up this cone shaped mountain. When the lookout needed supplies, the pack mules were loaded with the necessary provisions and taken to the start of the trail at the base of the mountain. They were pointed up the trail and given a slap on the fanny. They would then proceed all the way up to the lookout tower (by themselves) where the provisions were unloaded. Conversely, they were turned around and headed back down the trail where they were picked up again by the packer later in the day.

The Forest Service met with a sad experience up in the Trinity area involving a big black pack mule called Midnight. They had leased the mule from a cooperative rancher who admonished the Forest Service employees with explicit instructions to "always lock the corral gates with a chain" since this mule had an uncanny ability to open any kind of a gate latch, no matter how complicated. It wasn't long before a Forest Service employee got in a hurry and failed to properly secure the gate. That night old Midnight picked the lock and decided to head for home. It was a dark night, he was black and the road was narrow. A car came around a curve in the road, killed the mule and caused some fatal injuries to the vehicle occupants.

There was a big battle in the courts as to who should pay for the tort claims. The Forest Service tried to lay the blame on the rancher and his mule, but lost the case and was held liable for the damages because the rancher had given such thorough warnings on the mules proclivity for opening gates.

HOW TO BRIDLE A (ARMY) HORSE

Robert W. Cermak

Coalie was involved in another episode not long before his demise. One weekend Assistant Ranger Gene Murphy had some visitors who became excited when they learned that there were horses in our barn at the ranger station. All of them went down and admired the horses, and of course, wanted to ride them. Gene was reluctant since he was no better a horseman than I but he found a bridle and saddle in the tack room and got in the corral with Coalie to equip him. Now Coalie was a tall horse. Every time Gene tried to bridle him he would toss his head up. Otherwise he stood quietly just playing his game to Gene's increasing frustration. Finally, Gene remembered that my wife Ethel loved horses and knew how to manage them. He trudged up to our house and asked her for help. She agreed and went down to the barn with him. Now, Ethel is normally mild-mannered and is not noted for coarse language. But there she was, all five feet of her alongside that tall horse. She hoisted the bridle and Coalie hoisted his head. Again she lifted the bridle and again Coalie lifted his head. Fire in her eye, she grabbed his mane gave it a hard jerk and said, "Get your head down here, you sonovabitch!" Coalie's head dropped as if on an express elevator and Ethel hung the bridle on him with no more trouble. She turned to Gene, pointed to the U.S. brand on Coalie's hip and said, "Coalie was an Army horse. You just have to talk their language."

EARLY DAYS

Grover C. Blake

As I sit here in my easy chair reminiscing, my mind wanders back to the problems of the men who manned the Forest

Service during the years immediately following the creation of the national forests.

Perhaps the major headache endured by the early day forest ranger was straying saddle and pack horses. Don't tell me they were merely dumb brutes. These animals were plenty smart. They could dream up more ways to outwit their owners than any animal with which it has been my privilege to associate. They soon learned to manipulate a pair of hobbles until they practically lost their effectiveness. The hobbles, that is. They could fill up on the choice pasturage upon which they were placed, then when the night was dark and all was quiet and the ranger soundly sleeping, they would sneak away to find a hiding place in some far away rendezvous. Then next day, while the ranger owner sought their whereabouts, they would stand quietly in a secret nook, being careful not to move the head and sound the bell, meanwhile giving us the well-known "horse laugh." The poet refers to the horse as a "trusty steed" and I agree to a certain extent for I still love a good horse and think fondly of those who served me well. I also remember some of those of the early Forest Service as "tricky varmints."

Pasture fences were so scarce and so badly needed in those early days and we obtained them so slowly as horse hunting continued to occupy so much of our valuable time. It was a great relief when this problem was eventually overcome. On my district on the old Deschutes (then Ochoco) was a beautiful little meadow known as Carroll Camp, only a half mile or so from the summit of Mt. Pisgah. A nice and convenient place to camp with oodles of lush meadow grass. Nevertheless, our horses did not seem to like the place and would steal away at the first opportunity. I tried to get some material for fence making but improvement money came so slowly and the need was so great that we were obliged to do the best we could with what we had. About 1912, an idea came to me as how to obtain fencing material for a pasture at Carroll Camp. Over at the Trout Creek Guard Station, where I had been counting sheep into the forest each spring for several years, was a pasture enclosed with four barbed wires. It occurred to me that three wires were adequate for that pasture so I proposed to Forest Supervisor

Homer Ross that I be authorized to remove the bottom wire from the horse pasture and pack it on my pack horse to Carroll Camp as a starter for a fence at that place.

Homer approved and told me about two spools of wire left over from a fence building job at Derr Meadows some 15 miles southeasterly from Carroll Camp. My spirits perked up. I saw an opportunity to obtain a pasture fence without money, only work. I went to Trout Creek, removed the bottom wire from the pasture, rolled it into 20 or 30 pound rolls and packed it some 20 miles to Carroll Camp, then to Derr Meadows for the two spools of new wire. Then I made posts and set them and eventually a three wire fence developed around a small patch of rich meadow grass. Thereafter, the ranger or guard slept peacefully in the knowledge that he would wake up and find his horses in camp.

TWO MULES FOR TINY

Don Bauer

In the early years of the San Bernardino Forest there was an excellent lookout on Tahquitz Peak named Tiny Kemp. He had a very good sense of humor, was very jovial and served as a cook in fire camps. Tiny weighed 380 pounds. It took two mules to pack him up to the lookout each year. One would haul him about 100 or 200 yards and then he would switch to the other.

TWO LAUNCHINGS OF ED CLIFF

M.M. "Red" Nelson

In 1962, Ed Cliff became Chief of the Forest Service. It was only a few weeks after John Glenn had made his famous trip into space. A family meeting was held in the USDA auditorium which I&E promoted as a "Launching of the New Chief." They even had a dummy rocketship on the stage. Some of us were called upon to say a few words. I thought it might be a good time to say that this was not the first time Ed Cliff had been launched; and tell the story of the first launching.

In the late 1930s, one of our horses at the Redwood Remount Station was a beautiful pinto. His name was Agate. He was not a stallion, and really not a gelding either. That was because he had been "cut proud." We called him an "original." As such, he was kind of a nuisance. If in a corral with geldings he was always fighting with them. If in a corral with mares his stallion instinct became pronounced. But, he was a good strong horse so my packers and I decided he would be better useful as a saddle horse rather than being used in a pack string. They broke him to ride.

When Ed Cliff came to the Siskiyou as forest supervisor he needed a saddle horse to get around in that unroaded forest. He chose the beautiful Agate even though he had not been fully broken and tended to buck now and then. It became common knowledge that Agate would unload his boss, the supervisor, now and then on a cold morning or early in the spring.

On a back country inspection trip Ed was making with Ranger Boyd Rasmussen they had been gone a week and Agate had behaved fine. On their last day as they headed toward the Powers Ranger Station, Boyd commented to Ed something like, "I am not going to be satisfied until I see Agate buck you off." Well, they had not gone far and were riding a steep trail around a mountainside with a cover of thornbush, when sure enough Agate launched Supervisor Ed Cliff high into the air and down the hill into the thornbush. As you can expect, there was one mad supervisor climbing out of the brush patch and accusing his ranger of having jogged Agate with a stick to cause the bucking. Boyd steadfastly denied it for many years. Good thing he did for he was perhaps closest he had ever come to being demoted or fired.

When Chief Cliff took the podium he told the story in greater detail. Also, how he enjoyed that horse Agate, and had him transferred to the Fremont Forest when he moved to Lakeview to be Forest Supervisor. Agate still had his game at bucking but

Ed did not mind because Agate was still a fine, beautiful, strong horse and also made a good show in local parades. (Probably the local Lakeview people were like Boyd and looked forward to seeing a contest between Ed and Agate.) The regional safety officer, however, considered Agate as a safety hazard and recommended disposal. Ed refused, but it is said that when Ed left for Region 4, the new Supervisor Larry Mays, could not stand the pressure from the safety officer. That was the end of Agate's Forest Service career.

It is also understood in later years, Boyd did admit that all he had done was toss a small pebble that happened to land under Agate's tail. And that ends this tale!

THE HARMONICA

Gary Munsey

In the summer of 1959, I was assigned as part of the Sierra NF's CFI (continuous forest inventory) crew. Basically we were cruising timber using fixed plots. There were three of us who were pretty much on our own for the summer, camping out for days at a time and planning our cruise strips so that we would end the day at some high country lake.

We were initially packed in from the Wishon Reservoir area to Crown Valley by a pack string. The three of us rode horses with the string. I had always envisioned riding in the wilderness and playing my harmonica as I had watched many cowboys do at the movies when I was younger, a product of two back-to-back "oaters" per week at the 25 cent matinee.

Well, the ride went well until I pulled out my harmonica and started to play. My horse's response to the music was to stop dead in his tracks and slowly turn his head to look at me as if to say, "what the hell was that?" I tried this several times en route to Crown Valley only to have the horse react in the same manner. The result was that I was about an hour behind the rest of the crew by the time I rode into Crown Valley.

AN OREGON MULE STORY

Ira E. Jones

After I was married in 1912, I asked Supervisor Henry Ireland to give me a ranger district (both the North Powder and the Sumpter Districts were vacant). He said, "Yes, how would you like the Sumpter District?" I really wanted the North Powder District as Sumpter was the supervisor's headquarters and I was too handy and was sent out on jobs, but I said OK.

In 1913, Supervisor Ireland, who had been master of the Sumpter Masonic Lodge, was asked to conduct a funeral at Audry, about 30 miles south. We had a team of young and partly broken mules. We thought this would be a good trip for them so we had a two-seated hack, hitched them up and started off. The front seat was set high up and the brake was worked from it. I drove and Henry Ireland worked the brake. R. M. Evans and Harry Wilson (a local jeweler) rode in the back seat.

We made it all right until we reached the top of the Whitney Hill and started down. Henry shoved the brake handle forward but it jabbed the mule in his rump and away they went. It was about two miles to the bottom of the hill. Every attempt to use the brake only made them go faster. The road was narrow and crooked, but fortunately, it was early morning and we met no one. We made the bottom and after half a mile got them slowed down but we had lost our hats.

We made the rest of the trip OK. On the way back we gave a ride to a man who had been fishing in Camp Creek. When we stopped to let him off at the Whitney Mill, one of the single trees dropped off. The mule gave a jump, the tongue dropped down, and away they went again. After a short distance the tongue ran into the ground and broke. We all jumped out. I got mixed up with the lines and was dragged 30 or 40 feet before I got loose. Aside from ruining a suit and losing some skin, I came out all right. The team broke loose, ran into the slab pile at Whitney and stopped.

INSTRUCTIONS WITH NO BLUEPRINTS

Tom Wintringham

Working for the Forest Service entailed many functions, not the least of which was range management. This involved working with cattlemen, inspecting the range, counting cattle and probably the most odd job of all was estimating the deer population.

The Oak Knoll District of the Klamath Forest had its share of range jobs. Oak Knoll had its share of horses. We saw quite a bit of Al Crebbin and Harry Taylor. I remember one time when we, Mark Petty and I, rode with Al and Harry. Al had a beautiful little horse that he dearly loved. Al was the picture of a cowboy astride this little horse. But Al had to carry a stick in order for the two of them to get along. The horse had the habit of refusing to let Al remount after we had all dismounted to examine a transect or whatever. Al would put his foot in the stirrup and the horse would whirl in the opposite direction so that Al could not get mounted.

A few minutes of the stick, "horsemen's" language and lots of dust, Al would once again be astride his docile mount, a picture of the perfect cowboy. Then we would stop again. Mercy, it wasn't a pretty picture.

The Oak Knoll horses were usually of one mind. When they saw someone with a halter they knew one of them was going to get ridden that day. As far as they were concerned that was a bunch of nonsense. You couldn't catch one by yourself. Our tactic was, therefore, to get everyone before they left the station to form a skirmish line across the pasture and slowly work the horses into a corner. At this point the horses all became friendly with their nuzzling and snorting and acted as if the past forty-five minutes had been some kind of a game. Of course, by that time you were all sweaty and mad as hell. But they didn't care because now they were all buddy-buddy.

We had one horse named Laddie. He was a Tennessee walking horse. These horses are named for their comfortable gait. This was Mark Petty's horse. Unfortunately, Laddie had a congenital defect in that every once in a while his hind end would falter. Come to find out he was known to occasionally fall down.

Before we finally got rid of him, I had occasion to take him to the veterinarian in Yreka because the horse seemed to be "off his feed." The vet examined Laddie quite thoroughly and decided that he needed a stool sample. Well, there is only one way to get a stool sample and you should have seen the surprised look on Laddie's face as he looked over his shoulder to see what was going on back there!

I took Laddie back to Oak Knoll to await the results of the test and the vet's diagnosis. Meanwhile, the engineers needed a horse for some reason and Ed Jereb came and borrowed Laddie for a few days. While Laddie was gone, the vet called and said that he needed a fresh stool sample and to bring Laddie into town. This was too good to pass up so I wrote out very detailed instructions to Ed about getting subject specimen and to take it to Yreka as soon as possible. Since Ed was on the Seiad District, I knew that a few days would pass before I would hear about this.

Laddie returned to Oak Knoll none the worse for wear. In the trailer was a bale of hay with a note. The note said: "Here's a bale of hay. Get your own goddamn sample!"

A HORSE NAMED DOOFUS

Pat Harrison

OK, what's a horse named Doofus got to do with the national forests?

Actually, not all that much. Doofus did, however, get his big start as a rental to the Forest Service's wilderness program out of Pinedale, Wyoming, back in 1970. At the time, I was getting my "big start" as a fledging wilderness ranger. We were both attending a training school held at a dude ranch (this was before "guest ranch" was the politically correct term).

I'd barely noticed this short-coupled Appaloosa until, after several days of riding lessons in small corrals, all the assembled rookie wilderness rangers were supposed to run their oat-burning buddies through their paces in a big pasture. The instructor looked critically on. The pasture in question hadn't really recovered from several days of rain. Water stood six inches deep in the lower spots.

After I'd survived my go at it, the last horse in line was urged out into the field. We could all see some cheap entertainment was in store. A medium sized Appaloosa gelding was taking short little crow-hoppish steps, to the dismay of a very green trainee. Quick like, the critter was blazing across the field, homing in on the wet end of the pasture. When the water was hock deep, he set the brakes. The rider, observing elemental laws of physics, continued onward. He inscribed a nearly flat trajectory through the air, hit the shallow water at a slight angle and sorta skipped like a flat stone as he expended his kenetic energy. The horse went to grazing the swamp grass.

The rider went on to be nicknamed "Froggy" for the rest of his Forest Service career, which wasn't especially long. He quit the outfit after a few years, went into environmental consulting, and made a good living charging the Forest Service an arm and a leg for doing specialized environmental paperwork. I honestly believe that each dollar was gained in direct retribution for the indignity this horse had inflicted upon him.

But I degress. I was so impressed by this speckle-rumped nag that I sought him out to be my riding animal for the balance of the long summer season up in the Wind River. I figured he was lively enough (just ask Froggy) to step right along.

The first person I met ("contacted," in government-speak) was a very nice looking young lady, reading a book as she sat on a boulder beside the trail. Anxious to make a good impression, I stepped smartly off my critter and commenced to make rangerly remarks. About this time the horse carefully, but firmly, stepped down on my foot.

During the ensuing struggle involving the removal of my foot from under the hoof, the young lady sat entranced, perhaps having never heard such words from a government employee before.

Old spotted-butt got called Doofus after that, a North Carolina term for someone who really doesn't know what's going on. For some reason, I'd heard that term a lot, and thought I'd share it with my trusty mount.

Ol' Doof proved to be a pretty good mount that summer. He still had a thing about pond weed and sedge, though. He was plumb good about not straying far from camp overnight. In the morning all you had to do was walk to the nearest shallow pothole, and there would be Doofus, knee deep in cold water, grazing contentedly on the water grass. I suspect he had a little moose in his family tree.

When the summer was over, I didn't want to part with him, so I bought Doofus from the ranch that had leased him to the Forest Service. He put in a couple of years with me, working at a dude—er, guest ranch. The same national forest land I'd ridden Doofus through as a wilderness ranger also was the hinterland of this guest ranch, providing a great recreational experience to hundreds of people each year. Doofus' unerring ability to step on my foot also provided coarse entertainment to many of the dudes and fall hunters, not to mention a small fortune to a podiatrist.

I am happy to report that Doofus, after years of faithful service, ended his days in the high grass of northern California, as a pampered pet on my folks' place

But, getting back to the original question, what does this horse have to do with the Forest Service? I guess my not-too-profound point is that the national forest, providing us with everything from lumber, forage and clean water, can also provide us with another natural resource—good memories. Although memories might not stack up as one of the classic "multiple uses," I like to think that our national forests have allowed more than a few of us to acquire fond memories, whether from the back of a good horse, or just enjoying a camping trip with the family. Without all that unspoiled national forest land to ride around in, I might never have made the acquaintance of Doofus—and my memories. And my podiatrist would have been poorer as a result.

MULES

Harry J. Taylor

Anyone who has ever worked with pack and saddle stock ultimately has had to contend with that sure-footed creature, the mule. Mules are really not the "dumb" animals that they are so often described. Mules are not only intelligent, they are smart, dependable, sometimes gentle, sometimes mean, sometimes tricky, but always patient. As Al Crebbin used to say, "A mule will wait twenty years to kick you."

My experiences have been with the ones with the tricky streak in them. The first tricky one I had to work with was on the Modoc NF. Fittingly enough, he was named Modoc.

On the Modoc, my one ton Chevy pickup was outfitted with a stock rack, complete with manger and a wind screen. Our horses and mules were trained to jump into the bed of the pickup and then back down, or halfway fall out when unloading.

One day I was hauling the mule Modoc to the south end of the district (Surprise Valley Ranger District) down highway 395. As the mule and I traveled along, I noticed that as people drove by or passed us, they kept looking up at the front of the pickup. After a few miles of this, my curiosity got the best of me, so I figured I had better stop to see if there was anything unusual going on.

On the Modoc, when we hauled our horses or mules in our pickups, most often we did not tie them in with the halter rope, leaving them the freedom to eat their oats and hay. On this particular trip the mule took the liberty of putting his front feet into the manger, then standing on his hind legs. He was peacefully surveying the countryside as we drove along. If his ears had not been so long, one might have thought Modoc was a big dog. Ol' Modoc may not have been tricky on this occasion but he was just a bit on the unusual side.

Another memorable mule was Sarah on the Klamath NF. During the time we were working on range surveys in the Marble Mountain Wilderness, Bob Buttery the range technician had this little mule to carry his food and belongings while he was out. I only made one trip with this mule and it did not take her long to figure out that I was a greenhorn as far as she was concerned.

Most of the mules on the Klamath were trained to follow a horse, so most of the time the lead rope or halter rope was just tied to the pack and the mules were more or less allowed to roam free. Sometimes the mules would follow closely; at other times they would dawdle along until the horses were out of sight, then they would start trotting to catch up.

On the first trip I took with Buttery and Sarah, Buttery decided that he wanted to look at some feature off the trail a bit, so he asked me to continue on down the trail with Sarah.

This I proceeded to do, looking back now and then to see if Sarah was following. After riding a mile or so, I looked back for Sarah, but she was nowhere in sight. I waited a few minutes but still no Sarah, so I decided I had better go back and check. A short ways back I spotted Sarah but she wasn't jauntily trotting down the trail to catch up; she was laying down on her side, pack and all. As I rode up, she raised her head and rolled back her eyeballs. I just knew she was dying. Seeing her in such a sad shape, I jumped off of my horse and started to loosen the pack ropes to make her more comfortable.

Before I could get every rope undone, Bob came riding up. He just started to laugh when he saw what was happening. I don't remember Bob's exact words but in essence he said, "Sarah gotcha." Apparently, Sarah's little trick of "lying down on the job" was a trick on all inexperienced and uninitiated. Bob just pulled on her halter rope and she jumped right up, none the worse for the experience. She surely was a good actress and fooled me 'cause I just knew she was dying.

UP A TREE WITHOUT A SADDLE

Grover C. Blake

On July 3, 1920, on the Ochoco National Forest, I witnessed what I believe to be the most unusual of all the unusual spectacles of my career. I saw it with my own eyes and still I don't believe it, so I will not expect the readers of this tale to believe it either. I found a full grown horse fast in the forks of a tree.

Virgil Allison, foreman for Elliott, Scoggins & Wolfe, road contractors, and his wife were riding with me along the Vowell Trail near the summit of the mountain when we saw this horse in the tree not far from the trail. He was an unbroken range horse about three or four years old and probably weighed about 1,100 pounds. The tree forked about two feet from the ground and the spread at six feet was not more than 15 inches. The hind feet of the horse were on the ground on one side while the head, neck and shoulders were on the opposite side of the tree with the front feet about four feet from the ground. His body was wedged between the forks until he was pinched as tight as it was possible for him to get. His struggles had worn all the hair and most of the skin off his sides where they contacted the tree.

He tried to fight us when we came near. I took the axe off our pack horse and we started to chop off the smaller fork, about 16 inches in diameter. While we were so engaged, another man, Mr. Bill Peterson, came along and assisted. When the horse was finally released he was in a bad way and very wobbly. He was able to keep on his feet, however, and soon wobbled away without saying "thank you." No doubt he had been fast in the tree for at least two or three days. The question that bothered us was, "How did he get there?" The tree stood alone in an opening of considerable size and the only theory I could advance was that a bunch of range horses were standing in the shade of the tree, fighting flies as they would likely be doing at this time of year and started fighting each other and this horse was cornered somehow and jumped at the only opening he could see. It took a tremendous leap to get his body high enough to get between the forks of this tree. However, it may have happened some other way, I do not know. I have always regretted that we did not have a camera on that day of all days as I realize I need proof.

TWO HORSES

Joe Ely

My second ranger job was way back in the canyons of the American River country. Guerdon Ellis, the forest supervisor over in Nevada City was my boss. Soon after I arrived, he told me to get a horse so I could properly attend to ranger district affairs in the back country and other roadless areas.

So I came up with a big, black horse. He was a sturdy fellow, somewhat along the lines of a brewery wagon horse and suited my needs just fine. I must concede that his only gait was a walk, but he sure was strong. I would put my coffee pot, frying pan and groceries in one barley sack and grain in another. All that was needed was to hang the sacks over the horse's neck, ahead of the pommel and off we would go, clattering down the trail for a few day's or a week's work.

Horse and I were getting the work done all right. We were checking and measuring the work of the trail crew and the fence contractor and making our range measurements and appraisals. The only item I had overlooked was Guerdon Ellis.

Many of you remember that Guerdon was a spit and polish sort of fellow and he expected his rangers to be the same. His hat always had a jaunty angle and there was a twinkle in his eye. He rode a neat little mare and always kept her mane and fetlocks neatly trimmed.

So one day he was out checking on his American River ranger. His little mare was trotting up the trail with her neatly picked tail swishing crisply from side to side. And, of course, her rider had on a clean shirt, nice snug cowboy pants and sat lightly in the saddle, the very picture of an alert executive on a horse.

As he topped the ridge, what did he see? It was this big, old black horse with a barley sack on the side with the kitchenware clattering at every step. And on top sits the ranger with his badge pinned to a pair of bib overalls, his axe and bed roll tied behind the saddle. Well, there was a long, long discussion right there and a few changes were decided . . . .

So when the boss got back to Nevada City, he called up Ranger Pete Land over at Sierraville. "Pete," he said, "Go over into Nevada and get a good spirited saddle horse for Joe. Then he phoned me and told me what he had done and that I best get a pack saddle and pack bags for horse.

Well, as you know, Pete was a fine ranger and an excellent judge of saddle stock. I'm sure he had no inclinations toward being bloodthirsty. Let's just say he took the boss at his word and remember the word was "spirited."

Nevada horse stood still while I saddled him and got on. Then he threw me over the corral fence. Nevada horse just simply had to buck me off every morning. Then I would get back on and we would go about our day's work without further incident. When this was later reported to Pete, he couldn't understand it. He knew the horse well and insisted that a little girl had ridden him to school every day. Those little girls over in Nevada must be really something.

Guerdon also gave me my second lesson in horsemanship. We were riding one of the high country allotments and stopped in a green meadow to have a smoke. Guerdon said, "Now, you must be casual about horsemanship. Never tense up, because the horse will sense it. Take it easy, relax and do what you like; it doesn't matter what the horse likes, you are the boss." I wasn't quite sure that this was the whole story but I figured we'd find out pretty soon.

"Your back is sort of tired," the boss noted, "So hang one leg across the pommel and relax." I did and it felt good. "Now, get that folded map out of your shirt pocket." I did. "Now, unfold it and shake it out so you can study it."

I broke the tops out of a couple of lodgepole pines on my way to the ground.

TRAVELS WITH FOUR DONKEYS

C. P. Cronk

This installment deals with a unique feature of the Siuslaw National Forest in 1910-1911—the use of donkeys for packing. Supervisor Cahoon promoted their use in those days of almost no roads, few trails and little pasturage.

On a rainy day about November 1, 1910, I made the acquaintance of two of my traveling companions, the mother, May, and the daughter, Fanny. We started out of Eugene in style and ease, I riding May; Fanny trailing with my belongings stowed in panniers. This was my first acquaintance with the species. I found it highly educational; their actions unpredictable. After a few uneventful miles we came to a point where, due to rain, a waterfall was coming over the cliff from which the road was carved and landing in the middle of the roadway. The burros balked. Finally I pulled Fanny through; May refused to budge. There was nothing to tie Fanny to. The moment I dropped her halter rope she trotted back to her mother, paying no attention to the waterfall she had to go under again. Next I tried to pull May through the waterfall. By putting a half hitch around her nose and pulling steadily on it until she had to move to get a breath of air, I managed to move her about 10 feet at a time. As soon as she got through the waterfall, she became her docile self again and daughter Fanny dutifully followed her. Thus was completed the first of many lessons I was to learn regarding burros.

We continued on toward the coast as far as Indian Creek. Here I picked up the rest of the party. Vic, the biggest and most even tempered of our burros, and Bubbles, the jackass, smartest and smallest. These two had been used during the past field season to pack supplies to the trail along the backbone of the Coast Range from near Mapleton on the Siuslaw River to near Waldport on the Alsea River.

All burros seem to have a sense of humor. Unless led by a horse or bell mule, they delight in exploring all side trails to the discomfort of their driver. Bubbles had learned that he would be given candy if he walked up the steps of the store in Florence.

One of the trail crew told a story on Supervisor Cahoon. When approaching the camp riding Bubbles quite properly, they reached a mud puddle when the burro lowered his head to the ground and the supervisor slid off into the puddle, to the merriment of the crew assembled at the end of the day.

From the end of the ridge trail at the Corvallis-Waldport Road we turned east, there being then no road along the coast. From Corvallis we went north to Sheridan and along the road to Willamina to Dolph and Hebo, then up the mountain to the ranger station. This was approximately 225 miles and 22 days from Eugene. Because the night stops were more or less routine, only one stands out. I discovered that in the Willamette Valley, east over the Coast Range from the Siuslaw National Forest, a ranger was still an oddity. A bit north of Corvallis, I inquired at a house if I might put the burros in a fenced pasture I had noticed. There was hesitancy, but finally it was decided that the burros could be taken care of and I could sleep in the barn and get supper and breakfast. After supper the boys of the family brought out copies of "Youths' Companion" to show me a series of articles on the forest ranger and to ask questions about the life of a ranger. A couple of hours later, as I asked the man of the house if he would give me a call as he went out to the barn in the morning, he said, "If you don't mind sleeping with the boys, we can put you up in the house." I had talked myself into a bed.

The burros were used to pack supplies to the planting crew on Mt. Hebo during the winter of 1910-1911, but I had little to do with them as I was busy elsewhere. It is my recollection that burros, because of their thin skin and consequent tendency to get saddle sores in wet weather and their small hoofs which sank in the mud, did not prove as satisfactory as horses or mules in this region of high rainfall. I did use the burros during the summer and my last job on the Siuslaw Forest was to deliver Fanny and May to Ranger Durbin near Waldport. On September 14, my record shows it was "rainy" as I took the two donkeys down to the Hebo store, where, beside my duffel, I loaded on a mile of telephone wire, 25 brackets, 25 insulators and an extension bell. We stopped at Neskowin for the night, 18 miles. On the second day we left one coil of wire on the way up Neskowin, or Slab Creek and the rest in the Salmon River Valley, where adjoining ranchers were to erect the line. This time we stuck to the road, as on a previous trip to our sorrow, we had taken the shortcut foot trail through second growth hemlock over the ridge between the two streams. There, one of the burros went off the trail, up to her belly in mud from which she couldn't be extricated until I removed the entire load. Even then, it took much persuading and pulling to get her to exert herself to get onto solid ground again where she could be reloaded.

From Rose Lodge on Salmon River, we went up over the ridge and down the Schooner Creek Trail to Taft. It was on this trail, up from Rose Lodge, that I first met the 12 year old and 10 year old Pylkanen sisters (generally known by the American name they chose—Adams). The older girl had a 50 pound sack of flour on her back to pack up the seven miles to the family homestead. Another time when I passed that way, the two young ladies were "manning" a crosscut saw to replenish the fuel supply.

Having delivered all the telephone equipment, we had only my pack from now on. I got someone to row us across Schooner Creek trailing two unwilling burros behind. At Drift Creek and the Siletz River the performance was repeated. The record for this day shows "Sunday, September 17, 6 a.m. to 3 p.m., 19 miles and weather CLEAR."

Putting up at Newport, in the morning we ferried across Yaquina Bay. At Beaver Creek, I phoned Ranger Durbin. He took the Wald-Newport stage along the beach, and upon his arrival took a picture of me, arms around the necks of Fanny and May. I turned the donkeys over to him, thus completing my last act as assistant ranger on the Siuslaw. I took his place on the stage en route to Newport and Eugene.

GRABBING LEATHER

Bob Bjornsen

It was one of those bad yellow jacket summers on the Wallowa-Whitman. The critters were everywhere in the woods—neither man nor beast were safe from their stings.

Tom Griffith, Baker Assistant Ranger, and I were working our way horseback up Indian Creek below Anthony Lakes, when his horse stepped on a jacket's nest and all hell broke loose!

We were on a sidling hill when they started their rampage. Tom frantically tried to stay in the saddle as the "Speed" horse turned every way but loose to avoid the stings. Have you ever tried to stay with a bucking horse, head pointed downhill while swatting yellow jackets?

"Turn his head uphill," I cried, sitting calmly astride my "Smokey" horse as if such a feat were possible. About that time the yellow jackets hit me and I was grabbing leather too. Miraculously, we both stayed aboard our horses but not because of our skill at bronco busting.

We got out of there fast and found a safe spot where we rubbed our horses down, all the while dabbing ourselves and the horses with spirits of ammonia, a great remedy for neutralizing bee stings.

Our travails weren't over yet. As we reached a meadow near the ridge, it started to rain hard. The meadow soon became a sheet of water and we found ourselves in the middle feeling our way towards solid ground. Next "Smokey" went down in a bog to his hocks, pitching me into the mud and slime. I hollered to Tom to stop on solid ground until we could find our way out.

Next thing we knew, "Smokey" was on his back, legs in the air, gasping for breath and not responding to our trying to right him. This called for quick action because a horse doesn't last long with his innards pressing against his lungs. Somewhere I'd heard that a stick thrust in a horse's anus would cause a violent response—I guess it would with humans too!

I quickly found a smooth stick, and with Tom holding his tail aside, did the job. That horse did a 180 degree flip and in a split second landed on solid ground with all four feet planted! The rest of the tale was anticlimatic as we made our way safely to solid ground.

THE REMOUNT STATION

M. M. "Red" Nelson

In the mid-1930s, the Forest Service in much of the West, found that supplying fire camps on large back country fires was becoming a problem because the number of pack strings that might be rented for use on fires was becoming fewer and fewer. The answer was for the Forest Service to maintain some remount stations so as to be sure to have pack animals to go on large fires. Region 1 out of Missoula, Montana, established a remount station with brood mares and jacks and raised mules for their supply of remount pack animals. Later in the 1940s, their mule production was great enough so that they were even supplying mules for some ranger stations in Oregon. We used mules from such a shipment on the Umpqua NF. Region 6 decided to establish a remount station on the Siskiyou NF for use in the Northwest. In 1935, or spring of 1936, Ken Blair, the Redwood ranger, and Frank Folsom of the regional office made a horse buying trip to eastern Oregon for animals to establish the remount. I know it was in operation in 1936 because, as an assistant ranger, I was assigned as service chief on the large Sandy Fire (one of many being handled by the FS during the late fall conflagration situation). We determined that we needed to establish a fire camp a good distance back from any road. Otto Lindh was division boss in charge of that camp. My responsibility was to keep the camp supplied. I heard about the new remount station and ordered packers and pack animals to pack to Otto's camp. A couple of months later, I was made ranger with responsibility for the remount station.

It was then that I began to really learn about that remount. The animals bought for it were, in general, range horses and had not been broken to carry a pack. The remount packers had a big job just breaking horses. Some were impossible to break, so the packers and I were allowed to "horse trade," always trying to upgrade the pack strings. That was in the days before the Siskiyou rated an administrative officer on the staff. Later, Ernie Shank was assigned in such a job and discovered in the manual that "horse trading" was not allowed without getting out bids and other paper work that made it not worthwhile. By that time, however, we had a pretty good string of working horses.

When I took over the ranger district, I also assumed considerable responsibility for horses and mules! I had my district string of seven or eight mules, plus saddle horses and also five or six burros used with trail maintenance crews. I also had full responsibility for the regional remount station. I had about 65 head of horses maintained at my ranger station for use in packing on fires any place in the Northwest (also used some in No. California). In addition, each fall all of the string of mules and the saddle horses from the other five ranger districts were assembled at my ranger station. I was responsible for getting winter pasture for the hole herd, about 110 head. We usually got the pasture in the Medford area and drove the whole herd to the pasture and returned in the spring. It was a two day drive each way.

I recall one year when spring was late in coming and the rented winter pasture played out. We rented another pasture for a month but it was located nearly 40 miles away. One of my packers and a summer fire guard and I went over early one morning, caught us some riding animals and started the drive to the new pasture. The first 10 miles were at a full gallop. The route required crossing a ridge of mountains. As we neared the top of a logging road, the road divided into many branches and we had different horses taking different branches. It was a big roundup job before getting them headed down the other side on a narrow trail. It was well after dark and raining hard before we got them into the new pasture. Needless to say, part of me was too sore to comfortably sit down the next day. After returning the whole herd to my station in the spring, the other districts would come for their pack strings.

During my first year at the station, other improvements were made. The old standard ranger's barn was greatly extended on both ends, making a very large storage area for hay, and mangers divided by stall partitions were put in so that all the animals could be fed at the same time. We also built four pole corrals, one for each quarter of the barn. Also three large red pack animal hauling trucks were provided for use in sending pack strings to fire assignments. Special loading ramps were built to facilitate fast getaway.

There were many interesting experiences in operation of a remount. Pasturing the stock in winter was one already referred to. When at the station, the stock had to be fed twice a day. They ate a lot of hay in a season. I had to buy hay and some of that was done in the packer's "off season," meaning that I was the only one available for the unloading and stacking of the hay bales in the barn, a back breaking job! After each horse was broke to pack, they had to be shod before being used on the rocky trails. We hired a special horse shoer to help the packers with that job in the spring. Then it was up to the packers to replace shoes as needed. Horse shoeing went on for several weeks in the spring. Some horses did not like it and a special sling rig was used to hold up the horse and a special method used in tying up the flailing hind legs until the metal shoe could be heated in the forge, pounded out to fit the shape of the hoof and then nailed in place. Spring always had something interesting at the horse shoeing shed. If the animal had not yet been branded with the "US" that was also done at shoeing time while we had a fire going in the forge to heat the branding iron white hot. The bad odor of burning hair was common.

One year, we had a young jack burro and decided to try to raise a couple of mules using mares in our pack string. We built a special corral for the jack to keep him away from the jennie burros. We put mares in with him but he would have nothing to do with them. My packers claimed it was because he had previously been with jennies and liked them better. They could be right, for the next spring we did have a jennie come in foal with the cutest little burro colt you ever saw. In years after I had left the remount, it was reported that unexpectedly some of the mares in the remount did come in foal. That was a mystery until it was learned that one of the employees had been secretly experimenting with the use of artificial insemination—pretty new stuff in those days!

While I ran the remount station, the pack horses were used on many fires in all parts of the region. It was in days when dropping supplies from aircraft was just beginning and usually used only for those camps that had no trails near the camp. In 1938, we had one packer supply camp with 125 head of pack and saddle stock on the Illinois River. Use of pack animals was not without accident. I recall when one of our remount horses was killed when it fell over a cliff while packing to a fire on the Galice District. Later that year, when we had missing items in our annual inventory we usually said, "Lost when pack horse went over cliff." That was OK until someone in the office figured one horse couldn't possibly carry such a load.

BROWNIE: A HORSE OF ANOTHER COLOR

Russ Rogers

I would like to say a few words about Brownie. Brownie resided for almost 30 years at Brush Creek Ranger Station on the Plumas NF. Toward the end he mostly just stood around and did nothing. Brownie was a horse, the district ranger's horse.

I first became acquainted with Brownie in 1938, when I came to Brush Creek in a contingent of 50 newly enlisted CCC boys from Los Angeles. After two weeks of working on the road crew under Frank Church, Walt Graham and Jay Peterson, I was picked to work for the ranger in his fire warehouse. I hung axes and sharpened tools. Deene Stowell was the district ranger.

Deene would often ask me to go down to the corral and give Brownie some oats. I would do this and Brownie seemed to appreciate it. The time came when Deene needed to go to a ranger meeting in Quincy for three days. He asked me to feed Brownie while he was gone. Brownie liked oats so I gave him oats—lots of oats. (What did a kid from a beach town in Southern California know about feeding a horse?) In the afternoon of the third day, there were sounds like the firing of a shotgun coming from the vicinity of the corral. And then "whap," Brownie raced to the other side of the corral. This was repeated several times. It was then that I realized what had happened. Brownie had gas and I was responsible. Brownie did recover and I got smarter regarding the feeding of a horse.

I have known three people who, at different times, were district rangers at Brush Creek: Deene Stowell, Spike Slattery and Bill Turpin. None ever said that Brownie was a great horse.

I left in 1939, after a year at Brush Creek. On the last day, I gave Brownie some oats—but not too much. When I left, Brownie was standing in the corral. Years passed, nineteen years in fact. In 1958, I returned to Brush Creek as the TMA. On the first day, I wandered about the station trying to reconstruct the past. The CCC camp was gone except for the rec hall which was being used as a school. Pine and fir saplings were growing where the barracks had been. I walked down to the corral. There, in the middle of the corral, stood Brownie.

By then Brownie must have been at least 25 years old. He was seldom ridden. I would like to say that Brownie died peacefully of old age while eating oats, and that there was a solemn burial with a drum roll and a 21 gun salute. It didn't happen that way. About 1962, Brownie was sold to a guy in Chico who was in the business of buying old horses for reasons that I prefer only to surmise.

I know that Brownie was not a great horse. Secretariat he was not. There will never be a statue erected in honor of Brownie. But he was there every day for nearly 30 years. That is worth something. Happy grazing in horse heaven, Brownie, and eat all the oats that you like. Gas is no problem in horse heaven, or so I have been told.

BUSTER AND THE YELLOW BUCKET

Bob Irwin

About 1961, the ranger at Hat Creek on the Lassen acquired a new horse. It was a gelding named "Buster." He was young, spirited, and actually lived up to his name one day sometime later when he busted the ranger's ankle.

Shortly after he arrived, Buster developed physical problems. He couldn't walk well. The irritation caused him to start waddling like a duck, revolt at being saddled and getting downright mean if anybody tried to ride him.

The ranger called the local veterinarian to do an exam. The vet determined that the horse's private parts were in bad shape. There was crud and gunk inside the sheath of his penis that was quite irritating to the poor beast. He demonstrated the required cleansing technique after giving the horse a mild tranquilizer. He said to continue that process daily until the irritation was completely gone.

The ranger wrote a field purchase order for the vet showing that he had "cleansed Buster's prepuce" (the correct veterinary term). An SO purchasing clerk returned the FPO to the ranger with a speed memo asking for more details on exactly what services the Government received for this payment. The ranger's reply was, "He washed Buster's dick." There were no more requests for clarification.

I was timber management assistant at the time, but was given the daily follow-up task of cleaning Buster as part of the "other duties as assigned" portion of my job description.

The first treatment was not easy. I didn't have the vet's advantage of using a tranquilizer. The only tools I had were a rope, a clean towel, and a yellow bucket full of warm, soapy water. I had to get the ranger to help me the first time, and we finally roped Buster to the corral fence with one hind leg raised well off the ground. The second treatment went a little better; I only had to snub Buster's head to the fence. The third time I just dropped his halter rope for a "ground tie." After that, when I came up the road to the corral each evening carrying my towel and yellow bucket, Buster came to the gate to greet me! I felt fortunate that the routine only went on for a week or so, but I think Buster was disappointed!

One final note: Before this episode, Buster had always resisted loading in a trailer. Afterwards, all anyone had to do to get him to load was to put the yellow bucket up front in the trailer feed bin.

218

SOME OF EARLY FOREST SERVICE PERSONNEL

222

HUNTING
AND FISHING

TOUGH WORK, BUT THE
RANGER HAD TO DO IT

Dan B. Abraham

Range management was not a big part of the work on the Gold Beach District of the Siskiyou in the late 1950s. There were a few small cow allotments, mostly up on the high ridges where the timber and brush thinned enough to allow some grass to grow. The permittees were locals, mostly of the Agness area. Taking the cows into the back country at the start of the season and hunting them out of the brush in September was more of a tradition than it was a venture of profit. Those had to be tough cows, however tender their meat, in order to make a living in that rough country. They learned to eat brush, of which there was plenty.

At any rate, the range work was not a big deal, but it did provide the basis for the annual range inspection pack trip. By the marvelous magic of middle management manipulation, the trip always coincided with the prime part of buck season.

In those days we were beginning to build some timber sale roads into the coastal side of the district, but the interior was still wild and woolly. The only road in that part of the district was the old CCC road over the Coquille divide from Powers and down to the Rogue via Billings Greek and Illahee. At Agness the road crossed the Rogue on a five ton limit suspension bridge and went four miles up the Illinois to Oak Flat. Otherwise, travel was by trail or parachute, with little chance to go cross-country because of the heavy brush.

The pack and saddle stock were kept at Agness. The main trail to the high country east and south of Agness, where most of the range was, went up Snout Creek and climbed the ridge between Shasta Costa Creek and the north fork of Indigo Creek. It was a steep climb to the 5,000 foot high ridges around Squirrel Peak, Sugarloaf, Burnt Ridge and Fish Hook, because Agness is probably less than 150 feet above sea level. Fish Hook, about 15 trail miles from Agness, was the favored camp spot. There was a small meadow south and east of the abandoned lookout. The lookout spring was located near the meadow, and there was enough feed to keep the stock two or three days.

Late one October day George Morey, the veteran district assistant; Cy Wood, the born and raised at Agness packer and I, the bushy-tailed young ranger, pulled into the meadow and set up camp. The sun was down already behind Fish Hook ridge, but I was eager to try my luck before dark. I worked my way up through the brush almost to the lookout to where a sharp ridge ran down to the north. The ridge was covered with stunted trees, thick enough so that no brush grew under them. I heard some rocks rattle and looked down the ridge. There was a running buck, going away from me down the ridge and about to disappear over the nose of the ridge to the west. It was twilight under the trees, but I could see plenty of horns. The .30-.30 came up of its own accord, and a shot snapped off. The buck went out of sight around the nose of the ridge.

I scrambled up over the ridge also, hoping to get another shot at him as he came in view below me on the west side. Sure enough, there he was, standing and looking at me over his shoulder. Ka-pow! Down he went. By that time I was out of breath and shaking with buck fever but managed to get down the ridge to him in short order. It was a nice three point, shot through the shoulder.

I dressed him out and propped the carcass up against a tree. It was getting dark by then, so I climbed back up the west side of the ridge, almost to the lookout, then followed the lookout water trail down to the camp.

It was dark by the time I got to camp and I was pooped. I had the heart and liver of the buck in a bandanna, tied to my belt, so I was pretty proud of myself; a happy hunter. Soon we were feasting on strips of liver and heart along with slices of spuds with the skins on, fried in deep bacon fat. Could any gourmand ask for better? We thought not.

Next morning, Cy and I led one mule back up the mountain to retrieve the carcass. When we got to the north ridge I retraced my route of the night before, over and down the west side. Cy took the mule down the west side, planning to cross over at about the level where the buck had crossed, as it was easier going for the mule.

I arrived at the carcass and found it in good order, well chilled from the high elevation night air. I sat awhile and waited for Cy. When he did not show up I went around the brow of the ridge to where I knew he had to be. There he was, sitting by another carcass, another three point which was not dressed out! Cy was laughing and scratching his head at the same time. The great white hunter had shot the hind-most of a pair of bucks as they ran around the nose of the ridge, then managed to scramble over and shoot the fore-most. Damnedest thing he had ever heard of! I had to agree.

We dressed out the second carcass. The cold night air had saved it from spoiling much. We had to throw away only some of the side meat. That good mule was able to get both carcasses back to camp.

I don't remember if we were able to fill out the third tag on that trip, nor do I remember the condition of the range around Indigo Prairie, Sugarloaf and Burnt Ridge. Forty years later, though, I still can savor that late supper of heart and liver and fried potatoes around a campfire with my good buddies George and Sy.

It was tough work, but the ranger had to do it!

WADE'S BELLY ACHE

Randy Witters

At the time of these events, Larry Wade and I were assigned to the Inyo National Forest, Larry as resource officer on the White Mountain District and I as lands officer on the Mammoth Ranger District. We were both avid deer hunters but just amateur horsemen, even though we both owned horses and had spent a lot of time over the years on various back country pack trips involving a wide range of wilderness management activities.

However, when our yearly hunt along San Joaquin Ridge occurred it was always with mixed feelings. Was this going to be the year we ended up shooting a horse, or the year one of us comes off the ridge tied over the saddle. Our families, and we later learned the local veterinarians in Bishop, and Larry's dentist, always waited to hear of our latest misadventures. After our second seasons problems, and before our third hunt Larry's dentist had him reschedule his checkup until after our hunt. It was obvious that he wanted to hear Larry's tale of survival. However, the other possibility was he wanted to wait and see if Larry survived.

In 1978, I had an opportunity to visit for the first time what would later become a favorite hunt area. Southern California Edison Power Company had applied for a permit to reface the wooden upstream exterior and to make other repairs to their dam on Waugh Lake in the Rush Creek drainage. This was in the Minaret Wilderness (since renamed the Ansel Adams Wilderness). They initially requested an okay to use helicopters to move the required materials to the site, but because of wilderness restraints on use of motorized vehicles, and the politics involving local packers wanting a piece of the action to move materials, the final permit allowed only pack animals to bring in materials.

Because my job involved reviewing and inspecting use permits I needed to inspect the work in progress. To reach the dam I could either hike in or use a horse and pack animal for my overnight stay. I chose to ride, but rather than use a government horse I elected to use my own horse, a Morgan bay gelding named Flame, and an Appaloosa gelding that I generally used as a pack horse. I hauled the three of us to the trail head at Agnew Meadows, the jump-off point for the upper San Joaquin drainage.

During this trip I also needed to inspect a snow survey cabin near the head of the San Joaquin drainage once used by the California State Department of Water Resources. The cabin was allowed under a Forest Service use permit. The surveyors would either ski or helicopter in and stay overnight in the cabin. They would measure the snow for water content along an established course. This particular survey course was in a nearby meadow. The cabin was no longer used after the state modernized their operation by placing snow pillows just outside of the wilderness. The pillows weight the snow to determine water content. Telemetric devices then relay the data back to Sacramento.

Because the cabin was not needed by the state, I wanted to inspect for condition and to determine if it should be removed. To my surprise, it was in excellent shape and had never been vandalized by either man or bear. Likely, few people realized it was there. It was set some distance off of the trail in a park like setting of mature red fir and lodgepole pine and adjacent to a large meadow with stringers of alder, willow and ceanothus. The meadow looked like a stockyard from the heavy concentration of deer. Within the cabin there were barrels used to protect bedding and food from rodents. Even a Coleman lantern and a pint of brandy had been left behind. Since I had keys for the state locks, I was able to inspect the cabin both inside and out, but I made a note that for my next visit I needed to bring standard Forest Service locks to replace the state locks.

John Harmening, Forest Service Winter Sports Officer for the Mammoth Ranger District had also told me of a nearly level area near the crest of San Joaquin Ridge, at approximately the 10,600 foot level, once used as an airstrip to bring in deer hunters. Because this was new country to me, and possibly accessible by abandoned trail, I made it a point to look for the old trail once I had made the dam and cabin inspections. I wanted to make sure the airstrip was no longer being used and at the same time I planned to scout the area for deer sign. My conversation with John led me to believe this might be an excellent place to find deer.

The old trail was found but evidently hadn't been used for years and had sloughed in and was largely overgrown with brush. I used what portion of the trail I could before finally striking cross-country when it petered out entirely. In the process, I gained 800 feet of elevation before cresting from my starting point on the Pacific Crest Trail.

I almost gave up on locating what is most assuredly the highest landing strip in the United States, when I noticed a line of small boulders along both sides of a gray pumice covered flat. The strip had about a five percent gradient which allowed pilots to land uphill, turn around and then take off downhill. Balloon tired STOL equipped planes were once used to ferry deer hunters into the Minaret Wilderness, that is until the operation was discovered and this guide service was shut down by the Forest Service. From what I could determine the strip hadn't been used for years. No tire tracks were seen. However, in my horseback exploration of the ridge looking for the airstrip, I observed an abundance of deer sign and jumped several nice bucks. More importantly, I found several prominent rock outcroppings that provided a generous view of a large swath of the terrain I had traversed earlier to gain the ridge.

Just as importantly, I found a large spring not more than one third mile from the outcrops. The area around the spring had excellent horse feed and a dense thicket of whitebark pine and provided a sheltered campsite, something that I felt could be important on this windy 10,000 foot ridge during early fall. I certainly wasn't the first person to appreciate the juxtaposition of the spring to what later turned out to be an outstanding place to harvest deer and grouse. Obsidian chips liberally blanketed the grassy area around the spring. Indians certainly harvested deer as well as bighorn sheep in and near the San Joaquin ridge. Bighorn sheep no longer grace the terrain, but the California DFG has reestablished bighorn not much more than fifteen miles to the north in Lee Vining Canyon, the east entrance to Yosemite Park.

My first few hunting trips to the ridge were solo with just Flame and packhorse. It was only after my first two solo hunts that I confided in my friend Larry Wade about the good hunting and unique qualities of the San Joaquin country. However, we also talked about the abandoned snow survey cabin just below my ridge top hunting reserve. The thought of a warm cabin in the wilderness intrigued us both, so we made plans to use the cabin as hunt headquarters for next season. Since this was to be a midseason hunt I decided not to hunt the upper ridge by myself on opening day.

Later in looking back at our mishaps, I often thought that when I took in a partner was when the troubles started. Being superstitious, I reasoned that telling others of the magic of San Joaquin country, even if it was just to one person, may have evoked an Indian curse that protected both ridge and valley. In any event, about the time Larry was told of this quality hunting area, I found it possible to ride a horse to the camp site from where the road crosses San Joaquin Ridge at 9,500 feet, some eight miles to the south. At that point the road descends into Red and Agnew Meadows, the normal jump-off for the Pacific Crest Trail. Most of this ridge route is without trail, but even those areas where you have to cross fairly steep side hill, terrain is easily traversed. The mature overstory is largely scattered red fir, white bark and lodgepole pine, so it was easy to guide the horses around and over deadfalls.

Season Number One

For our hunt at the cabin, we elected to take the traditional Pacific Crest Trail route. We drove two vehicles to Agnew Meadow, where we saddled and loaded our one packhorse. In less than three hours we arrived at the cabin. Our stay at the cabin was almost too pleasant, having shelter, a good wood stove for heat and cooking, soft bed and Coleman lantern. We could have comfortably spent three seasons there. The horses were hobbled and staked out to feed. Close to our camp we noted numerous sign of bear, both scat and scratch marks high on nearby trees. The signs did not particularly alarm us. I had often ridden Flame by bear and was certain bear had come into our camps many other evenings. He had never shown much more than a curious interest in his long clawed brethren, so other than making sure our food and belongings were secure, we did not feel a need for extra precautions. The other two horses though, had not likely ever seen a bear up close. However, there was little we could do about their ignorance other than tie them up extra short so they couldn't easily break their halter rope.

That evening temperatures got below freezing, so making the most of the warmth of our little cook stove, we closed the cabin door. My Appaloosa gelding was a good packhorse, but was unreliable for riding. He would wait until you were about to fall asleep and then give a few bucking crow hops to the side, almost always lifting a person out of the saddle. When he started glancing back you could be certain he was taking your measure and figuring when would be the appropriate time to unload his cargo. He had gotten away with it enough times that there was no changing his bad habit. He wasn't especially high strung, but I suspect it was he that got spooked when a bear woke them. During the night we heard a sound of agitated horses, but only for a few seconds, and the warm bed and cabin made the sound seem less than urgent so we didn't get up to investigate.

When we awoke before daylight to get ready for the hunt, my two horses were nowhere to be found. Only broken halter ropes pointed to where they had been tied. Larry's horse hadn't moved. As it got daylight we quickly determined from tracks that they had headed down the trail to where we started, seven miles and more than 1,400 feet lower. Since they were my dumb horses and my responsibility, I grabbed a rope and headed toward Agnew, hoping that they had stopped to graze before reaching the meadows. Later, in looking back I was convinced that the Indian curse caused the horses to walk the entire seven miles back to Agnew Meadows. I found them feeding less than one quarter of a mile from the horse trailers.

Without a saddle or bridle, it was easier to lead them back to the cabin than to ride. Larry returned from a hunt just as I came into camp and was getting ready to go again, but my first priority was to put something in my belly followed by a nap. We still had plenty of time to make the evening hunt. The hunt was successful and Flame was put to good use again packing deer back to camp. That night we both slept well, but me particularly so, due my extra curricular 14 mile hike. Even then, we both slept with one ear open. The cabin door was also left slightly open.

Unfortunately, soon after our hunt I lost my sidekick Flame in a cattle guard accident. Somehow, the horses had gotten out of their enclosure, and with dogs chasing them, they tried to jump a cattle guard. One made it, but unfortunately Flame broke a leg. He was a true mountain horse, equally at home in the back country as he was in a fenced pasture. He was fool-proof, and was almost certainly what kept me out of trouble for so many years. I replaced him with a beautiful leopard Appaloosa mare, born and raised in the Sacramento Valley. Unfortunately she was a homebody and not happy when out of sight of pasture and barn. Because the Appaloosa packhorse wasn't safe for riding, she was sold.

Season Two – Second Horse Escape

For next season's hunt, I borrowed my daughter's mare. It was with her mare, used as at packhorse, and my new leopard Appaloosa, along with Larry's sorrel quarter horse gelding, that we set off on what was to be Larry's first overnight hunt on San Joaquin Ridge. The cross-country trek was made without incident but on arriving at the spring where we set up camp, l sensed we needed to take extra precautions in handling and feeding our transportation. Normally, with Flame and my other packhorse, I would hobble Flame and let the packhorse feed with 30 feet of rope tied to an ankle strap. No problems were ever encountered.

However, we quickly learned that neither Larry's horse nor my new horse had ever been hobbled, and it didn't seem like now would be the time to familiarize them to the subtleties of hobbles. My daughter's horse could be hobbled, but if she wandered out of sight while feeding, the other two became very agitated. The solution was to keep close tabs on the pack mare while the other two were tethered with leg straps. When we turned in, all three were tied up closely for the night.

This worked well for our first night. The next morning we were up before daylight, checked to make sure the horses were okay and still tied securely, and left for the rock outcroppings using flashlights to keep from tripping. The view of the area below allowed us to see other hunters that an outfitter had stationed in the forest nearly a thousand feet below. When they started hunting, the deer naturally moved up the hill ahead of them. Both of us had our California mule deer not more than an hour after the season opened.

I went back to camp, saddled my daughter's pack mare and brought her back so she could drag the deer to camp. Before noon we had both deer hung and cooling. The plan for the next morning was to lead the pack mare back to the trailers carrying the two deer while we rode. Our small camp would be carried behind us on our horses. This I had done many times before without any problems more serious than shifting pack loads. The rest of the day was spent exploring and making sure the horses had enough time to feed.

About dusk, when we were just about ready to bring the three horses in for the night, the pack mare wondered out of sight of the other two horses. Both became worried and the Appaloosa mare broke her tether. Instead of running to be with the hobbled horse, she decided it was high time to head for home or at the least back to civilization. We followed her tracks for awhile with flashlights, but could quickly see she was headed for the trail head some eight miles away. She wasn't slowing to graze.

The next morning we decided to implement Plan B, packing both horses. Each of us then led a horse. When we got to where we had parked, we could see where the mare had walked right by without stopping. We figured we would find her somewhere in the community of Mammoth Lakes, about five miles away, and were pleasantly surprised to see Gus Weber, an employee for the Mammoth Mountain Ski Area leading her alongside the road. She still had her leg strap that we used to tether her, but the long rope she had drug behind her was gone. I sold her before winter. Both of us had our winter's supply of venison and plenty of time to plan for next season. Next year, we vowed would be different. No rodeos or foul-ups were allowed.

Season Three – Another Chase

When next deer season rolled around, we were one horse short of what we had the year before. Larry had two other horses, but he didn't consider either usable for deer hunting. It was decided that we didn't need a pack animal. He would ride his gelding and I would ride my daughter's mare. If we got deer, we could load them and our camp gear on the horses and walk out, similar to what we had to do the previous year. We got to our camp the night before the opener. The horses were behaved and content with feeding. Before turning in we led them to water for their last drink before tying them up for the night.

The next morning our routine was similar to what we had done the year before. We were stationed on the rock bluff well before daylight and in time to watch the campfires in the valley below being doused. The valley hunters again put a deer in my cross hairs before the sun came over the ridge. This deer was well downhill from the outcropping, so it was decided to go back to camp, put saddles on both horses and ride them back to the outcrop. Larry tied his horse near the outcropping before we led the pack mare down to the dressed out deer. The mare had packed deer before, so we didn't anticipate any problem. We tied the mare to a tree while we slid the deer onto the saddle and tied it down. On the way back uphill, the load shifted, so Larry held the halter rope while I attempted to redistribute and retie the deer. What I was doing made the horse fidgety, so Larry dropped the rope to give me a hand. Mistake number one, don't ever drop the halter rope when you are handling a nervous horse. Said nervous horse decided to walk up the hill and go back to camp, while two winded hunters tried to catch her.

When she topped the hill, she didn't even stop long enough to say hi to Larry's nag. This naturally made his horse upset, and being curious as why she was headed back to camp without him, he pulled hard enough on his halter rope to uproot the sapling he was tied to. He quickly caught up with her and passed her on their rush toward camp. Fortunately, the weight of the deer again shifted, pulling the saddle to one side. This enabled us to catch up to the pack mare about half way back to camp, but their was no catching Larry's horse. The gelding though was reducing his load piece by piece in his headlong rush. Unfortunately, camp wasn't his destination. He passed camp in a cloud of dust and kept going.

We got to camp dropped the deer and tied the mare close, then took off in a rush to follow the tracks of Larry's horse. Since we didn't want to go clear back to the trail head we took off jogging in the hopes of catching the wayward nag. Because the horse was still dragging it's halter rope, we would periodically find pieces of the rope but no horse. However, we did soon find Larry's rifle that had slid out of the scabbard. Somewhat further on we found his coat that had been tied behind the cantle and other items that came out of the saddle bag that hadn't been closed. My daughter's fancy bridle that had been looped over the saddle horn, when we led the mare to the deer, was never found.

Larry had recently had his teeth pulled and was fitted with a temporary set of choppers. Jogging gave him a mouth full of cotton, so his solution was to yank out the temporary teeth. His new sunken cheek look caught me by surprise causing me to double over from laughing while at the same time trying to catch my breath at 10,000 plus feet. After about four miles of this comedy, the gelding's tracks led us into a thicket where we found the errant nag with the saddle under his belly and the halter rope caught up in a windfall. No worse for wear, either horse or man, we straightened the saddle and led him back to camp. The next day Larry bagged his deer without incident, and we were home before nightfall, vowing to do things differently next season. To our chagrin, and almost to Larry's demise, next season would be different.

Season Four – Larry's Belly Ache

Before next season Larry acquired another gelding, really not much bigger than a pony. The seller assured Larry the horse was a mustang, a tried and true mountain horse, as much at home in the mountains as in a barn, could leap wide streams in one bound and would carry any bloody mess a hunter cared to tie on its back. Besides that, his iron hard hooves never needed to be shod, something Larry later found he had special reason to be grateful for. It was just the animal we needed for our annual hunt. Larry did some riding that summer after his mountain horse purchase and couldn't find any serious faults, so was looking forward to deer season. Like the year before, we determined that two horses were sufficient for a three day pack trip.

Again our trip back to our high camp was without incident. Deer sign was numerous everywhere we checked, so we anticipated a good hunt. Larry drew first blood with a nice plump three pointer. Rather than have a repeat of last year's debacle we elected to drag the deer back to camp without the help of the horses. The drag was only about one third of a mile and that was with a slight downhill gradient. Everything went as planned (no stock involved). The deer was hung, dressed and covered with a deer bag. We continued with the hunt that day and next morning, but I wasn't able to connect with anything. That was fine, since my deer hunting season would continue and Larry could only dream about next season's hunt.

After the morning hunt on the second day, we returned to the spring to break camp and to pack. Since we knew my mare would pack a deer without too much fuss, we thought it only reasonable to use Larry's new wonder pony to allow him a chance to show us what he could do to earn his keep. We lowered the deer out of the tree and began to drag it up to his pony where he was ground tied. The pony was nervously observing us and the deer. When Larry got within firing distance, two hooves lashed out and caught him just above his belt buckle. He dropped to the ground like he had been gut shot rather than gut kicked. I'm not sure how long he lay on the ground writhing in pain, but I was beginning to become a little worried thinking that maybe he was seriously hurt and the kick had ruptured organs. As a nervous rejoinder to his predicament, I announced that he better get to his feet or I would have to gut him out too, so I could get him home. I'm not sure if it was my words of kindness or the lessening of his pain, but he put up his hand, and with me tugging slowly, got to his unsteady feet. His belly was skinned up and beet red.

Fortunately, Larry was making an effort to stop smoking with the normal results. He had gained nearly 15 pounds, all in his gut. If it had not been for the extra 15 pounds, I probably would have had to gut him out just so I could manage to lift him up and lay him over the saddle. A few weeks later after the kick, Larry raised his shirt to show me the impression. Two unshod imprints, one on each side of his naval, were clearly visible. Another three weeks passed before the hoof imprints disappeared. No doctor visits were required. Larry did though have to let his vet doctor know of all the fun he was having.

After this fourth and potentially serious incident, we debated the merits of continuing with our yearly San Joaquin outing. We blamed it all on the stock we had and determined that it couldn't happen again, at least an incident as serious as what happened this last time. At the time we hadn't yet fully considered the Indian curse possibility. While it was true that we no longer had the opportunity that we once did of spending a good part of the summer in the wilderness on horseback and working with our stock, we still felt confident that our run of bad luck was behind us. There wouldn't be any more foot races with the stock or opportunities for one of those 1,000 plus pound critters hurting us. We could accept getting a toe stepped on, but nothing more serious than that. With our confidence restored, we made plans for next season.

Larry sold his pony and renewed his acquaintance with his sorrel quarter horse. We both made short day rides to build our confidence. I was still using my daughter's mare as my steed. The old mare didn't have a mean bone in her body. Her problem, if she had one, was that she had better places to be than on some high mountain ridge in the Sierra's eating course mountain grasses and sedge, hardly the diet for a civilized pasture horse.

Season Five – Sitting Horse

For the fifth season we packed up, drove to the trail head and rode the eight miles to our high country camp site. In a few steep places, logs had to be pulled or pushed aside to allow passage. However, the ride in was as usual made without incident. Going in the day before the season opener, in a part of the wilderness seldom visited by anyone, was a treat for both of us. Prior to reaching our camp, we had to skirt two springs. Deer and grouse would almost always be present. We often thought about camping at the second spring, but we wouldn't have had the vantage point or have other deer hunters driving deer to us. I did though, on several occasions, go back on foot to bow hunt for deer, never with success primarily due to lack of skill with a bow. Our grouse hunting though was more productive.

The valley deer hunters again did their job. This year I was the first to score. About 11 a.m. we concluded that no more bucks were going to make an appearance, so together we pulled the deer back to camp where he was quickly strung up to cool. The hunt for a second deer continued but without success. Larry's horse was chosen this season to be the pack animal The plan was to take turns riding my daughter's mare, while leading Larry's gelding. I started out riding and leading. The mare sensing she was going home, started stepping it off. Larry, being from 4,000 foot high Bishop, quickly got winded trying to keep up. It didn't help that footing was in a loose volcanic pumice soil. Every step was labored. I would stop until he caught up, could catch his breath and then lead off again, all the time trying to hold the mare in check. About the fourth time I reined her in she decided to show her displeasure.

To let us know what she thought about our slow progress, she reared. Unfortunately, her head was pointed uphill, with back feet planted in the soft forest soil. Back over she came. I didn't even have time to cuss before I found myself under her. She scrambled to her feet while I lay there moaning. Larry thought it was going to be his turn to threaten me with a gut job in order to get me up. However, I determined that it didn't feel like anything was broke and slowly regained my feet. If it had not been my daughter's horse, that old mare may well have ended her days there. But common sense prevailed. We still had about seven and one half miles back to the truck and horse trailer, and half a ride was better than walking the entire distance.

While I hurt all over, I felt that riding was possible, so after a few minutes, got back in the saddle. After another one half mile, the mare decided to slow her pace. Larry took over the reins and I walked. Both walking and riding were uncomfortable, but nothing compared to the pain I was going to experience for the next month. Then, just as suddenly as the pain appeared, I awoke one morning and it was gone.

I guess this last incident broke the curse, for we hunted the ridge and upper Joaquin drainage after that but never again had to chase horses or experience severe pain. The deer herd has since nearly vanished. Where there was once a herd of over 6,000 deer, there is now less than 900. Some blame it on the mountain lions or a combination of mountain lions, man's inroads into their winter range, poaching, drought and increased road kill. I don't know the reason, but because of this change, there is only a limited chance of getting a tag to hunt the upper San Joaquin drainage. I have gone back since, but without a deer tag. Sometimes I go to hunt grouse, but more often just to experience the solitude. I hope that someday soon I will again be able to set on that high rock outcropping, that both hawks and marmots like to use as a perch and scan the hillside for deer. I look forward to again feeling the warmth of the sun as it crests the ridge, just after I have harvested my deer.

COW OR BEAR?

Hank Mostovoy

While stationed at Oak Knoll Ranger Station, Klamath National Forest, the suppression crew foreman and I were exchanging stories about all the deer we had killed so far that hunting season.

Our supervisor sat in on that conversation expressing a desire to hunt a bear. He was known not to hunt, so I asked him if he were to hunt, what type of a rifle would he use? He stated that he had borrowed his brother's 303 British half round, half octagon barrel bolt action. He admitted he wasn't too familiar with the rifle.

The foreman and I agreed we would take him hunting behind the ranger station because bear were known to be in that area.

The next morning off we went. Everything was going along well when "bang" went the old 303 followed by what I thought was a bull bellowing. I thought, "My God, he's shot a cow."

I started to go in the opposite direction, then thought better of it.

When I found our supervisor, he was frantically trying to load another shell into the chamber of the old 303. About 50 feet in front of him was a black bear bellowing. He had a broken back. I dispatched the bear and then confronted our newfound hunter. He was still trying to close the bolt on a shell that was being bent double!

Have you ever tried to carry a bear? Try picking up a 125 pound dead bear by the scruff of the neck and by the skin on the rump. Your arms and the bear's hide come up about waist high but the bear remains on the ground. You then wrap the bear around your neck and on your shoulders. However, he keeps slipping off one side, then the other. You wrap your arms around the bear's midriff (a bear hug), but he slithers to the ground. This goes on until it dawns on you to either butcher it right there or drag the sucker out! You don't pack it.

EVERY RANGER KNOWS EXACTLY WHERE AND HOW TO HUNT!

Harvey Mack

It was the 1948 deer season on the Cleveland Forest. As usual, virtually every hunter would stop at the ranger station to seek our advice as to the best place to get their deer. We tried to be as helpful as possible but also tried to distribute them around as much as possible to avoid crowding and to promote safety.

One weekend there was a group of three "city slickers" who obviously had never, ever been hunting. They had new guns and outfits and were ready for a kill. After talking to them for awhile, I decided that I had better send them to a place where there would be few hunters and they would not get hurt, shoot a cow or otherwise get into trouble. I sent them up the road about five miles into a relatively flat brush area and suggested that two of them go up the ridges of a small draw and that the third one go up the bottom of the draw. I felt that this would at least let them feel they had hunted and they would be busy and safe.

About three hours later, here they came with a nice buck to have it validated. When I started to weigh it, I noticed that its head was virtually destroyed by something other than gunshot wounds, so I inquired as to what had happened. One of the three proudly got out the remains of his new, very expensive rifle and showed it to me, explaining that he had brought the deer down with one shot. However, as he approached the animal, it obviously was still alive and trying to get up so he turned the rifle around and beat it to death with the rifle stock which now was completely splintered. They proceeded to thank me for all of the assistance and for telling them exactly where to go to get a deer. Of course, with crossed fingers and a guilty conscience, I took full credit.

STURGEON

Joe Church

The Klamath River, at least back in the early sixties, supported a pretty varied fishery such as salmon, trout, eels, steelhead and sturgeon. A lot of people came to fish the Klamath at Orleans on the Six Rivers National Forest. Sturgeon was a prime target. One summer among the multitude, was one of our foresters, John Nelson and his brother Bob, who was visiting the Nelsons on the station. One afternoon Bob, with someone else on the station, went up the river to the sturgeon hole where, lo and behold, they caught a keeper. After a suitable struggle, they beached it, all six and a half feet and plus or minus 100 pounds of it. They then trucked it back to the station where all those around admired it, ugly as it was. But, there was no place to immediately store it. Improvising, they lugged it into the Nelson's house and put it in the bathtub. Shortly thereafter, the Nelsons returned from wherever they had been. Unaware of the trophy, Nancy Nelson stepped into the bathroom, where she sat down on the throne and in a trice, saw that big fish staring at her. Her reaction was noted over the station followed by her immediate evacuation of both the bathroom and the house, followed then by her ultimatum to John to get it out of her house—NOW. And so he did. An operating table of sorts was set up in the yard and just about everyone on the station took part in the partition of the fish. Everyone got a little bit of the seventy or so pounds of meat that was netted. It looked a lot like beefsteak with small round cuts, but it still tasted like fish.

A REAL HUNTER

Hank Mostovoy

While I was stationed on the Happy Camp District of the Klamath National Forest, a young forester from Duke

University by the name of Tony Mollish showed up for his first assignment with the Forest Service. Tony had passed the entrance exam to the Naval Academy but chose to "come out west."

When deer season approached we hunters started feeding Tony stories about big bucks killed, etc.

One day Tony showed up for work with a brand new rifle, ready to go hunting. We old-timers decided we had gone too far with our stories and explained to Tony that sometimes bucks are hard to find and that we could go through a season without getting one.

The first day of hunting season I went out for a couple of hours without any luck. I came back to the ranger's office and there was Tony. He asked me if I would validate his tags and teach him how to dress out his bucks! He had shot two of them within the first hour of the first day of his first day of hunting season.

A HUNTING SEASON TRAGEDY

Roy R. Sines

Back in the days before search and rescue organizations, in the 1940s and 1950s, nearly every deer hunting season the US Forest Service was called to help find lost hunters. Usually the search only lasted a few hours, but sometimes a day or more.

Several deer hunting seasons my brother-in-law, Haven Stanaway, packed hunters into back country camps on the Entiat District of the Wenatchee National Forest. I was district assistant, responsible for fire, trails, recreation, etc., at that time.

One deer hunting season, Haven packed a young man and his wife into a campsite about seven miles up the North Fork of the Entiat River. He and the hunters agreed on a date to pack out their hunting camp and deer if they had hunting luck.

A few days after moving their camp in, Haven had a call from the husband on a Forest Service field telephone at the trail head. He said his wife had become ill and died suddenly while they were hunting on a ridge above their camp.

Haven called me to help him, so we gathered up several horses and asked two brothers, Don and Earl Roundy, to help us. Don worked for the USFS, too. We unloaded our stock at the North Fork trail head and rode up to the hunting camp. The husband told us how to find his wife and he remained at the campsite and started breaking their camp. Three of us hiked up the ridge above camp to where he told us we would find his wife. We carried her to their camp on a stretcher. At camp we discussed how to carry her out to the road where an ambulance would be waiting. By this time it was becoming dark. Some of the group suggested that we lay her across a packhorse and tie her on like she was a pack. Haven and I did not like that method so we came up with another idea. We set her in riding position on a saddle horse and Haven and I took turns sitting behind her and holding her upright. It was a long, hard ride in the dark, but we carried the lady out with dignity and reached the road before the ambulance arrived.

CLOSE CALL

Hank Mostovoy

Tom McKay, when finished with working for the Klamath National Forest fire department in the fall of the year, would fall back on living off the land.

Tom would show up in Hamburg and stay with different people. Late one fall he took a horse and went hunting up near Lake Mountain Lookout. He had some luck and on the way down Lake Mountain he ran into Game Warden Starr.

This was the depression era and Tom didn't have a license. It was not hunting season, anyway. The conversation went something like this:

Starr: "Hi, Tom, that's a good looking buck you've got there. Is it fat?"

Tom: "It sure is. It's blue and butterball fat."

Starr: "I'll bet it's going to be good eating. I haven't had a good piece of deer meat in quite sometime."

Tom: "Would you like a hindquarter of this one?"

Stair: "Can you afford it?"

Tom: "Sure." He gave Game Warden Starr a hindquarter.

Starr: "Thanks again, Tom, and good luck. Keep your powder dry."

Tom: "Thanks." And they parted.

Tom told the folks in Hamburg this story when he showed up with a hindquarter missing from his deer. Tom never lied.

THERE IS MORE THAN ONE WAY TO CATCH YOUR LIMIT

Harvey Mack

Bob Cron was an avid hunter and fisherman and almost always was able to get his limit. By contrast, I had never hunted or fished and Bob just could not understand how anyone could live on the Modoc and not participate in these wonderful activities. So—he took it upon himself to get me started in the fishing business. He outfitted me with rod, reel, line, flies, salmon eggs, etc., and we headed out for a stream he knew would provide good trout fishing in the Surprise Valley area of the Warner Range where he assured me that the fish were just waiting to be caught.

Upon arrival, he carefully explained just how we were going to fish the stream and its pools. We hiked upstream until we found a pool that he felt was just right for my first lesson which involved all steps of the Forest Service four step training method. He even cast into the pool and immediately caught a nice pan size trout. He really concentrated on trying to teach me the knack of fishing but soon realized that I wasn't showing too much progress, so he told me to work the lower part of the stream and he would hike up farther for his fishing. He once more picked out a prime spot in a pool and told me where to cast. Nothing happened so he said, "Here, let me show you," and he took my rod and immediately got another fish. I accused him of having the ability to think like a fish.

After a couple of hours of "exciting" fishing, catching most of the bushes and drowning all of my flies, here came Bob with his creel full of fish. He promptly asked me how many I had caught and I held up my one fish. He grinned and said that that was what he had figured so he had caught 29 just in case I had caught one as the legal limit for the two of us was 30. We got teased about this a lot and the staff accused Bob of taking me along to assure that he could catch a limit. Oh yes, he did let me keep my 15 limit! I think he only took me fishing one more time and gave up. I just could not learn to think like a fish!

DID I HAVE THE DEER OR DID IT HAVE ME?

Hank Mostovoy

All of the young veterans I have talked with agreed that one thought they have at discharge time was going home, hunting and fishing.

When I got home after being discharged, I went back to work for the Klamath National Forest on the Yreka District at Oak Knoll. That fall I was off and running when hunting season started.

One bright and early morning I took off from the ranger station walking on a contour, heading upriver. Within 15 minutes I had my buck in very steep country. I decided to drag him down to the Klamath River Highway where I would stash him, walk back to the station and get a pickup.

Everything went well until I got to the edge of the upper bank of the highway. There was a small cedar which I proceeded to wrap the buck around. All of a sudden I was holding on to the cedar with one hand and a buck's horn with the other. The deer was hanging free of anything except my one-handed grip. His horn had slipped into the placket of my shirt sleeve and was twisted tight so I could not let loose of him. Finally, the hand holding the cedar gave out and deer and I free fell about 15 feet down onto the highway. Right then our mail stage man drove around "dead man's turn" and saw the deer and me flying down off the bank.

When the stage man came up to me and found I was all right, he said that that was the damnedest thing he had encountered in the 30 years he had been driving the mail route. He said that it looked like a man was riding the deer down off the bank!

THE KAIBAB WILDLIFE PROGRAM

Jay H. Cravens

The wildlife program on the North Kaibab was a tremendous opportunity for me to follow in the footsteps of President Theodore Roosevelt, "Doc" Rassmusen and many other famous wildlife biologists. The area was also known as the Grand Canyon National Game Preserve and had a long history that had been studied by many generations of students and frustrated Forest Service and Arizona State game managers and wildlife biologists. Deer populations had exploded in the 1920s and devastated available food supplies. Attempts to drive surplus deer across the Colorado River by way of House Rock Valley and Little Saddle, to the south rim area of the Grand Canyon, had failed when many cowboys and Forest Service riders found the deer were not about to go into that big, deep canyon and ford the Colorado River. One old-timer told me when the deer approached the inner gorge of the Grand Canyon, they exploded all over, around and under the horsemen and headed back to the Kaibab and starvation that awaited them.

By the mid-1940s, the habitat had improved somewhat with the increase in logging by the Whiting Brothers' Kaibab Lumber

Company and the condition of the deer improved. In fact on my first hunt on the Kaibab in 1949, with friends from Williams, we killed four mule deer that weighed from 185 to 215 pounds, field dressed. They were fat and in good condition. By 1954, when I was transferred to the North Kaibab, deer numbers had sky rocketed and the habitat was again being eaten into the ground. Deer ate all available vegetation. Spruce trees were hedged up as far as deer could reach... an indicator of severe overuse and starvation. In fact the deer stood around waiting for the loggers to fell an aspen and then consumed all the twigs and leaves in a short time. Seeding for site restoration on skid trails and closed logging roads was unsuccessful since the deer slicked it off as soon as the grass and clover shoots appeared. We could count several hundred undernourished deer at one time in some of the overgrazed open park like areas on the upper summer range. In these areas the grasses and other vegetation were fully consumed. The critical winter range at lower elevations was hit heavily when the deer arrived in late fall only the intermediate range between the top of the Kaibab Plateau and the lower winter range was in fair shape. Deer being creatures of habit did not pause in their migration from the summer range on top, including those coming from the Grand Canyon National Park, until they reached the lower elevations above Kanab Creek, House Rock Valley and the Grand Canyon. Adding to the problem was over half a century of overgrazing by cattle, horses and sheep. The average field dressed weight of bucks harvested the fall of the year I arrived averaged 129 pounds and all were in poor condition. Does, which normally produced twins or triplets, produced none or only one which usually could not survive through the winter. These were some of the challenges we faced in the mid-1950s.

I worked with our Forest Service and Arizona State wildlife biologists on deer management. We made deer counts in the summer and winter. As on the Coconino, big game counts involved being on a survey route before dawn and coming in late at night. We also measured the amount of vegetation utilized on summer, intermediate and winter ranges. The Forest Service was responsible for operating 24-hour deer checking stations during an early and a late hunt. We weighed, aged, recorded sex and location of where each deer was harvested. We designed and constructed roads to improve hunter access, installed pipelines, developed springs, constructed earthen stock tanks, deer guzzlers (covered rain water catchments), cleared and burned low value vegetation, planted deer browse and reseeded thousands of acres with crested wheat grass and other suitable species. This work was accomplished through the use of cooperative funds coming from a deposit paid by each deer hunter. As with all other resource programs, and before funds were allocated, we prepared detailed work plans, budgets and made presentations to the Forest Supervisor and staff.

We conducted many show-me trips for hunters and state people to demonstrate our management program and the seriousness of the over population of deer. I made many trips to Phoenix with the Forest Supervisor Flick Hodgin in unsuccessful efforts to try and convince the Arizona State Game Commissioners to issue more permits and increase hunting pressure. We told them the consequences would be further destruction of the range resources and a winter die off. The state feared the political consequences and refused to increase the number of permits. They wanted improved and reduced livestock use, more water improvements, reseeding and the Arizona Fish and Wildlife Service to set up a predator control program. By working with the grazing permittees we obtained reduction in livestock numbers and improved management. We continued a program and installation of water development and reseeding. But we refused to permit a predator control program, including the establishment of poison (Compound 1080) bait stations to kill coyotes and mountain lions.

The deer were in poor condition when they migrated from the summer range. Our predictions came true that winter. We lost thousands of deer on the winter range. Deer carcasses could be found in every canyon and deer browse was fully consumed. With the large die off and a significant reduction of deer numbers, acceleration of reseeding and water developments, improved range management and continued timber harvest, the range and deer responded. Calves were fatter, does produced healthy twins and the average weight of male deer increased. The Kaibab was famous for its trophy deer. Antlers were huge, up to a 40-inch spread and almost the size of elk. When I saw coyotes I was pleased to think we had not been a party to poisoning them. After all, they helped eliminate the weaker deer and keep the numbers under control. I fell particularly good early one morning when I saw a mother mountain lion and two spotted cubs cross a woods road in front of me.

We had another interesting feature on the Kaibab... a herd of a few hundred buffalo. This use was permitted to the State of Arizona on one of our grazing allotments. Managing buffalo is a chore. If an animal decided that it wanted to go somewhere there was no fence, or any manmade structure, no amount of effort could stop it. There were times that these animals drifted miles out of their allotted range and had to be moved back,

We had turkeys on the forest. Some 40 wild turkeys were flown in by District Ranger Pat Murray from the Apache National Forest in 1948. They did well and by 1955, they had multiplied and spread all over the Kaibab Plateau, including the Grand Canyon National Park. The park superintendent was heard to complain about the presence of exotic birds that had never historically been known to inhabit the area. In confidence he admitted enjoying seeing these majestic birds.

One of our early deer hunts coincided with the turkey hunt. I had a turkey permit, but it was a busy fire season and I did not have time to hunt. On the last day of the season, we were putting out a small forest fire and one of the firefighters called to me and pointed to a flock of turkeys passing through the burned area. It was just about daylight and the light played tricks. The turkeys looked huge as I picked out and shot what appeared to be one of the largest. It turned out to be a young three pound hen! It was not much to be proud about.

After the fire season I did well fishing for trout. John Church, Pat Murray and I usually went to Idaho and fished the Salmon River for steelhead trout and the Big Lost and Little Big Lost Rivers for brook and rainbow trout. We had some great, exciting times and made many new friends in Idaho. John was an excellent German brown trout fisherman. He knew their habits and taught me the secret of catching these wily trout. The trick consisted of casting a fly or spinning lure into a likely spot, usually in a pool under an overhanging bank on a small stream, as many as 20 to 30 times... always in the exact same place! Most trout fishermen will tire of that practice, decide after a few casts there are no fish and move on. But repeated casts in the same location finally make the elusive German brown trout mad and it will finally lunge at your lure.

I fished Asay Creek which is 42 miles north of Kanab, Utah. This small stream heads in the Dixie National Forest and leaves the forest boundary just before it crosses U.S. 89 Highway. The area was heavily grazed by sheep and had the living daylights beat out of it all slimmer by fly fisherman. I could go there after work, about dark in late September, and come home with a limit of German brown trout as long as my arm. Of course, I told everybody I caught them out of a lake up on the Dixie. That also was part of John Church's training... be elusive like the trout and don't give away all your secrets! Never give away the location of your favorite fishing holes, except to friends, or like that friendly ranger on the Gunnison National Forest in Colorado did for a crippled soldier back during the war. Hunt, trap and fish, live in a cabin in the woods... I had it made, except I never went for the trapping part.

I DIDN'T KNOW THE GUN WAS LOADED

Hank Mostovoy

It was fall, fire season was over and slash burning finished for the year.

A group of men on the Gasquet District, Six Rivers National Forest decided to go deer hunting at Fort Bidwell on the Modoc National Forest. Although I always hunted alone, this time I acquiesced to go along with the gang.

When we arrived at camp a self-appointed leader made a ruling that all bolts would be removed from all rifles. I said, "No way." I was carrying a 308 automatic.

Another member was sitting with me in the back of a pickup and he agreed with me, stating that he knew when his rifle was empty. To prove his point he worked his bolt several times real quick without any shells extracting, pulled the trigger and shot a hole in the pickup tailgate. This confirmed my preference to always wanting to hunt alone, the way I was brought up to believe!

FINDERS KEEPERS!

Bruce Barron

Out in the sagebrush and juniper flats east of Mt. Hebron (on the Shasta Forest Goosenest District) were numerous vernal pools and natural ponds that were a welcomed respite for transient waterfowl. During duck hunting season we would often hike out to these ponds and camouflage ourselves behind some of the sprawling juniper trees. I got set up behind one of these big trees and was pleased to find a wood rat had built a nest with a huge pile of twigs entwined amongst the lower branches. It was a natural duck blind and as I shifted around making myself comfortable, I was puzzled by what appeared to be a piece of water pipe protruding above the nesting material. While waiting for ducks to fly in, I began moving the twigs away from the pipe and found it was a big single barrel 10 gauge shot gun. Since it was sheltered under a large limb, it had been protected from the rain and snow. The entire gun was in a remarkable state of preservation. The duck hunting was also good that day. When I got home I cleaned the gun and found that the firing pin had to be replaced. With some diligent grinding and filing on an 8 penny nail, I was able to fabricate a new pin.

After locating some 10 gauge shotgun shells, I went goose hunting at Tulelake and found the gun had an extremely reliable pattern with a tremendous reach. It is hard to conjecture how many years that old gun had been abandoned in that rats nest, or what had happened to the original owner, or why he had left it there?

MISCALCULATIONS

Lloyd W. Swift

About 1940, while in the regional office in Denver, I like many in the forest, had a deputy state game warden appointment.

During early spring, someone reported that rainbow trout in streams flowing into the Platte River, Pike National Forest, were unable to move upstream as they were blocked by beaver dams.

With a bit of curiosity and a desire to escape the office, I met Cliff Spencer from the forest and we made an investigation.

It was on a bitter day, with wind and snow but being hardy types, we carried on.

While on a stream we detected a whiff of smoke which we deduced to be man related on such a wet day. So, guided by the smoke trail, we soon spotted a man at a beaver dam with a warming fire and fishing out of season.

We approached carefully and when he landed a trout, proceeded to make an arrest. Much surprised, the man looked us over and wanted to know if we were forest rangers and wardens too. When we said we were both, he was disgusted, saying, "I figured you guys would have better sense than to be out on a day like this."

OLD BUCK

Hank Mostovoy

Johnny and Mary Reed transferred from the Salmon River Ranger District to the Yreka District of the Klamath National Forest and became the Deadwood lookouts. They brought with them a dog named Buck.

Buck was a medium sized, brown dog who looked as if he had been run through a thresher machine. His ears resembled the fringe on an old tattered curtain and his tail was as hairless as a baby's bottom. But what a deer hunting dog he was.

Johnny wanted me to go hunting with him so he could show off Buck's abilities. I did not like to hunt with anyone, yet I was interested in seeing old Buck at work.

Johnny, Buck and I took off from Deadwood Lookout one morning, hunting. We came to a logging road and Johnny told me to put my back against the uphill bank on the road and keep looking out across the road. He would turn Buck loose and Buck would circle me and Johnny, driving any bucks to us. Sure!

After a five or ten minute wait Buck came back and was above me, barking and yipping, when over the top of me a deer and Buck flew, down over the bank and out of sight before I knew what happened.

Soon after I heard Johnny whistling for Buck. When I finally caught up with them, Johnny had his palms up to his ears with his fingers pointing up into the sky explaining to Buck that they were no longer in the Salmon River country and that we wanted only bucks now, not does. Buck had run a doe over the top of me.

I WON A SPECIAL MODOC AREA DOE SEASON PERMIT!

Harvey Mack

In 1955, the California State Fish and Game Department decided that there was need to reduce the female deer population in the Modoc area and announced a drawing would be held for issuance of a limited number of permits. Most of the Modoc staff entered their names in the hopes that they would be lucky enough to get one of the permits. I did not hunt but they talked me into entering the drawing as it would be one more chance of getting one of those prized permits. As luck would have it, I think that I was the only one that won a permit.

The local ranger promptly propositioned me to join him in the hunt, using my permit, with the assurance that we would split the meat 50-50. Since I didn't have either a license or a rifle, it sounded good to me as he had an excellent hunting reputation.

Opening day we were on our way to what he considered one of the best hunting areas and he took us to the spot where he just knew we would get a doe as he had seen so many there every time he visited the area. As soon as it was time for hunting to begin, there was a barrage of gunfire all around us but none in the area in which he had chosen to hunt. As we approached his "favorite spot," sure enough we saw a doe standing still in front of a large rock. My official duty was to use the binoculars and keep quiet. I continued to watch the deer as he took careful aim and whispered that he could get a good head shot and not ruin any of the meat. The dear continued to stand and watch and I kept it fixed in the binoculars while Don took careful aim and fired. The deer flicked its left ear and darted behind the rock. He had put a bullet right through the ear. I am even sure I saw where it hit.

As the day progressed, the area become like a battlefield with hunters everywhere to the point where we decided it was no longer safe to be out there. We had not had another chance anywhere we looked and went home empty-handed with an unused special permit to remember that day. During the regular deer season, Don did get a deer and gave me a package of frozen steaks, venison, I hope!

A GAGGLE OF GEESE

Mark Petty

I remember when I was TMA on the Goosenest District of the Klamath National Forest and Chuck Burk was the ADR. One stormy morning Chuck headed out on a goose hunt. A couple of hours later I heard a knock on the back door and Chuck wanted to know if I could use any geese. He looked a little sheepish. It seemed that he had crawled up a ditch into a flock and fired three shots. He had flopping geese all over the place—something like 33 of them! Chuck was straight arrow and brought only one limit at a time back to residents of nearby Macdoel and Mt. Hebron. He spent a long morning shuttling between the hunting ground and the two small towns so that nothing was wasted.

TEN IS ENOUGH

Hank Mostovoy

One day while stationed on the Happy Camp District of the Klamath National Forest, I decided to take my three sons up the Klamath River to Grider Creek and teach them how to put a grasshopper on a hook to catch trout.

At that time the limit of trout was 10 and I made sure the boys understood the law and what the limit meant.

After we caught 10 trout we headed home. On the way I decided to stop at a good hole on the Klamath River and test it for trout. After a few casts I looked back up to the highway to see if the boys were okay. There stood my three sons and the game warden.

When I got back to the pickup the warden asked me how the fishing was and I showed him our 10 trout. We talked for a few minutes then he left. The boys were very proud at showing the warden our fish and how dad had taught them about the law and the limit.

I believe if I had lied to the warden I would have been cited. Children are guileless.

DUCK HUNTING

William G. Weigle

In 1909, when the late George H. Cecil was district forester of District 6, which covered Washington, Oregon and Alaska, he and the superintendent of public roads came to Alaska on an inspection trip. One day, when we were looking over a timber sale in a little bay on Zarimbo Island, George saw some ducks. This brought up the subject of roast duck for dinner. I gave each of the visitors a shotgun and took what was left, a rifle. A large stream came in at the head of the bay and the boys made a good killing on one side of that stream. Then I told them they could get some more on the other side of the stream but they would have to wade across. They refused, so I waded the stream and chased some ducks over to them. I then moved to higher ground, set my gun against a rock and in a nice mossy place, removed all of my clothing to wring it out. While I was performing this act I spied a deer looking at me. My gun was at least 50 feet away, and by the time I got it, the deer had moved. Although dressed only in the suit that nature gave me, I ducked around a little hill and again ran into the deer. One shot and he never moved off the spot! This kind of hunting was great sport for the visitors. I called to the Japanese cook on "The Tahn," our splendid six plus foot boat, and he came over on the skiff, picked us and the deer up and took us out to "The Tahn." So, for the next few days we had some exceptionally fine venison and roast duck and also plenty of hard shell crabs. Our visitors thought this was great fun.

INNOCENT TURKEY HUNT

Duane G. Breon

I was district ranger on the Pinedale Ranger District on the Sitgreaves National Forest in Arizona during the fall of 1961. A rancher named Ivan Williams had a good pond on his homestead. Turkeys came to it every morning and he gave me permission to hunt on his land.

Prior to daybreak, on a September morning, I drove to his ranch in a Forest Service pickup. At that time, Forest Supervisor "Lanky" Spaulding encouraged his rangers to mingle with the hunters using a government pickup for transportation and hunting.

I shot my very first turkey shortly after sunup. I proudly went back to the ranger station to display it as the crews came to work. Lloyd Mansfield, the Hopi Indian crew leader, asked if he could have the feathers to use when making Kachina dolls. (A small wooden doll representing the spirits.) Of course, he got the feathers.

That night another crew foreman, Henry Williams, came up to the ranger dwelling. He asked me what day turkey season opened. My answer was Saturday, September 30th. Henry asked what day it was today and after thinking, I said, "My gosh, it's Friday, September 29th." The turkey had been shot a day early! The foreman said to forget it and not to worry. What happened would not leave the station.

Frankly, I was scared! It could mean my job, which was dearly loved and worked hard for.

After talking at length with my wife, we decided not to turn myself in to the game warden. I went over to Ivan's ranch and told him what had happened. He laughed. It was not funny to me. He said that he would keep it to himself and suggested I come back the next morning and shoot another turkey. His offer was respectively declined.

Over a year later, some trash was dumped on the district. Labels indicated who the trash belonged to. Several attempts were made to personally contact the owner of the trash. We could not connect so a registered letter was sent giving him a choice of picking up the trash or going to court.

The owner of the trash came into my office a couple of days later. He was very angry and threw the letter on my desk saying, "I didn't dump that trash! I also know you shot a turkey out of season and if you insist on pushing this, I'll have your a__." He was informed most rangers who walk the face of this earth are suspected of poaching. After a few more words from him, he left.

Now, I was scared again. A ranger cannot afford to be confronted with accusations of breaking the law every time he or she has to enforce regulations. I went over to the local Arizona Game Warden, Harve Palmer in Snowflake. The turkey hunt was explained. He said, "Duane, I've known you long enough to know you did not intend to break the law. I also believe there is a one year statute of limitation on a case of this nature. You go and talk to Judge Gardner in Show Low and tell him I have no desire to prosecute."

The next day my story was told to Magistrate Judge Gardner. He just laughed when I was finished telling the story. Again, I found no humor in my story.

Judge Gardner said, "Let me tell you my turkey story. I was sitting on my back porch one evening plunking with my .22 rifle. A turkey walked along the fence line so I decided to see how close I could come to his head. I came so close I killed him. Furthermore, I ate him."

So, I explained to the judge about this man I wanted to bring into his court for dumping trash. I told him the man would bring up the turkey I shot out of season. The judge said, "You bring him in here and I'll let him know who is being charged with what!"

I went back to the accused trash dumper and asked him to be in court at 9 a.m. Saturday morning. He looked at me and said, "You're serious, aren't you?" I said, "Yes, I am." He paced up and down his living room floor and said, "I know you shot that turkey out of season. I have talked to your employees but none of them will say you did it. After a pause, he said, "Can I still pick up the trash and not go to court? Frankly, I really did not dump it. My wife did."

I said, "Yes, that is all I really want. The trash cleaned up."

A couple of days later I checked the trash area. You couldn't find even a postage stamp. He even raked the area clean.

THE GENDER GAP

Howard W. Burnett

In the 1950s, on the Chattahoochee National Forest in north Georgia, there were a number of wildlife management areas where managed deer hunts were held. The Georgia Game and Fish Commission was responsible for the game and the Forest Service for the habitat. Hunts were held each year with hunters selected by drawing. Hunters had to check in and out at checking stations manned by personnel of both the Forest Service and the Commission.

By the mid 1950s, the deer population was such that game managers (and foresters) could foresee the need for either sex hunting to keep populations at a reasonable level. At that time there was great public outcry over the idea of killing a doe (what, shoot a mother?) and so a long range public relations effort was begun.

In order to get information on the deer herd, and the hunting thereof, successful hunters were asked a series of questions when they checked their deer out. About where, when and how the kill was made, and so forth. The Georgia State Commission added a question one year: "What do you think about permitting either sex hunting?"

One of the hunters dutifully answered all the questions, but seemed pensive when he got to the either sex hunting question. Finally he asked: "Don't they allow women on these hunts now?" We had a good laugh but we all learned a lesson about not taking anything for granted about how we technical people word questions addressed to the public!

JUST SHOOT—WE'LL LOOK LATER

Hank Mostovoy

In the mid 1950s, I was the general district assistant at the Oak Knoll Ranger Station on the Yreka District of the Klamath National Forest.

One of my jobs was to validate deer tags, after a short course on how to do so held by the California State Fish and Game Department.

One day some folks from the San Francisco Bay area drove up and requested that I validate a tag for them. When I first saw the deer I told them to get out of there with that spike, which was still in velvet. As a group, they asked me to check out the small fork on one side. I did so and by pressing down on the velvet, a fork large enough to hang a ring on was evident.

The proud hunter said he was about 100 yards away when he shot and bragged about how well he did. I mingled with the group and found not a rifle scope in the crowd. A 100 yard shot at a spike in velvet, with iron sights—I would hope they named him "Hawk-eye!"

On the last day of hunting season in 1953, I went hunting at Humbug Creek on the Yreka District. Because dusk was settling I knew my hunting season was over so I headed for my pickup.

About then a shot rang out from the opposite wall of the drainage. I thought that it was late to be shooting. I sat down and waited to hear someone or something but heard nothing. About five minutes later I did hear a noise up the hill from where

I was sitting. I investigated and found a young forked horn breathing his last. It was so late in the evening that I thought I would have some fun. I hollered as loud as I could, "Who shot this doe? You better come over and get it." No one showed up and about 15 minutes later I hollered again. Still no answer. I took the buck home.

This is another case of someone shooting and not knowing what they were shooting.

TARGET PRACTICE OR OUR LOSS IS CASTRO'S GAIN

Robert W. Cermak

From 1970 to 1972 we spent two memorable years on the George Washington Forest in Virginia. I extracted, and embellished slightly, the following account from the December 1972 *GW Newsletter*. The GW had excellent relations with the Virginia Game and Fish Commission, so good that their regional manager had his office near mine in the SO and his game managers were located at each district headquarters. In the summer of 1972, Game Manager Sturgeon Funkhouser (yep, that's his name) visited a wildlife clearing on the Lee District near New Market and found that some of the apple trees planted in the clearing had been literally shot off by machine-gun fire. This agitated Sturgeon who reported the event to District Ranger Charley Huppach. In November, Sturgeon decided to check the area on a Sunday and sure enough he heard automatic weapons firing. He sneaked up on the clearing and found three men blasting away. He somehow got the attention of the shooters who ceased fire as he approached. With a bravery which later seemed foolhardy, Funkhouser began to lecture them on destroying game habitat. The eldest man introduced himself as Charles Tuller and indicated that the two others were his sons. He then informed Funkhouser that he was a GS-15 and an important official of the Commerce Department in Washington, D.C. Sturgeon allowed as how that didn't give him the right to blow away the apple trees and issued the three of them citations to appear in court for shooting out of season.

That seemed to be the end of the affair until several days later when three FBI agents appeared in Ranger Huppach's office. Charley was trying to think of what he had done that was a federal crime when one of the agents said that he wanted to talk to Sturgeon Funkhouser. "What for?" asked Charley. "Don't you read the newspapers?" replied the agent. "A man named Charles Tuller and his two sons tried to rob a bank in Alexandria. They failed, but later they killed an airline employee when they highjacker a plane to Cuba." Charley nearly fell out of his chair. "I thought that name sounded familiar." he said. Tuller and sons never made the court appearance for shooting out of season.

HIS FIRST AND ONLY ELK

Avon Denham

In the mid-1950s, Regional Forester Herb Stone was deeply concerned about multiple use. I was commissioned by Stone to organize a wildlife trip and to check into wildlife matters. I enlisted the aid of Larry Mays, Chief of Operations, and Earl Sandvig, Chief of Personnel (both had killed many elk, both legal and otherwise, in Oregon, Montana and Colorado), to help me organize the trip. The party consisted of Stone, Walter Lund, Chief of Timber Management, Mays, Sandvig and myself. We chose Sheep Creek, a branch of the Grande Ronde, above Tony Vey's ranch, for the location of our hunting camp. We put the camp up in about a foot of snow with plenty of wood, a heating stove for warmth, a cook tent and a bedroom tent. We went first class.

The night before the hunt was supposed to start, the regional forester asked that I counsel him on the fine points of shooting an elk, since he hadn't killed many elk in Milwaukee or Atlanta. I said, "Herb, first of all, you can only shoot horned elk. If you shoot one and get him down, don't rush in too close because he can kick like a mule. Just sneak up behind him and shoot him behind the ear."

So, to bed we went. Long before daylight, we were up and started on our trek up a mountain. About an hour after daylight, Larry Mays, who was fairly close to me, heard a single shot way up ahead of us up the mountain. Then, shortly thereafter, a second shot. We hurried on up the hill and found the skyline trail and there was Herb and Walt with a dead spike bull elk. I said, "Who shot it?" Herb said, "I did."

We decided to butcher the elk then. I volunteered to get my block and tackle from my pack so we could hang the elk up in a tree. It developed that, in our haste to leave camp before daylight, I left the block and tackle on my bed back in camp. But since Mays and I were experienced hunters, we started dressing the animal on the ground. We had the hide almost off and we hadn't yet found a place where the animal had been shot. We skinned him out and found one bullet hole about four inches from his ear and a second one about three inches away.

I said to Herb, "You might have missed him shooting him in the neck the first shot." He said, "No one could miss an elk as close as I was." I said, "He must have been pretty dead when you shot him the first time." To which he said, "He was." But he remembered my instruction the night before so he shot him the second time although he didn't think it was necessary. This was the hunt that Frank Wallisch described as being such a high level affair that no one less than a GS-13 (which was practically a supergrade then) could even pack water into camp.

THE NOVICE HUNTERS

Bruce Barron

It was early in the hunting season during the fall of 1950, when three young hunters came into my headquarters at the old Forest Service Bogard Ranger Station (located off Highway 44 northwest of Susanville). It was their first deer hunting trip and they were eager to find a good place to hunt. By their appearance and remarks it was obvious that they had little or no hunting experience.

Since the area around Bogard was favored by local hunters (myself included), it was deemed prudent to send these "city dudes" to some far away place where they wouldn't be a potential hazard to other people who frequent the out-of-doors. I directed them to a distant hinterland far back into a rough lava bed terrain known for its precipitous rimrocks and heavy mahogany thickets. Because of its mean reputation, it was a place usually avoided by local hunters.

A couple of days later, I recognized the three hunters as they came racing up the road in a cloud of dust. At first I had mixed emotions, fearful that they were returning to raise hell with me for my having sent them on a "wild goose chase." Instead, they jumped out of the pickup truck and hailed me with jubilance. They pulled back the canvas cover in the back of the truck and there lay three tremendous mule deer with huge racks that could have easily qualified for Boone and Crockett trophies.

As I validated the deer tags on these monstrous bucks, my mind was tormented by feelings of hypocrisy and deceit. I was especially chagrined as these exuberant hunters kept venerating me with their lavish praise and expressing their deepest appreciation for my having directed them to such bountiful hunting grounds. I did take solace in the knowledge that I had inadvertently located the area where the big bucks were congregating.

THE COUP DE GRACE

Avon Denham

Some years ago, while we were hunting elk in the Wanaha area, we were returning to camp at almost dark. Wright Mallery and Jimmy Wilkins signaled to Al Oard and me, who had just climbed out of a very deep canyon, of some elk grazing on a hill just ahead of us. I had the only scope on my gun so I tried to look through my scope to see if they were bulls. It took some time to get breath enough to hold a gun fairly steady. I finally saw that they were both bulls, one a spike and the bigger bull at least a five pointer.

The shooting then started, and after several shots, the big bull went down and the other acted like it was wounded. We gathered ourselves and took off to where the elk were last seen. When we arrived some 15 to 20 minutes later, the big bull was dead as a mackerel and was on his back under a windfallen tree. All you could see were feet and horns.

Mallery rushed in to him and shot the dead elk between the eyes, practically blowing the horns off his head. I asked Mallery why he shot the dead elk and ruined my trophy, to which he said, "I gave him the Coup de Grace." From then on, that area was known as the Coup de Grace Ridge.

THE GOOSE HUNTERS

Phil Lord

It was a bright fall day many years ago. Four forest officers, who shall remain nameless, were on annual leave and happily headed for a several days goose and duck hunt at Tule Lake. They were armed with, aside from their scatter guns and plenty of shells, a letter to a local farmer at Tule Lake, whose land bordered the lake and who raised grain. Their idea was that he might allow them to camp and hunt on his property since the letter was from an old army buddy of his, who now worked for the Forest Service. They had directions to the place and had little trouble finding it. The farmer read the letter, asked how good old so-and-so was and showed them a good place to camp near a harvested grain field, where he said honkers had been feeding. Their camp was quite close to the lake and they had visions of getting a few mallards also.

Camp was set up and it was still way too early for the evening hunt so they decided, never having been in the area before, to drive into the town of Tule Lake and see the sights, if any, and pick up a few items of food that they had left out of the camp outfit. They stopped at the ranger station to pay their respects but were informed that the ranger was in the field and wouldn't be back for a day or two. (I told you this was a long time ago.) So they proceeded on into town and took in what sights there were and wondered why the ground shook every time a truck load of potatoes went by. They did their shopping and decided to visit one of the local taverns and wet their whistles.

While engaged in this pastime, they got talking to some other waterfowl hunters (duck and goose hunters can and often will tell just as big lies as buck hunters or fishermen) and what with one thing and another they found when they went to leave that it was dark. So they decided to eat in town, which they did and then started back to camp. Not knowing the area they somehow took a wrong turn and pretty soon they were hopelessly lost. There were plenty of roads but no signs and the country was flat.

They stopped to talk it over and the driver said, "If we could just get back close to the lake I think I could find camp." Seeing a dim light in the distance and the road they were on leading towards it, they drove over to it. The light was in the window of a small one room shack. One of them got out of the car, walked over and knocked on the door. It was opened by a grizzled, hard looking old character who said, "What do you want?" The forest officer said, "We seem to be a little bit lost, could you tell me how to get to the lake?"

The old man looked at him kind of funny and said, "Take about three steps backwards son and you will be in it."

INSECTS

GOOD TIMES ON THE SHASTA TRINITY

David W. Scott

I'm not sure exactly when this happened but my best guess is Spring of 1963 or 1964.

Over the years a beekeeper had been trespassing on the national forest each and every spring. Numerous letters were sent admonishing the miscreant to apply for a permit with the assurance that one would be granted for 10 cents a hive per year. As you could guess the scoundrel ignored the power of the district ranger (myself) and continued to trespass each spring. After much advice and counsel from Dana Cox, Recreation, Lands and Range Staff, it was decided to invoke the trespass regulations. Yes, the same regulations used to impound cattle.

Step one was to advertise in a local paper that trespass was illegal and any animals found in trespass would be impounded. This was done in the Mt. Shasta paper sometime in the dead of winter. At this time we knew our trespasser lived in the state of Washington and his chances of seeing the Mt. Shasta Herald were slim to none. Well, come spring our beekeeper showed up just like clockwork and plunked about 500 hives down on the national forest near Lakehead.

Now what to do? How do you impound bees? Again after counsel with Dana it was decided to build a fence around the bees where they sat instead of trying to drive them into a corral. This was done with metal fence posts and snow fencing. A number of government property signs were hung on the fence and the supervisor's office brand new pickup camper was parked on site with Charlie Caldwell, the Lakeshore foreman in attendance twenty four hours a day.

When this was done a certified letter was sent to Mr. Beekeeper in Sunnyside, Washington, telling him what had occurred and that he could recover his bees with their removal from national forest land and the prompt payment of fees and penalties. I believe we sent the letter on a Thursday or Friday. On Sunday about noon I received a call at home from Charlie at the Lakeshore Guard Station saying Mr. Beekeeper was there and needed to talk to me. After much discussion and apologizing the Beekeeper asked if I would come out to Lakeshore GS (30 miles away) and we could settle up. My first response was NO, I did not work on Sunday. It was my time with my family. After some pleading on his part I finally relented and drove out but not before telling him he had best be prepared to pay all the fees, costs and penalties on the spot.

When I arrived and met Mr. Beekeeper I presented him with a handwritten itemized bill which included all costs including my time at the overtime rate, Charlie's time, mileage, phone calls, triple damages and just about everything else you could think of. I think it was about 500 bucks. He wrote me a personal check. In those days Mel Dimmick had trained me to not accept personal checks in payment of debts owed the Forest Service. Despite this training, I decided I had pushed this guy about as far as I could, so I crossed my fingers and took his check.

The guy next said he couldn't get any help on Sunday and could he leave the hives in place until Monday. I told him he could, but it would cost him so many dollars per hour to do so. He allowed as how he would remove them. I left the scene with his check and Charlie called me at home later that day to say the hives had been removed.

Somewhere in the middle of all this, Paul Statham had been informed that one of his rangers had apparently gone berserk and impounded a bunch of honey bees. The following Monday when everything had settled down and the check cleared, I spent the day in the field, returning to my office after everybody had gone home. There in the middle of my desk sat two quarts of honey. Early Tuesday I stopped by the SO and put one quart on

Paul's desk and one on Dana's desk before they came to work. I lurked in the hallways to see the reaction when they arrived. It was instantaneous. Paul headed directly for Dana's office mumbling something about "this damn honey." I discreetly left via the back door. Don't know whatever happened to the honey but I never saw it again.

Who said "rangering" can't be fun?

P.S. I read in later years that this same beekeeper was the recipient of the largest payment in history from the U.S. Department of Agriculture under their honey subsidy program. Maybe he won after all.

A YELLOW JACKET ORDEAL

Hank Mostovoy

This occurred in the late summer of 1951. That year, the yellow jackets were thick and mean. I was the fire guard/smokechaser stationed at Indian Dick Guard Station on the Covelo Ranger District, Mendocino National Forest. I had my own saddle horse with a government mule named Covelo to carry my tools, groceries and personal items.

Covelo was a very good mule to pack and never broke anything he carried. Ken Green's S-set radio, however, occasionally had its innards jarred. Covelo was easy to catch on the range and never lagged. His one bad habit was to fight being shod, which was a necessity in that terrain. We usually had to place a "flying W" of cotton rope on him and lay him down in order to "cold shoe."

On this occasion, a late September lightning storm passed through the headwaters of the Middle Fork of the Eel River. It left two isolated snag fires on Wright's Ridge. I was dispatched to these that evening and reached the first one before midnight. It was the easiest to put a line around and make safe. The other was almost to the top of Windy Mountain in a medium sized dead fir within a "dog hair" thicket. I had it ringed and the snag down by noon. So, of course, I had to mopup and be sure there were no smokes showing after 24 hours.

The next day, late in the afternoon, I headed home across Balm-a-Gilead Creek to report by phone. My usual practice was to let Covelo follow on the way home. He was nipping grass heads and clover as we ascended from the creek. We approached an opening and Covelo veered off the trail to the west side to grab some more clover. I watched him and noticed he stuck his nose real close to the ground. Suddenly, his ears went forward and he gave a great snort and whistle as he jerked his head up. Against the light I noticed yellow jackets boiling out of the ground and all over his face and ears. I knew he would run towards me, so I kicked my horse to run. I was able to keep ahead until I reached the upper pasture gate. By then, the yellow jackets had abandoned the pursuit.

At the hitch rail in front of the station I prepared to relieve Covelo of his pack and noticed that his halter was starting to choke him. I had to use my knife to carefully cut the throat latch and nose band. I then got some wet towels from the house and wrapped his muzzle and neck, being very careful not to infringe on his sensitive ears. I unpacked him and rubbed him down. By bedtime, quite a bit of the swelling had gone down but poor Covelo could not eat for awhile longer.

After that, Covelo was one shy mule whenever a bee or wasp flew around.

REDBUGS WILL GET YOU IF
YOU DON'T WATCH OUT

Harvey Mack

The San Juan Guard Station on the Cleveland Forest is located by the Ortega Highway adjacent to an area that had been a favorite hot springs resort prior to the depression years. By the late 1930s, nothing much remained but a series of hot tub pools with descending mineral water temperatures. The land belonged to the Star Ranch and had been fenced to discourage unauthorized use of these pools.

The fire crew had heard that this was a good place to do one's laundry and, since there were no laundry facilities at the station, it should be a wonderful asset both for doing one's laundry and getting a hot bath. The crew members started making regular trips for laundry and baths but soon they started turning red and itching in their more tender places as the vegetation surrounding these pools was an excellent habitat for tiny red mite larva, also call redbug. This became particularly uncomfortable when doing manual labor or fighting a fire.

Oh yes, some of the wives in the summer home area, as well as my wife, tried doing the same thing with the same results as the mites had no gender bias.

BUGS AND YELLOW JACKETS

Joe Church

Wood ticks were hardly ever mentioned at safety meetings. Ticks were common in the woods and carried a wide variety of serious diseases. They bit without causing pain, most of the time, and made no noise, were dangerous and this was before Lyme disease became popular.

On the Mi-Wok District of the Stanislaus Forest, I discovered by accident that after a day in the woods I had a tick firmly imbedded an the inside surface of my right thigh. High up. This was an, "oh, oh" situation to me so I removed the tick and next day filled out a CA-1 (the accident report form), couching it in, I felt, with nonprovocative language and sent it to the SO. Not too long afterward I received a note from Forest Supervisor Harry Grace asking me to explain further because a lot of people at the SO, including himself, were curious as to where I had actually been bitten. So, I sent in a supplemental explanation without the original vulgarities and that apparently satisfied their curiosity. And, by the way, I suffered no ill effects from the bite. Oddly enough, I was bitten by another tick a month or so later, only in a less delicate location. That CA-1 went though routinely and again I suffered no aftereffects. I felt then, and I still feel now, that ticks were far more dangerous than rattlesnakes or, for that matter, nearly any other forest animal except perhaps for humans themselves.

Mosquitoes were a daily scourge in spring and summer field work.

There was the time, the only time, my family and I visited Tuolumne Meadows one summer afternoon while on an exploratory trip to Yosemite National Park from Twain Harte by way of state highways 108 and 120. It was in the late sixties and, as we drove through the big meadow with its winding river nearby bordered by grassy banks, we wondered aloud why no fishermen were out making use of a great opportunity. We stopped to cheek it out. Two of my children, Clara and Sam, unlimbered their fishing gear and headed for the water with the rest of us close behind. We then discovered why no one was there. In a jiffy, about two and a half trillion mosquitoes rose out of the grass and set about using us for a meal. That got our attention pronto and we began a strategic retreat, which in about three seconds turned into an utter rout. We flung ourselves and equipment into the car, which because all windows were down, now also contained about half a trillion mosquitoes. We tore off down the road flailing and swatting. That didn't do much good, but the car's airstream did. It blew the bugs out of the car except for a few diehards that we hashed in hand-to-hand combat. Looking back on it, I'd bet that the river in Tuolumne Meadows had a lot of trophy fish, for there surely was enough food for them. On the other hand, it may have even been dangerous for the fish to expose themselves!

Ants certainly could be a problem if one chose carelessly a woodsy lunch spot. For a good scare, there was always the possibility of picking up fleas from wood rats or ground squirrels. But mostly I remember yellow jackets and bald hornets. My wife Ginny continues to call yellow jackets "meatbees," as do a lot of other people. I keep telling her they are not bees, they are yellow jacket and there is a world of difference.

When I was growing up in Buffalo, New York, my father kept a beehive in our backyard so as to have honey on hand. However, one winter, rats burrowed up into the hive, ate the honey and destroyed the hive. Those bees could sting too, and carried a pretty good belt. When I began working for the Forest Service in California in the summer of 1951, I was introduced to yellow jackets and their power. They could sting, sting again and keep on stinging until brushed off or killed. And they, like the lizard, would grab hold. If one was attacked by multiples of them, which was most of the time, one was in trouble. I quickly concluded that yellow jackets were at least ten times more powerful than honey bees and were far more aggressive. Then along came bald hornets. It didn't take long to conclude the hornets were at least ten times more powerful than yellow jackets and even more aggressive. I remember being belted twice by a hornet while cruising timber in Seiad Creek on the Klamath National Forest in the early fifties. It got me just behind the left ear. I never saw the hornet or its nest and didn't go searching for them either, but I did have an earache and throbbing headache for the rest of the day.

The encounter I remember more though, was one in which I didn't get stung, but did get a real fright. It too happened on the Seiad District, probably close to the same time as above when I had hiked up a logging road on Slinkard Ridge on the east side of Walker Creek. This road had a dog-leg, and for some reason the road was closed so I was afoot. During my return trip I decided to cut off the dog-leg by hiking downhill through the logging slash to the lower limb of the dog-leg, thus saving me time and energy. While pushing my way through the slash, I happened to look up straight ahead and picked up on a large, active hornet's nest right in my path about fifty feet away. Red flag conditions. Immediate retreat was my only option and I put that option in immediate action. About as soon as I noticed the nest, the nest occupants noted me and sent out a sortie. I ran uphill through the slash as fast as I could and when I reached the road, did the same thing, only faster. However, no matter how fast I ran, my escort of three or four hornets were faster, so much so that they circled me as I ran, buzzing loudly. I ran as fast as I could and after a hundred yards or so my escort, having done its job, peeled off and left me alone. I hadn't been stung nor even landed on, but I became a believer and in a way an admirer. They are terrific fliers; aggressive, determined defenders of their nest and all-around tough customers. Even now, forty years later, I can still hear the whine of those hornets as they circled my head while I was trying to break the world record one hundred yard dash.

INSECTS BOTHER EARLY TRAIL BUILDERS

Fred Wehmeyer

I often wonder if those who now use modern roads and trails ever fully appreciate the cost in pain and misery, besides dollars, of building them in the days long gone by. Every mile of trail was constructed by someone being stung by bees. Nearly every down log, if rotten, contained yellow jacket nests and the air itself was full of insects. Horseflies, deer flies, gnats, no-see-ems and mosquitoes were so thick that one breathed with difficulty. In those days, when exploring for future trail routes, we generally camped on a ridge and packed water. There we could clear a spot and build smudge fires for the horses. The horses would stand head to tail in the smoke and tears rolled down their cheeks. They would venture off to eat only when a breeze brought a temporary lull to the hordes of ravenous flies and mosquitoes. Keeping an eye on the horses was an endless job because, if they thought there was any chance of getting away, they would take off.

I remember a story of Ranger Jamison of Loomis, Washington, who was back in the Toats Coulee country, about his horses wandering off during the night. He started trailing them and soon met another person doing likewise. They struck up an immediate and casual acquaintance. Jamison introduced himself as the local forest ranger and the other fellow said, "I am a prospector, been prospecting these mountains for the past twenty years." He then added, "That ain't exactly the truth as I've hunted horses fifteen of those years!"

Painful adventures added many laughs to the ribald humor of the camp. I remember Glen Mitchell telling of the man they had hired to help cut the hay on their ranch at Molson. He said the hired hand passed him with his arms flailing like vanes on a windmill, cutting wild patterns through the hay field. As he passed, the hired hand yelled, "Ole Yesus, yellow yackets!"

On the way to a fire, about November 1, I had a Britisher in my crew, a soldier recently released from a Lancastershire lancer outfit. We were climbing up steep ground carrying fire tools. Attracted by our perspiration, a large bald hornet lit on the Britisher and changed the shape of the poor chap's ear. He let out a war whoop, but feeling somewhat conspicuous as a true Englishman, he tried not to be emotional. He then said, in a matter of fact conversational tone of voice, "I do believe that nasty insect bit me." Somehow, we "Yanks" lacked much in manners, for the affair struck us as being highly hilarious and we fairly rolled in dirt in laughter.

But back to bugs. I have read that there have been authentic cases of suicide by wild animals who could no longer endure the torture of the millions of voracious insects. I have seen range cattle, no longer able to endure the torture, let out a bawl and take off through the brush without any regard to injury, in the hopes of dislodging some of the insistent insects. I have also seen men working on a trail sit down and cry, completely worn out from the continuous battle of the bugs. I used to think that the devil surely created the insect world and if the time of retribution came about, I hoped to see the rascal staked somewhere on the Similikameen River with no protective net. That will be the day we can join Tug Boat Annie in saying, "Happy days are here some more."

A PET YELLOW JACKET

Don M. Stalter

I'm sure most people think that fire lookouts are peculiar people. Well, anyway, a little different. You have to be, to sit atop a 66 foot tower, which in turn, sits atop of a seven thousand foot mountain out in the middle of a forest. I know. I was there for seven seasons. You're not exactly alone all the time though. You seldom lack for company from your human friends. And you learn to commune with nature. You strike up friendships and relationships with various critters: deer, birds, wood rats, yellow jackets.

One warm, balmy afternoon, three of the fellows from the ranger station negotiated the tower to look over a certain area from my vantage point. While we were talking inside the 14 foot square glass house which I called home, an errant yellow jacket kept flying from one side of the room to the other. His flight path was just about nose high right between the engineers and me.

We kept a wary eye on him but after a dozen or so passes I mumbled, "Oh, that dumb thing," as I reached for an empty soup can. "That's about enough." As the yellow jacket came back from the far side of the room, I held the can up in its path and it flew right in. Showing no surprise at this easy capture, I covered the can, walked to the door, threw him out and said, "There, go outside and play."

By the way my friends looked at each other I am sure they were, and to this day, are still convinced that we lookouts are indeed a strange lot.

MAMMALS (MOSTLY RODENTS)

A SERIOUS CRIBBAGE MATCH

Howard W. Burnett

It seems there was a regional check scaler whose job was to visit various ranger stations and review the work of the log scalers. This often took him to remote ranger districts where he would spend the necessary time staying in the district bunkhouse. At one district in northern Idaho, he had an old friend with whom he enjoyed his visits. They had a mutual love of the game of cribbage and always looked forward to his visits so they could play a serious game or two.

On one visit, on the first night, they sat down in the bunkhouse to enjoy a good cribbage match, when a pack rat ran across the open ceiling beam. They realized that they wouldn't get much sleep that night as pack rats are noisy, so they agreed the pack rat had to go. In those days, when men were men, they were armed, so they agreed that the pack rat had to be shot and put their revolvers on the table. The idea was that the next time the pack rat ran across the beam they would shoot it.

The district ranger visited them briefly and remarked to the effect they must really be serious cribbage players. He, of course, was noticing the guns but they were concentrating on the board and didn't give the guns a thought. They agreed that they were both very serious cribbage players and looked forward to whenever they got together to have a good intense match.

After awhile the ranger left and eventually the pack rat made its reappearance, scurrying across the beam. Both cribbage players grabbed their guns and blazed away, doing away with Mr. Packrat. With the mission accomplished, and the assurance of a good night's sleep at hand, they got back to the cribbage board and were soon again lost in concentration.

The door opened a crack and the ranger stuck his head in, looked around, and said, "Everybody all right in here?" You don't have to have much imagination to guess his relief to find that the gunfire had been directed at the pack rat, do you?

RATS!

Roy R. Sines

Most folks who worked for the US Forest Service in the early days were vexed by pesky rats in camps, shelters, lookouts, guard stations or ranger stations. A rat, or rats, greeted me at my first Forest Service station, which was a lookout, the first day I worked for the Forest Service in 1940.

A trail crew foreman was scheduled to pack me into Cougar Mountain Lookout on the Entiat District of the Wenatchee National Forest the next day. That plan was scuttled by a lightning storm, so the protective assistant called me about 5 p.m. and said a CCC foreman and I would hike up to the lookout that evening. Other lookouts had reported lightning strikes around Cougar Ridge.

The trail to Cougar Mountain Lookout was steep and about a five mile hike. I carried lunches and water and the CCC foreman carried a firepack. As I recall, we reached the lookout about midnight and could see no fires. We finished our lunches then searched the lookout for sleeping gear. There were no sleeping bags and all we could find was a single metal bed and two thin mattresses. We built a fire in the cook stove, put on our coats, and each laid on a dirty mattress hoping to sleep a few hours.

From the odor of the mattresses, it was soon obvious some critter, likely a rat, or rats, had lived for a considerable time in the lookout. We were tired and sleepy, but before either of us had fallen asleep, we heard some critter scampering around the window sills. What else could it be from the smell and racket but a stinking rat? We would chase it around the lookout, then it would disappear only to return for another round about the time our tired bodies dropped off to sleep again. This went on until nearly daylight, so we gave up sleeping and rolled out of our makeshift beds.

The CCC foreman left in the morning, after a breakfast of firepack rations, and I started to house clean with the meager supply of water that we had left. I kept looking for a hole where the rat, or rats, came in. Cougar Mountain Lookout was only a couple of years old and in good condition. About noon the trail crew foreman Clarence Haynes arrived with my supplies so I borrowed a pack mule and went three quarters of a mile to a spring to get a good supply of water. After Clarence left, I continued cleaning and searching for a rat hole. No rats sneaked in all day long, but soon after I turned out the gas lantern that night the pesky critter was back again. The next day I cleaned under the firefinder stand and, of all places, I found a little hole chewed in the floor.

In those early days, some packers, trail crew foremen, and others, often carried pistols claiming they might need a gun to shoot a horse or mule if it fell and broke a leg. Well, I never knew of a gun being used for that reason. However, I have been awakened out of a sound sleep when camped in a shelter with a gun packing packer when he took a midnight pot shot at a pack rat.

I still do not like rats, even pet rats ....

CHRIS MORGENROTH TREED BY WOLVES

Rudo L. Fromme

Mr. E. B. Webster, in his book *The King of the Olympics*, furnishes a quite complete description of Ranger Morgenroth's harrowing experience of trying to keep out of the way of two seemingly vicious, or craftily curious, wolves—particularly the larger of the two. Chris' story was verified by Trapper Grant Humes, who accompanied the ranger back to the sight of this incident only a few minutes after it happened and checked tracks on the ground. It will probably be of interest to quote portions of this narrative, which is much as I heard it from Chris and Humes on the spot that same spring, around 1917 or '18.

After stating that Morgenroth was walking up a zigzag trail above the Elwha River with a view to meeting one of his guards who had been engaged in spring trail maintenance, the book reads, "Just as he reached the crest, there confronted him, only a few yards distant, an old' timber wolf—a giant of his race. Silently it faced Morgenroth, while a second and smaller animal as quietly circled around to the rear, in pursuance of tactics they doubtless had found universally successful. Without a gun, not even a walking stick, Morgenroth cast about for something in the way of a weapon. Picking up a couple of pebbles, he dropped them into his pocket and tried one dead branch after another; all were rotten.

"Meanwhile the big wolf edged a little closer, again waiting. Morgenroth yelled, waved his arms, threw his hat, tried everything he could think of, to no avail, and finally was forced to take refuge at the top of an old, smooth jagged-top stub, whereupon the wolf came up and sat down underneath, evidently with the intention of loafing around until he slid to the ground.

"All efforts, vocal and otherwise, having failed, and his grasp on the smooth limbless stub gradually slipping, Mr. Morgenroth reached in his pocket for his clasp knife, intending to slide down and give the old devil as hard a tussle for life as might be within his power. But, fortunately, the small rocks had gone into his pocket containing the knife. The first one thrown, the wolf being directly underneath, struck him on the head. Surprised, he jumped aside, whereupon Mr. Morgenroth dropped with a yell, then chased down trail as only a man whose life depended on his feet could run!

"For some reason, the wolves avoided the trail keeping alongside in the low brush until Morgenroth, out of wind, was forced to climb again. This time, however, he was able to pick up a club and thus, keep the wolves a short distance away until he was again ready to run. A better club, hastily grabbed as he flew along the trail, gave him greater confidence and the next time he stood at bay at the base of a tree.

The wolves seemed to realize that he was now armed and soon left. Mr. Morgenroth made the next two miles or so down to the Hume's ranch without catching another glimpse of them."

The article finishes by stating that "Mr. Morgenroth has concluded that a revolver has the same value in the Olympics today that it once had on the Texan Border." Chris told me, however, that in a calmer moment, he had decided that any kind of a gun is just too much of a burden, unless one is really out for venison in the hunting season. This was his first wolf encounter and he never expects another.

THE BOAR WAR

Howard W. Burneett

An older ranger told me this story about the Cohutta Mountain area of the Chattahoochee National Forest in Georgia. It took place sometime before I became the first ranger of the Cohutta Ranger District, which was established in 1958.

The Cohutta Mountain block is a very rugged, steep block of about 100,000 acres that is shown on the topo maps with very close topo lines. There is almost no level land and very little that isn't precipitous. The area had been railroad logged and then burned in the 1920s, but it was making a fast comeback, so fast in fact that much of it is now a formal wilderness area.

Hunting has always been popular there, and a hunting club from down state wanted to introduce European boars for a new source of sport. This suggestion of bringing in an exotic species was not met with approval by either the Forest Service or the Georgia Wildlife Commission, of course. After much talk, however, one gentleman took it upon himself to loose seven boars into the area apparently, and no one was supposed to be the wiser. However, as one might imagine, work of this deed soon got around and everyone know of the illegal introduction.

The gentleman in question apparently wanted to see how his project was coming along and spent a good bit of time riding the trails looking for some sign of his boars and asking local residents if they had seen them. They were just never seen and the introduction was a failure, but no one knew the reason why.

The former ranger was visiting a local farmer near the Forest Service land one day and after the obligatory conversation about crops, dogs, children and so forth, the local gent seemed anxious about something. Finally, he said, "Ranger, if you had worked all year to grow a crop of corn, harvested it, and put it in a crib so you could feed your pigs through the winter, and a wild hog came in and busted into your crib, what would you do?"

The ranger thought it over and finally answered honestly, "I believe I would shoot 'em."

The farmer said, "I did. All seven."

And that was the end of the exotic introduction of Prussian boars in the Cohuttas. I don't think this story has ever seen the light of day before, and I have left out names on purpose. I can't say it is the gospel truth, but I respect the older ranger who told it to me and I believe him. This is a case of sometimes learning more than you really want to know!

THE NEW BRIDE AND THE CHIPMUNK

Ken Weissenborn

I got lucky in 1950. I was one of a very few college graduates who were given appointments with the U.S. Forest Service. I reported for duty at Jacob Lake, Arizona, on June 12 of that year. I was given permission to leave school before graduation in order to accept this assignment.

Jacob Lake is located at the junction of the highway leading to the North Rim of the Grand Canyon, some 45 miles away, and the road to Kanab, Utah. During the summer tourist season it is a beehive of activity. Principal activities are filling tourists with food, trinkets, gasoline and charge card receipts for lodging. It also is the post office for the people who live on the mountain. During the winter season, the resident population totaled four— a young couple who were caretakers at the lodge, Natalie and me. The elevation was 8,000 feet. Winters were long, cold and snow-covered.

The North Kaibab Ranger District covered three quarters of a million acres. During the summer months, the Forest Service had a fairly large number of people working on the mountain. A crew of 12 to 15 forestry students were based at a work camp at Jacob Lake. Three lookouts were manned during fire season. A seasonal station was located at Big Springs. It had been the main quarters for years, before the ranger was officially assigned to Kanab, Utah. The facilities were old, but spacious and well maintained.

Big Springs was the summer headquarters for Assistant Ranger Bill Strawn and Range Conservationist Tuffy Swapp. Tuffy lived in Kanab, and his family stayed in town. Bill Strawn's wife Marjorie, was a medical student in Pennsylvania. She was able to spend her summer vacations with Bill, but had to return to her studies each fall. For Bill, it was a lonely existence.

The station was named after the large spring that flowed out of the cliffs which bordered the valley. It was the one dependable source of water for miles around. Groceries, entertainment and other amenities were available in Kanab, which was a long trip over sixty miles of rough dirt road. The following story tells of some of the problems of domestic life in the country.

> The ranger brought his brand new bride
> to his Arizona spread.
> He thought that she might be concerned
> about the life that lay ahead.
>
> "It will be different than you knew"
> he told his nervous spouse.
> "But we've gone up and piped the spring
> to bring water to the house."
>
> "I'll give you all the best I can.
> I do not mean to boast,
> Now would you kindly be so good
> as to pour our wedding toast?"
>
> It was not a sight for the faint of heart
> when she turned on the spout
> As chipmunk tails and legs and ears
> and other parts came out.
>
> He watched her as her face grew pale
> as she gazed upon the sight.
> He thought at once "This all might end—
> she may leave me by tonight."
>
> He called old Tuff, his faithful friend
> to see what he could do
> To calm the fears of his worried wife
> before his marriage was through.
>
> Old Tuff came back down from the hill—
> Said "Ma'am, have no more fear.
> Those legs and tails and other parts
> will never more appear."

The ranger thought "I'll show my bride
I know what I'm talking about."
He asked old Tuff "Did you box the spring
to keep the chipmunks out?"

Old Tuff said "Boss, seemed like too much work
to keep them from getting in,
So I've been up there all day long
teachin' those little rascals to swim."

THE GREAT PORCUPINE SHOOTOUT

Tom Glunt

In 1951, when I was the USFS log scaler for the Associated Box timber sale on Ball Mountain, I stayed in the cabin at Shovel Greek on the Klamath National Forest. It was near the main logging road and on the way to the landing on the timber sale.

The cabin was an old CCC shack that evidently was the cookhouse. Anyway, the floor around the wood range was soaked in grease from a lot of cooking. It evidently had soaked through the floor.

It all started the second night that I was there. About three o'clock in the morning I woke up to this awful crunching sound from under the building. Needless to say, I wasn't too thrilled about going outside to see what it was. It was pitch black, cold and spooky in the forest at night. I put on pants and boots, and with flashlight in one hand and .22 pistol in the other, looked under the shack and found Mr. Porcupine gnawing on the floor joists that evidently tasted like salty bacon grease. After he was dispatched, I went to bed thinking I had solved the problem.

Since I had no transportation, Louis Winfield, the Associated logging boss used to pick me up early every morning and take me to the landing. I put the porcupine in the back of his pickup and left it for the coyotes along the road.

It seemed that a bunch of other porcupines missed their buddy and showed up about twice a week between two and three a.m. and woke me gnawing on the floor joists. The empty building was a good sounding box and amplified the sound to a roar. I got tired going out at night and freezing you know what, so I tried a few sound shots through the old thin floor. Three well placed shots through the floor usually did the trick. In the morning Louis would meet me by the road as I waited with the night's floor kill. I think I thinned out the population around Shovel Creek Station as the talley rose to seven before they gave up. Louis Winfield seemed disappointed when I showed up by the road without my porcupine.

THE RANGER AND THE MONKEY

Chuck Hill

In the summer of 1953, the McCloud District of the Shasta National Forest had a lady from Los Angeles as a lookout on Grizzly Peak. That summer the Shasta Forest was replacing the lookout cab so the lady was enduring life in a tent on a high, windy knob. She had company all summer; a big ugly howler monkey. About midway through the summer she announced she'd had enough of Grizzly Peak. The ranger went up to the lookout, loaded up the lady and her monkey and brought them down to Bartle. He had called ahead and had us fire up the boiler in the bathhouse and alert Karl Larson the cook to fix up a nice meal.

When they pulled in, the lady took a long steamy shower while the ranger tuned on us firecrew members to mind our manners. After her bath the lady joined us for supper. She held the monkey on her lap while trying to eat. He kept grabbing the food before she could eat it so she asked the ranger to hold the monkey so she could get something to eat. The ranger took the monkey, the lady took a bite and the monkey took a leak on the ranger's lap.

The ranger smiled and said, "Think nothing of it."

After a little sweet talk, a hot bath and an excellent Karl Larson meal, the lady and her monkey returned to Grizzly Peak for the remainder of the summer.

Next day the cook changed the crew's work schedule. We spent the day giving the cookhouse a complete G.I. party. Karl had in the past been a cook with a carnival outfit and didn't have much good to say about monkeys.

THE PIG OUT

T. J. "Tom" Jones

Assistant Ranger William Clark, Assistant Ranger Wyatt, Charlie Duncan and I made a grazing reconnaissance in May of 1911 on the Mono National Forest. We arrived by pack and saddle horse in western Nine Mile Valley at a little brush draw where a small spring seeped from the ground and a narrow band of willows grew across the draw at right angles to its course.

Camp was pitched for protection from wind and sun on the north side of the willows. On going to work the next morning at about 7 a.m. we took the ordinary lunch of crackers, a little cheese and sardines. We returned to camp just as the sun was setting, which was about 6 p.m. at that time of year.

On arising that morning, Clark and Duncan, who had slept together, left their bed just as they got out of it, with covers thrown back. The grubstake, which consisted of a 25 pound sack of flour, a half sack of potatoes, the same amount of apples, some bacon, ham and canned goods, was stacked at the foot of their bed. Wyatt and I, who were more or less old-timers at camping, just by force of habit, had rolled our beds into the customary roll with canvas on the outside (sleeping bags in the Forest Service had not been heard of yet). Old China Tom, who lived over a little hill about 300 yards to our west, owned among other things, a red sow and five shoats. In our absence, those doggoned hogs had discovered our camp and hence this story.

When I rounded the willows that evening with a transit on my shoulder, the sight that met my eyes is impossible to describe. But anyone using his imagination and knowing a little about hogs can visualize how much dough they can make with a mixture of apples, potatoes, flour and bacon. And except for what they smeared on their exteriors, they had consumed the whole of it within a ten foot radius from the center of Clark's and Duncan's bed. To show their contentment at being fed, they went to sleep on the boys' bed. This created not only a comical situation but a serious one in that we were 25 miles from supplies, with all our food gone except for a few cans of fruit.

The human reaction of all concerned I remember best of all. On seeing the hogs, I set my transit down and was just taking in the situation in amazement when Ranger Wyatt, who was just behind me, saw it. He took one look and collapsed an the ground with a good-natured roar. Clark, who came next took one look, started to cry and made for the hogs. My old dog Friday, in sympathy with him of course, started to help him out. Duncan, who was a little behind, became extremely angry, ran to my saddle, grabbed a rifle off it and before he could be stopped, fired a couple of shots. But Friday by this time had put the hogs in the sagebrush and so far as I know, Duncan made no hits. When everybody quieted down, a council of war was held and we began to look for food. All we had left was some canned fruit; I remember especially canned cherries which had been somewhat mashed up but were still usable.

It was soon decided that Wyatt should take his packhorse and go to Nine Mile Ranch for food that night, which he did, returning the next day about noon. The balance of us stayed in camp and the next morning ran lines adjacent to camp, where the least walking would be required until we got something to eat.

BUNKHOUSE RATS

Wendall L. Jones

Any of us who stayed in pre World War II barracks or bunkhouses while working summers or otherwise, as a batching Forest Service employee, probably experienced some great stories about trying to coexist with a few pack rats. Actually, coexistence was not acceptable, so if someone heard, or thought they heard, a pack rat in the middle of the night, there was this very loud yell of "pack rat!" several flashlights went on, there was usually no power after 10 p.m. until breakfast and you could hear feet hitting the floor. Usually, almost everyone had a weapon of some sort handy—an old axe handle, broom handle or there was often a baseball bat somewhere in the bunkhouse. Now if you can imagine up to a dozen guys in their skivvies swinging these potentially lethal weapons in a mostly dark room, except for these darting flashlight beams, you can see there was great risk of loss of life or limb and I don't mean the pack rat's life or limb. However, I don't recall anyone suffering more than a stubbed toe. Oh yes, there was plenty of noise: "There he goes!" "I think he is over here!" "Look out, he's coming your way!" and, oh yes, some unprintable statements when toes were stubbed or bunks fell over. These were short-lived riots because we would give up within minutes as there were lots of escape routes for the pack rat through the built-in air conditioning system. On one occasion, there was the, "I got the s.o.b.!" and a brief ceremony of tossing the rat out the door before dashing back into our bunks and catching that much needed sleep before another hard day's work.

JACKRABBITS GALORE

Tom Glunt

In the evenings around the old Mt. Hebron Ranger station on the Goosenest District of the Klamath Forest in 1951, when things got a little boring, somebody would suggest that we thin out the rabbit population.

The formula was: take one pickup (I won't say what pickup we used) and fill it with armed men and drive the back roads.

The crew had everything from semi-automatic 22s to 30-06 with hand loads. One or two shotguns were usually present also.

As anyone who was ever at Mt. Hebron knows, the area is full of dirt back roads with weed covered ditches. We discovered that if you put a pickup wheel in the shallow ditches among the weeds at dusk, the roads erupted with jackrabbits in all directions. The ensuing sound of gunfire reminded the WWII veterans of the Battle of the Bulge. I believe it was Bob Freshour, the dozer operator, that had the 30-06 with scope and hand loaded ammunition. When a rabbit stopped out in a field, after escaping the road ambush, he thought he was safe at 50 yards plus. I swear the 30-06 turned the rabbits inside out or they just disappeared. Nobody really wanted to go look.

PORCUPINES

Wendall L. Jones

Many of us had great stories of hunting porcupine on government time or at least, with government furnished ammo. But there were also great stories of encounters with porkies at unexpected times. We all used to work alone in the woods a lot doing sale planning and sale layout, and we were a production outfit in those days. Anyone who went less than full speed would likely not see very good performance ratings. I often went at kind of a lope and usually did a sort of vault over big, old growth, down timber. You took lots of spills but learned to fall gracefully and, needless to say, we were tough! I clearly recall one of these vaults over a large Douglas fir blowdown about four feet in diameter. When I cleared it enough to see the other side, their was a big porky right where I was aimed to hit ground. Now, you have seen people change direction in mid-air in the cartoons—

Bugs Bunny, Donald Duck and others—but most people assure me that this was impossible, at least prior to the Michael Jordan era. But, I swear on a stack of bibles that I was able to either change direction or perhaps, even come to a dead stop in mid-air and alter my flight path. Anyway, I missed the porky and I was so grateful I let him waddle away.

THE DAM BEAVER OF THE SIERRAS

Lloyd W. Swift

The Plumas National Forest was my locale from 1930-35, first as chief of party on the range survey, then range staff.

Numerous Plumas stream and meadow types with willow and aspen looked similar to beaver occupied habitats observed in the Rockies but while California is the home of three subspecies of beaver, none occurred in the Sierra Nevada Mountains. The natives were all found in the lowland river systems—the Shasta beaver in the Pit and other drainages of upper northern California, the golden in the great valley and the Sonora beaver on the Colorado River.

Gradually the idea evolved that nature had overlooked opportunities for expansion of beaver populations and needed some help. Inquiries on the possibility of stocking native animals were not promising. Their numbers were very low and if the Sierras were suitable habitat, the California races would have spread into the mountains eons ago.

In pursuing the introduction proposal, it was concluded that sources outside California would be the route to go. Supervisor Dave Rogers supported the plan and Jesse Nelson, Chief of Range, perhaps recalling his early days in Wyoming and Colorado, approved. In the meantime Ben Beard, Milford District Ranger of the Plumas, and I scouted for a suitable release site. Our choice was Rowland Creek, a small permanent stream in a little valley supporting a thick stand of aspen, a regrowth following a 1926 fire.

During 1934, three pairs of Snake River beaver were obtained from Idaho. In anticipation of the introduction, Ben and I had two ponds created which served as the release sites. The beavers prospered and colonies appeared at increasing distances from Rowland Creek. Eventually the population was a source of stocking on other national forests in a cooperative program with the California Division of Fish and Game.

There was a release of California native beaver in Plumas County in 1923, but it seems to have been a failure. Idaho beavers were stocked at Wheat's Meadow on the Stanislaus National Forest in 1934. The numbers expanded, then declined. The 1934 Rowland Creek stocking would appear to have resulted in the first successful establishment of beaver colonies in the mountain streams of the Sierras.

BUGS AND RODENTS AT THE ANIMAL FAIR

Abe G. Turley

After two seasons at King's Pass, I was assigned to Sunset Peak Lookout. It is a high, rocky point on the same spur as King's Pass Lookout. It was a promotion of sorts, though not in pay, which remained at $105 per month, payable once a month, but in duties and responsibilities. It was a fully equipped weather station with anemometer/odometer, maxi/mini thermometers, sling psychrometer, rain gauge and fuel moisture sticks with scale. Daily observations were transmitted at 9 a.m. to Missoula and Coeur d'Alene with a little SPF radio. I could check wind speed at anytime with a push button, count the buzzes, consult the chart system. I recall that the highest wind speed I checked was in the fifties.

Fifty miles an hour was enough. The Sunset house was built about 1919. A cupola was added later. The whole thing moved in a strong wind. When I opened up, the floor was so chewed up by corked boots that just walking across it was an adventure. The knots stood up like little mesas in a desert. The finished floor was six inch pine shiplap. I tore up the floor, turned it over, moving the thinnest pieces to the edges, and painted it dark green to match the rest of the interior. Looked pretty good, too. I made a small sign, "No Corks, Please," a rather futile endeavor because the only visitors I had that summer, aside from resupply visits, was a five-man inspection team from the supervisor's office who checked me an everything, including cooking. They did bring their own groceries.

1937 was the year the wheels in Missoula decided that every primary lookout in the region should be equipped with a standard privy. A privy kit, with everything needed to assemble a precut privy, was delivered to each lookout. No instructions, diagrams or material lists were included and no one seemed to know why. By laying out all the pieces and determining ahead of time where each piece went, I was able to get it assembled with nothing left over but a few shingles. After I bragged over the radio that I had finished mine, I had a spate of calls over the privy network, seeking help.

This was also the year of the garbage can. I don't know if it was a regional, forest or district thing, but a five gallon, galvanized garbage can, with lid, was delivered to each lookout. I didn't bother to ask what it was for because I knew what the answer would be. "It's for garbage, stupid."

Because I burned what little garbage I generated and flattened my tin cans with the side of the lookout axe and skimmed them down over the side of the mountain like frisbees, I decided to use the can for storage of dry foods; navy beans, flour, sugar, salt, anything favored by mice. Worked great.

Sunset Peak was a razorback ridge that fell away in a broad, open area to the south. It was the only area that wasn't rocky. Over the centuries, a thin layer of dirt had built up and some families of ground squirrels had taken up residence there. They became quite friendly.

I was working outside one day, close enough that I had left the door open. I became aware of a sound, a sort of a clunk, and after listening to several clunks, decided it was coming from the cabin. When I was close enough to see into the cabin, the source of the clunk became evident. A ground squirrel had found the garbage storage can. It was standing on its hind legs, supporting itself with one front paw against the can and with the other, was trying to raise the lid. He was raising it, but when he had raised it to his maximum reach, the lid slipped shut with a clunk. He never would have figured it out, but didn't know that. I watched him for a few minutes until I felt sorry for him and scared him away.

Nobody warned me about the flying ants, so I was surprised one day to see a large swarm, almost like a cloud of black smoke, circling the chimney. They appeared to be discussing who would be first to come down the stack. I guess they came to an agreement because all of a sudden the whole swarm was crowding into the six inch pipe. I closed the door. I don't know why, because they showed no interest whatever in entering that way. I took a peek into the stove. It was filled with a pulsating mass of sex mad flying ants. I replaced the lid, hurriedly. By now, most of the buggers were either in the stovepipe or the stove. I lit a piece of newspaper and crammed it into the stove, followed by more crumpled paper until there was a good draft going. Wingless, charred ants were being carried up the chimney and out to fall back onto the roof in a motionless pile. There must have been thousands of them.

I've wondered what I would have done without paper. I wonder how lantern gas would work.

COOKIE SKUNK

Tom Glunt

A bunch of the crew was playing cards at Bob Marshall's place one hot night, having been drawn to the card game by the smell of fresh baked oatmeal cookies, thanks to Bob's wife. As the card game progressed the player facing the kitchen door froze and whispered in an undertone, "Don't move." A skunk with a cookie in his mouth trotted through the room and out the open back door. Being a hot night, the front and back doors were open and no screen doors were present. Everyone let out their breath and went on with the card game. About 20 minutes later the cookie loving skunk made another trip out of the kitchen with another cookie and out the back door. I believe it was Bob who said, "I don't care how hot it is, I am closing the door." Evidently the cookie aroma drew more than timber and fire crews at Mt. Hebron that night on the Goosenest Ranger District, Klamath National Forest in 1951.

PORCUPINES

Bob Gray

They make funny tracks in the dust, like dragging a broom behind a beaver. They're not very pretty, not very smart, don't look like they're enjoying life and I'm not sure their mother even loves them. They're too slow to get away from dogs, which aren't smart enough to let them get away, and they don't show up well enough in headlights to keep from getting hit. You don't know why your tire is flat until you take it off and find a porcupine quill in it.

What do they eat? Your saddle, your boot, your belt and the sweatband in your hat. Then your rifle stock, saddle blanket and other boot. From there it's the front doorstep and the bacon.

When deprived of these delicacies out in the wilds, it's the plywood sign you placed last summer and the routed sign with linseed oil.

But their favorite food is the 100 acres of pine seedlings planted last year or the bottom foot of the five foot trees in another plantation. Sometimes an acre of natural reproduction is their choice, where they girdle all the trees at nose height. Creeping destruction, they are.

District Ranger Dutch Sullaway and I were driving home from Medicine Lake one night when we saw a lumbering shape in the road. He must have been the granddaddy of all porcupines. "There's a shovel in the back, lets get him," says

Dutch as he came to a screeching halt. I grabbed the shovel and approached Old Grandad from the side, failing to see a round rock about baseball size. As I swung the shovel my foot hit the rock. It rolled and I fell right over that porkey's back, with the shovel flying. My body made an arch over him as he ambled on into the darkness. "Did you get him?" Dutch called from the cab. Well, no, I didn't get him, but I felt pretty lucky as I picked a dozen quills from the front of my shirt in the headlights of the pickup. Dutch just grinned and relit his pipe.

On another occasion I let one get away. We were looking for a lightning fire in the McCloud Flats and couldn't find it, though we knew it was nearby. I climbed a pine tree about 80 feet tall to get a look around. At about 50 feet I met a porcupine face to face two feet in front of me. He hardly even bristled as I detoured around him on the way up. Coming down, he was still perched on the same limb, with his dark beady eyes fixed on mine. We gave each other the once over for about ten minutes, just seeing what the other species looked like at close range, until my crew hollered, "What are you doing up there?" "Just communicating with a porcupine," I answered. "Oh, yes, the fire's about 100 yards that way," and I pointed to the fire. The crew hadn't seen the porcupine until I got down and showed it to them through the dense branches. "It could only happen to you," said one of the crewmen.

ROMANCE SAVES CONIFERS

Bruce Barron

In the mid 1940s, Ted Schlapfer took his first steps toward a highly impressive career in the U.S. Forest Service. He was a junior forester stationed far back in the hinterlands at a place called Shovel Creek on the Goosenest District of the old Shasta Forest. By long distance, Ted had been courting a winsome brunette by the name of Beth, an urbanite who resided in the Eastern U.S. The romance was serious and Beth kept the phone lines busy to the ranger district headquarters at Mt. Hebron.

As district fire dispatcher, I was an around the clock slave to a desk full of telephones, radios and log books. Beth was oblivious to the fact that there were no phone connections at Shovel Creek and it involved an hours trip over tortuous back country roads to deliver her message of ardor. I began to look forward to Beth's urgent calls and prevailed on the District Ranger, Chuck Abell, to designate me as an official messenger, thus giving me a welcomed respite from the office tedium.

By coincidence the Shasta Forest was being besieged by a plague of porcupines that were devastating the forest with their voracious appetite for young pine trees. A bounty of 25 cents per snout had been placed on these destructive animals. With a .22 caliber rifle and sharp hunting knife, I often collected a dozen or more "porky snouts" which helped defray my vehicle expenses.

I have always taken pride in being a good shot with a rifle, however, in this instance, I feel that I also did a fair job in helping to keep "on target" those legendary arrows that were twanged from cupid's bow! Ted and Beth have now been happily married for over a half century. Ted's distinguished career ultimately took him to the top of the ladder as a regional forester in Alaska.

The Schlapfers "long distance" courtship no doubt saved hundreds of young conifers from porcupine devastation.

THE GOAT

Tom Wintringham

This is the story of a euphemistic goat (and other tales). The event happened many years ago, circa 1959.

I was under the excellent tutelage of Phil Intorf and Russ Rogers in the field of blister rust control. At the time of the episode I was stationed at Challenge on the LaPorte District of the Plumas National Forest. The big boss was Bill "Goodwin" Peterson; "Bill Pete" to his lackeys.

These were my halcyon days in the good 'ol USFS. I was a beginner in 1957. Because of my age, I was Bill Pete's "senior" junior forester. This was because I had spent ten years in lumber mills principally as a dry kiln operator. The real beginning was in Quincy where I learned the rudiments of BRC from Russ Rogers.

For example, we made our own maps for contract control purposes. One day Russ and I went to a place I believe was called P Creek to do a little pruning and to make a map. Russ showed me the proper way to prune a sugar pine tree and then sent me merrily on my way to compass and pace a particular road. I would meet him back at the pickup in the afternoon.

When I left on my mapping job, Russ was busily pruning a young sugar pine. I compassed and paced and paced and compassed and ate my lunch and then compassed and paced some more. Eight miles and several hours later I arrived back at the pickup, exhausted, only to find Russ, almost as fresh as in the morning, still busily pruning the same tree! I think he heard me coming.

Later, I went to Challenge as "Blister Rust Control Officer." Jack Moore was the ramrod then and a little later Bob Cermak. This was a great time in the early part of my career since no one I worked with knew exactly what I was supposed to do! Jack and Bob may deny this but it is true. I came and went as I pleased and, essentially, worked for Phil Intorf.

The contractual part of the job was very interesting. I met people from all walks of life; there were students, older couples and people who enjoyed working out-of-doors. Sometimes when I would walk into a semipermanent camp at noon eating a peanut butter sandwich, it was difficult to the extreme to turn down a home cooked lunch/dinner of roast meat, fried chicken, or whatever, with all the trimmings. These people worked hard and ate accordingly. There was one older couple who set up a 16 by 32 foot canvas and netting campsite. One half of this was living quarter and the other half was the kitchen/dining area. And, boy, could the Mrs. cook!

300

This contractor had difficulty getting one of his lots passed by our checkers. It was always the same bush that eluded him! I went out with the checker one day after about four failures and he pointed out the bush. Well, it was like a tree; the stem was about three inches in diameter. The contractor walked under it every day. He was an experienced digger and neither he nor I had ever seen anything like it.

At Challenge, we had a side camp, if you will, at a place designated on the map as "Cascade." It was the site of an old logging camp. There was a barn in a meadow, a house and a bar plus several small cabins. These cabins were rented out during hunting season. It was a rather pretty place even being located in a cutover area. Today's environmentalists (the unwashed) would consider the area to have been ravaged by "person" kind, yet the trained eye could see signs of adequate recovery everywhere.

The caretaker of the place was a man named John whose last name escapes me after all these years. I remember him as having a miserable accent, two dogs and the key to the bar. Around that time there was a singing group called "Three Dog Night." I hadn't the foggiest idea what the group name signified. However, in talking to John, he told me that in the winter he covered his bed with a canvas upon which his two dogs slept, effectively warming his bed. Ah, the light bulb! Now I knew.

We, the USFS, rented what was left of the logger's barracks. It was somewhat dilapidated but offered protection from the weather, a place to sleep and a place to cook. It was homebase for the blister rust eradication crew.

It was also loaded with mice. They were brave little fellows and scampered all over the place, even on the table when we were eating. After opening the place up one early summer, we decided something had to be done about the mice or they would cart everything away. The first idea was mouse traps. But this became tedious because no sooner had you set out the traps than you had to start emptying them. And the mouse population didn't seem to decrease at all.

The second idea was to use wheat laced with 1080. (This was back in what you might call the "experimental days" before we understood the far-reaching effects of some of the stuff we played with.) After we came in from our field work we would set out handfuls of our bait in strategic places and go on about our business of eating and getting ready for bed. This worked beautifully for no sooner would you locate the wheat than here would come the little rascals for din-din. Some never made it back to where they came from! But it temporarily reduced their numbers.

When I first met John he was complaining bitterly about having to move all of the "cuhtam muhtrasses" out of storage and into the cabins. Neither Phil nor I knew what he was talking about. Apparently, John had spent the better part of the day doing housework and was tired of it. It wasn't until later that Phil and I concluded John was cursing the "goddam mattresses."

There was another time that sticks in my memory. Several of us from the ranger station were spending the night at Cascade for some training purpose or another. We were all erudite, literate people. We could sip tea and eat scones with the best. And, because most of us were veterans, we could talk like sailors on shore leave if the occasion warranted.

At this time, Sputnik was on the tip of everyone's tongue. It was THE thing to watch for. On a moonless night that was as dark as the inside of a cow we were sitting on the hoods of us our pickups waiting for Sputnik to pass overhead. Sure enough here it came, right across the night sky. Not a word was said as it made its traverse. We were in utter awe! When it disappeared from sight there was a moment of thoughtful silence and then Hal McElroy said, "Well, I'll be dipped in s___!" Somehow the expression, as crude as it may seem, reflected the wonderment of the moment.

Oh, I almost forgot the goat.

One night after Phil and I had visited John at the house and had accomplished some business, John suggested that we repair to the bar for a nightcap. It was dark and as we threaded our way along the trail from the house to the bar, John suddenly dashed off the trail into the darkness and bushes saying that he "had to milk his goat." A little farther on, Phil broke the quiet by saying, "I didn't know that John had a goat!"

MOUNTAIN ENCOUNTER

Michael A. Borysewicz

As I drove past Halfway Hill on the St. Joe River Road, I felt very tired and looked forward to my bed at the ranger station bunkhouse. The vinyl seat of my old 1968 Camaro was not the most comfortable for long drives. I shifted my weight on the seat and rolled the window partway down so the cold night air would help me stay awake. A bright moon lit up the top third of the tree covered slopes above the road The road itself was in darkness, temporarily lit by the twin cones of my headlights. In the gorge below me I knew the black waters of the river were spilling over boulders and swirling in deep, bedrock lined pools. It was already late October. I had just two or three weeks of work left with the U.S. Forest Service before being laid off for the winter. I was driving back from town after a long weekend of carousing and enjoying the company of friends. The river road was by then very familiar to me. My mind measured the trip more as a passage of time than of distance over the earth. There was a lot of time to think on that drive,

How unlike my first trip up this road! At that time I knew very little about mountains and places empty of people. I was a relative newcomer to Idaho, having recently moved out from the east coast to finish college. My introduction to the St. Joe River Road was the result of my being hired as summer help by the Forest Service. I was headed to my first job in the woods. I had virtually no idea of what my newly landed job would entail. There was no way for me to know that I was starting what would become a lifelong attachment to mountains.

I thought back to that drive, only three short years earlier. On that day, I had left late in the morning from the town of Moscow where I was attending the University of Idaho. Gray and white cumulus clouds cluttered a blue June sky, casting large shadows over the rolling wheat fields that started on the edge of town. The farther north I traveled from Moscow the more relief the landscape gained. The patchwork quilt of agricultural fields became torn here and there by woodlots of ponderosa pine and Douglas fir. Every so often, a tall butte or ridge covered with dark evergreens appeared, inevitably drawing my attention.

Eventually I left the farmlands behind and came into the tree-covered foothills of the Bitterroot Mountains. The road here was a swath cut through the dense forest, occasionally straight when the topography allowed, but mostly as curved as a stretching cat. The green on the map identified this area as part of the Idaho Panhandle National Forest of which I was soon to be an employee. Periodically, the highway dropped down into open valleys containing tiny hamlets of a few scores of residents. The logging town of St. Maries was the largest of these and marked the main course change of my journey. From St. Maries I turned onto the St. Joe River Road for the first time, heading due east.

Here the banks of the lower St. Joe River were lined with stately cottonwood trees, like the neat columns of a southern mansion. I was to later learn that the shade of these trees on the water had inspired the popular name for this stretch of river—"the Shadowy St. Joe." Although I had never seen it before, this river looked familiar to me. Its slow moving deep water meandering through a wide flood plain seemed reassuringly like the waterways of my native New Jersey. As a teenager, I first learned to fish in a small, lazy tributary of the Raritan River. My best friend and I would go down to a favorite sheltered cove on this stream to try for perch, bass and even an occasional pickerel. After a heavy rain the water would run brown with silt. Only catfish were likely to find your bait in those turbid conditions. The St. Joe seemed just like a bigger version of this brook I passed so many hours on in my youth.

From St. Maries it was roughly 90 miles east and southeast to Red Ives Ranger Station, my destination. Between St. Maries and Red Ives there existed exactly two towns that had a combined population of less than 300. As an easterner, not used to large wild spaces, I was struck by the isolation of the area I was entering. Tall hills quickly tightened up the river valley. Over time, the hill slopes became mountainsides. The forests went on and on! How could there possibly be so much vacant land left in the 20th century? After a half hour or so of driving, the winding, two lane highway turned into a gravel road. The farther I drove up the St. Joe drainage, the wilder the country seemed to get. The river slowly shed any resemblance to a sluggish, east coast stream and took on an entirely new identity. I began to see most of the rocky stream bottom as the water picked up speed. Rapids and chutes were already common by the time I passed the town of Avery.

From Avery it was about 40 miles to the ranger station. The road clung to ever steeper mountainsides above what was now a deep gorge. Here the St. Joe was a whitewater river. Thundering rapids alternated with bottle green pools that looked like perfect resting places for trout. Every bend in the road treated me to a new view of the St. Joe. While I appreciated the beauty of the river gorge, I also remember feeling a bit uneasy. The tree covered mountains seemed to close in around me. The immensity of this (what seemed to me) trackless wilderness was a little overwhelming. I began to wonder what I was getting myself into. Would I really adapt to working in such an environment? The terrain looked fit for mountain goats but not particularly so for two legged animals. How would it be living so far from civilization? I knew only time could answer these questions.

Of course, I look back on that summer at Red Ives as one of the adventures of my life. Over the four field seasons I spent there, I learned how to use a contour map and compass to navigate in places far from any road. I learned about the tree species native to the area and how to measure their growth and assess their health. I gorged on fat huckleberries in late summer and heard bull elk bugling on many frosty autumn mornings. Climbing the hills in that country toned my leg muscles and increased my stamina. The money I earned helped me to finish school. Most importantly, the time I spent there made me realize that I would always prefer to live and work where there are mountains, even though I grew up in the flatlands.

Now on this late October night I was nearing the end of my last season at Red Ives, possibly making my last drive up the St. Joe River Road. I had completed my B.S. degree the previous spring and the future ahead of me seemed more uncertain. I knew I needed to start looking for a more permanent work situation, at least seasonal work that was more in line with my chosen profession of wildlife management. These things were on my mind as I drove east of Halfway Hill under the moonlit night sky.

The high beams of my headlights lit up the road but did not penetrate far when they shone into the trees. I knew I would not see another car for the next hour or so until I pulled into the ranger station parking lot. Up ahead I noticed my lights reflected off the membranes at the back of some small animals' eyes. Two little orange coals glowed in the dark off the right hand shoulder of the road. I took my foot off the accelerator and gently braked the car, in case whatever it was decided to run in front of me. You sometimes get a sense for what an animal will do in these situations and I felt the need to stop and let him make up his mind. As soon as the car came to rest, he jumped out into the road, as if on cue. I saw him perfectly in my headlights. He didn't run across the road so much as bound with an arched back that made him look like a liquid sine curve. His feet were paired, with the front feet touching the ground very close together, followed by the hind. I immediately recognized the characteristic gait and long sleek body as belonging to a mustelid; a member of the weasel tribe. But this was no weasel. His body was much more substantial, his tail impossibly bushy.

Then this furry little slinky toy did something very unexpected. Instead of simply crossing to the other side of the road, he bounded over to my side of the car and stopped just below my door. My window was half way down and I slowly lowered it, trying not to make a sound so as not to spook him. He was no longer in the headlight pool but was still visible, dimly lit by the amber parking light on the left front fender of the car. The little creature was standing on his hind legs looking directly at me! His eyes were black onyx. I could tell his nose was working by the movement of his whiskers. Perhaps he caught a whiff of car exhaust, brake lining, and human. Momentarily, I recognized the little orange patch of fur on his chest that identified him as a pine marten.

I had seen marten before in these woods. Always they had been up in the trees, jumping between branches and scrambling up trunks with incredible speed and grace. Marten make their living chasing down tree squirrels, wherever they can find them. They will chase them through the treetops or ambush them on the ground. An animal that specializes in catching squirrels on their own terms is truly a quick and determined predator! In the winter they enter the dark, close world beneath the snow to hunt small mammal in the spaces between fallen logs and other forest debris. I feel certain that pine martens are regarded as holy terrors by the tribes of arboreal and land based rodents.

As if his curiosity was finally satisfied, my little visitor turned from me. He retraced his bounding, two by two steps back across my headlights and melted into the trees. I noticed my mouth was open, so I closed it and involuntarily smiled. There was an almost surreal quality to the encounter now that I was alone. An eerie feeling came over me that I had just been visited by a spirit of some kind. Had this creature felt the same sense of mystery regarding me as I did him? It was a meeting that took, I would guess fifteen seconds, but one that is seared in my memory.

I have been fortunate to have had other memorable close range encounters with wild beings in my life. Each moment was a precious gift. As a biologist, I am trained and accustomed to thinking about wildlife in terms of populations and habitat needs. But this is a narrow, two-dimensional view. It relegates individuality to mankind only. It denies the possibility of joy and wonder and awareness in animals other than ourselves. Encounters like the one I had with the marten keep me in my place, they help me to register my colossal capacity for self-centeredness; so much a trait of my species. I have been blessed to live and work where there are mountains.

WORK AS A FOREST GUARD

C.C. McGuire

On May 1, 1909, I was appointed as a forest guard on the Mount Baker National Forest. The forest supervisor fitted me out with a badge, the "Use Book" and a marking hatchet. He told me to go to Finney Creek and establish headquarters at the Finney Guard Station. Sixteen miles of trail from Sauk City the end of rail transportation to the guard station had been built the previous year and the winter storms made it impassable except on foot. The one major bridge at Gee Creek was out and in many places the trail was obliterated by slides.

I was told that $300 was set aside to repair the trail and build a bridge across Gee Creek. I was to spend the entire amount and if any surplus was left after maintenance work was done, I was to build a new trail continuing on to Little Deer Creek.

I arrived at old Sauk City at night. The next mornirg with a pack of beans and bacon on my back, I set out for the Finney Guard Station 16 miles away. Found many logs and slides in the trail and noted that Gee Creek ran through a box canyon about 60 feet wide.

The Finney GS was an old log cabin on an abandoned homestead claim. Never before or since have I seen so many mice. They were as thick as flies around a honey pot.

As soon as I had fixed something to eat I started killing mice with a stick of stove wood, but headway was slow. So I took a five gallon oil tin and cut the top out. Next I got a piece of wire and strung a milk can on the wire and laid it across the opening in the oil can. I put about four inches of water in it and placed a small rock in the water so that just a small portion of the rock extended above the water line.

Then I was ready to bait the trap by tying two pieces of bacon on opposite sides of the milk can. Then, with a flat stick leaning from the floor to the top of the oil tin, I was ready for business.

In a few minutes a mouse ran up the stick and not being able to reach the bait, he jumped the few inches necessary to get the bacon. When he lit, the can rolled on the wire axis and Mr. Mouse was in the drink. Soon another went after the bacon and he too went into the drink. Then the war was on. The rock extending above the water was only big enough to accommodate one mouse and a battle started to see who should have the perch. Their squeals attracted others and soon a procession was moving up the stick, some jumping for the bait and others just diving in to see what the commotion was all about.

Twice that night I emptied the can of dead mice. My first count was 62 and at least as many more on the second count. Business tapered off then, for even a mouse will get smart. I spread my bedroll on the old bough bunk and crawled in. In a few minutes mice were in bed with me. That I couldn't take, so I moved outside. Mice were even nesting in my boots by morning. The next morning I hiked out the 16 miles to Sauk, hired a man to help me, purchased about 60 feet of one and one-half inch rope and so started to spend the $300. The season was pretty well over by the time I got the mice thinned out enough so I could be comfortable in the cabin.

RANGE AND GRAZING

THE SUGAR PINE DRIVE

George Harper

The sugar pine drive, taking Ethel Steele's heifers up the Sugar Pine Creek Trail to graze in the Trinity Alps Wilderness on the Shasta-Trinity National Forest for the summer, has produced numerous episodes and incidents that are told and retold wherever horsebackers, cowboys and girls and Forest Service people gather.

The trail to the first meadow, Cabin Flat, climbs steep all along its five mile length with the lower half traversing side slopes of 60 to 80 percent in loose, decomposed granite.

My wife Alice and I had the pleasure of participating in one of the more eventful drives in 1979. This drive started as usual with forty, two year old heifers (the teenagers) plus one mature cow (the den mother) with her four month old calf. This bunch was held overnight in a small corral on the Coffee Creek Road near the site of the old Gold Field Guard Station which was lost in the 1964 flood.

The drive started shortly after daylight and proceeded the short distance up Coffee Creek Road to the Sugar Pine Trail Head which was a bridge across Coffee Creek at the mouth of Sugar Pine Creek. That bridge and trail head have produced several memorable events, but an this day the cattle trooped across it with no problems. As we began our way up the trail, the cattle were forced into a long string formation because the

310

brush and trees along the trail were pretty dense and the side slope progresses rapidly from sloping to really steep.

Two factors came together at this point in the drive that were to shape our fate for the balance of the day. The old cow became separated from her calf. The calf ended up at the back of the string with the cow toward the front, and as the trail narrowed and footing became more critical, it became obvious that the calf had been overcome with a severe case of pink eye and was essentially blind!

As the drive progressed up the trail, it rapidly evolved into two pieces. The one piece containing the heifers and the cow plus myself, Ethel's husband, Bill and Bob Carpenter, was a semiorderly file of cows and riders plodding up the narrow steep trail. The other piece, containing the blind calf, degenerated into a running scramble on and off trail as the calf would walk off the trail into space, fall down the hill and Ethel's over enthusiastic cow dogs would descend on it, often running the calf farther down the hill. After awhile, Ethel and Alice were ready to kill the dogs, (luckily for the dogs, neither had her gun that day) and all the animals were exhausted. Ethel and Alice caught the dogs, not very gently, and tied them up. Then they went down the steep hill and roped the blind calf, which by this time was completely exhausted and wouldn't move for anything. The hill was too steep and loose to drag him up with the mules so they decided to let him rest while Ethel caught up to the main bunch and returned with help.

While they were embroiled in catching dogs and the calf, both got off their saddle mule, tied up the dogs and got the calf secured. Ethel took her mule Roxy and temporarily tied her to a tree. A few minutes later as they were finishing with the dogs and the calf, Roxy spooked and went flying by, towing the tree. She stopped a short distance away and, after they caught her and calmed her down, they discovered that in her haste to return and help Alice, Ethel had tied Roxy to a dead tree which must have been held up by only a sliver because shortly it fell, giving poor old Roxy a significant emotional experience and this was still early in the day.

About two hours later, Bill, Bob and I were just pulling into Cabin Flat with the cattle when Ethel caught up to us. The plan at this point was to separate the old cow from the heifers and take her back down the trail to her calf and then bring the two of them back to rejoin the herd. That sounded simple enough but the cows didn't buy into the scheme. The four of us became embroiled in a wild round of cow cutting, trying to separate and then keep separate the old cow from the heifers. On about the third revolution around the meadows and through the dense clumps of lodgepole pine, I remember having a split second of eye contact with a dark haired, young backpacker and his female (I think) companion. My chestnut horse Ruby and I were about three jumps behind the old cow, and closing, when she dove into a clump of trees. Ruby didn't hesitate and dove in right behind her, still gaining. Riding a running horse through lodgepole isn't very smart, so I'm not sure whose eyes were widest in excitement and fear, mine or the backpacker, who had a big, old cow crashing past him a few feet away on one side and a crazy horse and rider crashing past a few feet away on the other.

We were successful in isolating the cow a short time later and started down the trail. I never saw those people again but I suspect they had a closer encounter with the wild west than they ever bargained for.

The next and final incident of the day lay ahead of us not too far up the trail where Alice waited with the blind calf. As we descended down the trail, the cow was plodding along in the lead, then Ethel, then me, then Bill and Bob. We were down into the steep, loose granite portion of the trail and rounding a sharp bend, when we met a family of backpackers coming up the trail, a man, a woman and a boy, maybe 10 years old. The meeting place was in the head of a small ravine. The trail across the head was crescent shaped and probably extended only a little more than 100 feet from one edge of the ravine to the other. The family was in the ravine about 30 feet when we rounded the corner. The cow was in the ravine about the midpoint when she came to a sudden stop, realizing there were funny looking people with big humps on their backs a few feet away blocking her path. By this time, all four riders were also inside the ravine and stacked up behind the cow. The trail is on a 70 percent loose granite slope and about a foot wide. This is no place to be turning cows or horses around.

Ethel immediately saw that we had a tense situation and in a calm, but authoritative voice, asked the family to back up to the edge of the ravine and move off the trail on the lower side. The woman in the family group bristles up and says, "No," that they will step off the trail behind a small, six foot tall pine tree on the outside edge of the trail where they are standing. Ethel asks them again to move back to the edge of the ravine, but even as she does, the woman took the boy and moved behind the tree. The man followed. They had difficulty keeping their footing an the steep, loose slope and slid downhill several feet, sort of en masse.

At that point, the cow decided that enough was enough and started to move rapidly down the trail, but to add spice to the situation, she tried to go above the trail as she crossed above the family. She made it uphill for one jump but lost her footing and fell, rolling and bellowing down the hill directly toward the family. The woman gave out with a choking, bloodcurdling scream and threw her body over the boy and they both slid farther down the hill!

By the time I was pointed down the trail again, the cow had caught her footing as she rolled across the trail and surged to her feet, showering the family in a cloud of loose dirt and pebbles. Ethel put spurs to her mule as soon as the cow went barreling down the trail and Ruby and the other horses weren't about to be left so they bolted after Ethel and the cow and we were outta there!

For the balance of the day, as we gathered up the calf (and left those @#!$ dogs tied up) and drove him and the cow back up the trail to Cabin Flat, we never saw the family again. However, I'm certain they had a significant emotional experience. That cow had to look bigger than a cow, when it was rolling and bellowing down the hill and appeared certain to roll right over the top of them.

I worked for Bob Devlin for a number of years when he was ranger at Sawyers Bar. He was fond of saying, "It's all part of the wilderness experience." I guess that would apply to all of us that day on Sugar Pine Creek in the Trinity Alps Wilderness.

OPEN RANGE ON THE KISATCHIE NATIONAL FOREST, A BULL STORY

Don Blackburn

When the Forest Service finally decided to get serious about the trespass livestock problem on the Kisatchie NF in central Louisiana during the mid-1960s, I just happened to have one of the "best seats in the arena." As Evangeline district ranger I knew first hand the problems being created by some 2,500 plus head of cattle, horses and goats (and a bunch of wild feral hogs) illegally making these federal lands their home, over grazing, competition with the deer herd (hungry cows eat browse too), eroding fragile soils and trampling of southern pine plantations. Since this was open range country and had been before and since the establishment of the Kisatchie NF, we also knew that these livestock owners, tough independent folks who did not have a lot of use for the "feds" were not going to raise the white flag without a struggle.

After years of contacting, explaining, cajoling, pleading and threatening owners of trespass livestock to get a permit or remove their animals from national forest lands it was action time! Time to make a statement! A new corral had been constructed at the Evangeline Work Center, a stock trailer acquired, a tranquilizer gun located, and four experienced "cowboys" lined up. And what a crew it was—Forest Supervisor Hans Raum, Special Agent Jack Boren, Range Staff Officer Clyde Peacock and yours truly. Had we only known the tribulations ahead of us, we probably would have sought the help of some real cow (bull) boys.

314

A trespass herd of predominately Brahman cattle had been located at the junction of highway 112 and the Twin Bridges Road. This livestock owner had rejected a grazing permit and ignored all notices that his cattle would be subject to impoundment if they continued grazing on national forest lands without a grazing permit, ear tags and fee paid. It was a warm late May morning when we made our move. We surreptitiously eyed the herd while discussing the various techniques to use in tranquilizing and loading several of the animals. (This is where we made our first mistake, or was it the second?, forgetting the potential difficulty in loading by hand, semi-conscious, full grown Brahman cows.) About this time a big beautiful Charolais bull caught our eye (yet another mistake?).

As the herd grazed along, filling their bellies with free national forest grass, switching flies with their tails, we moved in. The decision had been made, take the Charolais bull and three of his harem. Our trusty tranquilizer gun was put to use, and before we realized how easy it was, the bull and three cows were down on their knees, wobbly and half-dazed. And then the fun began. Somehow we got the four animals loaded, moved to the work center, off loaded into the previously unused corral, and the corral gate locked. And I thought the hard part was over!

As I waited at the work center for whatever repercussions might occur that day, one highly overwrought livestock owner confronted one very nervous district ranger, as night began to fall. After the owner completed his stormy demonstration of cussing and threatening, he pulled out a wad of bills that could have choked his 2,000 pound Charolais bull, and informed one verbally abused Forest Service officer that he was ready to pay his impoundment fee of some $115 plus. The verbally abused forest officer (me) had to call Special Agent Jack Boren in nearby Alexandria, requesting he bring change for some $20 bills and some backup (preferable something big like a machine gun) to support one lonely district ranger.

I reckon you could say "All's well that ends well." The Kisatchie National Forest range program did successfully get most trespass livestock removed or under permit (and with ear tags in most of the permitted animals), but the big bucks to manage the range program—the incentive that Regional Director Wayne Cloward used to dangle in our faces every time he visited—they never arrived in any of our later budgets. And that concludes a Louisiana bull story, Charolais variety.

Except for a footnote. As I was closing out my bank account a couple of weeks later, in preparation for a transfer to the National Forests in Alabama, guess who walked into the bank as I was preparing to leave that June day? My friend, the impounded livestock owner (and yes, we had become friends—of a sort), informed me that we had sterilized his world champion bull when we tranquilized him. He wanted to know what I was going to do about it. I was able to tell him (and with a straight face), that he could pick up claim forms from the district ranger's office in Alexandria, bid him good-bye, got in my Pontiac and pointed it towards Alabamy. My cowboying days were over, I had survived the Kisatchie livestock trespass challenge.

LARCENY ON THE RANGE

Harold E. Smith

When I took over the Pine Mountain Ranger District, Deschutes National Forest, I was told that I might expect some trouble from the lawless elements operating in that area. Antelope Spring seemed to be the operating center for at least one gang. The so-called spring was merely a water hole, scooped out in the center of a sand flat. Pine Mountain, just north of the spring, separated the Antelope Spring area from Millican Valley where George Millican operated his cattle and horse ranch. Pine Mountain was prime grazing land. Thus, the Millican stock grazed the north side of the mountain while the Katzman boys, John and Charley, ran horses on the south slope, adjacent to Antelope Spring. Both outfits paid the usual grazing fees.

The nearest water to Antelope Spring was Sand Spring, five miles to the south. Therefore, Antelope was a rather strategic location as it virtually controlled the grazing on the south and west sides of the mountain. Katzmans were not the first to recognize the value of this location. A few years prior to my entry into the area, John McPherson had homesteaded the land surrounding the water hole and engaged in the horse business. Being a new beginner and therefore a small operator as compared to Millican, John considered it proper range ethics to brand as many Millican colts as he could get his rope on. Millican being too lazy or too old to ride the range and look after his stock, did carry some clout with the Oregon Livestock Association of which he was a member. On hearing that there was a $500 reward being offered by the stockmen for his arrest and conviction, McPherson and his cohorts fled the country, taking along what loose stock they could hurriedly assemble. Thus, the Katzmans seized the opportunity to move into the vacuum created by McPherson's sudden, nocturnal departure. McPherson's homestead entry was still of record in the land office so the Katzmans were unable to tie up the water. They did, however, file on 320 acres of Sage Blush Flat adjacent to the spring. As soon as McPherson's time for offering final proof expired, the Forest Service had the entry canceled and the area, although outside the national forest, was set aside as a public service site.

The summer of 1915, I was allotted $600 with which I built a four room house at Antelope Springs. Katzmans had switched from horses to sheep. Millican had sold to a man named Sloan, who had disposed of the Millican horses and cattle and converted to sheep. Charlie Katzman had been drafted into the Army so John was handling the sheep by himself.

One day a half dozen or so of Sloan's sheep drifted over the divide onto the Katzman range. Discovering this, John seized the opportunity to increase his own flock with little effort and no cash outlay. He allowed the Sloan sheep to mingle with his own band, then drove the combined flock down to his corral, not withstanding the fact that the Sloan sheep wore the Millican Heart Brand and were all weathers, sort of setting them apart from Katzman's ewes and lambs. As soon as the sheep were corralled, John set to work with a pair of shears, slipping the black tar markings from the Sloan weathers. He also used a pair of heated blades to alter the ear marks. The hot metal seared the cuts and prevented bleeding.

Sloan's headers were soon alerted to the fact that some of their sheep had strayed over the divide so they began a search, which ended at the Katzman corral where John was engaged in the art work of altering the identity of Sloan sheep. Looking over the flock, the Sloan men had no trouble identifying their own sheep. The clipped portion of wool showed white and identified the animal as plainly as though it still wore the black tar. Two of the Sloan men stood guard at the corral while the third rode over to the ranger station and had me notify the sheriff. Within an hour the lawmen arrived accompanied by Mr. Sloan. They picked me up at the station and took me to the Katzman corral as a witness. There we separated the Sloan weathers from Katzman's herd, loaded one in the car as evidence, left a man to look after the sheep, took John into custody and left for Bend.

Justice was swift and decisive. John was tried the next day before Judge Jim Duffy. Harley DeArmond was the prosecutor, assisted by Vernon Forbes. I do not recall Katzman having an attorney, or what his plea was. Anyway, he was found guilty and sentenced to a year in the pen. S. Hudson of the First National Bank, interceded for John, explaining to the judge that help was scarce due to the war and that John was needed there to care for the sheep, in which the bank had a financial interest. On this presentation, the judge suspended the sentence, placed John on probation and allowed him to resume his sheep herding.

THE PLAN

T. J. "Tom" Jones

In early May 1918, I was transferred to the Plumas Forest as deputy supervisor. One of the highlights of the transfer was the fact that, although I had met Supervisor Rogers once before, he not only did not recognize me but didn't even know which one of the Joneses I was or where I had come from. There was a Ranger Jones on the Eldorado at that time known as "Deacon Jones," and Dave Rogers' first greeting to me was, "Oh yeah, you're Deacon Jones." With a somewhat suppressed laugh I replied, "No, not Deacon Jones—just merely God-fearing Tom Jones from the Mono." I was assigned to take charge of grazing as I had expected. Just how fully Dave wanted me to take charge of grazing I never knew, but I always surmised that I went further than he expected. The season of 1918 was spent with a pack outfit and in many places on foot or with a burro where a regular camp outfit could not get into the country. At any rate, when the season had ended, I think I knew every grazing permittee and range and how the stock were being handled, if at all.

To begin with, the valleys which contained practically all of the meadowlands, were owned by sheepmen and so used. Many hundreds of cattle were allotted to the ridges between the valleys. This was particularly true of the east side of the forest. Difficulties experienced were that the sheep, especially the lambs, were not doing well down in the meadows and there weren't enough cowpunchers to keep the cattle on the ridges. I therefore originated a plan of land waivers by which the hill range was occupied by the sheep and the valleys by the cattle. The plan, being to the advantage of all concerned, appeared quite satisfactory.

On the southern part of the forest there were a few prosperous cattlemen, practically all of whom were enjoying better than average summer range—mostly in the high country. Along the foothills were many small ranches, what Lou Barrett used to term "poison oak" ranches, with anywhere from 25 to 100 head of cattle, inbred and looking as though they had never had enough to eat. The boundaries between these ranges were not observed. The cattle ran where they ran because of having been their for generations and not because of any applied scheme of management whatsoever. Their range boundaries and capacities as applied to units meant nothing. It was in conjunction with this problem that I got Supervisor Rogers into considerable hot water, at least for the time being. During his absence to San Francisco, I was acting in his stead and I broke the news to the people using the Merimac and LaPorte Districts that some method of management was going to be put into practice which would be quite different from what was then in vogue. This resulted in the permittees getting together immediately to form a protective association—to protect themselves against the Forest Service. I well recall Supervisor Rogers' reactions on his return. Convinced that some method of cooperative management was going to be necessary, I started to prepare the ground by writing to permittees on the Mono for whom I had organized a plan of community management whereby they ran the stock collectively as if of a single brand. They elected one of their number to hire and fire the necessary labor and actually administer the stock, regardless of ownership. I received a large number of letters from these people acknowledging the benefits they had derived from the plan and their unqualified approval of the method. These letters, I believe, were finally printed and bound into little pamphlets which were distributed to the Plumas permittees who were on the warpath.

Grazing administration on the southern half of the Plumas developed rapidly and in a few days the permittees had called a meeting of their protective association at Bangor, inviting us, inferentially, to come and "take our medicine." Chief of grazing Chris Rachford, Dave Rogers and I attended. This was a memorable meeting in my grazing administration in that I finally produced a plan which met with the universal approval of the people concerned. If I remember correctly, almost every permittee there took the floor at one time or another. For about two hours they berated the Forest Service management. Finally, however, they ran out of material and there had not been what I could call a constructive suggestion from the entire group. Whereon I merely presented my plan, described the class of livestock they owned, the reason the stock were of that class and told them I was not particularly eager to put my plan into effect but that if they had a plan which would improve the condition, especially benefiting the small permittees in the foothills and improve the quality of breeding, I would have no objection to trying it. I immediately got a favorable response and before leaving the meeting, they had agreed to at least the major features of my plan and had ordered three carloads of registered bulls to replace the scrubs then in use by most small owners.

SHEEP, CATTLE AND HORSES

Gilbert T. Brown

In December of 1907, I received orders to report to the supervisor headquarters at Lakeview. Leaving my family at Silver Lake, I rode horseback the 100 miles and assumed the duties of deputy supervisor. Upon the resignation of Supervisor Guy Ingram, I was promoted to supervisor.

In the meantime the Goose Lake and Fremont Reserves were united, with headquarters remaining in Lakeview and I was asked to select a name for the new forest, the name "Reserve" having been discontinued and "National Forest" substituted. I chose the name "Fremont," since General John C. Fremont had traversed the entire length of this forest during the 1840s, and the further fact that the greater part of this area had originally been called Fremont. This combined reserve area then extended from the California State line on the south to a point just south of Bend, Oregon, a distance of almost 200 miles.

The grazing problems remained the big issue and it was necessary to reduce allotments from 127,000 sheep and 27,000 head of cattle and horses to approximately one half these numbers. While some small timber sales were being made, there was also much free use business to care for, but the big problem still was how to reduce the stock on the range without bankrupting the permittees. The big timber companies, especially Weyerhaeuser and other landowners, cooperated in fixing allotments so that it was easier to handle the stock on the range. There were many thousands of acres, in alternate sections, of railroad land extending across the forests and stockman claimed that they had private land as well as their forest allotments and were therefore entitled to more stock on the land. This question was finally settled by real estate men renting the private land from the owners and subleasing it to the stockmen, under which arrangement it was possible for the Forest Service to issue on and off grazing permits, depending on the amount of private land leased and the acreage of national forest land within their grazing allotments.

The wild horse problem on and adjoining the Fremont National Forest was solved by a big roundup and sale. After advertising in the newspapers that all unpermitted horses found on the forest would be rounded up and sold unless claimed by their owners, I proceeded to secure three men who were skilled in such work and started the roundup. Some of the horse owners thought that it could not be done so were not in too much of a hurry to get their unpermitted stock off of the range. However, we gathered approximately 300 head of horses, proving that it could be done. I was accused of hiring horse thieves for doing this work and in one instance this may have been true!

Some of the horses were claimed by the owners who paid $5 per head to cover the cost of gathering. The rest, mostly unbranded and of little value, were sold and removed from the area.

Many of these difficulties continued somewhat until I left the Fremont Forest in April 1931, where I was supervisor for over 20 years.

THE STONE JAW RIDE

Ken Weissenborn

The national forests are managed for multiple uses—for the production of goods, services and amenities for the benefit and enjoyment of the people. Not all activities may occur on each and every acre, but provision is made for the compatible use of forest lands.

Grazing of domestic livestock is one of the permitted uses. Forest lands suitable for livestock use are divided into manageable units, called allotments. People who hold permits to use these lands are called permittees (what else?) There may be one or more permittees assigned the use of each allotment.

District forest rangers, in cooperation with permittees, develop plans for the management and use of each allotment. Grazing activities are monitored to ensure compliance with the terms of the permit and the annual plan. Failure to comply may lead to adverse actions against the permit, including reductions in the numbers allowed to graze, or complete revocation of the permit in extreme cases.

The Sierra Mosca allotment on the west side of the Pecos Mountains had been a problem for years. The ranger, Chris Zamora, had developed a management plan that required a reduction of 20% of permitted numbers per year, until the vegetation stabilized. A number of individual permittees were involved. During the first year of the plan, no numbers were to be reduced. Future reductions were to be based on the condition of the range, based on an on-the-ground inspection. Any adverse decision was sure to be appealed by the pemittees. A formal appeal process was in place, but we were aware that the Congressional delegation would also be involved.

The allotment ranged in elevation from about 7,000 feet to over 12,000—above the timberline. It was harsh and unforgiving country. Mechanized access was prohibited, since it was a proclaimed wilderness area. (The country itself made it impossible to use motorized vehicles.)

The ranger arranged a horseback inspection for mid-October, the end of the grazing season. The group was to include Ranger Zamora, Forest Supervisor Bob Latimore and me (I was the technical support staff for range and wildlife management.) All of the permittees agreed to join us on the ride.

Chris, Bob and I packed into Panchuela West, a cabin within the allotment, at an altitude of 10,000 feet. We were to meet the permittees at 9 a.m. the next morning.

On the scheduled day, the weather was miserable. A sharp, cold wind blew steadily from the north. Snow fell intermittently.

It was obvious a major storm was imminent. The permittees did not appear. I didn't blame them—I wasn't too thrilled with being there. We waited until about 10:30 in the morning, at which time the boss (Bob) decided we would make the ride without the permittees being present. It was a dangerous decision, but away we went.

You may know what it's like in the mountains
When you ride in a wild winter storm,
When you'd rather be back in your cabin
By a fire that's cracklin' and warm.

You wouldn't be ridin' this country
If you had any God-given sense
With nothin' 'tween you and the North Pole
But a single-strand barbed-wire fence.

The wind whistles down from the heavens
And cuts through your bones like a knife.
It makes you feel so doggone happy
That you've chosen this good ranger's life.

Your ears start to feel like they're frozen.
An icicle forms on your nose.
Your hands will not move and you wonder
If by now you still have any toes.

Your slicker's froze fast to the saddle.
Your feet in the stirrups like lead.
Your mind starts to think, "This is livin'?
I just might be better off dead."

Your face feels like it's made out of granite.
You're cold—and that's no mistake.
You can't even talk to your partners.
Just try it, and your face will break.

We were ridin' the Sangre de Cristos
Up high where the trees do not grow
When a nasty old norther starts blowin'
With its wind and its sleet and its snow.

We caught up with what we were after—
Three cows, two calves and a bull—
And what with the wind and the weather
We really did have our hands full.

We finally got all those dumb bovines
On the trail to the valley below.
Found a bunch of small trees in a hollow
To get out of the wind and the snow.

We chipped ourselves loose from our saddles
Stepped down onto hard frozen ground.
Bob pulled out a pint of Jack Daniels—
With thanks we all passed it around.

We warmed up a bit after drinkin'.
I checked out the face of my pard.
The worst must be past, so I'm thinkin',
It seems he ain't shakin' so hard.

He put the cap back on the bottle.
Said "It feel's good, this fire within."
I says "It sure ain't the whiskey,
What you had dribbled right down your chin."

There's a moral to this story—
Of this there should be not a doubt—
Before you tip up that old bottle
Be sure that it's firm in your mouth.

ON THE OLD MONO

T. J. "Tom" Jones

I remember very well that in 1909, there was no stenographer in the supervisor's office at Gardnerville and Charlie Border, who happened to be a fair typist, was doing this class of work for Supervisor Wells. Bob Settles, the Mono National Forest's first clerk and stenographer, arrived in January 1910. Border and I secured saddle and pack stock and journeyed to the Alpine County headquarters at Markleeville where we started to work as full-fledged officers of the Forest Service. Border, also, had been in the Service only a few months. I was on the tail end of the Mono force, being their only assistant ranger.

I bought a pack horse and, as was usually the case in those days when buying cheap stock, I discovered she was so loco she wasn't worth a dollar. The first time I packed that animal I found that Ranger Border was not an experienced horseman. When we were about half packed, somehow he got in the way and the mare trampled all over him, injuring one of his feet quite badly. He was about six feet four inches tall and just about as awkward as he was tall. Like the proverbial Texan who couldn't ride home in a wagon when drunk, I finally put the pack on my saddle horse and the riding saddle on the locoed mare and rode her. I continued to do this until I was able to trade her off for a better animal.

New permittees were then being allotted range for the first time, and our most difficult job was to keep the two classes of stock—sheep and cattle, from trespassing on one another. With the strict application of penalties prescribed by the regulations, respect for the enforcement of range boundaries was accomplished with only minor infractions. At this time we found it difficult to prevent sheep infested with scabies from entering the forest. Both the state and federal governments, through the Bureau of Animal Industry, were cooperating very closely with us and demanding that scabies in sheep be eradicated in California and Nevada. Sheep being worth only $1 or so a head, the cost of dipping for scabies was quite an item and the sheepman would drive nights if he could get his sheep on summer range without the expense of dipping.

By unfailing application of the law, all of our stock were finally on their respective allotments with all conditions, up to this point, complied with.

WAR ON THE SISKIYOUS

Al Parker

In 1941, the grazing problem was one of the factors that occasioned the Oak Knoll District headquarters move from Yreka to Oak Knoll down the Klamath River in Siskiyou County, California. It was felt that we would be closer to the people who were actually grazing permittees on the forest. There was friction between the people who were grazing cattle in the Siskiyous around Mt. Ashland and Donomore vicinity. This was mainly between the grazing permittees on the Klamath River side of the Siskiyous within the administrative area of the Klamath National Forest and the grazing permittees on the Applegate side of the Rogue River National Forest. Some of the best grazing areas were in our area on the California side, the choice areas being roughly from Donomore Meadows— Dutchman Peak down into Cow Creek and up the slopes toward Mt. Ashland. The grazing rights for the various allotments were previously established by the Forest Service. This meant that the Klamath Forest determined the number of stock that could be ranged in their administrative area, as well as the number that each permittee could have on the grazing allotment. Likewise, the Rogue River Forest made similar determinations for their grazing permittees.

The facts were that cattle do not read and, naturally, drifted to where they could find the best feed. Even though there were drift fences, they were not too effective. Thus, there was mixing of cattle from the Oregon side of the Siskiyous with those on the California side. Furthermore, there were two cabins in Donomore Meadows, one owned by the Oregon stockmen and the other by California stockmen. This, in itself, was not a real problem except that it could well have given the Oregon stockmen a sense of actually belonging on the California side. With this background information, it may more readily be understood why there was conflict of interest, even to the point of feuding between the Oregon and California stockmen at the time that I came on the scene.

Several of the stockmen wore guns while riding the range. I often wore a side arm myself. It was merely the custom of the times, and little thought was given to it. I recall an instance that occurred shortly after having moved to Oak Knoll. As I sat at my office desk one day, one of our grazing permittees drove to a skidding halt out front and barged in, saying, "Look at me. Look at me." He was a sight. He was all covered with blood, his face was badly bruised and his eyes nearly swollen shut. "What happened?" I asked. He then informed me that one of the stockmen from the Oregon side confronted him at the gate that went into his Cow Creek pasture enclosure, an argument ensued, and the fight was on. While he had claimed to have been a pretty good prize fighter or boxer in years past, he was afraid to take the offensive because of the gun his opponent wore. He seemed to have felt that discretion was the best part of valor and thus was knocked down and pummeled unmercifully before saying "enough." He was a sight but I could not fault him too much for not fighting back since he wore no gun as a possible further equalizer.

At this point, I felt that there was a minor range war going on in the Siskiyous and was a bit apprehensive regarding the explosive nature of the situation, especially since I seemed destined to be in the middle of it. It became more apparent that I should get out with these folks and actually ride with them over these controversial areas. In other words, these range problems could not be solved even from Oak Knoll, but out there where the action was. This decision was further confirmed by the supervisor's office in Yreka. Thus, it became an annual practice, especially during round-up time, for the ranger to spend most of a week riding and mingling with our stockmen as well as the Oregon stockmen. In fact, my wife Mae, being an old-time cowgirl from eastern Oregon, always went with me. This was a plus in our favor, as several of our stockmen's wives would also ride with us. Since our stockmen had a cabin at Donomore Meadows, we were invited to bring our bedrolls and move right in with them. This was really a rather cozy arrangement for eight or ten people in a small one-room cabin. Incidentally, anyone who snored too loudly might be awakened by being clobbered with someone's cowboy boot.

Perhaps the most significant factor in smoothing relations with these people was the fact that the ranger had been headquartered at Oak Knoll and was now out there among them. We were now able to meet on common grounds, ride with them and discuss problems mutual to them as well as the Forest Service. The fact that we could be with them to note range conditions and help plan salt ground and watering troughs for better distribution of the cattle was something that they really appreciated. Prior to these expeditions, our stockmen seemed to have developed a feeling that the Forest Service with headquarters in Yreka felt too important to mingle with them and made all these range decisions with little or no consultation with them. Not only were we involved with our own stockmen but the Oregon stockmen, together with Lee Port, District Ranger at Star Ranger Station on the Applegate of the Rogue River Forest, rode with us. Even though many of them still wore side arms, after three or four years, the animosity seemed to have subsided and peace returned to the Siskiyous. Our range war was over.

THE ADDISON SCHUYLER IRELAND STORY

Grover C. Blake

I doubt if any supervisor in Forest Service history ever shouldered a heavier load then did A. S. Ireland when, on April 1, 1906, the vast Blue Mountain Forest Reserves was dropped in his lap. He was entirely unfamiliar with the area. Since 1896 or 1897, he had been a ranger on the Cascade Forest Reserve but had not seen the Blue Mountains. With his office and headquarters in the residence he had rented for himself and family on the banks of the Ochoco in Prineville, he faced the responsibility of bringing under Forest Service regulation a vast and strange territory which later contained several present day national forests. His domain was the most intensely grazed area in the West. His job consisted in part, the settlement of grazing disputes, regulating the grazing of vast herds of sheep, cattle and horses and establishing allotments for each separate unit. While dealing with this explosive problem he was expected to change the existing unfriendly public sentiment to a friendly one. An examination and separate report was demanded on each of the many land claims (many fraudulent) within the forest reserve boundaries. The supervisor was required to appoint and train a staff of field men to enforce regulations and help with general administration of the ranges.

Supervisor Ireland was authorized to open the ranges in 1906 to all stock grazed the previous season upon payment of the grazing fees. The opening of the grazing season was to be deferred to June 1 for cattle and June 15 for sheep. It was estimated that 30,000 cattle and horses and 340,000 sheep had grazed the ranges in 1905, but the numbers to enter this range under permit in 1906 were 32,170 cattle and horses and 247,004 sheep. The opening up of the ranges to all stock in 1906 gave Mr. Ireland and his field force a little time to become familiar with the ranges and study the grazing problems. Besides himself and one forest assistant, Mr. Ireland had an authorization of seven field men for his vast territory for the field season of 1906 as follows:

1 Supervisor at $1,200 – 11 months	$1,100
1 Forest Assistant at $1,456 – 12 mos.	1,456
1 Deputy For. Ranger at $1,000 – 12 mos.	1,000
2 Asst. For. Rangers at $900 – 12 mos.	1,800
4 Forest Guards at $720 – 6 months	1,440
	$6,796

Expenses

Travel	Equipment	Communications	Shelter	Protection
$150	$50	$50	$75	---0---

With the knowledge gained during the 1906 grazing season, Supervisor Ireland began formulating plans to increase the efficiency of the reserve and to improve administration for 1907, which included the reduction in numbers of permitted stock on the badly overgrazed ranges.

Many stockmen were bitterly opposed to government regulation of grazing and the way in which administration was being conducted. Many complaints were made to the supervisor as well as to the Washington office. They seemed to feel that the government was not only depriving them of their established rights but unjustly charging them for something that was already theirs. Meetings were held and problems and complaints weighed and considered. Objectives of the Forest Service were explained and future benefits to both the ranges and the users thereof were pointed out, but the demands on the forest supervisor continued to be very great. He had his hands full and naturally made mistakes. He was between two fires—the Washington office demanding compliance with regulations on one hand and the stockmen opposing this procedure on the other. Forest officials met with the stockmen at The Dalles in November 1997. This meeting was followed by another at Prineville in January 1908, with L. F. Kneipp, Chief of the Office of Control, in attendance. Mr. Kneipp later made a lengthy report on his observations and findings from which I will quote the following paragraph:

"Supervisor Ireland was a stranger in the country. His Rangers were not familiar with the work or were they particularly good men, and the grazing conditions were so complicated and involved that the stockmen despaired of ever getting them straightened out. In fact they refused to attempt to do so at the first meeting held by the Supervisor. Mr. Ireland, inexperienced and a stranger to local conditions, then had to undertake the work of sifting out the chaotic mass of claims and counter claims. Something like twenty of the stockman present at the Prineville meeting stated that he had done better than anybody had expected him or any other man to do. Numerous mistakes were made, but not as many nor as serious ones as were expected."

Schuyler Ireland did a magnificent job of putting into effect the Forest Service regulations in face of many handicaps, some of which reached great magnitude. When he resigned an April 30, 1911, much development had been accomplished. Buildings, trails and telephone lines had been completed or were in the raking. The pioneer stage was passing in all lines of activity including grazing and all had settled down to a smoothly running and permanent basis. His successor took over a well-organized forest with most of the kinks and tangles ironed out. After leaving the Service, Mr. Ireland retired to the old Ireland Ranch at Olalla where he was born December 8, 1867.

THE EARLY DAYS OF THE WENAHA FOREST

J. M. Schmitz

On August 8, 1905, I arrived in Walla Walla to act as ranger in charge and soon thereafter as supervisor of the Wenaha National Forest, having been transferred from my position as ranger on the Rainier National Forest. I found a few supplies, a typewriter and a letter press awaiting me. As there was no office, I did all the work in my room.

Stockmen began to call to see what it was all about. Most of them had the idea that their stock would be excluded from the forest. I assured them that such would not be the case. I also learned that the forest was practically surrounded by small stockmen and that a large part was being heavily overgrazed. The main reason for the overgrazing of the interior was that each spring, long before the range was fit to graze, there would be a race to get the sheep over the divide and located on the best camps. I then realized the hard work it would take to get things organized and on a good working basis.

A stock meeting was called for December 18-25, at the Walla Walla courthouse. A great number came, although only about 300 of them had stock on the Wenaha Forest.

Superintendent D. B. Sheller was there. He was a good organizer and kept the crowd in a fine humor.

We finally arranged a committee of three cattlemen and three sheepmen to divide the sheep and cattle ranges. Each group tried to claim about all the range. Finally, after an all day confab, an agreement was reached.

Then came the tug of war for the individual sheep allotments. All admitted that a reduction of sheep was necessary and as the one band men couldn't be reduced, it fell on the two and three band men. This was accomplished without much trouble. The division into individual allotments took some time.

The Oregon men claimed all the Oregon range for Oregon sheep. Both Mr. Sheller and I told the committee to disregard the state line and allot the range according to prior use. The Washington sheepmen were in the majority and so could outvote the Oregonians, leaving out some of the Oregon prior users for personal reasons.

The last day of the meeting was mainly used for making out applications for grazing permits. After they were all stacked up, I asked Superintendent Sheller what to do with them. He said if it were up to him he would send them to Washington, D.C. and let them do as they pleased with them. However, by the regulations, I would have to approve or disapprove them anyway, which I did. I do not remember the number of stock applied for or approved nor the permits issued. Approving applications and sending out notices took about two weeks work for Mr. Foster and me.

The committee's rejection of Oregon sheep applications was going to cause trouble and a move was being made to exclude Washington sheep from Oregon. As I did not want to leave room for a just complaint, I called a meeting at Pendleton, for which I got an old-fashioned call down from the Washington office saying I had no right to call a second meeting and that if the committee had made a mistake, let them shoulder the responsibility. However, the meeting was a success and all were fairly well satisfied. Apparently all the Oregon legislature could do was to pass an inspection law saying all Washington sheep had to be inspected at the state line but the actual inspections died out after a few years.

The foregoing will give some idea of the amount of work it took to get an overgrazed forest organized. The field work was yet to come. The cattle were given a general allotment in each locality, the permits ranging from one head up to a few over a hundred head. The sheepmen were given individual allotments with a description and map. All this was no small task.

As grazing protection was of the utmost importance, the early field men had to know stock and range. They had to be woodsmen and able to take care of themselves and their horses under all conditions. They must see that each sheepman got located on his allotment. The fact that there were very few infringements on each other's allotments or of sheep on cattle range, shows the good work of the rangers and the find cooperation of the stockmen, especially of the sheepmen. But some of the herders were not too careful as to the boundaries of their allotments.

All disputes were quietly and satisfactorily settled in the field by getting the parties interested on the disputed area. Although it cost me several rides to the heads of Walla Walla River and Mill Creek, I did not want to give the impression that the forest was being run in a high-handed manner but was willing to overlook little mistakes and to treat the stockmen in a friendly and neighborly way. By doing so we received their cooperation in fire protection which was of great value.

SHEEP SHOOTERS

Gilbert T. Brown

Learning that the Fremont Forest Reserve in eastern Oregon was to be put under administration, I applied for a transfer and in April, 1907, was assigned to the Fremont at Silver Lake as ranger in charge of that district.

Upon arriving at Silver Lake, I found a vast area of forest without telephone lines, roads or trails, and transportation was entirely by saddle horse and pack outfit.

The work consisted of running and posting forest boundary lines, reporting on June 11 claims (most of which were fraudulent and had been filed in order to get timber and were later rejected), forest improvements, grazing trespasses, issuing range stock crossing permits, etc.

The fire problem was not great on the Fremont for several years, partially because of the overgrazing. In later years there were several large fires, the worst one covering about 8,000 acres, burning much reproduction and considerable mature timber.

The Silver Lake District at that time included an area extending from a line west of Paisley, Oregon, westward to the Klamath Indian Reservation, to a point south of Bend, Oregon, west to the summit of the Cascade Mountains and east to the desert.

Thousands of sheep and cattle were grazed an this area and the range was rapidly being depleted. This condition of the range led to great friction between the cattlemen and the sheepmen, to the point where several thousand sheep were shot by organized cattlemen, calling themselves "Sheepshooters." These killings occurred over much of south central Oregon from 1900 until the forest was put under administration.

The greatest slaughter of sheep in central Oregon was probably on the desert north of Silver Lake town in 1903, when 2,400 head out of a band of 2,700 were killed. That night the storekeeper who had sold the ammunition to the cattlemen was taken out of his store and shot and his body left in the sagebrush west of town, presumably because they were afraid that he might squeal. No arrests were ever made for these killings.

The Oregon Journal of Portland, Oregon, in its Sunday edition of July 25, 1948, carried a story by Elise King, titled "Oregon's Bloodiest War," telling of the many disputes between the cattlemen and sheepmen, and of the killings, etc., and quoted excerpts from a letter to the *Portland Oregonian*, dated December 29, 1904, and signed "Corresponding Secretary, Crook County Sheepshooting Association of Eastern Oregon," which reads in part:

"Our annual report shows that we have slaughtered between 8,000 and 10,000 head during the last shooting season and we expect to increase this respectable showing during the next season provided the sheep hold out and the governor and the Oregonian observe the customary laws of neutrality."

The article goes on to say:

"But the growing feeling that there was need of supervision and the allotment of grazing rights inclined many stockmen favorably and as more and more were becoming informed of the purposes and intentions of the national government, the opposition melted away."

A DELICATE SITUATION

Submitted by Al Groncki

FOREST SUPERVISOR - Klamath   August 13, 1958
A.K. CREBBIN - Resource Manager
A-INSPECTION - Audit

Please refer to the attached Notice of Audit Exception #20 and the L/T for payment by Louisa Young.

Mr. Feustel requested me to write a letter explaining the additional payment to the Youngs. The circumstances in this case are as follows:

Record of use by Youngs' cattle

Year	Permitted Use	Actual Use
'48	600	358
'49	"	410
'50	"	385
'51	"	480
'52	"	506
'53	"	none
'54	"	528
'55	"	613
'56	"	549
'57	"	612

1953 was a very late season—opening date July 24th—and Youngs made other arrangement for pastering their cattle after payment of fee.

1955 was an early season with an opening date of July 5th and resulted in 13 animal months higher use than permitted.

1957 was a very severe year with three to four feet of snow falling in two storms 10/3 to 10/10, and 10/12 to 10/14.

The Young Brothers were gathering during the storm. The cattle were scattered by the storms and with a great deal of work, the main herd was moved out before the end of the grazing season. Twenty-five stragglers were got out October 23 and after much work, two head on December 9th. The allotment is

5,000 feet to 7,000 feet in elevation and there was no cattle feed available after the first storm.

The two head of lost cattle taken out on December 9th resulted in the $1.68 charge demanded by the auditor.

Because of these trying circumstances, and my 25 years of pleasantly cooperative relationship with the Youngs, I couldn't write a friendly letter requesting payment.

I decided to deliver the bill personally and try to explain the cast iron thinking of our auditors.

At the Young Ranch, while waiting for Lee to come out of the field, I chatted with Mrs. Young. She told me of the hardships Lee endured fighting the snow to get the cattle out of the high country—she wondered if it was worth the physical hardships that are often encountered in the fall to graze cattle in the wilderness area. I fingered the L/T for $1.68 in my pocket and wondered too.

To start the conversation with Lee about the $1.68 L/T, I said "Do you remember the two cows you got out on December 9th?"

Lee said, "Al, I'll never forget those two poor old cows. I damn near froze to death getting them out. Bud Davis spotted their tracks in the snow from his plane. So we went in after them—bucked four to five feet of snow and finally staggered them out to a truck at Finley Camp."

"Both cows had lost their calves and were just able to navigate. They were in the head of Uncles Creek and had been eating pine cones, trees and bark for weeks. I couldn't get them into shape for breeding this spring and they are not grass fat yet. I sure lost a lot of money on those cows, but I feel good because I didn't let them starve to death."

I stood and fingered the L/T for $1.68 in my pocket and talked about routine Advisory Board matters.

After talking to Lee, I don't think the bill for $1.68 is under grazing. Don't you think it should be handled as a timber trespass as the cows were eating trees?

May I suggest that Bill and I make an investigation of all the cow flops eliminated on Uncles Creek from 10/15 to 12/9/57, inclusive. If we determine the cow flops are made up of splinters and inhabited by wood ticks the case should be settled as a timber trespass. If the cow flops are bull and inhabited by doodle bugs I will be willing to pay the $1.68 personally and forget the 1958 audit.

A PIECE OF PIE

Phil Lord

Since this episode out of the past more or less features S. Cooper Smith, maybe a brief character sketch is in order for the benefit of those that didn't know him.

His full name was Samuel Cooper Smith but he said there were already far too many Sam Smiths in the world, hence the S. Cooper Smith. He was born in Mexico, raised in Utah in the livestock business, went to forestry school in Utah and at the time I am remembering was the range management staffman on the Shasta Forest. Coop, as he was known, was good at his job, was a very good horseman and horse trader, loved to argue and would argue with anyone about anything at the drop of an opinion. He was a fellow who had many strange adventures. When he related them many people, myself included, didn't believe them but later would find out they had really happened.

As usual, I'm not sure of the exact date but Gus Hormay was just well started with the demonstration of his five pasture rest rotation grazing plan at Harvey Valley on the Bogard District of the Lassen NF. Pete Hook was the district ranger at Bogard. Gus was busy proving his first premise—that cattle would do just as well on the feed in the timber as they did on feed out on the open flat but that fence would be necessary. Most stockmen in the mountains had been aware of this (the old wild cows that stayed in the timber up in the mountains usually came out fatter than those that stayed on the flat) but Gus, a true researcher, if there ever was one in the world (many a researcher would do well to pattern after Gus) had proved this premise with actual weights taken periodically over the grazing season. He had done it with 45 head of open heifers belonging to one of the Lassen permittees.

Ranger Pete Hook and I and one of the permittee's men had brought the cattle in well ahead of the regular grazing season and now, well after the close of the season, we were to take them out. Gus wanted the drives made as the permittee would have made them and would take the final weights when we reached the ranch. Gus wanted a complete weight curve and Gus Hormay, to my knowledge, never did anything by half. Well, it was a four day drive; we hauled hay to the night stops, gathered the cattle into a large field at Squaw Valley and set a date to go. Gus wanted to go along but he had other commitments. (He would have been a good hand, too, if he went at it like he did everything else.)

Pete Hook and I would just as soon have had another man along as heifers like that usually don't have any leader and take a lot of driving. Coop Smith some way heard about the deal and wanted to know if he could come along. He didn't have to ask twice, and we told him the date, the time and the starting place.

The fatal day came, as fatal days have a habit of doing and Pete and I went to Harvey Valley the night before so as to get a good, early start. Coop didn't show up and he hadn't by the next morning. We were saddled up by daylight and by dint of standing close and talking fast I got Pete to wait for about 30 minutes figuring Coop might still show. But, he didn't, and 30 minutes was all I could get out of Pete. Pete Hook was the kind of man that if he had an appointment at 9 o'clock, he was there by 8:30 and he had little or no patience with people who tended to be late. So, knowing I was beat at the end of this 30 minutes of grace, we crawled up on top of our fuzztails and lit out across country to the field at Squaw Valley, about three miles. We gathered the field, got all the cattle the first go around and took off for the horse camp at Eagle Lake which was to be our first night's stop. Along about 9:30, my horse looked around behind us, so I did also, and here came someone on a brown horse. It was Coop Smith; he had experienced tire trouble which made him late. It had not bothered him that we were gone when he got to Harvey Valley, he had not expected us to wait. He had saddled up and followed our tracks to Squaw Valley, no mean feat in that country at that time of year. When he got to Squaw Valley he just rode around the fence until he came to the gate where we went out and from there on he had 45 cattle and two horses to track. Coop was not exactly what you would call a greenhorn.

With his help, things went a little faster and when we went through Champs Flat we picked up an old cow with a big calf that belonged to what was known in Lassen County as the Scattered Cattle Company. The owner of this outfit, hearing that we were coming through had told me, "If you see anything of mine, bring it along." This old cow and her calf stepped right up into the lead and the heifers strung out and about all we had to do was ride along behind and lie to each other.

The rest of the day and the next past without incident except that Coop was really giving me a sales pitch on that brown horse he was riding, which belonged to him. It was a good looking horse, all brown, no white on him and he acted gentle and sensible. He was a little soggy built for Coop's taste; he favored tall, leggy horses. This I knew, but of course, Coop never said anything about that, only how well broke and gentle this horse was and how I would love him if only I owned him. Well, I was at that time, as I have been most of my life and still am, horse poor. So, I wasn't about to fall for Coop's pitch. Also knowing what a horse trader he was I knew there had to be a "hole" in that brown horse somewhere because if he was as good as Coop said, why did he want to sell him? I had noticed once when Coop shook his rope down to recoil it, he was kind of careful. The horse stepped around a little and showed the white of his eyes and Coop held him up pretty good.

The third day started just like the others except that we had lost our old lead cow. She got to thinking about all those haystacks in Honey Lake Valley, I guess, and figured we were not traveling fast enough, so she and her calf just walked off and left us. But the heifers were driving a little better now, anyway. We were going down Rice Canyon toward Honey Lake Valley. At that time the stock driveway turned to the east around a fence corner and went out across a big sagebrush flat (a medium security prison sits right there now). I asked Coop if he would go ahead and turn the cattle at the fence corner and Pete and I would do the rest. So, he went ahead and turned them and then he pulled way back and let them go pretty wide around that fence. When Pete and I got there with the tail end I saw why. Right in the fence corner was a big coyote in a trap and he was very much alive and quite angry. Coop was getting his rope down and he put two half hitches over the saddle horn. Coop was a "tiefast" roper. The brown horse didn't seem to like all this too much. Coop said, "I'm going to put a rope on that coyote, jerk him out of that trap and drag him to death." (Coop had herded sheep as a kid and hated coyotes.) I said, "Please don't do that, that's one of Milt Thompson's traps and it's not fastened solid, it's just hung up there, the drag has caught in the brush or the coyote is tired. You won't jerk him out of it and if you do he may get away and then old Milt will read the tracks and find out who came by here this late with cattle. I will be on his nasty list and he is the kind of a guy that I'd just as soon not be on his nasty list."

So I got off and got a stick and hit the coyote on the nose and killed it, the way trappers do; it saves time and doesn't leave holes in the hide. So Coop said, "OK, just so he's killed," and coiled his rope up and put it in the strap but he didn't take the half hitches off the horn.

It was about noon and Pete and Coop had lunches. I didn't. Very early in my misspent career I found that if I packed a lunch when I was riding, noon always caught me about two miles from water and since I never carried a canteen I usually ended up throwing the lunch away. However, I never have any objections if anyone else carries a lunch and I'll never take part of anyone else's either. (It's my own private "code of the west;" I figure a fresh chew of tobacco is about as good as a dry lunch, anyway.)

Pete was already eating his lunch, riding along, and Coop said, "I guess I'll eat," and he did. So I took out my plug of Star and had my lunch. Coop was about finished eating except for a piece of pie which he unwrapped and took in his right hand. Just then I looked over and saw his rope was about to fall out of the strap. I said, "Coop your rope is about to fall." He said, "Let it. I can't lose it, it's tied to the saddle horn and this horse is gentle." Well, just then the rope fell and that nice, gentle, brown horse bagged his head and lit in to bucking like he was trying to qualify for the finals at Salinas. Coop had had the bridle reins just lying over the saddle fork while he was eating his lunch so they were gone the first jump. But, let me tell you that Coop was a bronc rider and a good one; he sat up there and rode and scratched, strictly on his balance. I tried to herd that brown horse out of the worst of the sagebrush (it was about six feet high there) but I wasn't doing much good. Coop was really doing OK and I believe to this day he would have ridden that horse to a standstill but his cinch was loose and the saddle kept working ahead. Coop could feel it and knew it was going to turn soon. He had been laughing; I think he was really enjoying it, but then he said, "I guess I'm bucked off," and off he went on the left side where I couldn't see him in the big sagebrush. The brown horse kept on bucking and I saw the rope tighten up. Coop hollered, "Stop the horse!" There was no time for much of anything and my only thought was maybe I can put that horse in a circle. I couldn't see what was happening to Coop. Just then the saddle turned and the brown horse faltered a second. I rammed the spurs to my horse and he jumped a big sagebrush and lit right beside the brown horse. I got hold of what was left of the bridle reins and just at that second Pete Hook put his horse right against him on the other side. We got the saddle off and went to see what had happened to Coop. He was sitting up, leaning against a big sagebrush. He still had the piece of pie in his hand and he said, "I paid 35¢ for this piece of pie and I'm going to eat it," and he did.

What had happened during all the bucking, Coop had got two turns of that rope around his right leg and the rope was still tied hard and fast to the horn. So, Coop just had time to get a good hold on a big sagebrush stem with his left hand and managed to hold on when the horse hit the end of the rope. If the saddle hadn't turned when it did, I hate to think of what might have happened. Coop had a game leg for a day or two but his heavy chaps saved him from any real injury. Coop was a cowboy

343

though, he was on horseback the next morning, game leg and all. But the fact remains he didn't lose the pie—and I didn't buy the brown horse.

REPTILES (MOSTLY SNAKES)

A SPOOKY NIGHT

Ed A. Grosch

The Indian Dick Guard Station, Covelo Ranger District, Mendocino National Forest was set on the upper edge of a grassy pasture. To the west side was a large rock outcrop, almost a butte. This spot was home to what I believed was a rattlesnake den, something I discovered during the summer of 1951. The pasture was also home to many ground squirrels and field mice.

The house I lived in had a nice porch across its only entrance. This porch was used for saddle storage in bad weather. There was a nice screen door over the wood door and I had the habit of leaving the wood door open for cross ventilation during the warm summer season. I had been warned about the snakes in the area by Roy McCombs, the packer. So, before stepping out through the screen door, I always looked to see if "Mr. Friendly" had slithered along the door edge of building and porch.

By September, I had killed 14 rattlers on the porch with my pistol. I still have the jar of rattles. Along in late September, I met up with Roy McCombs at Soldier Ridge and Minnie Lake Trail Junction. The mules were carrying used fire equipment from a couple of smokejumper fires and I was headed for Indian Dick from a small one-man fire near French Cove. Darkness overcame Roy and me before we got to the guard station but we plodded along and finally got through the pasture gate and made it to the hitch rails at the station.

Roy stumbled in the dark up to the small gate in the yard fence to gain entrance to the porch where I kept a lantern. As he touched and moved the gate latch, he let out a yell, "Rattlesnake ##*!@!*!" I moved to my lead mule Red, and fumbled into the pack for my head lamp. I got the light on and stepped over to where Roy was frozen in his tracks, pistol in hand. There was not a rattlesnake to be seen on the ground. The gate had swung open and, pointing the light around, we discovered the body of a three foot rattler hanging on the gate. Some visitor must have killed the snake and hung the remains on the gate for me to find on my return.

The incident left Roy pretty upset. Even though he had many close calls over the years with these silent visitors, he was scared by having encountered one in the dark.

MORE RATTLESNAKES

H. M. Lilligren

The Tiller Ranger Station on the Umpqua National Forest seemed to be a convention center for rattlesnakes during my tour of duty as ranger from 1954 to 1966. It probably always was and still is. Residents were advised to keep a garden hoe handy, usually by the back door. It was one of the safest tools to use to kill rattlers.

We also had madrone trees in some yards. They would shed all summer and when you walked on the dry leaves they sounded just like rattlesnakes. They also made so much noise you couldn't possibly have heard a rattler rattle!

Late one afternoon I killed a rattlesnake near the old CCC built office, now replaced. I was standing talking to several people with the dead snake draped over the blade of the hoe. A dead rattler always drew a curious crowd of onlookers. I heard someone approaching from behind me and turned to see who it was. As I did so, something struck my leg about snake high. I went straight up in the air, did a quarter turn to the right and came down looking Eva Poole straight in the eyes. My uncontrolled and unplanned remark was a very loud and distinct, "Jesus Christ!" Those were words I would never use in vain in a conversation with the lovely lady Eva Poole. My dog had run between my legs and struck my calf with his tail!

I cannot remember the exact number of snakes killed on the station grounds in the 12 years I resided on the ranger station, but a map I kept of kill locations showed no regular pattern— the map looked like it had been hit with a blast of bird shot. The snakes showed up beginning in the first real warm days in April and only left after the first frosts.

I would estimate that more than 36 rattlers were killed on the grounds during my tenure, and probably 10 or more times that number got by unobserved. The problem seemed to come from two known dens east of and above the station, and the fact that the rattlers food supply migrated down to the river bank during the hot dry months.

During my years at Tiller the station was a dual district headquarters. One of my fellow rangers was "Black John" O. Wilson. His nickname was given to him because of his very black beard, not because he didn't bathe. John was extremely unfond of snakes, rattlers being at the bottom of his list. After work one evening I was walking along the access road within the station bounds when I saw two of John's summer crewmen busy at something near the ditch line. I approached and they volunteered the information that they were trying to catch a rattlesnake. It was in a hole in the cut bank, and all that showed was the rattles and several inches of tail! They had an empty burn barrel (an oil drum with the top cut out) in the ditch line. They planned to pull the snake out by the tail, drop it into the oil drum and take it to the bunkhouse where they could raise it as a pet.

Knowing Ranger Wilsons' feelings, and also realizing I could not condone any actions that might jeopardize the safety of Forest Service employees, I advised the young men to dig the snake out and kill it. I explained that a cornered rattler will often expose his tail, but his body is usually doubled back in striking position and will strike if molested.

The end of the story? The lads killed the snake. I was told that William "Beef" Hunter cooked it and John Wilson helped eat it.

On another summer evening a group started gathering at the Don Olson residence to admire a rattlesnake freshly killed in their front yard. As the usual crowd gathered, a youngster came running to tell us another rattlesnake had just been killed at the Clausen residence, several hundred feet away. Not to be outdone, one of the Olson children then got his parents and showed them another live rattler coiled under the rear axle of their car parked in their driveway. I'd say three snakes in about 10 minutes set the record at that time.

The biggest snake I personally killed on the ranger station was 42 inches long, had almost no rattles, and was probably very old. It was lying coiled in the horse trail about 50 yards upriver from the barn. My dog stepped over it without seeing it and it didn't strike. It was in the process of digesting a rather large rodent.

If it is any consolation to the present residents of the Tiller Ranger Station, as of the time I transferred in 1966, there was no record of anyone living on the ranger station or employed by the Forest Service at Tiller ever having been bitten by a rattler. The station was established at Tiller in 1919.

There were many interesting stories of encounters with snakes in the field—too many to tell in their entirety. One cool morning, Al Wilm, a young junior forester, was accompanying a soil scientist doing a soil survey in the upper South Umpqua River drainage. They were walking up a trail to get into some of the back country. The soil scientist in the lead stepped over a snake lying in the trail without seeing it. Al didn't see it either—until his foot skidded on an unfamiliar surface. I was told that Al went several feet straight up in the air, started swinging his shovel, and had the snake chopped into several sections before his feet ever returned to the ground.

One Saturday, early in the spring when the South Umpqua River was low enough to wade knee deep, my teenage daughter

Sandra and I decided to check out a possible aboriginal campsite on the left bank of the river below Dumont Creek Campground.

We waded the river and started climbing over some pole sized flood felled timber along the banks. I stepped up on one pole, then down and proceeded onward. My daughter was about 30 feet behind me. Then I heard a soft voice say, "Daddy, there is a rattlesnake here!" I looked back and saw her standing on the pole I had just left. I said, "Where is it?" She pointed towards her feet and said, "It's under this log!" I said, "How do you know it's a rattlesnake?" She said, "It rattled and I can see the rattles!"

I told her to slowly walk up the fallen pole, and when she was six feet away from the snake, she carefully checked the ground and then stepped down. I then looked for a weapon. All the tree limbs and other chunks of wood debris were too heavy to lift, and all the rocks were large and deeply imbedded in the river sand. There wasn't anything to use on the snake.

I was about to admit defeat when suddenly I remember I was carrying a U.S. Army Colt .45 semiautomatic pistol in a shoulder holster. In the rush of searching for a crude weapon, I had completely forgotten it.

I shot the snake, severed its head, and put the remainder in a cloth sack we had with us.

RATTLESNAKES

Joe Church

In all of my time in the woods, I think I actually saw no more than a dozen rattlesnakes and, come to think of it, not many more of any kind of snake. Of the few I saw, I killed only one and that one only because it was in a logging area where choker setters were working and it was under a recently bucked log. If I could have come up with a way to resolve the situation without killing the snake, I'm sure I would have done it, but such was not the case. Also, I always have had the feeling that far more snakes saw me than I ever saw and that they watched me pass without indicating their presence.

One rattlesnake sighting that does stick in my mind took place on the Mi-Wok District of the Stanislaus Forest in the late 1960s when I had stopped for lunch in a small clearing along a creek, both of which were bordered by a dense brushfield. As I sat on the low bank of the creek, a movement to my right caught my eye and, turning only my head, I saw the snake about forty feet away. A prime specimen of a timber rattler, looking about the size of a small python, though actually about five or so feet long. It apparently had come out of the brush behind me, crossed the road and now was approaching the stream. Completely unaware of me—I think—it sort of ambled along through the dust and sparse grass, periodically raising its head to look around and test the air with its tongue, acting like it owned the place. Come to think of it, it probably did. Gliding up to the bank, the snake paused briefly, then went down the shallow slope and into the creek. The creek wasn't deep, so with its head held up, it quickly crossed and started up the other side. The thing that really impressed me was that, even though the head had crossed the creek and was moving up the far side, the tail had yet to enter the creek. But the tail with rattles, held high, finally did enter the water. By that time, the head moved up the far bank and into the brush, soon to be followed by the tail with rattles still held high. The entire episode took perhaps five minutes and to me, was like poetry in motion. As I finished my lunch, and I did finish it, the thought popped into my mind, "What would have happened if it had come up right behind me? Yeah, what?"

FROG HUNTING WE WILL GO

Harvey Mack

Supervisor Neal Rahm lived across the street from our house in Alturas on the Modoc. Our families spent lots of time together. One evening we were at their house for dinner and I commented on what unusual fried chicken legs we had eaten. He was somewhat insulted as they were frog leg delicacies that he had caught and prepared. This inspired Neal to talk me into going on a frog hunt with him on a dark night.

He was certain that we had to go on a night when there was little moonlight and when that night came, we went to the pond of a local sawmill armed with bright flashlights, spears and boots. The objective was to find the frogs with the light and let it blind them long enough for us to get close enough to spear them. It was an exceptionally good pond for frogs and we soon had what we wanted. We also managed to fall into the pond a couple of times when we tried to walk out on logs. We weren't exactly pond men, especially at night on wet logs.

We came home overjoyed and proudly showed our wives what we had gotten. We met with a very cold reception as neither wanted anything to do with a couple of dozen large dead frogs. It was about midnight so Neal told me to go on home and that he would take care of the frogs. About a half hour later after he had gotten dried out, he proceeded to remove the legs and put them into a pan of salt water and called me to come over immediately to see what was going on. The salt had activated the nerves in the legs and they were "jumping" wildly, even coming out of the pan.

The wives still would have nothing to do with them so Neal cooked them the next day and they were delicious but for some reason, he never suggested going frog hunting again.

A SNAKE OR ARM?

Ralph G. Johnston

This story relates to an experience of mine in 1949 while serving on the trail crew on the Valyermo District of the Angeles National Forest.

We were working the Lupine Trail that originated in Prairie Fork of the upper end of the East Fork of San Gabriel Creek. This trail proceeded from there over Pine Mountain ridge and down the south side to Fish Fork of the San Gabriel Creek.

This six man crew under Trail Foreman Don Biederbach utilized an old cabin site in Prairie Fork as their base camp. The sleeping area consisted of the floor of the old cabin. On our job we killed at least one rattlesnake each day. One of the men on this crew named John Merrill was deathly afraid of snakes. One night while we were asleep I was awakened by Merrill, who I was sleeping next to, holding my arm and screaming, "Snake, snake, where's my knife?" He always carried an eight inch sharp hunting knife. Apparently, in my sleep, I had thrown my arm over his chest and he woke up thinking it was a snake. Fortunately he didn't find his knife or I could have had a serious problem.

SNAKES ALIVE

Wendall L. Jones

On a major fire in the Salmon River country, we established a zone firecamp along a tributary of the Salmon River. The Salmon River and this tributary had been fairly recently declared a wild and scenic river. We had heard that there might be rattlesnakes along this nice stream so our camp team quickly posted signs along the stream warning of rattlesnakes. About that time some local liaison folks arrived on the scene and said, "Who told you there were rattlesnakes here?" Of course, we couldn't identify the starter of the rumor but the local folks did say there were a few snakes another several miles downstream. More important to the local resource manager, was the protection of this wild and scenic stream from pollution by firecamp activities. No one was to bathe, wash clothes or otherwise contaminate this nice stream along the firecamp. There was much discussion about how we would control several hundred people at all hours of the day and night from taking advantage of this inviting mountain stream. Our service group never lacked for imagination. Someone suggested, "Hey, let's just put up more and bigger rattlesnake signs. That should keep most folks away from the creek." And, you know, it worked nearly 100 percent.

WHY A WATER MOCCASIN IS CALLED A COTTONMOUTH

James L. McConnell

Being a junior forester in the USFS in 1956, could lead to all kinds of adventures. I worked on the Catahoula Ranger District of the Kisatchie National Forest. Being a bachelor at the time, I rented a room in a large, old house in Pollock, Louisiana. Miss Mattie owned the house and charged $30 per month. She lived downstairs and rented four bedrooms upstairs. Miss Mattie had a twin, Miss Molly, who had been married. When her husband died she came to live with her sister. Miss Mattie had never married. One of the requirements for living in the house was you had to report in at least once a week and give an account of yourself and what you had been up to. Their nephew owned a local sawmill and Miss Molly's husband had worked for Weyerhaeuser company so they both knew a lot about forestry and the USFS.

One day in early fall I ascended the stairs and entered my room. There sat two men on my bed. One was Paul Russell and the other was Bart Kennedy. Paul was later to become supervisor in South Carolina. Paul introduced himself and said he was project leader for the Mississippi River and Tributaries Study. The Corps of Engineers had contracted with the Forest Service to cruise certain forested areas along the river and determine timber values. Simple job—if you were a duck. He also said, "You are working for me now. I've already cleared it with the ranger and forest supervisor."

Monday morning I reported to Bart Kennedy in Alexandria, La. Bart gave me a couple of days training on how to cruise the plots they had devised and how to grade hardwood trees for lumber quality. After the training he supplied maps with cruise plots on them and off I would go into the swamps and flatlands of Louisiana. At that time we worked alone in areas that were two and three miles off a dirt road. That's not a long way by some standards but in the flatwoods of Louisiana it could be the backside of hell. No one knew where I was, except Bart in a general way. When I had cruised all the plots on the maps he had given me, I would report in, turn in my plots sheets and pick up a new set of maps. Usually the water was not over waist deep. We tallied plots from Concord to Opelousas and from Tallaluh to Coushatta. Someone else was responsible for the area north of the Louisiana line.

One day in early spring, which comes early in Louisiana, I was following my compass line through an area which had some relief. It was still cool weather but sunny, the leaves were about as big as squirrel ears. I came to a stream which had a four or five foot bank. My eyes were on a tree across the stream that was on the compass line I was trying to follow. I jumped down and started looking for a place to cross without getting too wet. I thought this was a bit of luck, it was a sunny area and the water wasn't too deep. All of a sudden my eyes landed on a fat, dark looking shape that seemed out of place. Water moccasin— OK I thought, go around. Then I picked up another—and another. Gee, this is no place to be. I stood quite still and counted—fourteen, fifteen, sixteen water moccasins, all quite happy in the springtime sun. TIME TO LEAVE JIM! I really don't remember how I vacated the area, how I got up the bank or really where I stopped running. I do remember one huge snake (all snakes are huge to me) opening its mouth and slowly try to strike me. Being cold-blooded it moved too slow that spring day. That mouth was pure white, just like a boll of cotton.

YIPES!! A RATTLESNAKE

Stan Bennett

While working at Twisp on the Okanogan Forest, I had the good fortune to rub elbows with Lloyd (Bernie) Bernhard. One of the great joys Bernie had was to show off his collection of rattlers he had in a box in his desk drawer.

On one of those first sunny days in spring when the rocks start warming up, we went out to check on the grass on one of the nearby allotments. We had eaten our lunch and started down a small creek on foot. Bernie was ahead and suddenly the frantic whirling of a rattler echoed through the trees. It was as if there were a number of them all around us. Bernie froze, not knowing which way to go. For a moment it looked like Bernie was mesmerized. I then spotted the snake above him on the slope and yelled to Bernie to move downhill. He did, fast. It's peculiar how fast a rattler can make one move. After the dust settled, Bernie had the rattles of another snake to add to his collection.

Have you ever noticed how a rattlesnake swims? He always keeps his rattles turned up out of the water to keep them dry. That's a plus for us, for wet rattles are not very effective.

When working on trail maintenance an the Galice District of the Siskiyou Forest, the topic of rattlesnakes came up while we were sitting around the campfire one night. Of course we were very much in rattlesnake country and the question as to how could we protect ourselves while sleeping was tossed around. Being a greenhorn, I took in all these stories. As we were preparing to crawl into our sleeping bags, I began looking around as if a snake was behind every tree and bush. Claude Keyte said the best protection one could have would be to coil a hair rope around his bag. The theory being, a rattlesnake does not like to have his belly tickled by the horsehairs so won't crawl over the rope. Well, the upshot of that idea proved fruitless because we didn't have a hair rope. I've never used a hair rope or seen anyone else use one, nor have I had any rattlers as bed fellows.

Everett Lynch, District Ranger at Tonasket, when I came on the Okanogan, had an incident that was pretty scary. He was in the Mt. Hull area north of Tonasket climbing up through steep rocky country. As is normal, he was taking hold of rocks above from time to time to help himself up the steep terrain. All at once he got bit on the back of his hand by a rattler. Everett was extremely woodswise and he immediately sat, rested and forced the bite to bleed with his knife. He stayed there until late in the day and then made his way slowly back to his pickup and home. Everett said that he was somewhat sick and his hand was sore for awhile, but nothing else.

LIZARDS

Joe Church

On the Mi-Wok District of the Stanislaus Forest, I was driving along the North Fork of the Tuolumne River near Riverside at the end of the day when I spotted a creature in the middle of the road where it could be run over. I pulled to the side of the road, parked; turned off the engine and walked over to it. It was an alligator lizard, an excellent specimen, at least a foot long, half of which was tail. My aim was to get it off the read and to a safer place. I picked it up halfway between the front and hind legs. It immediately whipped around and bit my index finger, and not only bit, but also chewed by thrashing its head back and forth, quickly causing a rasping effect. I was surprised and dropped it. I checked my finger and noted scratch marks—abrasions—from which tiny drops of blood oozed. And, there it was, still near my feet, unmoving and studying me with those pitless black eyes. It was still in the road so I again picked up the lizard and again it whipped around and got me, but this time for only an instant for either I shook it off or it let me go. Then it occurred to me that I was lucky it wasn't ten times bigger. But on the other hand, if it was, I surely wouldn't have stopped— well, maybe for an instant to get a photo but I would have been famous. The lizard was still there so once again I made my move. Only this time, with a little more forethought, for I used both hands, one at the belly and the other at the neck just behind the head. It really thrashed hard and I could feel how strong it was. This time I got it to the side of the road and released it. It was gone in a flash. I had accomplished my goal but had been bitten by a lizard. Wow!

SNAKES ALIVE AND DEAD

Lloyd W. Swift

While on the Plumas range survey, the summer of 1931, I was on the west slope of the Middle Fork of the Feather River on a warm afternoon when a rattlesnake was discovered in a shaded retreat.

It occurred to me the situation was suitable for a test of the ability of snakes to endure exposure to direct sunlight on a hot day.

In preparation for the experiment I scooped a basin like depression, then with a walking stick, moved the snake into the sun. With my watch and a note pad in hand I observed and recorded the actions of the rattler. This was 66 years ago, yet I retain a memory of the snake's discomfort and demise.

The snake was immediately concerned with finding cover but was restrained. Its vigorous efforts to escape gradually subsided, being interrupted by irregular movements, sometimes convulsive in character; then in a final effort, stretched out with mouth open and expired in 12 minutes, as I remember.

This experience was described in a letter to Dr. Tracy Storer at U.C. Davis. He sent an edited version to a herpetology journal, resulting in publication of my first technical paper!

CA-1 OR NOT?

Ralph G. Johnston

Fred Post, who worked on the Angeles National Forest phone line crew years ago, was asked if he had made out an accident report (CA-1) after being bit by a rattlesnake. He said, "Hell no, it wasn't an accident because the snake bit me on purpose."

"NEED ANY ASSISTANCE RANGER?" "NO THANK YOU, EVERYTHING IS JUST FINE"

Chuck Smay

I knew and worked with Ken Ready on the Saugus Ranger District when the incident is alleged to have occurred. I do know for a fact that Ken was definitely afraid of anything that looked like a snake, moved like a snake, or sounded like a snake. He definitely wished to rid the world of this creature. Something in his past work in the southeast had imprinted him for life in his working relationship with snakes. This snake encounter certainly gave Ken legend status with his coworkers. Here's the story about Ken's encounter with a western snake. This story showed up in numerous forest newsletters in 1968-69:

Project Forester Ken Ready learned a lesson about snakes and trucks last month. He was driving his FS truck along the Interstate 5 project, which was somewhat wet from rain. Looking ahead through the fogged windshield and flapping blades, he saw a huge snake sliding across the wet dirt.

"Ah ha!" he said, "I'll squash him under the mighty wheels of old 3548." He aimed his truck, made a pass and turned to survey the crippled remains. The snake couldn't have been hurt less if it had been bombarded with a paper cup from the height of three feet. The road was clear and straight so Ready decided to make another pass in reverse—this time sliding the wheels under locked brakes. Again the snake showed no signs of pain or even a desire to get off the road. The only thing left to do was park on the thing and chop it up with a shovel. When Ken was sure the truck was atop the reptile, he got out and looked under. Things were not the way they should have been.

The elusive snake was worming from beneath the wheels and poking its head around the tie rods and wheels. That thing is going to crawl into my motor, Ken thought to himself. He jumped back into the truck to take off, but it was too late. The snake was under the hood. Racing forward and stopping the truck abruptly didn't shake it loose. Backing and stopping did no good either. The snake hung on. Ken got out and peered beneath the truck (at a safe distance) but saw nothing. Using a shovel, he managed to open the hood, but there was no sign of the snake. It was at this time with the hood up, that a passing motorist stopped and asked if he could be of any assistance. "No, thank you," Ken replied. "Everything is just fine." What else could a U.S. Forest Ranger say?—"Yes, I've got a snake in my motor."

The last remaining hope was that it would fall out from under the truck while driving. He started back to the cab and noticed that all this time the door of the truck had been open. "That darn thing could have crawled into the cab by now." It took 20 minutes to clean out the interior and inspect all the little nooks and crannies. "I never realized my truck was this littered up," he thought. When the job was done, Ken slipped in behind the steering wheel and eased down the road with an uncomfortable feeling that at any minute the snake would poke its head through one of the many holes in the fire wall or drop from under the dash into his lap. After traveling about one mile there was a violent thumping noise from under the hood, and something slammed against the fire wall and dropped to the road. It was the snake. Wherever it was hiding, it wound up in a spinner with the radiator fan and came out second.... third.... and fourth best.

An autopsy was made, but the remains were unidentifiable. The moral of this story is (1) don't try to run down snakes on a wet road, (2) keep the inside cab of your truck clean in case you have to hunt for snakes and (3) stand clear when the snake hits the fan!!!

MULTIPLE SPECIES

THE LAST TIME I SAW BILLY

Bob Irwin

In 1953, I lived on the Georgetown Ranger Station (Eldorado NF, R-5). My house had a small lawn all around and a cyclone fence encircling the yard. The fence was completely overgrown with an evergreen hedge that was about five feet high. There were walk-in gates on the north and south sides of the fence and each had a cowbell hung on it to announce visitors when the gates were opened.

After I moved into the house I acquired a young puppy that I named "Danny." It didn't take Danny very long to recognize that the clanging cowbells meant visitors. He would race to whichever gate made the noise, barking and wagging his tail all the way.

At the time I was the district prevention patrolman with added responsibility to service all the lookouts. One early summer evening Robb's Peak called in and reported that he and his wife had found and rescued an "orphan" fawn on the road to their spring. They had heard shots the night before and there were guts, blood and leftovers about a hundred yards from the fawn. (There was some suspicion that they knew more than they told about the event, but nobody ever followed-up.)

They were feeding the fawn bread and condensed milk in the lookout, the fawn was doing well but they were running out of both supplies. I was asked to get more of those items to them "pretty quick." I did that the next day.

They named the little fellow "Billy Boy." He wasn't all that strong but he was able to move around in the lookout cab and he sure knew how to get to his feed pan after the lookouts hand fed him for only one day! At this point in time it was pretty well determined that Billy Boy would stay at Robb's Peak for awhile and then get turned loose. That didn't happen.

A short time later a message came through for the lookout that his mother was about ready to die in Texas and he needed to get home. They left and that left me covering the lookout and caring for Billy Boy. In a few days a relief lookout was assigned and I took Billy home with me.

I wasn't sure how a dog and a fawn would get along and I kept Danny on a short chain for awhile. I made a bed of oak leaves and pine needles for Billy Boy on the front porch and Danny got to sleep in the kitchen. I don't think it was much more than a week before it was very clear that the two were compatible. I took the chain off of Danny; no problems. Danny even took to napping on Billy's front porch bed and Billy just laid down on the boards.

I still kept them separated while I was gone. Danny was outside hooked onto a wire run between the garage and the fence; Billy was inside the fence and gates. When I was home, Danny was let loose and the two of them just sort of "hung around" the inside yard together. When I saw that Danny seemed to have a protective attitude toward the fawn I had no more concerns about Billy Boy's safety. I left the two of them alone in the yard whether I was home or not.

Danny always barked and ran to the cowbells when someone pushed a gate. The first few times he did that it scared hell out of Billy and he tried to hide under the porch. That terror only lasted two or three times that I saw. After that, Billy got used to Danny's eruptions and he just sort of "spooked" for a minute, (jumped up but stayed where he was) and watched Danny do his thing.

Then Billy Boy figured out what was going on; the cowbell rang, Danny ran barking to the bell on whichever gate it was and people came in. People petted Danny and talked to Billy. Some of them even brought goodies from their gardens for Billy. He was less than two months old when he started running with Danny to the sound of cowbells! No more hiding, no more spooking, *just see who could get there first!*

Later on I put Billy outside the fence to give him more freedom. That was OK with him, he had eaten the grass, severely cropped the hedge on the inside, and chewed on what few flowers still survived. He was ready for a change of scenery and diet but he was usually around when I got home. Sometimes he would come to the gas house when I was servicing my vehicle. When I parked for the night and went in the gate, Danny would meet me from inside and Billy would be behind me from the outside. Once the two of them got together, I was forgotten. I usually put Billy outside at bedtime.

The older the two animals got, the more they liked to play together. After Billy figured out the response to cowbells, the two of them developed a game that was played with great energy. The routine went like this:

Four, five, six times a day, Billy would come up and kick or butt a gate. Danny didn't know whether real people had shown up or not, so he responded as usual. By the time Danny got to that first gate, Billy would have run around to the second gate and was clanging that bell. Danny would respond, only to hear the first bell ring again. The dog wasn't dumb. By the time he got to the first gate with nobody there, he knew he was chasing the phantom fawn but that seemed to be more exciting than meeting people!

After about three rounds of this wild race (Danny on the inside, Billy on the outside), Billy would take off and hide behind the garage. Danny would make another fast trip or two around the inside of the fence looking for the deer that wasn't there and finally give up and lie down panting. Just a few minutes later Billy would strike again, always on the opposite side of the yard from the spot where Danny rested.

Once it started, this circus went on daily. It didn't take long for the news to get around. During one period, station personnel and some of our local neighbors were on my porch every evening. As I recall, the animals seemed to play harder with an audience. Activity (and audience) died off as winter closed in. On midwinter days that were warm and sunny, there was still contact between them, even with snow on the ground and the same hilarious game would be replayed at a slower pace.

In the spring of 1954, Billy heard the "call of the wild" and he was gone more than he was around the station. When he did come back, he "announced" himself by clanging a cowbell. Danny always came to that call and the game began again. Billy probably came back once a week, then once a month, during the summer and fall. Then nothing. I was certain that I had seen the last of Billy and I think Danny sensed the same thing. Without a live playmate to run after, Danny took to chasing logging trucks coming down the road in front of the station. He lost one of those races in the late fall of '54.

And I was wrong about not seeing Billy Boy again. Toward the end of the 1955 fire season (close to a year after I saw him last) I was working with some of the fire crew in the warehouse yard. One new member of the crew who had never heard about Billy suddenly said something like "Wow, take a look at this" and pointed to a (just barely) forked horn strolling up the road from the pumphouse.

It was Billy, of course, and he came right up to me, in the midst of several others who quit work to watch the show. I asked one of the crew to get some bread and condensed milk from the barracks. When that got delivered, Billy scarfed it down like he remembered how hungry he was the first day at Robb's Peak!

Billy and I visited with one another long enough for one of the crew to take our picture. Then he went on over to "our" house and banged on the north gate. The cowbell clanged but there was no response. He banged again with the same result. He went to the south gate and banged it twice. No response. He didn't try again, he just wandered away without even looking back. That was the last time I saw Billy.

The Last Time I Saw Billy Boy.

NATURE IN THE RAW

James R. Pratley

In the extensive brush fields of the forests of Southern California, the pack rat and the rattlesnake live side by side, one the victim of the other in the natural balance of nature.

A confrontation between these two forest dwellers allowed me to witness a very dramatic life and death encounter on a lonesome trail one warm and sunny day early in my career.

Pack rats acquired their name as a result of their natural habit of collecting twigs, leaves and other forest debris and building a large mound which then becomes their home. These mounds are often eight feet in diameter and as much as four feet in height, and are the focal point of their inhabitants' constant search for vegetable matter, the pack rats' principal source of food. These rats are also avid collectors of junk, mans' discards, and one can often find in their nests bottle caps, buttons, empty cigarette packs, broken pieces of glass and many other lost and stolen items of man, as they are not above stealing whatever it is that they deem desirable. And, being prolific breeders, they comprise one of the principal food sources of the resident rattlesnakes.

Rounding a small ridge late in the afternoon, I startled a pack rat that was foraging for food, causing it to bolt headlong down the trail toward its protective mound somewhere in the immediate vicinity. And, unknown to both the rat and me, a patiently waiting and coiled rattlesnake was just off the trail, ready to take advantage of any small creature or man that might pass within striking distance.

As the rat ran past the snake, it struck with deadly accuracy. As the fangs penetrated and then were immediately withdrawn from the side of the rodent, the rat squealed in terror and at the same time, leaped into the air in a futile effort to escape its ultimate doom.

Even as it came back to earth from its terrified leap, the effect of the venom was beginning to take its toll. Unable to run, it fell on its side and staggered to its feet as the poison enzymes began to digest the still living tissues as they spread throughout the small body. It was obvious from the actions of the rat that it was not going to go far in its death struggles. Within a minute or two, it was lying motionless on the trail about ten feet from where the fatal bite had taken place.

As the final moments of life ebbed away and the little body began to slowly relax, the snake, obviously unaware of my presence and witness to the drama, began to slither toward the meal that was now available. Being somewhat poor sighted, it began to flick out its tongue to pick up the scent of the rat and thus direct itself toward the now lifeless creature. The effect of the venom is such as to prevent smaller victims of such snakes from going too far before they perish. Otherwise, the snake might well kill the animal but be unable to find it, even with its keen sensory organ.

Arriving at the now dead rat, the snake worked its way to a position where it could engorge the small body head first to facilitate swallowing.

Disengaging its hinged jaws, it literally began to walk itself around the body using small convulsive motions to assist in the endeavor. This headfirst approach is necessary to avoid the possibility of the snake being unable to get past the rear legs of any four-footed creature if it began with the tail. The front and rear legs of most small creatures tend to fold easily backward along the longitudinal axis of the body, allowing for easy passage through the jaws and down the throat. A rear end approach could be the death of the snake. If it could not get past the extended rear or front legs of its victims, the backward curving teeth of the serpent would prevent it from disgorging the partially swallowed body. The snake would either die of starvation or become the victim of another hunter of the forest.

With the serpent lying fully extended along the trail after its meal, all that remained of the rodent was a small bulge in the snake's body as it underwent the final digestive process. In due time, a day or two at most, all that would be left of the pack rat would be a compact residue of bones and skin, passed out of the rattlesnake somewhere on the forest floor.

After this meal, the snake would not eat again for many days, perhaps a week or more, and only after another successful encounter somewhere in the elfin forest.

HERE KITTY

Harvey Mack

In 1942-43, I was the fire crew foreman at the El Cariso Guard Station on the Cleveland Forest. This was a relatively remote location at that time with mostly scattered local people in the area as gasoline rationing curtailed most travel but we did have lots of animals. One early morning, my wife started out to put some trash or garbage in the garbage pit behind the house. She got about halfway when she notice a large cat trying to get into the pit. She was familiar with bobcat and didn't think too much about it but decided to wait awhile. However, she did call me on the intercom phone so I came to see just what it was and, to my surprise, it was a large mountain lion. It saw me but continued to paw at the lid trying to get to whatever it thought might be inside. I was pretty much at a loss as to what to do but remembered that we had a fire standpipe with 100 feet of hose for station protection and decided this would be a good way to scare the animal off. I started pulling the hose around the house and instructed one of the crew to turn on the water when I told him to. However, when I came around the corner there was no sign of the lion and I never was able to convince anyone that there had been a lion as they thought I was pulling some kind of a joke on them.

At the same station, we frequently had deer that would come up onto the porch of the house and look in the window as we often put food out for them. The porch was badly damaged by termites and rot so I proceeded to repair it and replace all of the supports, joists and floor. I finished the job late in the afternoon by putting on a heavy coat of paint. After dark, we heard a lot of commotion but, since we had no electricity, we could not see what had gone on but the next morning it was obvious that a couple of deer had skated around and fallen on the fresh paint and really made a mess of it. We sure wondered what they may have looked like but, to the best of our knowledge, we never saw them again.

MOTHER NATURE'S ALLIANCES

Bruce Barron

Loneliness is often a haunting companion to people stationed on remote Forest Service fire lookout towers, however, they soon learn ways to cope. When visiting these lonely stations, a person would often be greeted by a raucous Steller's jay (or other bird) that would land on one's shoulder and demand to be fed. It was also a common occurrence to have to step lightly in order to avoid crushing a contented golden mantled squirrel or a chipmunk placidly sprawled out on the stairway. They would be so fat they could barely waddle, let alone scamper out of the way. It soon became apparent why some lookout personnel always included a copious order of peanuts or sunflower seeds on their provision list.

Whenever you spied a conspicuous salt block on a nearby rock or stump, it was obvious the lookouts also enjoyed the company of deer, porcupines or other salt loving animals congregating at the "saltlick!"

Table scraps were often utilized to attract raccoons or opossums, or perhaps a docile family of skunks. The amusing antics and camaraderie of these wild creatures helped relieve the feeling of loneliness in these isolated surroundings and more than made up for the lack of the amenities of urban life.

Many lookout personnel brought domestic pets with them but found they were not always compatible with the native wildlife.

There was an amusing incident that occurred on the Orr Mountain Lookout on the Shasta Forest. A fox terrier dog fell from the 32 foot high tower. He landed astride the clothesline below, which stretched like a bungee cord and eased the dog to the ground without a scratch.

A less fortunate lookout on Black Butte near Mt. Shasta had a cat named "Snowball." Late one evening when gale-like winds were blowing, the lookout stepped out on the catwalk to appease his kidneys before retiring for bed. Snowball stepped out with him and the last he saw of the cat was a ball of white fur glistening in the moonlight, sailing in the air at 5,000 feet headed in the direction of Dunsmuir. It was hoped that the cat may have landed in a thicket of soft fir trees and perhaps is still trying to find its way back home to the lookout?!!

IN THE BACKWOODS

Lura Esther Cooley Osborne

Editor's Note: During the summer of 1909, Mrs. Esther Osborne, a bride from New England, accompanied her husband, William B. (Bush to his friends) Osborne, a young forest assistant, while he was making the first extensive timber reconnaissance of the Oregon (now Mt. Hood) National Forest. Mrs. Osborne wrote long letters home, many of which were so interesting to her relatives and friends that they were published under the title Experiences of the Inexperienced in the Backwoods. *What follows are a few paragraphs from that publication.*

Bush Osborne, referred to as the forest assistant, was a keen observer. He later became a leading forest fire technician in the Northwest, developed the "Osborne Fire Finder" and was the author of a series of Forest Service handbooks on fire behavior and control that were long standard tests.

I watched gleefully the packing of the alforjas and saw the malignant glance of our new horse, Gypsy, who well understood that a trip awaited her. With ears laid back, she fastened her good eye upon the ribs of the forest assistant and gnawed viciously at the nearest tree. Joyously I assured the storekeeper and early loafers that, of course, I could ride to the ranger station, 82 miles distant, little guessing it meant eleven hours in the saddle. The trail led abruptly up the slope, and the tiny shacks were quickly lost from view. The morning sunshine filtered through the tall trees, making bright patches among the shadows. A great stillness lay over all. The horses' hoofs made little noise on the soft brown earth and needles, and the occasional snapping of a twig or the babble of a swiftly flowing brook only accentuated the silence. Missing the grass, low spreading hardwoods and underbrush of wood lots, I still felt the greenness about me. Towering far overhead—180 feet perhaps—the tops of mighty Douglas firs shut out the sky. It was a mature stand and the lower branches had been shaded out long ago. There was nothing green about the gigantic trunks, the thick, dark brown bark roughly broken into red-brown furrows. Their size and number prevented any sense of perspective, but the feeling came to me that, in the distance, tree tops and earth drew nearer and nearer, shutting us under a vast dome of green. This comparatively level plateau and absence of brush proved not to be characteristic.

At first the ascent was gradual but I realized we had been climbing when the path came out along the side of a ravine and two hundred feet below rushed a mountain river. The sheep herder, who was making this part of the journey with us, remarked cheerfully that if a horse slipped there, it would be the end of him. The crystal, pure water made the colors of the rocks beneath clearer than those of the ledges. At that point the roar was like the passing of the wind. Beyond this point the trail seemed precipitous, but later I learned it was a Broadway in the woods. It was eight o'clock when we reached the ranger station and too late to make a bough bed. We spread our blankets on the ground and slept beneath the stars (the first time I had ever slept in my clothes and hat).

The next day the ranger left and we took temporary possession of his quarters.

The gay crossbills hopped fearlessly near. There was no need for the bird lover to tiptoe in the woods and squint through a field glass only to catch the distant flutter of wings. The chipmunks, too, were friendly. I enjoyed having one sit boldly beside me and others scamper around the cabin while I ate my luncheon. Then I tried to sleep in the afternoon, however, the little thieves made such a disturbance that I sat up in the bunk and drew my revolver. Greatly to my surprise, I killed one at some distance outside the door, and being gratified by praise, I thought I would repeat the performance next day. This time the rogue was on the table only a few feet from me. I shot and heard something drop to the floor, but hating to see the little creature writhe, I waited a few minutes before looking over the edge of the bunk. There was a rope and punctured water bottle, but no other victim. Investigation showed a bullet hole through the lard pail back of which these articles had been hidden. One chipmunk's tail was my only trophy of the season.

People often ask if I wasn't afraid of bears, bobcats, wolves and so on. They were more timid than we, and I saw nothing except tracks. Only one night, when I was lying under a huge cedar, watching the moon glide above its top, I heard again and again the slowly rising howl, long drawn out, of a wolf far away.

OF DOGS AND CHICKENS AND CHICKEN KILLING DOGS

Robert W. Cermak

Dogs were always a problem on ranger stations, and the Challenge Ranger Station (Plumas NF) in 1960 was no exception. I didn't appreciate scooping up gifts left by station canines, refereeing spats between dog owners or washing off the front door after some mutt left his mark. But then we didn't have a dog until that spring when I brought home a Siberian husky female pup named Tatoosh. My whole attitude changed from intolerance of all dogs to intolerance of all dogs but ours. As

Tatoosh grew she became quite a traveler like many sled dogs. Which was okay until we began to hear rumors of a wolf dog chasing a neighbor's chickens. Then it was alleged that this dog had killed some of same. The allegations became fact when Tatoosh brought home a bedraggled chicken that she had assassinated. We went through the old cure of tying the chicken around her neck until it stank. She didn't care. What stank to us was perfume to her so what the hell! The complaints continued and threats of dog shooting began. We tied Tatoosh up but couldn't do that for long. She had far too much energy.

One day we happened to tune the TV in on a dog "expert" explaining that dogs attacked chickens because they fluttered and ran when chased. The remedy was to stake the dog out near chickens until the dog became used to the way chickens acted. Sounded logical, but we had no chickens. What we had, however, was Mrs. Soames the milk and egg lady from down the hill at Rackerby. We enjoyed fresh eggs and raw milk that she brought every week never realizing that we were dooming ourselves and our children with high cholesterol and other dread diet factors. When wife Ethel explained the problem, Mrs. Soames said, "Why, we always have a few henpecked chickens that we have to get rid of. You can have them. Some of our eggs are properly sexed and turn out to be roosters. I'll give you one of them, too."

I built an A frame chicken coop in the back yard and fenced it. When Mrs. Soames brought the chickens I began to have doubts. For some reason chickens, like people, persecute certain others of their kind. Our chickens had really taken a beating; puny and pecked free of feathers on head and neck, they looked like POWs. However, after a few weeks of food and freedom from their oppressors they were fat and fully restored to featherdom. Meanwhile, the little rooster had blossomed into an imposing white cock of the walk. Then the hens began to produce eggs and I became a believer.

We began the chicken experiment by tying Tatoosh close to the pen where she could watch the chickens but not reach them. She lay there and quivered as the chickens went about their nonsensical ways, clucking and fluttering around. We continued this for several days moving her closer to the chickens by stages. Then we put her in the chicken pen She never made a move toward them even when they ate from her food dish, an act that would result in instant bloodletting with any other creature. Soon we could put her loose in the pen and she never molested a chicken. Thrilled, we held a graduation ceremony for Tatoosh and all was right with the world. Naturally, I bragged around the district office about the successful training of our wonderfully smart dog.

A few days later I was in my office when Dale Hall, Challenge Experimental Forest manager, hollered from the front office, "Bob, come take a look at this." I walked up and looked to where Dale was pointing, a grin on his face. "This" was Tatoosh trotting across the yard in front of the office with a live banty rooster in her jaws heading for our house. I left the office in a hurry, the sound of giggles and guffaws ringing in my ears. I chased Tatoosh around one side of the house while Ethel cut her off on the other. Tatoosh saw that she was trapped, stopped dead in her tracks, laid the rooster down and looked at us in wonderment. What was the problem? She hadn't taken one of OUR chickens had she? Meanwhile, the rooster got up and ran squawking across the yard toward its home, indignant as only an assaulted rooster can be. We concluded that Tatoosh had indeed been well trained. She had learned that she was not to take our chickens but her training didn't cover the neighbor's chickens. In fact, the training worked because Tatoosh never had another relapse.

ANIMALS IN THE SNOQUALMIE NATIONAL FOREST

R. W. Smith

In the summer of 1954, I worked on a survey crew on the Naches District of the Snoqualmie National Forest. One Sunday I decided to hike up to Mt. Aix from the Rattlesnake Guard Station. I walked up the road from the guard station to

McDanial Lake. From there I followed the trail in a westerly direction. About four miles up the trail I rounded a corner and 300 feet ahead of me was a gray colored shaggy bear with a hump between his front shoulders. He was in the middle of an open meadow eating grass next to the trail. All the bears I had seen before that, always ran away at the sound of a human voice. So I backed down the trail just out of sight of the bear and yelled, "Wahoo!" The bear heard me, looked first left then right and since he didn't see me, he went back to nonchalantly eating grass. Since he did not run away as I expected him to do, I wet my finger to see which way the wind was blowing and detoured downwind around the meadow.

About an hour later I was traversing across a steep grassy meadow. Glancing up about 500 feet above me on a rock ledge, I saw a large cougar sitting there looking over the countryside. I decided that he must have already seen me and he was sitting there calmly, so I continued up the trail. A quarter of a mile farther up the trail I looked back up the hillside. The cougar was still sitting in the same place.

On the east side of Mt. Aix the trail disappeared under snow that had not yet melted from the previous winter. With no trail to follow, I climbed up the slope. When I got on top of a ridge that projected out east from the summit, I saw a lot of white fuzz on all the bushes. A mile father west, I found the source of the lint like fuzz. I was in the middle of a herd of wild goats. The fuzz was goat hair. I was amazed that I could walk right into the middle of the herd and they just milled around as if I wasn't there. I have always had a thrill in seeing wild animals in the woods.

On another day later in the summer I had followed a trail south to Bethel Ridge and decided to follow the road down to the guard station. About three fourths of a mile north of Bethel Ridge and 300 feet lower, I heard a loud screech. I looked up and saw a hawk diving straight toward me. The hawk dove at me three times, each time screeching real loud and each time pulling out of its dive about 20 feet above my head. I found that more unnerving than the next encounter.

A half mile farther down the road I heard a noise above me, looked up the hillside to the west and saw about 20 cow elk with about 10 calves. They were running parallel to the road. As I rounded a corner in the road the herd of elk crossed in front of me. Most of them ignored me and continued on their way but one cow elk crossing the road 25 feet ahead of me stopped in the middle of the road, lowered her head and pawed the dirt. I knew I could not outrun the elk so I stood my ground in the middle of the road, neither moving toward or away from her. After a few seconds the cow took off with the rest of the herd and I continued on my way.

ANIMALS AT THE LOOKOUT

Bob Gray

Rattlesnakes were plentiful. Of course, one or two of them are plenty. In the early summer they showed up at the most unexpected moments. The first one greeted me about 10 o'clock one morning as I stepped my bare feet out the front door while holding a pan of dishwater. Instinctively, or at least with little thought I drenched him with the suds as he slithered away into the rocks. This one got away but several others were disposed of with a long handled shovel before the summer ended. There were the remains of an older lookout building about 50 feet from the one I occupied, which proved to be the home of about ten baby rattlers when I tore it down for firewood and kindling. These were only about a foot long when I found them but were really on the peck, kind of like a bunch of Bantam roosters.

Barefoot was a way of life at the lookout but a wary eye checked the area before stepping out the door each time.

Quite often I spotted snakes while going to the spring about one fourth mile away. No, I wasn't barefoot on these trips, which were almost daily, with a five gallon backpump to pack back up the hill. These trips kept me in good shape as the climb from the spring was about 400 feet in elevation.

Grouse are somewhat less than the smartest creatures, with habits which can lead to an early extinction. On nearly every trip to the spring I would see a grouse or two, sometimes more. They would be running down the trail ahead of me or perched on the same limb of the same fir tree most anytime I passed. One day the thought occurred that one of those grouse might make a good meal and since they sat on the limb like a bottle in the baseball throw at a fair, I'd try to knock one off. If I missed, they're so dumb they wouldn't fly away unless I hit the limb. Armed with three egg sized, round rocks I went grouse hunting. This time they weren't on the limb or anywhere to be seen, so I started back up the hill. Then I saw one on the ground in front of me about twenty feet away. When I wound up to throw he decided to fly. That was his mistake because he flew right into that rock which would have missed him a mile. With the oldest grouse and a pretty bad cook combination, I had the toughest, most unsavory meal I ever ate. No more grouse hunting after that!

Grizzly Peak is bear country, no longer inhabited by grizzlies but plenty of California black bear of various shades, even one whose shaggy coat made him look like a tan and black pinto. Most of these were sighted about one fourth to one half mile away with binoculars, but one of them decided to check on what was gong on at the mountain top. In late June, daylight lasts until about 10 p.m. at 6,000 plus feet. I had gone to bed, still lying there awake when I heard a noise at the door. Glancing over my shoulder, I nearly had a heart attack as a huge bear stood up looking into the open front door through the screen He probably was as startled as I as he turned to amble away down the trail. Had he been accustomed to humans as those bears in national parks, he could have been a problem but real wild bears are quite fearful of men and he never came back.

Evidently all animals have curiosity about man. Even a big buck appeared one night and I saw his large antlers scraping the window and side of the building just beside my bed. The building had no catwalk as most lookouts do and the buck was walking on the ground which was a narrow ledge between the building and the shear dropoff into Devil's Canyon on the east side. My movement and the flashlight beam frightened him away in a hurry. Does and fawns came by the salt regularly but only one other buck came into view of the lookout during daylight hours all summer long.

Chipmunks, golden mantled ground squirrels and digger squirrels abounded in the area. One gray squirrel became friendly but never really tame. Much of my food supply went toward these little rodents, which added company to an otherwise lonely job.

My favorites were the golden mantles, which were the easiest to tame and became noisy and belligerent when they felt I was neglecting them. After a short time there were about six of these which I could hold in my hands, put in my pocket and let climb all over my head and shoulders with the reward of a stale biscuit or piece of bread. The chipmunks, little sharp-nosed varmints, were never real tame but would eat out of my hand, even search my pockets but never let me pick them up. The digger squirrel (also called ground squirrels) became quite tame and would let me stroke their head and back while feeding them but never liked to be picked up.

The gray squirrel was a real challenge. For weeks he would watch me from the rocks about 15 feet away and would eat what I left out for him. After several weeks he would come to me by following a trail of crumbs and eventually eat from my hand but always holding my fingers with his front feet. Sometimes I could stroke his head with the back of my hand but not the palm. He seemed to know that I couldn't grab him so long as I was using the backside.

One morning I heard a noise in the cupboard and found a chipmunk in the flour container. I had left the lid off and it was funny to see the furry streak of white with a dust cloud of fine flour as he took off for the front door. Needless to say, I only used that flour to cook for the little ones after that.

During late summer, the squirrels and chipmunks were not so tame and I feel they were trying to become less dependent as winter and hibernation season approached.

HOGS, DOGS AND HORSES

James L. McConnell

I graduated from college in May 1956, and went to work for the USFS in June. The first of many duty stations was the Catahoula Ranger District on the Kisatchie National Forest in Louisiana. John Beal was the ranger. New professionals in those days were called junior foresters. John's idea of training JFs was to put them in charge of experienced crews. The JFs would plan the work, do the paper work and learn which end was up. The job of the crew was to do the work correctly and keep the JFs out of trouble. It could also work in reverse. If the crew did not like the JF, he was in hot water all the time.

One of the first jobs I was assigned was the annual hog roundup. Louisiana had been open range for many years. Local farmers had allowed their hogs and cattle to run wild in forested areas. What a scrawny bunch they were. The Forest Service had constructed barbed wire fences in many areas that were in different stages of pine regeneration. Wild hogs and cattle are certain failure to planted pine trees. The Forest Service tried for years to run cattle in plantations and finally decided it had to be one or the other but not both in the same area. The barbed wire fences would keep the cattle out, except where it had been cut, but it didn't slow the hogs down one bit. Hogs ate the hard mast and rooted up the seedlings, especially longleaf which was difficult to plant anyhow.

Each year the district would put a small crew together to roundup the hogs and cattle in certain fenced plantations. Usually the animals were returned to the owner, sold or otherwise disposed of. A couple of horses and a pack of dogs were rented from local people to accomplish the job. I was not a horse rider and, anyhow, riding a horse through Louisiana woods is not for everyone. Both the horse and the rider have to really know what they are doing or somebody is going to get hurt. The horses and dogs were paid for on a field purchase order and that was one of my jobs as crew leader. I asked how many dogs made up a pack and was told not to worry about it. Each horse was $1 a day and the pack of dogs was also $1 a day. I was told to bring the truck, keep up with the number rounded up and make sure the owner of the horses and dogs got paid. The ranger took care of the captured animals.

I was also told if I would learn how to ride I could go with the crew next year on the fun part of job. Jim Doughty, the tower man, had a mare and said I could use her to learn how to ride. We were introduced one day after work. Jim said to hold the bridle while he picked the ticks out of the mares ears. She put up with it for about 30 seconds and then tried to rear up and buck. All I can remember was Jim Doughty yelling, "Hold her Jim, hold her." Later when I tried to actually ride her, she ran out of control and would have nothing to do with me, so I gave up on that adventure. Before the next roundup I was drafted into the Army and never did learn to ride a horse properly.

ANIMAL PALS

Harvey Mack

In the 1930s and '40s, the Cleveland Forest would open three fire lookouts prior to the beginning of the fire season as a precaution for possible early preseason fires. I was a seasonal employee at the time and really appreciated an extra month or two of additional work, so I welcomed the assignment. With my little dog "Stinker" we started the season on Santiago Peak with a 75 foot tower, cabin and garage.

Since I generally was in the tower most of the day, I payed little attention to what my dog did around the lookout area until I noticed that he seemed to be spending a lot of time with another animal. On closer look, I realized that it was a fox about his size and they appeared to have made friends, including its eating part of his daily food rations while he stood by. They would take turns following each other around and would lay in the shade of the garage or cabin but they never seemed to get closer than three or four feet at anytime. While they appeared to be friends, they really didn't seem to trust each other. Hardly a day went by that they were not together and I'm sure they missed each other when I went to my regular summer assignment.

ANIMAL ANTICS

Blanche L. Phillips

Editor's Note: Mrs. Phillips was the former wife of Charles Knight, who was in charge of building trails into the Marble Mountains in the early 1920s.

After our marriage in 1926, we lived in a small two story house at the mouth of Collins Creek, near the lower end of the John Campbell ranch on the Klamath River.

Later that summer Charley was stationed at Kelsey Creek. We had the usual box of utensils—pots, pans and dishes—all nested together. When we went to move, it took me quite awhile and many tries to make all of it go back the way it came out. We had a sheet iron stove and a small tent big enough to put a cot in. All the other things including the stove were standing outdoors under a big maple tree. A table and benches were built and this was home while Charley built trails in the Marble Mountains.

At first, when cooking with hot grease in a frying pan, small green worms came down a web and dropped into the pan. The minute they hit the hot grease they swelled up twice as big. I threw the whole thing out, but it wasn't long before I just took a fork, tossed them out and went on cooking.

A higher bench was set up for a wash basin under the fly and we had to take soap out every night. We used green hand soap. The deer came into camp at night and would knock things over in their curiosity and chew our soap. We found balls of it all over the ground where they chewed it, then spit it out. Every night was the same. When they found out it didn't taste good, we thought they would stop, but they never did.

Kelsey Creek, ice cold and clear, flowed within a few feet of our camp, so butter and canned milk etc., was kept in a bucket with a tight lid in the creek. Even fresh meat kept for days.

Several long hikes were taken back into the Marbles. Charley checked salt licks for stock. He also checked cattle in the summer range and I went along for the pleasure of the beautiful country. One day after a fifteen mile hike, I was following Charley down the trail. He passed a swarm of yellow jackets in the ground (just a hole). I was about ten feet behind and arrived just in time for one to nail me on the leg right at the top of a sixteen inch boot. I was so mad that I went back and tried to stamp them all out. I guess you know who was winning when Charley came back to get me out of there.

Another time I caught eleven fish out of Scott River, but Charley took one look and said go throw them all back—they are all under four inches! About broke my heart and I lost faith in my fishing ability. Besides I couldn't see where throwing them back helped—we could just as well eat them—they were dead anyway.

While building the trail for the Forest Service in the Marble Mountains, Charley heard the big shots from the city were coming and would be there about noon. The cook said they were out of butter and there wasn't any chance of getting any. At dinner time a bowl of butter sat at each end of the table! As told to Charley later, the cook took shortening (Crisco) added salt, beat up an egg yolk for color, and it really tasted like butter!

Charley told of one man, one of the crew, who had spent most of his spare time trying to climb a steep rock about fourteen feet high. The rock was almost straight up and down and was called "Good Luck Rock" if you could climb it! One day he saw some bear cubs near the rock, so decided to catch one. He chased it around and around and finally caught a cub. About that time, he looked up and saw mama bear coming straight in his direction, walking, standing straight up and looking like she planned on giving him a rib cracking hug. Now he didn't mind the ladies hugging him, but she had a gleam in her eye that she also planned on puncturing his hide with her teeth and tearing out chunks large enough to throw a baseball through. He dropped the cub and the nearest thing in sight was that rock, where he found himself sitting on top. Hearing his yells, Charley and some of the men went to see what was the matter. The mama bear with a determined look in her eye, was walking around and around the rock looking up. After chasing the bear and family away, they helped him down and the rest of the season, he spent all his spare time trying to climb that rock but never made it!

POETRY AND POTPOURRI

SHORTY

James R. Pratley

When you came to live next door that day,
  You never knew that you would stay;
And when we met as chance would be,
  you decided to live with me.
To romp the paths and range the hills
  Despite the heat and winter chills,
To hike the trails of life each day
  With merry steps along the way;
To scale the mountains side by side
  And cross the rivers often wide.
A faithful friend until the day
  Our paths did part along the way.
Though peaceful on the slope you lie,
  My thoughts of you will never die.

And now that you are gone so long,
  I've finally finished this simple song;
A tribute to a gracious friend
  who loved in full until the end
The Ranger that you chose that day,
  When all you did was come to play.
Your story lives, as well it should
  For those you touched with all your good;

But the day will come when we shall meet
　　Along some trail that's known our feet
To live again in another place,
　　To greet each other with a warm embrace.
So when we meet around some bend
　　Please chose me again to be your friend.

HAZARDS ON THE TRAIL

Stan Tixier

There always has been danger
To a mounted Forest Ranger,
　　When ridin' on a rocky mountain trail,
There's slippery slopes and gravel,
The surface might unravel
　　And cause his equilibrium to fail.

Occasionally he'll tire
When ridin' to a fire,
　　Though it's essential that he not delay,
To keep the flames from spreadin',
And so you'll see him headin'
　　Right up the trail and in the swiftest way.

Sometimes when he's patrollin',
An ATV comes rollin'
　　On down a steep and twisty kind of slope,
The fumes and noise and clatter
Might make his pack string scatter,
　　Or least-wise tighten up the old lead rope.

His horse and pack mules never,
Or rather, hardly ever
　　Get spooked of other creatures that they see,
Like deer and elk or other

Big game they know won't bother,
  Or do them harm while runnin' wild and free.

I guess those equines figger
There ain't no spook that's bigger
  With hoof and hide and tail and pointy ear,
Than those they've seen a-plenty,
More'n fifteen times or twenty,
  Familiar sites, they're not about to fear.

But seldom have the Ranger
And horse seen somethin' stranger
  A-comin' towards 'em right around a bend,
Than some back-packers herdin'
Exotic beasts of burden
  That looked like anything except a friend.

The Llamas' heads were noddin'
As swiftly they came trodin'
  With small pack loads, they didn't have a care,
That horse got so afraid, he
Just turned a quick one-eighty,
  And left the Ranger hangin' in the air.

He tumbled down a grade there,
His pony should'a stayed there,
  But don't you see, he'd had a mighty fright,
He headed down the trail there,
Showed nothin' but his tail there,
  A-tryin' to get away with all his might.

The Ranger did some checkin',
No bones were broke he'd reckon,
  He started down the trail to find his steed,
He finally found him waitin'
By some old drift fence gate, 'n
  He figured that his luck had changed indeed.

But when the Ranger studied
Why he'd been bruised and bloodied,
    He knew it was because his horse was 'fraid
Of some strange lookin' beasty,
And so he knew at least he
    Had best assure some remedy be made.

He figured that he needed
A program that exceeded
    Those routine safety plans he'd always seen,
He wanted innovation,
So sent an invitation
    To breeders of the brutes that looked so mean.

He knew his saddle horses
Were terrified of forces
    Of unfamiliar beasts however meek,
To minimize the trauma,
He put a rented Llama
    In his horse pasture for about a week.

For several days those ponies
Were cornered up alone, he's
    A devil that might eat 'em all alive,
But finally they concluded
The monster that intruded
    Might just perhaps allow 'em to survive.

The moral of the story,
Is neither sad nor gory,
    Is simply that—it can be clearly shown,
There's nothin' half as scary,
Or more gol-darned contrary,
    Than fears you have of that which is unknown.

A RANGER'S JOYS

A. R. Ivey

Did you ever for a Summer, try a "bachelor stunt"
    alone,
  In a lonely mountain meadow, forty miles away
    from home,
Where mosquitoes wore no muzzles, and the flies
    knew how to bite,
  And the rattlesnakes were plenty, and the
    coyotes howled at night?
Did you ever cook your "flapjacks" in a house so
    full of smoke,
  That your tears dripped in the batter? It is
    funny, but no joke.
Have you burned your beans and bacon, wished
    devoutly for a wife?
  If you haven't, then you're missing half the joys
    of Rangers' life.

Have you tried to catch your horses in a meadow
    wet with dew,
  Where the grass grew rank and luscious, that
    wet your clothing thru'?
Watched them kick their heels with pleasure, and
    then start on a run
  Across that same wet meadow, till you wished
    you had a gun?
Did you finally corral them in a corner of the fence,
  Stamping, snorting, wildly eager, looking for
    another chance
To dash by you, kick their heels up, just as though
    you were stranger?
  If you haven't, then you're missing half the joys
    of a Forest Ranger.

Have you ridden for an hour, by the side of a
      roaring brook,
    Watching trout jump in the sunlight, when you
      didn't have a hook?
When the shadows on the water were alluring as a
      dream,
    Did you mutter a few "cuss words" as you left
      that tempting stream?
Did you swear by all that's Holy, that as sure as
      Sunday came,
    You'd be back there with your fishrod and mix in
      that little game?
Did you roll out Sunday morning, half awake and
      half asleep,
    To get this little message, "Can you go count
      Freeman's sheep?"

Have you ridden through the Forest with the
      shadows at your feet,
    While the grouse were drumming 'round you, and
      you hadn't any meat,
And the quail were thick as spatter, and you
      couldn't take a shot,
    Did the "badge" on your suspenders help your
      feelings out a lot?
And at night when you're so tired you can hardly
      even eat,
    Does some tourist "drop in on you," take your
      only easy seat,
Stick his feet up on your stove hearth, and
      although he is a stranger,
    Tell you calmly as he lolls there, "It's a snap to
      be a Ranger?"

RECREATION

James H. Sizer

When the hunting season opened I cleaned my
    trusty gun,
For my annual leave was coming and I planned to
    have some fun.
I bought a lot of cartridges and stuck them in my
    belt,
Loaded up my pack horse, and Gee, how proud I
    felt!

I rode up in a canyon to a mighty pretty spot,
Found tracks of deer and turkey and I knew I'd get
    a shot.
Got up early in the morning in the frost so cold and
    wet,
And started out a-hunting to see what I could get.

I struck a bunch of turkeys and my old gun sprung
    a leak,
But the blamed infernal turkeys was a-runnin' like
    a streak.
I exploded seven cartridges, a-runnin' as I shot,
But a little bunch of feathers was the only thing I
    got.

Next day I rimmed a mountain side for many
    weary miles,
Through brush and lava boulders thrown up in
    awful piles;
Then I heard the rocks a-rolling down hill and to my
    right,
And saw a buck a-runnin' but he soon was out of
    sight.

The next four days I ambled through timber, brush
    and park
From daylight in the morning till sometime after
    dark,
Looking very careful and stepping mighty light,
But never seeing nothing till I come to camp at
    night.

The seventh day, for breakfast, bread was all I had
    to eat,—
With a cup of black coffee, I sure was needing
    meat;
So I made an extra effort to try and kill a buck,
But never saw nothing, as was just my luck.

All the game had quit the country and the only
    living thing
That was capable of moving on either foot or wing
Was me and my two horses; so I packed my bed
    and steel
And hiked it back to Springer and a good square
    meal.

Though I got no deer or turkey, and my feet are
    bruised and sore
From walking through the malpais some forty
    miles or more,
My trip was not all failure as some folks may have
    guessed,
For one thing that I did get was a darned good rest!

'Twas relief from official worries and the regular
    daily grind,
And the high cost of living that had occupied my
    mind;
And I came back feeling younger than when I went
    away,
And I take a keener interest in the business of the
    day.

SPRING HAS CAME

J. A. Larsen

Being a Comedy in Three Acts

DRAMATIS PERSONAE

FOREST RANGER (*wishing for Spring to come*)
BRUNO, a young Houn' Dawg

ACT I

SCENE I. Sunday, a warm, bright, happy day.
RANGER sitting behind a pipe, and a large desk, in picturesque disarray, on which are 6 stacks of grazing applications each 1 foot high. Crayons, ink, pencils, gem clips, fire warning pen-wipers, tobacco cans, erasers, blotters, grazing manuals, circulars, pocket-knives, and match stubs scattered about in the interstices. Packages of Garden Seed on one corner of the desk, and a Seed Catalogue in the RANGER'S pocket.
THE RANGER (*looking out of the window*): "Damn!"
(Curtain)

ACT II

SCENE I. Sunday, a warm, bright, thawy day.
RANGER, on the sunny side of his barn, digging furiously with a happy smile, tools scattered about, packages of Garden Seed in his pocket.
BRUNO on an eminence in the background; looking on.
RANGER completes digging of ground, which is in a hotbed frame, and sows many rows of seed carefully and with a smile. Finishes sowing, and stands up.
THE RANGER (*happily*): "Damn!"
BRUNO (*Wags tail and smiles from the eminence in the background*)
(Curtain)

ACT III

SCENE I. Monday, early morning. A raging blizzard. The snow flies in whirls and gusts, and the wind howls in the eaves of the barn, on the south side of which, on the sagging tarp which covers the hotbed, sleeps BRUNO, curled up in the warm hole which he had to turn around nine times to make. The wind howls, and BRUNO curls up tighter.
Enter, THE RANGER, heavily wrapped, from the house.
THE RANGER (*vehemently, seeing BRUNO*) "DAMN!!!"
(*BRUNO, scenting the vials of wrath, retires apologetically to the eminence in the background, where he reluctantly sits down in the cold snow, slowly wagging his tail. THE RANGER looks long and sadly at the hotbed; then turns to BRUNO.*)
(Curtain)
THE END

THE RANGER'S SADDLE

Wendall L. Jones

This is stretching it some to call it an animal tale, but it does have something to do with horses and/or asses. Back in the late '50s, the big thing going was the splitting of ranger districts. Someone decided that this was the right thing to do and may have been at the time. Anyway, it involved some specific logistics and supply problems which seemed to be a pretty important issue at times. We usually tried to divide things up evenly or else say, "OK, you guys take the big power saw and we will take the little one." However, the great dilemma that seemed to have no answer was, "Who gets the ranger's saddle?" Nobody was about to make that decision for the rangers. One young forester, who probably came close to ending his professional career when the word got around, said, "Hey, all we need to do is get a couple of half-assed rangers!"

THE OFFICE SWEET

Hank Mostovoy

One day I drove up out of the bowels of the Klamath River to deliver "things" to the new supervisor's office in Yreka, California.

When I entered the SO, the first thing I noticed was that there weren't any direction signs. I proceeded down a long hallway, opening each door to see who was occupying the space.

I opened one door and I new immediately that I was up to my a__ in alligators. The rug was plush and a large, beautiful desk with an expensive chair occupied a corner of the room.

As I backed out of the room a voice behind me said, "May I help you, Hank?" There stood Forest Supervisor Joe Thornton. Although Joe was a forester, most of us believed his heart was with the cattle and grazing aspects of the job.

I asked Joe what he was going to do when he held a permittee hearing in his office and people showed up with manure on their boots and walked on that beautiful rug. He said that if they showed up with too much on their boots they would have to leave them outside his door. However, he thought a little would be fine. It would sweeten up the place!

BIGFOOT SKEPTIC

Harry White

While reading an issue of *The Oregonian*, I ran across an article entitled "Sasquatch season ends with big Bigfoot feet in Washington." Although my apartment was warm, cold chills ran up and down my spine as I pondered what could have happened to me 54 years ago and later when I walked the trails or scrambled through the brush in the Gifford Pinchot National Forest, alone and defenseless.

When I was assigned to that forest on July 1, 1920, I began traveling to the ranger districts to get acquainted with the personnel and help them with their work, and to become familiar with the forest terrain and cover. In August, I took off from the Wind River station northward. After pulling myself across Lewis River on the basket ferry, I walked eight miles down river to a station near Cougar. From there I went upriver to Pine Creek, thence north to a trail construction camp and later to Spirit Lake along the east side of Mt. St. Helens. After completing work there, I walked to Cougar along the west side of the mountain.

What if one of these reportedly eight foot, 800 pound beasts had appeared while I was eating my lunch beside upper Kalama River or was resting at the top of a long grade on the mountain? That's Bigfoot country. It makes me shudder to think of it.

Seriously, I wonder if it has ever occurred to the Bigfoot hunters that the Mt. St. Helens and Lewis River areas have been in national forest status for most of the present century, and hundreds of forest personnel have roamed and worked all over it, constructing roads and trails, telephone lines and other improvements, cruising timber and fighting fires. Not one of them, as far as I know, ever saw the beast's tracks, reported to be as much as 18 inches in length.

If it be said that the Bigfoot invasion is of recent origin, I would point out that he was reported as early as 1924, when a miner's cabin on the east slope of Mt. St. Helens was bombarded with big rocks one night and large tracks (manmade) were found near the cabin the next morning. That caused what I call "The Great Ape Hunt of 1924." Among many others from Portland and other points, L. H. Gregory went to the area and wrote a fantastic story for *The Oregonian*, in which he said the purpose of his trip was to try to capture one of the apes, train him as a baseball pitcher and sell him to the manager of the Portland Beavers for a million dollars.

When will these expeditions and wild tales of huge beasts, known variously as Sasquatch, Bigfoot or Hairy Ape, end? Probably not soon, if ever; they have been going on for a long time and not only tracks but sightings continue to be reported in California, Oregon, Washington and Canada.

Well, they give reporters something interesting to write about. Even the *National Wildlife Magazine* got into the act. There is a profusely illustrated tale in the October-November, 1970, issue, written by the managing editor, no less, who was in an expedition to the Mt. St. Helens area the previous summer.

THE FOOD WAS LOCAL
THE TALE OF KLONDIKE CHARLEY

Edward C. DeGraaf

Being the first ranger on the newly created Manistique Ranger District of undeveloped Hiawatha country was interesting and challenging. In addition to the protection and development of the resources of the area, it was important to cultivate the friendship of the scattered residents who lived in the occasional hunting lodge, resort or isolated cabin. Each of these isolated back country residents often were highly individual characters. One such individual was Klondike Charley.

I never knew him by any other name than Klondike Charley. To reach his isolated cabin one had to take a narrow winding road from the Steuben community to a little farm back in the hardwoods where Phil Hermann kept a few cows, raised some hay and potatoes, as well as a few chickens and a fat pig. (Incidentally a son of Phil Hermann went to Michigan State College and became a nationally known dairy authority.) Although the Hermann farm appeared to be the end of the road, if one went to the far end of the clearing, a barely passable single track road continued on through the woods.

After a mile or two of this road one came to an old clearing with one remaining logging camp cabin where Klondike Charley lived. At the far end of this clearing the old Manistique and Lake Superior Railroad had a rusty set of railroad tracks where occasionally carloads of pulpwood were hauled to market. In addition a weekly mail car, consisting of an old automobile on a nosy handcar chassis, provided postal service to pulpwood camps and kept up its franchise.

Klondike Charley lived in his cabin in almost complete harmony with nature. He himself had a neat personal appearance and this standard prevailed in his housekeeping and in the clearing. Besides his garden of potatoes, strawberries, radishes, carrots and onions he had a flower bed of nasturtiums and zinnias.

One of Charley's special qualities was his communion with the wild animals of the area. The deer, grouse, rabbits, bear and other creatures accepted him as one of them. Next to his cabin door was a bedded down spot where a large whitetailed buck slept each night like a watch dog. This was in spite of the fact that Charley had a salt lick about 150 yards away from his cabin where he would shoot a deer from his doorway when he needed a supply of meat. Grouse hung around his cabin clearing like farmyard chickens while local birds were everywhere.

A short walk from his clearing was a beaver dam and pond where Charley liked to watch the beavers. Here Charley showed me something I'd never seen before or since. On a small stream he pointed out a little dam made of small sized aspen limbs which he said was a practice dam built by young beavers. The adult beavers trained the young ones to cut sticks and secure them with mud so as to dam the small stream.

One special relationship of Charley's was with a big black bear. This bear's territory included Charley and his clearing with the surrounding woods, trails and wild berry patches. Charley told me about this bear and how they got along. They passed each other on the trails and at times the bear would move aside to let Charley pass. The bear came to Charley's clearing periodically to give it a curious inspection. It appeared the bear had accepted Charley as one who shared his territory. However, on one of his berry picking ventures, Charley encountered the bear who acted very surly and would not give way to Charley. The bear was very threatening so Charley retreated down the trail with the bear shuffling a few steps behind. Charley got to his cabin door without the bear rushing him. Once inside, the bear left. Charley in the meantime had gotten his loaded rifle. He went outside and returned to the trail they had just come down. The bear was hiding beside the trail waiting for Charley. He raised up to make a lunge at Charlie who made a quick shot, killing the bear as it reared on its hind legs.

I happened to call at the old man's cabin shortly after the shooting occurred and Charley was still shaking. He took me to the trail and showed me the dead bear. He could not understand what had changed the bear unless it was a variation of the old Indian remark that "any bear is jealous in a berry patch" since it was in berry season. It ended with Charley skinning out the bear and having bear meat to eat for awhile.

One thing that needed to be considered when calling on Charley was that he cooked and ate any of the local creatures. This would include mud turtles, porcupines, woodchucks, rabbits, etc., as well as grouse, deer and bear. If you arrived near meal time you were expected to eat hearty of whatever was in the pot. I once ate mud turtle stew from a kettle that included head, feet and shell. Muskrat in turn tasted as good as snowshoe rabbit. Trout were available in the creek and Charley caught fish on occasion when he wanted a mess.

In thinking back on Klondike Charley's way of life, I marvel at his primitive way that was in close harmony with nature. The creatures of the woods had accepted him, his cabin and the clearing as part of their environment. Charley lived out his days on this basis.

PINCHOT STARTS GRAZING FEE

From "History Lines," WO

Gifford Pinchot was determined to make livestock men using the reserves pay a nominal fee for the benefits they were receiving. A fee clause had been in two previous transfer bills which got stalled in Congress. He was sure Congress would not approve a fee so he decided to do it by regulation under the authority of the 1897 Act. First, he sought through Secretary Wilson, the legal opinion of Roosevelt's Attorney General, W. H. Moody. But to make certain of a favorable opinion he also spoke personally to Moody and to Roosevelt, who then urged a somewhat reluctant Moody to approve the idea.

Moody issued his favorable opinion on May 31, 1905. This was just in time for a paragraph to be included in the grazing section of the first manual of regulations and instructions issued by the Department on July 1, *The Use of the National Forest Reserves*, notifying livestock men that a fee would be imposed on and after January 1, 1906, for all classes of stock using the reserves. This notice caused a violent reaction from Western Congressmen and stockmen which took several years to subside.

THE SMOKEY BEAR STORY

USDA Bulletin, January 1963

Once upon a time there was no Smokey Bear. Although, today, Smokey is known far and wide as the symbol of fire prevention in our national forests, it was not until 1945 that he came into being.

Since the beginning of the Forest Service in 1905, there has been a continuing effort to teach the public the basic principles of fire prevention. When World War II brought the extra danger to the Pacific Coast forests from enemy shells and bombs, the aid of the Wartime Advertising Council was sought. The program is still sponsored by the council, ranking with savings bonds as one of its oldest public service projects.

At first, posters and other materials stressed war themes, but in 1944 the posters featured Walt Disney's Bambi, Thumper, and Flower. The animals had strong appeal and led to the creation of a new animal figure to serve as a permanent symbol of fire prevention.

The idea of a bear as fire prevention symbol developed in a conference of Forest Service and advertising industry representatives. The bear met all the requirements. He was a forest animal and could assume a humanlike posture, enabling him to be shown practicing fire prevention. The name "Smokey" was taken from a New York fire chief called "Smokey Joe."

Albert Staehle, a *Saturday Evening Post* cover artist, drew the first Smokey Bear poster, showing a cub in dungarees and ranger's hat, pouring water on a campfire. Although many artists have drawn Smokey, the man responsible for how he looks today is the Department artist Rudy Wendelin, who is art coordinator for the entire campaign. He serves as "caretaker" of Smokey's image.

The living Smokey was found, a dazed and badly burned cub, in the wake of a forest fire on the Lincoln National Forest in New Mexico in 1950. Nursed back to health, he was placed in the National Zoological Park in Washington, D.C.

EARLY LETTER FROM RO WILDLIFE AND RANGE MANAGEMENT

Glenn E. Mitchell

Your secretary made a cross-country jaunt early in the season. The wildlife men from all regions met at Chattanooga, Tennessee and from there drove through several eastern forests looking over wildlife developments.

When the eastern forests were created, they were about the only land of stable ownership in those states where wildlife program could be started. Deer and bear had been about eliminated and so had wild turkey. There remained only a few squirrels, rabbits and the usual predators on those lands. Because of land ownership, the State could do nothing as there was no assurance that the land would be available the following year.

Thus the creation of the National Forests made a habitat for wildlife in those states. The State Game Departments, together with the Forest Service, set to work to build up wildlife population. Deer were imported at considerable expense. Bears were liberated and protection laws were set up and enforced. At first it was not difficult to obtain good law observance. Everyone wanted to see game animals return to the woods. That the management was effective is proven by the fact that all states now have an open deer season and wildlife hunting is increasing each year. With the return of game they also have some illegal hunting.

The States of North Carolina, Virginia, Tennessee and West Virginia get good money for their game. As an example, we will consider game fish.

The streams are fairly cold and many of them maintain a good flow of water all year. But there is insufficient food to grow catchable fish within a period of two to three years. So the game department and Forest Service arrange rearing ponds where the baby fish are kept and fed until they reach legal size (about one year). It costs about 15¢ per fish to grow to legal size and plant.

The fisherman pays one dollar per day to fish and the limit is 8 to 10 per day, depending on the stream. The average catch is 6 fish. Both the fisherman and the agency are satisfied. Some fishermen in this region would be happy indeed if they were assured six legal fish each time they went out.

Deer hunting is controlled to the extent that a hunter can only hunt on a certain area for four days, then he is through. If he wants to 'wilderness' hunt, which means camping out on the forest, he is also limited to area and time. Then they have 'still' hunting and hunting with dogs.

Bears are hunted in parties of 7 to 15 persons with a maximum of 7 dogs. Two dogs are allowed for a hunt and the party must pay $50.00 as a special fee. This is an extremely popular hunt.

One of the big problems for nearly all kinds of wildlife is winter cover. The vast hardwood forests are wonderful cover and food providers in summer. But when the leaves are off in winter they are a very naked place for game of any size to hide.

We really don't appreciate all the natural advantages our region has in the variety and supply of game and game habitat. As an example, I can imagine Ira Jones and John Kuhns following a patch of hounds after deer with a guide offering to help them over logs and across creeks. So lets keep our forests and our game so we can hunt and fish as we want to within limits of good management.

SOME THINGS NEVER CHANGE

Submitted by Robert W. Cermak

This is a copy of a letter regarding use of homing pigeons for reporting fires discovered by the Army Air Patrol established in 1919 in District (Region) 5. Other methods used were to drop messages, which usually missed, or in later years, use a wireless telegrapher's key to transmit to receivers at each SO. The SO sets were manned by teenage radio "nuts" or what we would call today, "nerds." The only other option was to report the fire after landing by which time the fixed lookouts had already reported. The Air Patrol was not a success in reporting fires except after lightning storms, but was the first to use aerial scouting, dropping supplies and even "bombing" fire from the air. Note that the RO in 1919 thought they had all the answers until corrected by the forest. Some things never change!

United States Department of Agriculture
FOREST SERVICE
DISTRICT 6

Post Office Building
Portland, Oregon

0
Fire Cooperation   October 24, 1919
Use of Aircraft
(Homing Pigeons)

District Forester
San Francisco, Calif.

Dear Mr. DuBois:

Reference is made to Mr. Rachford's wire of October 6 and our reply of the same date.

There being no one in this office familiar with the care and training of pigeons, it was supposed that feeding, watering and keeping the loft in sanitary condition would comprise all the work necessary, and that some caretaker could do this in an hour or so a day at a nominal cost to the Service.

Today a letter has been received from the Acting Supervisor of the Cascade at Eugene in which he outlines what is really necessary. Among other points he states that at present it requires the entire time of four men to properly care for the pigeons, including their training. Training, or a part of it at least, requires that the birds be taken a distance of about thirty miles every day for practice flights. The work and expenses, therefore, of handling the birds is far beyond that which this office supposed necessary, and, with much regret, it is desired to withdraw from the undertaking, since neither funds nor men are available for such an extensive operation.

Very sincerely yours,
GEO. H. CECIL, District Forester,
By /s/C. J. Buck Acting.

WORDS OF WISDON

Anselmo Lewis

Editor's Note: The following two official Forest Service memos are exactly as they were written years ago by long-time Mt. Baldy District Ranger Anselmo Lewis. Our thanks goes to Phil Kromer for preserving them and Chuck Lundeen for submitting them.

To: FOREST SUPERVISOR, Angeles   March 25, 1957
From: DISTRICT RANGER, Mt. Baldy
G-STUDIES - Capra hircus (Goats)

Reference is made to your recent memorandum concerning the use of goats for maintenance of firebreaks on the Angeles in 1917.

After considerable research and investigation, we find that goats were used on the Angeles on an experimental basis for the maintenance of firebreaks during this period. Although the preliminary hypothetical theory appeared sound in that the goats would pay their keep with milk, meat and manure, certain biotic factors and relationships as well as administrative difficulties precluded the successful application of the theory in practice.

As you know, the goat originated from the pasong, an animal related to cattle and characterized by a long beard and rather poignant odor, especially among the males. These attributes appeared to be contributed to others through association and offered some difficulties to Forest Officers who were administrating the project. Unfortunately, these contributable qualities caused some confusion on the part of the general public and resulted in a degree of social ostracism to the Forest Officers which had not been anticipated.

In addition, the animals were possessed with a degree of perversity which can only be equaled by a frustrated Russian delegate to the U.N. Herding was most difficult, with the animals constantly scattering through the brush adjacent to the firebreaks. One herder reported that it would be simpler to herd a swarm of bees across the desert than to keep the goats on the firebreaks. Applicants possessing this ability were immediately solicited from among the local apiarists, but unfortunately the Forest Officers conducting this phase of the study made their initial approach to an apiarist who was in the process of "robbing" his apiary of honey. Reports indicate that before questioning could be initiated, the Forest Officers became concerned with other matters and rapidly lost interest in pursuing this phase of the problem, which on their recommendation was terminated and not reopened.

The harvesting of the by-products to pay the maintenance of the animals caused considerable difficulty. Although the goats could be driven out and the meat utilized, approved methods for the harvesting of the milk and manure proved economically unsound on the basis of cost-benefit ratio as well as inherent biotic weaknesses.

As the firebreaks were located in country of steep and rugged topography, and inaccessible, except by foot travel, means of harvesting the milk and manure proved an insurmountable obstacle.

At first, the goats were milked and the milk transported to the nearest road by pack train. Unfortunately, the milk, on arrival at the road, had attained definitely undesirable characteristics. Further study indicated that due to the churn-like action of pack stock, plus the high temperatures sustained by the containers in transit, it encouraged the process of bacterial action under anaerobic conditions, which caused the milk to become curdy and with an odor which was definitely objectionable and reminiscent of primitive sanitary facilities.

Preliminary studies were then initiated to handle the milk by pipelines, but due to the pipes heating up during the heat of the day, it was manifestly impossible to get the teats of the goats into the pipes because of the sensitivity of this particular organ to outside stimuli.

Harvesting of the manure proved most discouraging. Reports indicated that the manure was deposited in prodigious quantities. However, the method of deposition did not lend itself to statistical analysis. Deposition on the most part was in small piles. However, each band contained a high percentage of uninhibited animals, who evidently remained in motion as deposition was made, resulting in a deviation from the norm, thus negating all efforts on the part of the statistician to arrive at a normal curve or to present, schematically, the problem for study.

In addition, due to the rapid desiccation of the small, round pellets and their lack of cohesion when dry, when combined with the effect of the hill-creep, they were easily dislodged and under the pull of gravity were in constant movement toward the valley floor. Due to their shape and the steepness of the topography, some of the pellets attained considerable velocity in their movements. There are numerous reports of eye injuries to administrative officers from this cause, as well as sprained limbs due to the insecurity of footing and agility demanded to avoid this "fall out."

The project was abandoned during the first Santa Ana wind, when the pellets along the high ridges became airborne and were deposited in the adjacent cities in the form of "Black Rain," causing considerable agitation among the local citizenry as well as stimulating research which resulted in the development of such present day products as Air Wick and other aerosols.

By and large, and in the long run, and not withstanding the fact that this study was abandoned, we feel that with modern technical developments, such as the vacuum cleaner, etc., that this project has definite possibilities and merits reconsideration. Recommend that funds be requested for a preliminary study, to ascertain whether or not we are sufficiently technically advanced to utilize this resource to the best interests of the body politic.

A. Lewis

———

To: Sim E. Jarvi, Forest Supervisor   April 27, 1964
From: A. Lewis, District Ranger, Mt. Baldy
Subject: Aerial Operations

    Reference is made to the letter received from Mr. William E. Bovard, of the Falcon Aviation, Inc. of El Monte on March 13, 1964, concerning his proposal to dispose of cow manure from the local dairies through the medium of air drops on the Angeles National Forest.

    We have investigated this situation and find that this by-product is produced by the local dairies in such prodigious quantities that it is veritably comparable to the Mt. Vesuvius lava flows which destroyed the Roman cities of Pompeii and Herculaneum in ancient times. In fact, one could say that the task confronting Hercules in cleaning out the Aegean stables pales into insignificance when compared to the magnitude of the disposal problem confronting the local dairy industry. In addition, we were informed that one dairy alone pays over $2,000 per month for disposal of this material, which has definite economic significance to the local body politic.

    Since the cow population in Los Angeles County is one of the largest in the nation and increasing daily, the effect on the local environs to these production centers becomes of real importance.

    Disposal of the product through regular commercial channels is not feasible due to the fact that the supply far exceeds the demand. Unfortunately, the demand is also seasonal, reaching its peak in the Spring gardening months, whereas the production centers produce at a constant high rate, round the clock and on a yearlong basis, with no seasonal peaks or dips.

    Give away programs to the general public have not proven feasible due to the fact that the material must be treated to destroy noxious weed seeds before it is suitable for home use. Further, this method of disposal is complicated by the morphological characteristics of the product in its raw state, which varies from fines to large solid chunks, to the extreme of a fluid state of gel-like consistency. The latter state offers considerable difficulty to the inexperienced collector, as well as creating a definite safety hazard in the form of insecure footing while harvesting the crop. Of particular hazard is when the product is in the semi-solidified state. When lifted overhead in loading with a fork or shovel, the brittle outer shell tends to crack permitting the semi-fluid interior to cascade down on the inexperienced harvester with disconcerting results. When in the latter state the material is cohesive, imparts a more or less permanent greenish tint to fabrics and produces an aroma varying from ammoniacal to unique.

Due to the rapidity of the urban growth in county areas, the possibilities of purchasing and using disposal areas in the vicinity of the production centers are prohibitive, both from the standpoint of the cost of the land involved and the health problems created. In addition, but of equal importance, the aesthetics of the situation involved cannot be ignored. With large piles of this product in the immediate path of encroaching subdivisions, the reaction of the local urbanite, whose view from his Arcadia window is suddenly cut off by a large "pyramid of Cheops-like" mound of this product and whose children may inadvertently use the mounds for sand pile activities, has sinister portents for both the local public administrator and the owner of the mound involved from the irate citizenry.

In lieu of the above, the ocean has been suggested as a place for disposal. Unfortunately, preliminary studies indicate that the distances involved make the transportation costs excessive and, consequently, uneconomical. In addition, large volumes of this material dumped into the ocean may create unique problems for the Sunday bather, both from the standpoint of the discoloration of the water, and if washed ashore before complete disintegration and assimilation by the plankton and pasture fish takes place, could create a narrow, odiferous, green, gel-like belt along the beach, similar to the foraminifer ooze, which would deter all but the most intrepid bather from access to the sea.

If the wave action should bulk up the material in lagoons and inlets where chemical decomposition would take place without benefit of aeration, the creation of marsh gas and hydrogen sulfide gases are a definite possibility. Such gases would have a very poignant effect upon the olfactory organs of those unfortunates who encountered the downwind sea breezes from such areas.

It is Mr. Bovard's plan to use a PBY plane to dispose of this material. He feels that he can handle about 11,000 pounds a flight, which needless to say is a lot of material. If the Forest is used, the close proximity to the production centers insures that it will be economically feasible to all concerned.

From an edaphic and ecological standpoint, the proposal has considerable merit to the Forest. Under the present physical conditions, it is estimated that it takes over two hundred years to create an inch of soil on our mountains. Under the optimum conditions of plant growth produced by these cascading loads of material from the local dairies would result in the development of plant communities with a definite greater erosion prevention potential as well as increasing the rate of soil depth growth commensurately.

If the Forest is used as a disposal site, certain management directives and practices would have to be included in this permit to avoid bulking of the material and to assure that it is distributed in fine layers. It is obvious that from a fire standpoint, the bulking of this product would hold fire, produce pungent odors, be difficult to extinguish and tend to return to its gel-like consistency when subjected to water. On steep slopes this could be a distinct safety hazard to our personnel.

No dropping would be permitted on windy days, since fines carried into the adjacent valley towns could result in possible tort actions against the government for eye irritations and the discoloration of the painted surfaces of houses, due to the action of early rain on the accumulated fines on the rooftops. This would be especially noticeable on the lighter colored houses.

In checking with the medical profession, a particle of this material in the eye is said to be most irritating. In addition, the world, when viewed through such an irritated eye, tends to take on the tone and tint of the material involved.

Of equal importance to the physical aspects of this product cascading down upon the Forest in rather large amounts are the psychological connotations involved, which are certain to have a deleterious effect upon the administrators of the Forest.

This program would have no effect on routine administrative matters. However, it is obvious that when controversial matters were under discussion an energetic and imaginative antagonist, by use of the allegations, metaphors and inference, could with Machiavellian intent transfer the imagery of the amount and extent of the material on the Forest to the administrator himself with devastating effects. This sinister aspect of the situation should not be discounted prematurely.

In conclusion, we feel that this proposal is of sufficient economic importance and potential from a multiple-use standpoint that it warrants additional investigation. To that end we suggest that the Experiment Station be assigned the project for further study. We feel that due to their past experience and knowledge in studies of this type that they are uniquely qualified to appraise the value of the use of this material as proposed, and to advise administration as to the procedures and techniques to be used to obtain the maximum benefits to the Forest.

A. Lewis

ABBREVIATIONS

ADR	Assistant District Ranger	JF	Junior Forester
ATV	All Terrain Vehicle	LO	Lookout
AWOL	Absent Without Leave		
BLM	Bureau of Land Management	NF	National Forest
		ORRR	Outdoor Recreation Resource Review
BRC	Blister Rust Control		
CA	Compensation Act	OSC	Oregon State College
CCC	Civilian Conservation Corps	PIO	Public Information Officer
		POW	Prisoner of War
CFI	Continuous Forest Inventory	PWA	Public Works Administration
CHP	California Highway Patrol		
C&M	Construction and Maintenance	R5	Region Five
		R6	Region Six
		RF	Regional Forester
DA	District Attorney	RIP	Rest in Peace
DFG	Department of Fish and Game	RO	Regional Office
DR	District Ranger	S	Superregenerative (Radio Model)
FBI	Federal Bureau of Investigation	SO	Supervisor's Office
FCO	Fire Control Officer	SPF	Semiportable Fone (Radio Model)
FMO	Fire Management Officer		
FPO	Field Purchase Order	STOL	Short Takeoff and Landing
FPT	Fire Prevention Technician	TMA	Timber Management Assistant
FS	Forest Service		
GFI	General Functional Inspection	UC	University of California
		UN	United Nations
GI	Government Issue	US	United States
GII	General Integrating Inspection	USDA	United States Department of Agriculture
GMC	General Motors Corporation	USFS	United States Forest Service
GS	Guard Station or General Schedule	VIP	Very Important Person
GW	George Washington	WO	Washington Office
		WWI	World War I
I&E	Information and Education	WWII	World War II

NAME INDEX OF CONTRIBUTORS

Lewis, Anselmo
Lilligren, Hillard M.
Lord, Phil
Lundeen, Chuck

Mack, Harvey B.
Masonheimer, Edwin "Ed" W.
Mathews, Norman F.
McConnell, James L.
McGuire, C. C.
Menanno, Susan
Merritt, M. L.
Mitchell, Glenn E.
Moisio, Fritz
Morey, George W.
Morford, Lee
Mostovoy, Henry "Hank"
Munsey, Gary

Nebeker, Dwain
Nelson, M. M. "Red"

Osborne, Lura Esther Cooley

Parker, Alvin "Al"
Petty, Mark
Phillips, Blanche L.
Pratley, James "Jim" R.

Reeves, Ralph A. "Sparky"
Rogers, Russ

Sabol, Emil
Schmitz, J. M.

Scott, David W.
Shaw, Charlie
Shelley, R. S.
Sines, Roy R.
Sizer, James H.
Smay, Charles "Chuck"
Smith, Harold E.
Smith, R. Kenneth
Smith, R. W.
Space, James "Jim"
Spencer, Jack
Spivey, Robert "Bob"
Stalter, Don M.
Stevenson, Andy
Swift, Lloyd W.

Taylor, Harry J.
Tixier, Stan
Tubman, R. H. "Dick"
Turley, A. G. "Abe"

Waite, David M.
Walker, Gordon Jesse
Wehmeyer, Fred
Weigle, William G.
Weinzinger, Phil
Weissenborn, Ken
White, Harry
Wintringham, Thomas "Tom"
Witters, Randy
Worthington, Richard "Dick"

Ziegler, Robert "Bob"

Gilbert "Gil" W. Davies worked for more than 30 years in the U.S. Forest Service, retiring in 1990. All except the first six months were spent on the Klamath National Forest in Yreka, California.

Florice "Flo" M. (Hebard) Frank worked for more than 23 years in the U.S. Forest Service, retiring in 1985. The first 15 years were on the Klamath National Forest in Yreka, California. The remaining years were on the Winema Forest in Klamath Falls, Oregon and the Lassen Forest in Susanville, California as the forest contracting officer in both places.

Davies and Frank founded **HiStory ink Books** in 1992. To date, they have either authored or edited 17 different books, all connected to history.

FOREST SERVICE MEMORIES

Stories of Past Lives and Times in the U.S. Forest Service

More than 300 stories, letters, poems, biographies and essays from 1891 to the present. It's a huge *648* pages cover to cover with 30 old black and white FS photographs and references to more than 90 specific national forests from 144 contributors.

❖ It's a book of history—of an agency, a people and the land they took care of.

❖ It's a book that preserves the wonderful and unusual stories of an agency that consisted of dedicated, strong willed, brilliant, loyal and courageous men and women.

❖ Stories are often humorous, sometimes tragic and sad, usually dramatic, frequently poignant. A few are suspenseful and a handful are unbelievable.

❖ Chapters are mostly by decades and chronological in order.

❖ Many stories are from early (now deceased) pioneers in the Forest Service.

❖ Dozens of topics and subjects are included—from air tankers to wildlife.

❖ ❖ ❖ ❖ ❖

Sale Price: $26.95 each book
Shipping Price: $2.50 for each book
(California residents add $1.95 sales tax for each book)

ISBN: 1-887200-03-7

Personal checks, money orders, government third party vouchers all accepted.

Make checks payable to:

FREE SHIPPING AVAILABLE: Order two or more books to same address. Titles may be same or mixed

HiStory ink Books
P. O. Box 52
Hat Creek, CA 96040

Free flyers on our other Forest Service and history books if requested.

FOREST SERVICE HUMOR

More Than 300 True Stories

With a Four "H" Rating—HUMOROUS • HILARIOUS • HYSTERICAL • HUGE

*Stories, Yarns, Vignettes, Anecdotes, Poems and Cartoons About People,
Places and Events in the U.S. Forest Service*

146 Contributors • A WHOPPING 568 TOTAL PAGES COVER-TO-COVER

*Adventures in more than 75 National Forests • Stories from 1905 to the Present
6" x 9" soft-covered perfect bound book • ISBN 1-887200-01-0*

CHAPTER HEADINGS

- Animal Amusements
- Accident Adventures
- Bosses Behavior
- Camping Capers
- Character Charms
- Communication Comedy
- Engineering Encounters
- Fire Follies
- Hunting Happiness
- Inspection Insights
- Land Lines
- Language Lingo
- Law Enforcement Litter
- Lookout Laughs
- Money Madness

- Mining Mirth
- Miscellaneous Merriment
- Office Oddities
- Personnel Performances
- Procurement Pandemonium
- Property Procrastinations
- Public Platitudes
- Range Ramblings
- Retirement Rapture
- Timber Tales
- Training Tidbits
- Travel Troubles
- Water Wonders
- Wildlife Wit
- Dictionary Definitions

- **Plus ...** Name and Abbreviation Index

Sale Price: $24.95 each book

Shipping Price: $2.50 for each book

(California residents add $1.81 sales tax for each book)

FREE SHIPPING AVAILABLE: Order two or more books to same address. Titles may be same or mixed

Payment:

Personal checks, money orders, Government third party vouchers all accepted.

Make checks payable to:

HiStory ink Books
P. O. Box 52
Hat Creek, CA 96040

Free flyers on our other Forest Service and history books if requested.

MEMORABLE FOREST FIRES

200 Stories By U.S. Forest Service Retirees

- More Than **75** Years of Forest Fires from **1910** to **1988**
- Fire Stories From All Over the United States by **57** Retirees
- More Than **200** Stories Written in the Retirees Own Words

A Perfect Bound 6" x 9" Book with 506 Pages and 80 Photographs

---

Stories about dispatching, demob, firelines, aircraft, fire camps, initial attack, equipment, communications, smokejumping, travel, crews, slash disposal, trespass fires, law enforcement, training, command, safety, weather and much more.

The book describes accidents, tragedies, humor, close calls, snafus, fire gods, characters, goof ups, drinking, food, friendships and unforgettable experiences.

Sale Price: $21.95 each book

Shipping Price: $2.50 for each book

(California residents add $1.59 sales tax for each book)

FREE SHIPPING AVAILABLE: Order two or more books to same address. Titles may be same or mixed

ISBN: 0-9634413-9-6

Payment:
> Personal checks, money orders, Government third party vouchers all accepted.

Make checks payable to:
> HiStory ink Books
> P. O. Box 52
> Hat Creek, CA 96040

Free flyers on our other Forest Service and history books if requested.